D0930170

Improving the Elderly's Housing:

A Key to Preserving the Nation's Housing Stock and Neighborhoods

Improving the Elderly's Housing:

A Key to Preserving the Nation's Housing Stock and Neighborhoods

Raymond J. Struyk
and
Beth J. Soldo

Ballinger Publishing Company • Cambridge, Massachusetts
A Subsidiary of Harper & Row, Publishers, Inc.

International Standard Book Number: 0-88410-495-8

Library of Congress Catalog Number: 79-3008

Printed in the United States of America

Library of Congress Cataloging in Publication Data

Struyk, Raymond J
Improving the elderly's housing.

"Written to provide the Department of Housing and Urban Development with set of carefully documented alternatives to its current housing programs."
1. Aged—United States—Dwellings. 2. Housing policy—United States. I. Soldo, Beth J., joint author. II. United States. Dept. of Housing and Urban Development. III. Title.
HD7287.92.U55S77 301.5′4 79-3008
ISBN 0-88410-495-8

Contents

Foreword

In the first chapter of this book, the authors call their effort a "new look" at the housing situation of the elderly—strong language, perhaps evoking a sense of *déja vu* in those of us who have found housing to be a steady component of the literature in gerontology for twenty years or more. Potential readers may be assured, however, that practically all of the volume is truly new and, what is even better, cogently complementary to the substantial body of previous work in housing for the elderly.

Viewed in this perspective, the effect of the book lies in the bridging functions it performs at a variety of levels. A demography of aging has grown during the past decade, and the economics of housing has been a major issue in both the policy and the academic worlds since the New Deal. However, we have not had an economic or a demographic treatment of housing for the elderly to put into better perspective the primarily social-psychological or service-delivery contributions of gerontologists to the housing literature. Thus the combination of these disciplines insures some element of a "new look."

Perhaps it is a sign of the times that this field now moves from concern with determining the optimal characteristics of the residential environment to concern with "satisficing," that is, gaining the optimal tradeoff rather than the best of all possible worlds. In this vein, Struyk and Soldo repeatedly emphasize the many opportunities where services can be improved at reasonable cost by more efficient use and coordination of existing resources. Clearly, the future will not bring sweeping, new, and costly programs. The authors assume this and show, in a highly rational, cost-conscious manner, a variety of ways in which improvements in the efficiency, effectiveness, equity, housing stock preservation goals, cost, and ease of administration may be attained.

But to emphasize the economic and demographic aspects only is to do an injustice to the book's highly successful ability to bridge the gap between these factors and the social-psychological aspects of the residential environment. Thus the authors address concepts such as familiarity with the neighborhood, attachment to a home, informal support systems, and especially the intricacies of the interaction between personal competence and the housing environment.

The research presented here is highly original; it mixes variables from the economic and behavioral levels and is based, in large part, on new, rich data. The authors have utilized existing resources (public data files) rather than generate more expensive new data. More specifically, they shed light for the first time on such matters as the determinants of active home maintenance—the relationship between in-home supportive services and home maintenance activity and housing quality. Similarly, their demonstration of the concurrence of neighborhood blight and high age concentration provides data in support of one of their major points, namely, that improving the housing situation for the elderly will contribute to the preservation of neighborhoods for all people.

After highly informative discussions of current programs aimed at the community resident elderly, Struyk and Soldo identify the elderly homeowner lacking liquid assets and the rural elderly (as well as the black aged person) as the natural targets for new programs. A variety of such programs are discussed, again in a way that genuinely qualifies as new.

The authors' concern for bridging gaps also concludes the book, as they point to the overlap, sketchiness, and wasted effort inherent in maintaining federally distinct home-maintenance programs in local areas. They suggest that there are gains to be made in reducing the necessity for local agencies to piece together federal programs. Such a reduction is consistent with an important motivational aspect of a successful local effort: A sense of commitment is likely to result from a common problem-solving effort *if* the process itself is not too frustrating. Their final suggestion of having a single integrated housing-assistance plan rather than separate ones in Community Development, Social Services Title XX, and the Older Americans Act Title III plans is most welcome and should provoke earnest consideration at every level. Such consideration might even penetrate the federal bureaucracy, about which the authors are less than optimistic.

Perhaps the most obvious example of the book's new look at elderly housing is its almost total concern with nonprogrammatic housing. This is where 90 percent of all elderly people live, and the authors have contributed greatly to their well-being by writing this book.

M. Powell Lawton
Director of Behavioral Research
Philadelphia Geriatrics Center

Foreword

When my colleagues and I joined the Carter Administration to manage the research program at the Department of Housing and Urban Development, we were struck by the heavy emphasis—both in the research and in ongoing department programs—on assisting elderly-headed households to improve their housing through the use of specially developed, newly constructed rental housing projects. Certainly, new rental housing for the elderly is an essential element of any housing strategy. There are, however, several facts—documented in this volume—that argue for additional assistance to the elderly in the community, or the independent elderly, that is, those neither in subsidized housing projects nor in institutions. Most elderly prefer to remain in their own homes and neighborhoods where social ties are strongest and the security of familiarity is present. Three of four elderly-headed households are owner-occupants, as are a majority of those income-eligible for housing assistance; yet no systematic assistance is furnished to the needy elderly homeowner. Finally, many of the elderly live in neighborhoods that are beginning to deteriorate. Assisting these households would help stabilize such "fragile" neighborhoods.

Our training taught us that a major shift in emphasis for the research program was critical to developing the factual basis necessary to support any discussion of new policy initiatives in this area. This incisive volume is one product of the shift in emphasis.

Two other major initiatives have been launched in our research program that are closely related to this book. First, we are conducting a two-phase demonstration and evaluation of the feasibility, cost, and effectiveness of the provision of in-kind maintenance services to elderly-headed homeowners. In this pilot program the homeowner receives, in exchange for a nominal $10 fee, an annual inspection and necessary minor repairs (e.g., caulking, weatherstripping, fixing cracked windows, installing handrails, replacing worn-out faucets) and is entitled to emergency services. A key factor of the program is its longevity: it is hypothesized that the cumulative effect on dwelling quality will be substantial. This type of program is suggested in Chapter 9, and we are developing the necessary systematic experience with it to determine whether a national program should be considered.

The second initiative is a ten-year, longitudinal survey of elderly-headed households in two metropolitan areas. We, along with the Administration on Aging, have undertaken this large effort because of the lack of an adequate data base for detailed analysis of the housing adjustments of elderly-headed households. Note that "housing adjustments" are defined here to include both those made without moving, such as change in the functions of rooms and delayed maintenance, as well as those affected by relocation. We view the development of these data as essential if thoughtful, efficient, and sensitive policies for helping the elderly to make timely housing adjustments are to be forthcoming. As the baby boom generation matures, the search for such knowledge will become increasingly important.

These projects, of course, represent only first steps in our continuing effort to develop a comprehensive housing strategy for the department. Fortunately, other agencies and a large group of dedicated scholars and persons at foundations are also working on those problems.

The early drafts of this volume as well as the opportunity to work closely with Dr. Struyk during the first two and a half years of the Carter administration has profoundly changed my own thinking. It has also broadened my own agency's debate on elderly housing needs. *Improving The Elderly's Housing* is an excellent example of first class policy analysis growing out of the federal government's serious efforts to improve the quality of its programs that serve needy Americans. It should prove to be a valuable resource for all of us now and in the years to come.

Donna E. Shalala
Assistant Secretary for Policy Development and Research
U.S. Department of Housing and Urban Development

Preface

This book was written to provide the U.S. Department of Housing and Urban Development (HUD) with a set of carefully documented alternatives to its current housing programs, alternatives that emphasize helping the elderly who are residing in the community to live in adequate housing. During the research for the book Ray Struyk was the deputy assistant secretary for research at HUD and was responsible for research on improving the department's efforts in housing the elderly. Beth Soldo was a senior research scholar at the Kennedy Institute, Center for Population Research, at the Georgetown University. Some of her research was performed under contract to HUD. Both authors gratefully acknowledge the support provided for this work by the Department of Housing and Urban Development.

Ray Struyk wants to thank Debbie Devine for her assistance in preparing two chapters and Ed Dolbow and Mark Sanblanet for help with computer programming. Sandra Newman was a consistently helpful critic of early drafts. Much of the policy thrust in the volume has been strongly influenced by long discussions with Dave Garrison and Donna Shalala and by the experience of arguing proposed new programs through the department's budget process for fiscal year 1980. The following people provided background material and data and/or commented on various drafts: David Einhorn, Debby Greenstein, Howard Hammerman, Barbara Haug, Jill Khadduri, James McCollum, Terry O'Connell, Elaine Ostrowski, Julie Pastor, Howard Sumka, and Harold Williams. The RAND Corporation provided special tabulations of data from the Housing Allowance Supply Experiment. Special tabulations from the 1973 Annual Housing Survey were generously prepared by the Philadelphia Geriatrics Center, and Neil Mayer provided special tabulations of the Census C-50 data.

Beth Soldo acknowledges the competent assistance of Carol DeVita and Jaana Myllyluoma in preparing the basic demographic profiles of the elderly. Mahesh Sharma provided programming support. Richard T. Campbell, Department of Sociology, Duke University provided methodological guidance. The Center for Demographic Studies, Duke University, prepared the initial extract from the 1970 Public Use Sample of Basic Records.

We also would like to thank those who provided the necessary behind-the-scenes support: Barbara J. McClelland and Barbara Armstrong typed initial drafts of chapters and patiently endured countless revisions. Audrey Wyatt edited and prepared the final drafts. Barbara Armstrong also coordinated the preparation of the manuscript.

While numerous individuals contributed to the final publication of this volume, all errors or omissions remain the authors'.

List of Tables

List of Figures

Improving the Elderly's Housing:

A Key to Preserving the Nation's Housing Stock and Neighborhoods

Part I

The Elderly and Their Housing

❋ *Chapter 1*

The Elderly in the Housing Market

By many standards, older people in the United States appear to be well-housed albeit in somewhat older, more modest homes than the rest of the population. Clearly, this is the view held by most older persons themselves: approximately 80 percent of older household heads rate their house as an excellent or good place to live.[a] The vast majority of older persons also enjoy the independence of owning their homes and four out of five of these do so mortgage free. To compensate for reductions in income following retirement, real estate tax laws in many areas ease the property tax burden on older homeowners.

Contradicting this overall favorable impression is a continuous stream of stories like the following:

> Mrs. Sally Gruen, a seventy-eight-year-old woman holds tenaciously onto her home, which is now dilapidated, in the inner city slum areas of Washington, D.C. Mrs. Gruen and her husband had worked long and hard to own their own home, which she now possesses "free and clear." Her husband died ten years ago and she is living on his minimal Social Security income together with some babysitting money. She can no longer afford repairs for her deteriorating home. She has no electricity, no heat, no water. In order to stay warm she has closed off most of the house except for one downstairs room . . .[b]

[a] In contrast, only 68 percent of younger household heads offer a similarly positive evaluation of their house.

[b] The name used here is false. Paraphrased from Butler (1975: 104).

> Eighty-year-old Mae Dayton rents a crumbling one-bedroom apartment in an old hotel in Chattanooga. She says she is there against her will. She explains that a year ago her landlord moved her out of a much nicer apartment to make room for a gift shop "and into here in two days without notice." Ms. Dayton says she wants to move to a better place but fears moving to a strange neighborhood. She is waiting for a new federally subsidized apartment building to be completed a few blocks away. If she does not obtain space in that building she has few alternatives. She cannot afford to pay much more than her current rent of $90 a month. Her sole source of income is a $240-a-month Social Security check.[c]

These case histories aptly illustrate the types of housing problems confronting many counterparts of Mrs. Gruen and Ms. Dayton. Whether housing problems stem from undermaintained units or the limited availability of good low-cost housing, the effect on older occupants is the same: life satisfaction is reduced, good health is compromised, and safety is threatened. Although society has made a commitment to the well-being and care of its older members, the interrelated problems of inadequate housing, low income, and poor health define the life-style of an embarrassingly large segment of our older population. The U.S. Senate Committee on Aging estimates that "at least 30 percent of the elderly live in substandard, deteriorating or dilapidated housing" (U.S. Congress 1977: 66).

HOUSING OF THE ELDERLY

High rates of homeownership and high levels of expressed satisfaction among all older persons mask comparatively high rates of observed dwelling deficiencies for some groups within the older population, particularly for the black elderly, the impoverished elderly, and those in rural areas. Of the 1.2 million households headed by an older black, for example, 162,000 households lack complete plumbing facilities. In total, approximately 1 million units occupied by older individuals or families have one or more of six major housing deficiencies.

The high incidence of mortgage-free homeownership is a key factor in keeping the average housing expense burden of the elderly at 23 percent of income, close to the 20 percent average of the nonelderly. Still, 2.3 million elderly spent more than 35 percent of their income on housing in 1976. Housing costs consume an excessively large share of monthly income for almost two out of every five older renters and one in three older homeowners. The cost of housing is a particularly severe strain on the monthly budgets of older blacks and those below poverty

[c] The name used here is false. Paraphrased from J. Koten (1978: A1).

level, those living alone (who, for the most part, are widows), or those living in nonmetropolitan areas.

The pervasive pattern of mortgage-free homeownership (and resulting low annual housing costs) conceals other types of housing problems among the elderly. Homeownership, for the majority of the elderly, does not constitute a strong asset position: the value of homes owned "free-and-clear" by 25 percent of the elderly was less than $15,000 in 1976, and an additional 25 percent had accumulated equity of less than $25,000. The homes owned without mortgages by one-third of older persons living alone and one-half of those below poverty were valued at less than $15,000. Frequently older persons or families with near-poverty-level incomes suppress annual housing costs by neglecting or postponing basic maintenance or needed repairs on their mortgage-free homes. The overall picture that develops is one of the elderly devoting a substantial share of their income to housing of quality slightly below that of their nonelderly counterparts. In recent years the share of income necessary to maintain this standard seems to have risen.

Broadly and reasonably defined, housing also includes aspects of the residential environment and neighborhood. When asked directly if they are satisfied with their neighborhood, most older persons, like those younger than they, respond with a favorable evaluation.[d] Both Lawton (1976) and Carp (1975) warn, however, against the easy acceptance of subjective evaluations that are likely to be contaminated by the perceived lack of realistic alternatives, by reduced aspirations, and by self-protective denial.

In neighborhoods with excessively high proportions of older persons, the dwelling units themselves tend to be old and of comparatively poorer quality. The average property value in these neighborhoods is relatively low. Coupled with high vacancy rates, these facts suggest that the neighborhoods where the elderly cluster are those with (excessively) high rates of building abandonment or sluggish real estate markets. Areawide housing problems are accompanied frequently by other characteristics that define decaying areas: high rates of unemployment, poverty, and crime; poorly maintained streets and sidewalks, and limited municipal services.

Despite similarities in neighborhood characteristics, the elderly are disproportionately represented in two distinct and very different types of neighborhood settings: older, core cities of major metropolitan areas and small rural towns (communities of 1,000 to 2,500 inhabitants).

[d] See Lawton (1978) for a summary of survey results on subjective neighborhood satisfaction and the elderly.

Patterns of residential inertia by the elderly and attrition of younger families by outmigration have transformed both the older sections of our cities and small rural communities into the functional equivalents of "gray ghettos" (Cowgill 1978).

Obviously, not all older persons are inhabitants of downtown areas or isolated rural communities. Yet although the older couple gardening outside their well-cared-for suburban home may be a familiar sight, the more typical house in such neighborhoods is likely to be one occupied by a young or middle-aged couple with children. Elderly residents in such highly age-integrated neighborhoods are not likely to have severe housing problems, and, if they do, they are likely to be isolated cases. Where dilapidated housing is a common neighborhood pattern, a "hostile" residential environment compounds the housing problem of older residents.

For some older individuals, inadequate housing and unsafe, threatening neighborhoods are problems confronted throughout the life cycle. The human aging process is characterized much more by stability and persistence of living standards than by dramatic change and disruption. Postretirement incomes below the poverty level are typically a result of limited midlife financial resources (Henretta and Campbell 1976, Soldo 1978)—resources that were, in all likelihood, too meager to sustain residential repair, maintenance, or renovation activities even before the onset of old age. Among older persons with a life history of chronic housing deficiencies, age-related changes in health status or marital status may indeed exacerbate housing problems, but, for this group, it is incorrect to attribute housing inadequacies to life events associated with old age.

For those whose housing was of good quality at the threshold of old age, housing deficiencies observed during the seventh or eighth decade of life reflect changes that accumulate with old age, most notably, reduced financial and physical abilities. Often living on relatively low and fixed incomes, the elderly face the dilemma of devoting an increasing share of their inflation-plagued incomes to adequate housing or "purchasing" inferior, but less costly, housing. Renters exercising the latter option may move sequentially from one small, inadequate house or apartment to another, even less desirable unit. For the majority who persist as homeowners and age "in place," inferior but less expensive housing can be "purchased" by reducing or eliminating the allocation made to home repairs and home maintenance. Moreover physical impairments often prevent the older homeowner from compensating for reduced maintenance expenditures by making his or her own home repairs. Lacking the knowledge or experience, even a physically fit older widow living alone on a reduced income may neglect proper home maintenance.

For many elderly homeowners, their old age coincides with what Gottesman (1970) describes as the "aging of the physical plant in which they live." The elderly own and occupy some of the oldest dwelling units in the national housing inventory: less than one-third of all owner-occupied homes in 1973 were built prior to 1940, but more than one-half of the units owned and occupied by older persons were of this early vintage. Older homeowners also tend to be long-term neighborhood residents: the median duration of occupancy for an older homeowner was 22.25 years in 1976 but only slightly more than six years for nonelderly homeowners.

Those who age in place acquire a comfortable and secure working familiarity with their neighborhoods. Community ties develop and informal helping networks evolve. Perhaps as a consequence, the elderly (particularly homeowners) have very low rates of residential mobility, and if a move is made, it is likely to occur within the same area (Siegel 1976). Even those elderly who express dissatisfaction with their housing and neighborhood are reluctant to abandon their familiar neighborhood when offered alternative housing (Lawton 1978). Because of the elderly's marked tendency to age in place in older units and resist relocation, the need for substantial home repairs may peak at a time when the older homeowner is least able, physically or financially, to meet this demand satisfactorily. The aging and incipient decline of individuals, their dwelling units and neighborhoods often occur simultaneously, exacerbating the rate of "aging" and functional loss in each.

The ill-housed elderly are as diverse a group as the older population itself. It includes the older homeowner as well as the renter, the physically fit as well as the impaired, those in rural areas as well as in urban areas. Their "housing problems" also assume many different forms: structural deficiencies, excessive rental or repair costs, decaying neighborhoods. For the elderly with acute housing problems, the changes in marital status, income, and health that "intensify shelter needs" (U.S. Congress 1978) also reduce their coping resources and limit their realistic alternatives for securing improved housing situations.

THE FEDERAL RESPONSE

An adequate standard of living for the elderly is accepted by society as a social necessity, if not a moral responsibility. In pursuit of this ideal, the federal government has made a substantial commitment to the care and well-being of older citizens. During fiscal year 1977, $112 billion of the federal budget—25 percent of the total budget and 5 percent of the GNP—were allocated to the elderly. At least $1.2 billion was spent on subsidizing housing costs alone. In reviewing federal housing programs, however, Congress has concluded that despite the amount of government assistance directed toward housing programs, many elderly continue to live in inadequate housing. The United States has accumulated forty years experience with housing assistance programs. For the most part, these programs have attempted to supply adequate housing alternatives either by financing construction/management costs or by subsidizing monthly rental costs to those in need. The absolute number of elderly-headed households who currently benefit from these programs is impressive: 750,000. Yet this figure accounts for only 3 percent of the older population. The vast majority of the elderly (at least nine out of every ten) are neither patients in long-term care facilities nor residents of subsidized public housing, but rather, live in privately owned housing within the community. Most of the poorly housed elderly, for one reason or another, have fallen through the net of federal housing programs and remain in the community.

We judge current initiatives in housing assistance programs to be inadequate, at least in part, because the demand for low-cost rental units of acceptable quality far exceeds the supply of such units. For every federally subsidized unit completed and occupied in 1971, there were one and one-half times as many older persons on waiting lists (Lawton and Nahemov 1975). Even if projections of the older population did not indicate a dramatic increase in the size of the older population as the baby boom cohorts age, it would be many decades before the current demand for subsidized units could be met (Lawton 1978). The cost alone of a large-scale construction effort commensurate with demand challenges the viability of the traditional approach to upgrading the housing of the elderly.

Most attempts to remedy the housing deficiencies experienced by older persons have involved relocating them in newly constructed multiunit buildings. In addition to the supply issue, this approach can be criticized on other grounds: the 600,000 older persons rehoused under various programs of the U.S. Department of Housing and Urban Development (HUD) are self-selective and unrepresentative of the older population in need of housing assistance. The applicant pool, by definition, excludes older persons who are unwilling to relocate or ignorant of the option. In addition to meeting an income eligibility criterion, applicants for subsidized units also are screened for their capacity to function independently. The self-selection of the applicant pool and the screening procedures themselves "produce resident groups of relatively well-informed, independent, persistent and perhaps even aggressive people. It is likely that, among the elderly with limited options, they tend to be the most capable of exercising the options which are available" (Carp 1976:248).

Perhaps the most serious charge that can be leveled against the major housing programs is the systematic disregard for the preference of many older persons, particularly homeowners, to remain in their own homes as long as possible. The older homeowner who wishes to stay in his or her long-familiar, but deteriorating, home and neighborhood has few alternatives: friends or relatives can be encouraged to assist in home maintenance or repair chores; if a government-funded "Handy-Andy" repair assistance service is available locally, application can be made; or, more likely, the home can be allowed to deteriorate still further. Even if an older homeowner can secure home maintenance-repair assistance, related neighborhood and environmental problems, where they exist, will continue.

A single-program approach is inadequate either to remedy the different types of housing problems that are found within the older population or to accommodate the range of housing preferences.

HOME MAINTENANCE AND NEIGHBORHOOD PRESERVATION

A coherent housing maintenance program is acknowledged by many, including the U.S. Senate (U.S. Congress 1975), as a needed supplement to the repertoire of existing housing assistance programs. Home repair proposals are justified as being not only cost-effective but also compatible with the preference of many older homeowners to age in place in familiar environments. For example, the Senate Select Committee on Aging argues that, "old neighborhoods need not be swept aside. A combination of existing housing programs, preservation legislation and tax breaks could result in the successful recycling of sound structures into model housing for the elderly at costs considerably below those of new construction" (U.S. Congress 1978:109).

Because the poorly housed elderly are disproportionately concentrated in our inner cities and rural areas, programs supporting residential repair-maintenance are likely to spawn neighborhood revitalization in areas blighted by deteriorating or abandoned housing units. It is clear that the elderly, as a group, have a stake in preserving the housing and character of their neighborhoods. At a minimum, checking the process of decay in their neighborhoods would provide the elderly a safe, pleasant, and familiar environment in which to live out their lives. Unchecked, neighborhood deterioration might mean living in fear of crime in the midst of abandoned structures or sustaining a major capital loss upon sale of the property. Moreover, the rest of society should have a stake too in assisting elderly homeowners to maintain their homes adequately. Home maintenance is inexorably linked not only to housing stock conservation but also to neighborhood preservation. The upkeep of units occupied by long-term residents, many of whom are elderly, is a critical ingredient in sustaining a favorable neighborhood image. The case for providing housing assistance to the elderly may be especially strong if it can be demonstrated that the elderly convert such assistance into housing improvements at a higher rate than other households.

Society has enunciated preservation of its neighborhoods as a national policy, although it has not aggressively pursued such a goal. Neighborhood preservation appears as one of the goals of the Department of Housing and Urban Development under the Carter administration and also is a key element in President Carter's urban policy. The Congress for its part has funded the Community Development Block Grant and related housing and rehabilitation programs at increasing, though insufficient, levels.

This consensus stems from the recognition of several facts: The escalating cost of new housing and associated infrastructure makes the utilization of refurbished existing housing a bargain. Housing repair, particularly in the inner cities, also is seen by some to be the *sine qua non* for the ultimate improvement of inner city public services, both because it enlarges the tax base and because a stable resident population exhibits greater community concern. Also, there has been recognition of the massive capital losses, typically unrequired, accruing to the individual property owners in severely depressed neighborhoods. Finally, the intrinsic worth of certain settlement patterns and architecture has come to be appreciated.

Simultaneous with the emerging recognition of these factors, the development of several favorable circumstances gave a solid, positive impetus to the neighborhood preservation movement: the price of new housing driven upward by higher quality and more severe building codes coupled with the reduced level of building in the mid-1970s made housing in the inner cities (often discounted in price compared to suburban properties because of conditions in the neighborhood) very attractive to would-be homeowners. Household formation was at full tide as the children of the baby boom reached adulthood. The price of suburban properties escalated as the metropolitan highway building program reached completion. These factors fostered a remain-in-the-city movement for young families who ten years earlier would have moved to suburbia to raise their children.

Despite these favorable signs and despite pockets of revitalization in most major cities, on balance the major cities continue to lose population. The strengthening of many presently "fragile" neighborhoods is imperative, and one way to accomplish this, as argued throughout this study, is to adjust the type of housing assistance being provided to households headed by the elderly.

STUDY OBJECTIVES

This study evolved from a simple premise: a cluster of home maintenance programs, targeted at the elderly, is a logical and cost-effective solution for extending the umbrella of federal housing assistance to those currently outside that coverage while concurrently stimulating housing stock conservation and neighborhood preservation. This proposal is not unique.[e] As noted previously, both the executive and legislative branches of government, in addition to numerous researchers, have made similar recommendations. But before any recommendation or broadly stated public policy objective merits translation into actual program initiatives, adequate answers must be supplied to three fundamental questions:

1. What is the scope and nature of the problem under consideration?
2. Who is the population to be served?
3. Which of several types of program strategies are most likely to affect the desired results?

Framings answers to these three questions is the overall objective of this book.

The first two questions are examined in Part I of the book. A complete understanding of the housing situation of the elderly involves knowing not only how many older individuals confront severe housing problems of various types, but also the socioeconomic characteristics of the poorly housed elderly and the reasons that current program strategies are insufficient to satisfy their housing needs.

Improving the immediate housing situation of the elderly is a worthwhile and well-accepted objective of public policy. This study shows, however, that improving the housing of the elderly through home maintenance-repair assistance also serves the needs of policies directed toward neighborhood preservation. To demonstrate the compatibility of these two objectives, we examine the location of the elderly, particularly the location of those with housing problems, and the characteristics of the neighborhoods in which older persons congre-

[e] See, for example, recommendations of varying specificity proposed by Carp (1976), Lawton (1978), Myers (1979), and the Senate Committee on Aging (U.S. Congress 1978).

gate, either by choice or default. If it can be shown that neighborhoods with large concentrations of the aged overlap substantially with neighborhoods in which the quality of housing is deteriorating, then defining the target population for repair-maintenance programs as the "poorly housed elderly" is justified.

In initiating a home maintenance-repair program to improve housing of the elderly, the United States has several working models from which to choose. The Swedish approach is to supplement the monthly income of the elderly living in poor-quality housing with a housing allowance. This approach will serve the twin maintenance-preservation objectives of U.S. policy only if the elderly recipients voluntarily allocate an appropriate share of their incremented income to home repairs. Under the Norwegian system, older homeowners with dwelling units in need of repairs qualify for low-interest loans restricted to financing maintenance-repair activities only. If loans, even with relaxed repayment schedules and low interest rates, are the only vehicle for assistance, however, the elderly most in need may be systematically excluded. Another option might be financing and extending the coverage of home repair services (such as "Handy-Andy") currently available in some municipalities. Analyses of the determinants of home maintenance activities in Chapters 4 and 5 suggest the appropriate structure and organization for programs supportive of adequate home environments for the elderly *and* neighborhood preservation.

As the United States enters an era of potential economic slowdown and reduced federal expenditures for social programs, only nonredundant and cost-effective proposals should be considered. Through inventories of existing housing assistance strategies, originating primarily from the Department of Housing and Urban Development and the Department of Health, Education and Welfare (HEW), Part II shows the limitations of existing home maintenance programs. Although a large number of federally funded programs attempt to improve the housing situation of the elderly through upgrading occupied dwelling units, neither the scope nor budgets of these programs are sufficient to stimulate home maintenance on a scale necessary to brake neighborhood deterioration. Given this situation, one might be tempted to recommend a large increase in program budgets. But, a simple budgeting increase is unlikely to produce the desired effect because of the structure of existing programs and the sharing of responsibilities between HUD and HEW. Thus, in the final chapter, a series of new program initiatives designed to complement and supplement existing housing assistance programs is described and evaluated.

In summary, this study is not just "another look" at the housing situation of the elderly but a "new look" at the determinants of the existing situation and the efficacy of potential remedies. Studies of housing for the elderly have relied almost exclusively on data bases developed locally; national data, where available, have achieved breadth of coverage at the expense of depth. Seldom are the two perspectives balanced adequately. The object of the following chapters is to introduce such balance into the growing body of literature on the subject of housing for older persons. Both local and national data, most of which were collected specifically for resolving issues in housing policy, are used. With few exceptions, these data have not been published previously and were current as of 1978. Rigorous statistical techniques to analyze these data are used consistently. For example, two-stage least squares regression is used to evaluate the determinants of housing behavior among the elderly as reported in Chapter 4; profiles of neighborhoods with high concentrations of older persons are drawn with the techniques of discriminant analysis in Chapter 6. To preserve readability, all technical discussions are reserved to footnotes or, if greater detail is necessary, to appendices following relevant chapters.

Although those charged with formulating housing policy for the elderly are concerned about the ways in which the community environment and housing services can prevent or postpone institutionalization of older residents, overt discussion of this topic is omitted. It is possible that by improving the housing situation in which the elderly reside, their ability to lead healthy, independent lives in the community may be shored up, but we have made no attempt to trace the linkage between housing conditions and functional health. Nor have we assessed the relative merits of age-segregated versus age-integrated housing sites. The proposals set forth in this study concern the elderly who occupy inadequate dwelling units, many of which are located in neighborhoods with large concentrations of their peers. In recognizing a neighborhood dimension in housing assistance programs this study does not endorse age-segregated communities but simply advocates programs consistent with the preference of many older persons who wish to age comfortably and safely in their neighborhoods of long-standing residence.

REFERENCES

Carp, F.M. 1975. "Ego Defense or Cognitive Consistency Effects on Environmental Evaluation." *Journal of Gerontology* 30: 707–11.

———. 1976. "Housing and Living Environments of Older People." In R.H. Binstock and E. Shanas, eds., *Handbook of Aging and the Social Sciences.* New York: Van Nostrand Reinhold Co.

Cowgill, D. 1978. "Consequences of Changing U.S. Population: Demographics of Aging." Written testimony before a joint hearing of the Select Committee on Population and the Select Committee on Aging, U.S. House of Representatives. Washington, D.C.: U.S. Government Printing Office.

Henretta, J.C., and R.T. Campbell. 1976. "Status Attainment and Status Maintenance: A Study of Stratification in Old Age." *American Sociological Review* 41: 981–92.

Gottesman, L.E. 1970. "Long-Range Priorities for the Aged." *Aging and Human Development* 4: 393–401.

Koten, J. 1978. "Aged and Alone." *Wall Street Journal,* October 17.

Lawton, M.P. 1977. "Methodologies for Evaluation in Environment and Aging." In P. Suedfeld et al., eds., *The Behavioral Basis of Design*. Stroudsburg, Pa.: Dowden, Hutchinson and Ross.

———. 1978. "The Housing Problems of Community—Resident Elderly." In *Occasional Papers in Housing and Community Affairs*. Vol. 1. Washington. D.C.: Government Printing Office.

Lawton, M.P., and L. Nahemov. 1975. "Cost, Structure and Social Aspects of Housing for the Elderly." Final Report to the Administration on Aging. Philadelphia: Philadelphia Geriatric Center. Mimeo.

Myers, P. 1979. *Neighborhood Conservation and the Elderly: An Issue Report.* Washington, D.C.: The Conservation Foundation.

Siegel, J. 1976. "Demographic Aspects of Aging and the Older Population of the United States." *Current Population Reports,* Series P-23, No. 59. Washington, D.C.: Government Printing Office.

Soldo, B.J. 1978. "Incomes of Black Aged: Their Determinants and Consequences." Paper prepared for the conference on Blacks and Retirement: An Untapped National Resource, sponsored by the Council on Minority Planning and Strategy. Washington, D.C.: Center for Population Research. Mimeo.

U.S. Congress. 1977. "Developments in Aging: 1976, Part 1." A Report of the Senate Committee on Aging, United States Senate. Washington, D.C.: U.S. Government Printing Office.

———. 1978. "Developments in Aging: 1977, Part 1." A Report of the Senate Committee on Aging, United States Senate. Washington, D.C.: U.S. Government Printing Office.

❋ *Chapter 2*

Who Are the Elderly?*

Frequently, reference is made to "*the* older population" or "policy for *the* elderly," as if to imply that older persons were a collection of like individuals. Celebration of a sixty-fifth birthday does not erase the numerous social, psychological, or economic differences recognized among middle-aged adults. If anything, the effect of different experiences, life-styles, and economic opportunities endure and accumulate over time, so that those who are the elderly may be the least homogeneous age group within the population. Because of this diversity, it is not surprising that "legislation in aging traditionally has suffered from a lack of understanding of the clientele it intends to assist" (Kerschner and Hirschfield 1976: 353).

Human aging is a continuous process; previous life-cycle experiences and decisions affect the choices and options of later life. An older woman who has remained childless, for example, does not have the option of living with an adult child or relying on such a child for financial assistance or personal care. Similarly, a person with a life history of low or poverty-level income is not likely to have accumulated the assets necessary to escape poverty status in later life. For the most part, life-styles persist, rather than change, as one makes the transition from middle age to old age (Maddox 1968).

The later part of the life cycle is characterized also by a number of abrupt, and often unwelcome, external changes. Spouses and friends die; children, friends, and neighbors move away; the neighborhood changes; work status and frequently health status change as well. The

* This chapter was co-authored by Carol DeVita.

ways in which an older person copes with such events is predicated to a large extent on what has come before in the life cycle.

Housing needs also change: a home that is suitable during the young adult and middle-age years may not be desirable later in life. The elderly widow living alone may not require, or desire, as much space as when she was married and raising a family; excessive space may even put a heavy burden on her financial resources. With age, the possibility of chronic disease and associated impairments in functional ability increases (Shanas and Maddox 1976), and the ability to perform household chores may diminish. Major repair work cannot be accomplished readily, and the older person may request assistance from relatives, friends, or community agencies. Some individuals, however, arrive at the extremes of old age with few physical or financial problems. For this segment of the older population, housing needs change only minimally over the later part of the life cycle.

Policy and service initiatives focused on the older population need to be sensitive to both the diversity and similarities that exist among elderly individuals. Such sensitivity evolves only if knowledge and understanding replace traditional stereotypes.

In the next section, the social and demographic characteristics of individuals in the older population are inventoried and discussed. General patterns, and the exceptions to these patterns, are noted. The third section focuses on the economic status of the aged. Emphasis is given to characteristics that affect the housing needs and consumption patterns of the elderly. Because the need for and receipt of housing assistance is often predicated on low income status, the elderly poor are singled out for a detailed analysis in the fourth section of this chapter. Even a brief review of the sociodemographic and economic characteristics of the elderly suggests flaws in the orientation of current housing programs and policy. These problems are summarized in the final section.

SOCIODEMOGRAPHIC ASPECTS OF THE OLDER POPULATION

Diversity of the Older Population

During the twentieth century, the population of the United States "aged." Demographically, there has been an increase, not only in the absolute size of the older population, but also in the proportion of elderly in the total population. In 1900, 3.1 million persons were age sixty-five or older, representing 4.1 percent of the population. By 1960, this number had grown to 16.7 million, and by 1977, 23.5 million. Proportionally, the elderly accounted for 9.2 percent of the population in 1960 and 10.9 percent in 1977.

Not all groups have shared equally in this growth. The "aging" of the black population proceeded at a somewhat slower rate during this time, with the proportion of blacks sixty-five years of age and older increasing from 6.2 to 8.2 percent over the seventeen-year period.[a] In absolute numbers, the percentage increase translates into 1.9 million older blacks in 1977, or a gain of approximately 378,000 elderly blacks between 1970 and 1977.

Since 1960, the older population has grown faster than the population as a whole; the aged segment has increased by 21 percent while the total population has increased 13 percent. Although the recent growth rate of the older population is impressive, it is substantially less than that of the 1950s when the elderly recorded a 35 percent increase. Projections by the U.S. Bureau of the Census anticipate a continued growth in the size of the older population, but at a slower rate than is currently observed. This slow growth pattern will persist until the year 2020, when the baby boom cohorts begin to reach old age and rapid growth among the older segment of the population will reappear (Siegel 1976).

The older population itself is aging. Among both the older white and black populations, the growth of the oldest segment (those seventy-five years of age and older) has exceeded the rates of increase for either the older population as a whole or for the younger age groups (those aged sixty-five to seventy-four). As the data in Table 2-1 show, in 1950, only 12.8 percent of elderly males and 14.9 percent of elderly females were eighty years of age and older. By 1977 these percentages had increased to 17.1 and 22.9, respectively. Concurrently, the proportion of males and females at the youngest age group (age sixty-five to sixty-nine) diminished slightly. Although the black population showed more concentrated growth at the older ages than did the white population, the older black population is still "younger" than the comparable white population. In 1977, proportionately more blacks (66.4 percent) were in the younger age groups (sixty-five to seventy-four years of age) than were whites (61.8 percent).

The gap between the number of elderly males and the number of elderly females has widened over time. Less than fifty years ago, the number of males approximately equaled the number of females, but since that time there has been a dramatic increase in the number of females. A useful way to monitor the increasing imbalance between the sexes is to track the sex ratios over time, as shown in Table 2-1. The

[a] Although changes in mortality patterns have contributed to the aging of the population, downward trends in fertility have been of greater significance in producing higher proportions of the aged (Spengler 1972; Cowgill 1970; Stockwell 1964). The lower rate of aging in the black population reflects sustained levels of higher fertility, relative to the white population, rather than any racial differential in mortality per se.

Table 2–1. Age Structure of the Population Sixty-Five Years of Age and Older, by Age and Sex, and Sex Ratio: 1950–1977[a]

	1950			*1960*			*1970*			*1977*		
Age	*Male*	*Female*	*Sex Ratio*	*Male*	*Female*	*Sex Ratio*	*Male*	*Female*	*Sex Ratio*	*Male*	*Female*	*Sex Ratio*
65–69 years	41.8%	39.8%	108	39.1%	36.7%	114	37.1%	33.2%	124	39.1%	33.8%	126
70–74 years	28.0	27.6	112	29.1	28.2	117	27.5	26.9	135	27.1	25.4	136
75–79 years	17.3	17.7	117	18.1	18.7	125	18.5	19.5	146	16.6	17.8	156
80–84 years	8.7	9.6	125	8.9	10.1	138	10.4	12.1	161	10.3	12.7	179
85+ years	4.1	5.3	146	4.8	6.3	156	6.4	8.3	179	6.8	10.2	217
Total	100.0%	100.0%	...	100.0%	100.0%	...	100.0%	100.0%	...	100.0%	100.0%	...
	(5,734)[b]	(6,523)	114	(7,503)	(9,056)	121	(8,416)	(11,650)	138	(9,569)	(13,925)	146

Sources: U.S. Bureau of the Census. "Estimates of the Population of the United States by Age, Sex, and Race: 1970 to 1977." Current Population Reports. Series P-25, No. 721, April, 1978, Table 2.

U.S. Bureau of the Census. "General Population Characteristics, United States Summary PC(1)-B1." 1970 Census of the Population. Table 52.

U.S. Bureau of the Census. "Detailed Characteristics, United States Summary." 1960 Census of the Population. Table 158.

[a] The sex ratio is calculated as the number of females per 100 males.

[b] Numbers in parentheses in thousands.

sex ratio indicates the number of females per 100 males. In 1950, there were approximately 114 females per 100 males in the older population; by 1977, the sex ratio had increased to 146. The number of females also increases with age (as can be seen from the table). In 1977, for example, the sex ratio in the youngest age group (sixty-five to sixty-nine) was 126 while the excess of females eighty-five years of age and older was an astonishing 217 females per 100 males.

Implications of Population Change

The changing age structure of the population might be little more than an interesting demographic fact except for what it implies for almost every aspect of our national social and economic life. In housing patterns, the increased size of the very old population (aged seventy-five and older) has particular significance. Housing needs and expectations change with age, and impairments in the activities of daily living are more common. Going to the grocery store, preparing meals, climbing stairs, all may require more effort for the "old-old" than for those elderly in the younger age groups. Maintaining one's own household may become progressively more challenging.

Changes in the sex ratios of the older population have two obvious implications: first, there are, and will continue to be, more older women in the population; second, more older women will head their own households. Most older whites, particularly women, advocate maintaining their own homes and will attempt to do so as long as finances and health allow (Shanas et al. 1968; Lopata 1971). Comparable studies have not been done for older blacks, and therefore, it cannot be determined what proportion of older blacks live with relatives because of financial default or because of an actual preference.

Minority-group elderly, particularly blacks and Hispanics, tend to be in relatively poorer health than their white counterparts. A higher proportion of elderly nonwhites (24 percent) than whites (17 percent) report some type of limitation in mobility, and more older nonwhites living in the community are housebound. Whereas whites with similar impairments tend to be institutionalized, nonwhites remain in the community and need to rely on their families or social services for meeting their physical, social and psychological needs (Soldo and DeVita 1978).

THE OLDER POPULATION AND INCOME

Financial Status of the Elderly

The total income of the elderly is illusive to measure accurately because tax exemptions and various public and private transfer systems constitute an important share of the aged's total personal income. The U.S. Bureau of the Census in 1973 estimated that persons age sixty-five and older received $95.2 billion in income—11.2 percent of the aggregate household money income in the nation.

On an individual basis, financial well-being can frequently be used as a reliable indicator of a person's autonomy. Limited financial resources restrict the range of alternatives an elderly person has for adjusting to old age. Simply stated, money enables the older person to purchase needed, or desired, goods and services.

On the average, the elderly have much lower incomes than younger age groups primarily because of a decrease in income that usually accompanies retirement. Brotman estimates that "retirement brings a reduction of between one-half and two-thirds in money income as retirement benefits replace earnings as the principle source of income" (1974: 5). In comparison to older whites, aged blacks have tended to receive even lower incomes. In 1974, the median income of families with heads age sixty-five or older was $7,298 compared to $12,836 for all families—three-fifths of the national norm. Families with an older female head had lower median incomes than those headed by an older male. The median income of unrelated individuals (those not living with a relative) over age sixty-five was only $2,956 in 1974 (Siegel 1976).

Table 2-2 shows the distribution of total money income for families headed by an older person and elderly unrelated individuals in 1976. These data indicate a broader range of income level for family heads than for persons living outside a family unit. The median income for families with the head age sixty-five or older is approximately $9,210; for unrelated individuals, the median is less than $4,000.

Henretta and Campbell (1976) have demonstrated that the factors that predict income in retirement are the same ones that determine income before retirement: family background, education, occupation, duration and consistency of employment, and marital status. Although retirement is usually associated with a reduction in income, old age does not reduce the importance of the variables involved in the status attainment process itself nor does it minimize racial differences in status maintenance (Jencks et al. 1972). The primary difference between the determinants of pre- and post-retirement income levels is that the effects of midlife status attainment are absorbed by differential access to Social Security claims, pension benefits, savings, and investments. Such forms of unearned income constitute the major income sources of older persons (Bixby 1970).

Money income is defined in official government statistics to include the amount of income received from earnings, Social Security, railroad

Table 2-2. Percentage Distribution of Total Money Income for Persons Age Sixty-Five and Older, by Family Status: 1976

Total Money Income	*Head of Family*	*Unrelated Individuals*[a]
Under $2000	1.3%	10.5%
$2,000–$3,999	9.9	47.5
$4,000–$5,999	18.1	19.8
$6,000–$7,999	15.9	9.2
$8,000–$9,999	12.2	4.5
$10,000–$14,999	19.6	5.1
$15,000–$19,999	10.6	2.0
$20,000–$24,999	5.1	0.5
$25,000+	7.4	0.9
Total	100.0% (8,141)[b]	100.0% (7,027)[b]

Source: U.S. Bureau of the Census. "Money Income in 1976 of Families and Persons in the United States." Current Population Reports. Series P-60, No. 114, July 1978, Tables 20 and 21.

[a] Over 95% of these persons are classified by the Bureau of the Census as primary individuals, most of whom live alone.

[b] Numbers in parentheses, in thousands.

retirement and other pensions, public assistance and welfare programs, and interest and dividends. Income-in-kind such as food stamps, subsidized housing, health benefits, and farm products for home consumption is specifically excluded. As the data in Table 2-3 indicate, the majority of older persons rely on income sources other than earnings. Over three-quarters receive some income from the Social Security system, with as many as one-fifth exclusively dependent on these payments. A family with the head age sixty-five or older is three times more likely to receive its income from a combination of earnings and other income than is the older person who lives alone. Eighty-two percent of the elderly who live outside families and outside institutional settings receive income from sources other than earnings. Although most receive support from Social Security benefits, one-quarter report income solely from sources other than Social Security, such as pensions, public assistance, and property income.

There is little difference between the proportions of blacks and whites who receive Social Security benefits. However, these benefits constitute proportionately more of the average post-retirement income for older persons of low economic status, and blacks and other minorities tend to be overconcentrated in these low-income groups (Abbott 1977). Furthermore, the average retirement and dependent benefits paid to older blacks and other minorities tend to be considera-

Table 2–3. Percentage of Persons Age Sixty-Five and Older Receiving Income from Selected Sources, by Family Status: 1976

Source of Income	*Head of Family*	*Unrelated Individuals*[a,b]
Earnings Only	1.3%	1.4%
Wage or salary only	76.9	94.9
Self-employment income only	6.7	2.0
Wage or salary and self-employment income	16.3	3.0
Earnings and Income Other than Earnings	47.3	16.1
Other Income Only	51.4	81.9
Social Security only	14.8	20.7
Public assistance income only	0.3	0.3
Pension income only	[c]	0.4
Pension and property income only	1.0	1.7
Social Security and other income	62.2	50.9
Other combination of other income, excluding Social Security	21.6	25.9
Total	100.0% (8,141)[d]	100.0% (7,027)[d]

Source: U.S. Bureau of the Census. "Money Income in 1976 of Families and Persons in the United States." Current Population Reports. Series P-60, No. 114, July 1978, Tables 31 and 32.

[a] Over 95% of these persons are classified as primary individuals.

[b] Includes a small number of persons reporting no money income.

[c] Base less than 10,000.

bly below the median benefits received by whites. Under the scheme used to calculate Social Security benefits for retired workers, those who retire before age sixty-five, with low lifetime earnings, and/or interrupted work histories receive minimal benefits. The minority-group elderly frequently fall into one or a combination of these categories.

Receipt of minimum Social Security benefits does not indicate, in itself, inadequate post-retirement income. Social Security benefits can be supplemented, for example, by income from another pension plan. However, analysis of the Social Security Administration's Survey of Newly Entitled Beneficiaries (Rubin 1974) showed that 65 percent of elderly men and 79 percent of elderly women did not receive, nor did they expect to receive, a second pension. The sex differential was more exaggerated for blacks.

Savings, investments, or insurance also can supplement post-retirement income, but relatively few older persons report receipt of income from these sources. According to a survey by the National Council on the Aging, approximately four of every ten older whites had accumulated savings for retirement; but only one of ten elderly blacks had done so. Less than 10 percent of the elderly drew post-retirement incomes from investments. Although the proportion of elderly receiving income from insurance policies is low in general, whites are seven times as likely to have income from insurance than are older black individuals (Jackson and Wood 1976).

Purchase of a house is probably the largest expenditure a family ever makes, and, for the elderly, it is a source of accumulated equity. Nearly three-quarters of persons age sixty-five and older own their home, and over 80 percent of these properties are mortgage-free. The value of the elderly owned homes, however, tends to be decidedly lower than property owned by most other age groups (Baer 1976) and of somewhat poorer quality.[b] (Struyk, Housing Situation, 1977). Black elderly are less likely than white elderly to own their homes, and if they do, the value of the home tends to be lower. Although the accumulated equity of a home may represent a sizable portion of an elderly person's net worth, this asset is not readily accessible and cannot be converted into the income necessary to meet daily living expenses.

Despite the fact that the average annual income of retired persons age sixty-five and older is reduced from their pre-retirement income, their pattern of consumption expenditures does not change considerably. It is typically true that for some items, such as education or transportation, the elderly household spends less than a younger family, but in other areas, namely food, housing, and medical expenses, the elderly spend proportionately more. The latter items also have been among the items hardest hit by inflation. A study by the National Council on the Aging (1978) revealed that between 1972 and 1976, the percentage increase in the cost of food, fuel oil, housing, medical care, and hospital service charges—all items heavily consumed by the elderly—rose at a faster pace than the overall Consumer Price Index for the same period. As costs for the necessities of life increase, less of the annual income is available for discretionary expenditures such as home improvements and maintenance.

Table 2-4 shows the amount and percentage distribution of income spent by two households for common items in 1973. One family is headed by an individual aged fifty-five to sixty-four, while the other head is age sixty-five or older. Although the average income for the older household was approximately one-half (52 percent) that of the younger family, the expenses of the older household were almost two-thirds (62 percent) of the pre-retirement family's expenditures. In seven categories, similar or identical proportions of income were expended.

[b] The quality of housing occupied by older persons is the focus of Chapter 3.

Table 2–4. Annual Consumer Expenditures, by Age of Family Head: 1973

	55–64 years		65+ years	
Family income before taxes	$13,080.00		$6,841.00	
Average annual expenditures, total (current consumption expenses)[a]	$ 7,992.03		$4,888.01	
	Dollars	*%*	*Dollars*	*%*
Food, total	$1,607.99	12.3	$1,113.29	16.3
Alcoholic beverages	72.21	[b]	30.65	[b]
Tobacco products	138.61	1.0	61.39	1.0
Housing, total	2,143.26	16.4	1,600.05	23.0
Clothing, total	608.74	4.7	311.17	5.0
Transportation, total excluding trips	1,691.74	12.9	727.87	10.7
Health care, total	560.01	4.3	497.47	7.3
Personal care (selected expenses)	132.22	1.0	84.74	1.2
Recreation, total	674.53	5.2	353.23	5.2
Reading materials	47.79	[b]	31.37	[b]
Education, total	118.59	1.0	9.76	[b]
Miscellaneous	126.36	1.0	67.03	1.0

Source: U.S. Department of Labor. "Average Annual Expenditures for Commodity and Service Groups Classified by Nine Family Characteristics, 1972 and 1973." Consumer Expenditures Survey Series: Interview Survey, 1972 and 1973. 1976.

[a] Excluding personal insurance, gifts, contributions.

[b] Less than 1 percent.

In three categories (food, housing, and health care), the elderly allocated a greater proportion of their income than did the younger family, and in only two categories (transportation and education) did the elderly spend less.

These data indicate that housing expenditures consume the greatest share of the elderly's budget. Detailed analysis of housing expense burdens is presented in Chapter 3, but we wish to note here that a prior study (Struyk Housing Expense Burden 1977) found that, in contrast to all households, twice as many elderly-headed households were paying an "excessive" amount (beyond 30 percent) of their income for housing.

The proportion of income that must be spent on property taxes is of particular concern for elderly homeowners. For the elderly household faced with a reduced and often fixed income, increasing property taxes can be an onerous burden. Data from 1971 indicate that the elderly paid a substantially greater proportion (8 percent) of their annual income on real estate taxes than did younger homeowners (4 percent). Recently, state governments have attempted to reduce this disparity through tax exemptions for the elderly.

THE ELDERLY POOR

Comparing total money income distributions, or statistics based on such distributions, can be misleading unless controls are introduced for the size of the family and size of the place of residence. Because the cost of living varies between urban centers and rural areas, total money income does not indicate the adequacy of a specific level of income.

A simple poverty definition also presents conceptual problems. As Aaron has noted: "Any fixed poverty threshold is arbitrary . . . It disregards wealth, especially owned homes. It gives as much weight to a family one dollar below it . . . It covers a period too brief (to capture a "normal" income concept) or too long (because hardship from six months of poverty can be severe for families with few assets) . . . It ignores significant amounts of in-kind benefits under an increasing variety of growing Federal and State programs" (1978: 37). Although a more comprehensive income definition is desirable, it is difficult to derive or apply. Despite their shortcomings, the available poverty definitions are convenient and standardized summary indicators of income adequacy.

Originally developed by the Social Security Administration in the mid-1960s, the poverty cutoff is adjusted for such factors as family size, sex of family head, number of children under eighteen years of age, and farm versus nonfarm residence. The poverty-level income cutoffs are revised each year with reference to the annual Consumer Price Index.

In 1976, of the 25 million persons living below the official poverty level, slightly over 3 million (or 13.3 percent) were elderly. This proportion increases to 15 percent when the population age sixty-five and older is used as the denominator. Thirteen percent of all white elderly and 35 percent of older blacks are classified as poor. Translated into absolute numbers, 2.6 million older whites and over 0.5 million older blacks subsist on minimal incomes.

Table 2-5 displays various characteristics of the elderly population and indicates the proportion of elderly below the poverty level in each category. The data show that proportionately almost three times as many older blacks as older whites live in poverty and nearly twice as many women as men are considered poor. Forty percent of older black women and 16 percent of older white women are classified as having income below poverty levels.

Although 12 percent of the elderly in metropolitan areas are poor, the problem is more acute in the nonmetropolitan regions, where one in five older persons lives in poverty. Particularly hard pressed are the rural nonfarm elderly; that is, those persons living in small communities away from an urban center. Approximately 1.2 million white

Table 2–5. Percentage of Elderly below the Poverty Level, by Race and Selected Characteristics[a]

Selected Characteristics	All Races Total	All Races % below Poverty	White Total	White % below Poverty	Black Total	Black % below Poverty
Sex						
Persons age 65+	22,100	15.0	20,020	13.2	1,852	34.8
Males	9,132	10.8	8,238	9.1	776	28.0
Females	12,968	17.9	11,782	16.0	1,076	39.6
Location						
Metropolitan areas	13,846	12.1	12,459	10.5	1,226	29.4
In central cities	6,842	15.1	5,720	12.8	1,017	28.9
Outside central cities	7,004	9.3	6,739	8.6	209	31.8
Nonmetropolitan areas	8,254	19.8	7,561	17.5	626	45.2
Farm	1,009	13.2	949	11.3	53	[b]
Rural nonfarm	7,245	20.7	6,612	18.4	573	45.0
Tenure						
Owner-occupied units	10,647	14.7	9,845	13.1	725	35.0
Family, head 65+	6,690	7.6	6,152	6.1	482	24.9
Unrelated individual						
Males	781	19.0	716	16.9	59	[b]
Females	3,176	28.7	2,977	26.7	184	59.2
Living alone	3,813	26.9	3,571	25.0	223	56.1
Renter-occupied units	4,170	26.8	3,608	23.9	514	46.9
Family, head 65+	1,439	15.0	1,201	11.5	211	24.9
Unrelated individual						
Males	614	31.2	497	28.1	109	47.9
Females	2,117	33.4	1,910	30.6	194	61.2
Living alone	2,670	33.0	2,357	30.3	292	55.8

Source: U.S. Bureau of the Census. "Characteristics of the Population below the Poverty Level: 1976." Current Population Reports. Series P-60, No. 115, July 1978, Tables 8, 9, 11, and 24.

[a] Numbers in thousands.

[b] Base less than 75,000.

elderly and 0.25 million black elderly live in poverty conditions at nonmetropolitan nonfarm locations.

A profile of the elderly poor by housing tenure shows that 15 percent of all elderly owner-occupied housing units and 27 percent of all elderly renter-occupied units are classified below poverty. For blacks, these proportions increase to 35 and 47 percent, respectively. Table 2-5 also indicates that elderly poverty rates vary not only by race but also by type of living arrangement. Regardless of tenure, the poverty rate for the elderly living alone is higher than that for families headed by an older person.

Variations in the 1976 poverty rates of the elderly by region, place of residence, and family status are shown in Table 2-6. The data

Table 2–6. Poverty Rates for the Population Age Sixty-Five and Older, by Region, Metropolitan-Nonmetropolitan, Place of Residence and Family Status: 1976

Metropolitan and Family Status	Percent of Total below Poverty Level		
		Regions	
	United States	North and West	South
Total			
Persons 65+	15.0	11.3	22.5
In families, head 65+	8.9	5.8	15.0
Not in families	30.3	24.3	43.5
Metropolitan			
Persons 65+	12.1	10.1	18.0
In families, head 65+	6.6	5.2	10.7
Not in families	25.6	21.7	37.7
Nonmetropolitan			
Persons 65+	19.8	14.0	26.8
In families, head 65+	12.4	7.1	18.8
Not in families	38.7	30.4	49.4

Source: U.S. Bureau of the Census. "Characteristics of the Population below the Poverty Level: 1976." Current Population Reports. Series P-60, No. 115, July 1978, Table 9.

indicate that the rates of poverty among the older population are twice as great in the South as in the North and West regions, and that metropolitan areas show lower proportions of elderly in poverty than do nonmetropolitan areas, regardless of region. The major predictor of income adequacy appears to be family status. Depending on region and place of residence, one-quarter to one-half of persons age sixty-five and over who are not living in a family have incomes below the poverty level. In contrast, only 9 percent of all families with the head age sixty-five or older are in poverty. The highest poverty rates occur among the elderly in the nonmetropolitan areas of the South who do not live in a family environment. Almost 50 percent of these persons have incomes below minimal standards.

References in the literature often speak of the "near poor," those persons with income close to, but not below, the poverty line. The U.S. Department of Health, Education and Welfare has established this measure as persons with income 25 percent above the poverty threshold. In 1975, 5.5 million elderly, or one-quarter of the older population, were considered near poor. For a two-person family headed by a person sixty-five years of age or older, the near poor income level in 1975 was $4,040. For an elderly individual it was $3,215 (National Council on the Aging 1978). The near poor must also be considered to have inadequate incomes, and thereby add to the magnitude of the problem of housing for the elderly poor.

The issue of income adequacy has received much attention in the past two decades, and some success has been achieved in reducing the proportion of older persons who maintain households below the poverty level. The differential in the proportions of elderly blacks and elderly whites who live in poverty also has declined since the mid-1960s. Recent data, however, seem to indicate a slight increase in the proportion of families with an older head living in poverty. Nevertheless, depending on region and place of residence, elderly persons not in families are two to four times more likely to have poverty-level incomes than are those in families headed by a person sixty-five years of age or older.

The income of poor elderly is largely dependent upon publicly financed sources. The majority of elderly receive some income from Social Security benefits, but for those below the poverty threshold in old age, the benefits are the primary source of postretirement income (Soldo 1978; Soldo and DeVita 1978). Although automatic cost-of-living increases have adjusted the Social Security benefits each year since 1975, the average monthly benefit barely keeps pace with inflation and in some cases falls short of the poverty-level threshold (National Council on the Aging 1978).

Some elderly are able to qualify for the Supplemental Security Income (SSI) program—a federal welfare program that provides a minimal level of income for aged, blind, and disabled persons. In 1976 approximately 2.4 million persons age sixty-five and older—about 10.5 percent of the elderly population—received SSI payments. A greater proportion (13 percent) of unrelated individuals, primarily persons living alone, received SSI benefits than did older heads of households (8 percent). Proportionately more blacks than white were SSI recipients.

Other welfare and public assistance programs are available to the elderly poor, including food stamps, health benefits, and subsidized housing. Low-rent public housing is the largest and perhaps best known of the federal housing assistance programs. Although not officially designed to aid any particular age group, the program has benefited the elderly substantially. Myriad rent supplement programs are also available to assist the elderly in obtaining adequate housing. A detailed discussion of these programs can be found in Chapter 7.

Many of the low-income elderly, particularly blacks and members of other minority groups, have experienced a lifetime of poverty. Because of this, it could be assumed that many poor elderly are renters who were unable to purchase their own homes earlier in their life. On the contrary, 70 percent of the 725,000 elderly-headed families below the poverty line in 1976 lived in owner-occupied housing. The data in

Table 2–7. Percentage of Elderly Living in Owner-Occupied Housing Units, by Living Arrangement, Age, and Poverty Status: 1976[a]

	All Incomes		*Below Poverty Level*	
Living Arrangement and Age	*Number*	*% in Owner-Occupied Units*	*Number*	*% in Owner-Occupied Units*
Persons in Households	22,100	74.8	3,313	59.6
Age 65–71	10,838	77.3	1,372	63.0
Age 72+	11,262	72.4	1,942	57.1
Family Head	8,128	82.3	725	70.2
Age 65–71	4,316	84.2	355	73.5
Age 72+	3,813	80.1	370	67.0
Living with Relatives	7,100	81.3	560	64.3
Age 65–71	3,748	82.5	282	72.3
Age 72+	3,351	79.9	278	55.8
Living with Nonrelative	390	67.7	122	64.8
Age 65–71	190	62.1	60	60.0
Age 72+	200	73.0	62	69.4
Living Alone	6,482	58.8	1,906	53.8
Age 65–71	2,585	59.3	675	53.9
Age 72+	3,898	58.5	1,231	53.9

Source: U.S. Bureau of the Census. "Characteristics of the Population below the Poverty Level: 1976." Current Population Reports. Series P-60, No. 115, July 1978, Table 15.

[a] Numbers in thousands.

Table 2-7 show that, regardless of living arrangement or poverty status, a majority of elderly reside in owner-occupied housing. Even among the poor elderly living alone, 54 percent, or 1.9 million individuals, own their own homes. This proportion was higher for elderly females (56 percent) than for elderly males (44 percent). With advancing age, the proportion of older persons in owner-occupied housing diminishes only slightly.

SUMMARY

With an increasing proportion of the population age sixty-five and older, the needs and concerns of the elderly have become more visible to the public. Not only are there more older people, but a demographic profile of the aged reveals that many more are living beyond age seventy or seventy-five. There are many more females than males in these older age groups, and with advancing age, chronic illness and functional impairment become more prevalent.

Socially and economically, the elderly prefer, and attempt, to live independently. During recent decades an increasing proportion of older persons maintained their own households, either as a husband and wife team or alone. This trend has been possible partly because of a rise in income among the elderly, even though the elderly's median income is substantially lower than that of the population as a whole. The proportion of older persons living below the poverty line has been falling sharply. In 1976, only 15 percent of the older population were poor, compared to 35 percent in 1959. Data show, however, that the very old have a greater probability of being functionally impaired and financially poor.

It is significant that three-quarters of the older population reside in owner-occupied housing. Although these units are frequently of less value and of lower quality than the housing stock occupied by the younger age groups, the homes represent a major financial asset for the older person, as well as social and psychological security. Reduced retirement income and inflationary price spirals combine to restrict the quality and quantity of repair and maintenance work that can be undertaken by the elderly homeowner. Not only are the lower-income elderly unable to undertake home repairs, but the middle-income elderly defer or eliminate such expenses when faced with budget constraints. Such action frequently results in a gradual reduction of housing comfort for the older individual as well as in a deterioration of the housing stock.

REFERENCES

Aaron, H.J. 1978. "Politics and the Professions: The Great Society in Perspective." Washington, D.C.: The Brookings Institution.

Abbott, J. 1977. "Socioeconomic Characteristics of the Elderly: Some Black-White Differences." *Social Security Bulletin* (July): 16–42.

Baer, W.C. 1976. "Federal Housing Programs for the Elderly." In M.P. Lawton, R.J. Newcomer, and T.O. Byerts, eds., *Community Planning for an Aging Society,* pp. 81–98. Stroudsburg, Pa: Dowden Hutchinson and Ross, Inc.

Bixby, L.E. 1970. "Income of People Aged 65 and Over: Overview from the 1968 Survey of the Aged." *Social Security Bulletin* (April): 3–25.

Brotman, H.B. 1974. "The Economics of Aging." Paper presented at the Conference on Aging, University of Miami, Coral Gables, Florida.

Cowgill, D. 1970. "The Demography of Aging." In A. Hoffman, ed., *The Daily Needs and Interests of Older People,* pp. 27–70. Springfield, Ill.: C.C Thomas, Publishers.

Henretta, J.C., and R.T. Campbell. 1976. "Status Attainment and Status Maintenance: A Study of Stratification in Old Age." *American Sociological Review* 41: 981–992.

Jackson, M., and J.L. Wood. 1976. *Aging in America: Implications for Black Aged.* Washington, D.C.: The National Council on the Aging, Inc.

Jencks, C.; M. Smith; H. Land; J. Bane; D. Cohen; H. Gintis; B. Heyns; and S. Michelson. 1972. *Inequality: A Reassessment of the Effect of Family and Schooling in America.* New York: Basic Books.

Kerschner, P.A., and I.S. Hirschfield. 1975. "Public Policy and Aging: Analytic Approaches." In D.S. Woodruff and J.E. Birren, eds., *Aging: Scientific Perspectives and Social Issues,* pp. 352–73. New York: D. Van Nostrand Company.

Lopata, H.Z. 1971. *Widowhood in an American City.* Cambridge, Mass.: Shaenkman.

Maddox, G. 1968. "Persistence of Life Style Among the Elderly: A Longitudinal Study of Patterns of Social Activity in Relation to Life Satisfaction." In B.L. Newgarten, ed., *Middle Age and Aging,* pp. 181–83. Chicago: University of Chicago Press.

National Council on the Aging, Inc. 1978. *Fact Book on Aging: A Profile of America's Older Population.* Washington, D.C.: National Council on the Aging.

Rubin, L. 1974. "Economic Status of Black Persons: Findings from the Survey of Newly Entitled Beneficiaries." *Social Security Bulletin* (December): 16–35.

Shanas, E., and G. Maddox. 1976. "Aging, Health and the Organization of Health Resources." In R.H. Binstock and E. Shanas, eds., *Handbook of Aging and the Social Sciences,* pp. 592–618. New York: Van Nostrand Reinhold Company.

Shanas, E.; P. Townsend; D. Wedderburn; H. Friis; P. Milhoj; and J. Stewhouwer. 1968. *Old People in Three Industrial Societies.* New York: Atherton Press.

Siegel, J.S. 1976. "Demographic Aspects of Aging and the Older Population in the United States." *Current Population Reports,* Series P-23, No. 59. Washington, D.C.: Government Printing Office.

Soldo, B.J. 1978. "Incomes of Black Aged: Their Determinants and Consequences." Paper presented at the conference on Blacks and Retirement: An Untapped National Resource, sponsored by the Council on Minority Planning and Strategy. Washington, D.C.: Center for Population Research. Mimeo.

Soldo, B.J., and C.J. DeVita. 1978. "Profiles of Black Aged." Paper presented at the conference on Blacks and Retirement: An Untapped National Resource, sponsored by the Council on Minority Planning and Strategy. Washington, D.C.: Center for Population Research. Mimeo.

Spengler, J.J. 1962. "Aging Populations: Mechanics, Historical Emergence, Impact." *Law and Contemporary Problems* 27: 1–21.

Stockwell, E.G. 1964. "Some Notes on the Changing Age Structure of the United States." *Rural Sociology* 29: 67–74.

Struyk, R.J. 1977a. "The Housing Situation of Elderly Americans." *The Gerontologist* 17, no. 2: 130–39.

———. 1977b. "The Housing Expense Burden of Households Headed by the Elderly." *The Gerontologist* 17, no. 5: 447–52.

Chapter 3

The Current Housing Situation

A prerequisite for discussing the maintenance and improvement of the physical environment in which elderly Americans reside—even for discussing the need for some improvement—is to know the current situation.[a] Remarkably, until quite recently the housing circumstances of Americans over age sixty-five were poorly documented, which permitted a wide range of characterizations to exist unchallenged, side by side. A broad-brush description of long-term national housing trends is given below to provide the context for a detailed discussion of the current situation of the elderly.

A NATIONAL PICTURE

In 1976 there were about 79 million dwelling units in the United States designed for year-round occupancy: 31 percent in the central cities of standard metropolitan statistical areas (SMSAs), 34 percent in the balance of the SMSAs, and the remaining 35 percent in smaller towns and farms outside of SMSAs. Furthermore, there has been a

[a] The decennial census has been the traditional source of such data. For a description of the data gathered in 1970, see the appendix in U.S. Bureau of the Census (1972). The most detailed tabulations of the decennial census data for the elderly are in U.S. Bureau of the Census (1973).

Data from special surveys have also been useful; one of the best of these special surveys is described in Beyer (1961). Another important paper uses data from the 1973 Survey of the Low Income and Disabled: see Schieber (1978).

The most recent analysis, using the Annual Housing Survey, has been by Struyk (1977).

sharp increase in housing stock (17 percent between 1970 and 1976). While these counts are interesting, of greater concern is what has happened to the quality of housing.

Data from the 1950–1970 decennial censuses are displayed in Table 3-1, showing several quality indicators for renters and owners and for three separate income groups. The incomes are expressed in 1970 dollars for all three censuses, making it possible to compare, for example, how a household with a $5,000 income in 1970 would have been housed with the same purchasing power in 1950 and 1960. The point made resoundingly by these data is the broad improvement in occupied housing. All three indicators of deficiencies—lack of plumbing, delapidated structure, and crowding—show marked reductions. Further, indicators of improved housing quality—the median number of rooms occupied and the presence of air conditioning—generally increased. Finally, because of the sharp rise in homeownership and the better average housing of owner-occupants over the period, the improvement experienced by the average household is understated in these data.

Similarly, in setting the stage for examining more recent data, it is important to know what has happened to the percentage of income devoted to housing in the postwar period. Table 3-2 provides rough documentation; it is imprecise because of the assumptions one must use to convert the data on the value of owner-occupied housing into an equivalent rental or expenditure figure. In summary, these data suggest no change in the percentage of income devoted to housing. When one looks at the situation for individual household types, however, it becomes clear that this constant housing expense-to-income ratio has two elements: (1) the ratio has been falling for many of the household types while remaining roughly constant for the others; and (2) there has been a shift over time into those household types that have traditionally had the higher expense burdens. Overall, the picture for 1950–1970 appears quite favorable. For the period since 1970, however, there has been much debate about the true cost of housing, particularly of homeownership. Because much of this debate concerns first time homeowners—not typically elderly households—it will not be reviewed here.[b] Recent trends for the elderly, including homeowners, are described below.

THE HOUSING OF THE ELDERLY

Three aspects of the housing situation of the aged are documented in this chapter: (1) the physical characteristics of the dwellings occupied,

[b] For a discussion of the debate see Follain, Katz, and Struyk (1979); also, Weicher (1978).

with special emphasis on a set of conditions that is fairly commonly accepted as being deficiencies; (2) the characteristics of the neighborhoods in which the dwelling is located for urban households; and (3) the housing expense burden, defined as the percentage of current income spent on housing services. Exploring these aspects in considerable detail will provide essential facts for the discussions in the remainder of this study and will permit a closer analysis of the present situation than previously available, an exercise useful in its own right.

The data employed are from the 1974 and 1976 Annual Housing Survey, a national survey of approximately 70,000 dwelling units that has been fielded by the Department of Housing and Urban Development and the Bureau of the Census[c] since 1973. Each year an enumerator returns to the same group of dwelling units, thus creating a longitudinal record for those households who have not relocated. The survey as a whole gives a longitudinal record of the entire housing stock, including demolitions and new construction.[d]

Not all elderly are included in our tabulations. The study excludes those elderly who are living in a dependent status and are not designated as heads of households, such as the widow living in her daughter's household, in whose case the quality of housing depends heavily on the housing preferences of her daughter and son-in-law. The present focus is on the relation between the economic and personal resources of the elderly and their physical environment. We have termed the subpopulation studied here the "independent elderly" in an attempt to keep the distinction before the reader.[e]

The elderly population is disaggregated along several different lines: homeowners and renters are distinguished; households are separated into three types (husband-wife families, individuals living alone, and individuals living with nonspouse relatives and/or nonrelatives); and units occupied by blacks and whites are contrasted.

In some instances, households are divided into a three-class system based on current incomes: those in poverty, those between the poverty cutoff and 200 percent of the poverty cutoff, and those with incomes greater than twice the poverty definition. Poverty is defined for each

[c] The survey is described in U.S. Bureau of the Census (1975). The figures in the present report have been compiled from a users' data tape of these data, not from the printed reports, which do not distinguish aged from other households.

[d] The survey adds new units as they are built and keeps them in the survey. The reader might also note that the 1973 survey is not being used here because (1) a change in geographic definitions made it impossible to link the 1973 records with later years, and (2) the income and housing expenditure data was greatly improved in the 1974 survey.

[e] The "hidden" elderly are certainly of interest in themselves, given that many are economically constrained to be part of larger families. For an analysis of the choice of living arrangements of the elderly see Soldo (1978).

Table 3–1. Trends in Selected Measures of Housing Quality by Tenure for Constant Real Income Groups[a] Proportion of Units

Tenure and 1970 Income	Mean Number of Rooms	Lacking Some Plumbing[b]	In Dilapidated Condition	Crowded[c]	With Air Conditioning		Share of All Households Owner-Occupant
					central	room	
Income under $5,000							
Renters							
1950	3.5	.21	.13	.20	[d]	[d]	
1960	[d]	.19	.08	.15	.01	.05	
1970	3.4	.08	[d]	.09	.06	.17	
Owner-Occupants							
1950	5.0	.16	.06	.10	[d]	[d]	.41
1960	[d]	.09	.04	.06	.01	.09	.42
1970	5.2	.06	[d]	.03	.07	.24	.42
Income $5,000–$10,000							
Renters							
1950	4.0	.07	.04	.17	[d]	[d]	
1960	[d]	.07	.03	.15	.01	.09	
1970	4.2	.03	[d]	.11	.09	.25	

Owner-Occupants							
1950	5.3	.05	.07	.05	[d]	[d]	.53
1960	[d]	.02	.01	.10	.02	.12	.60
1970	5.6	.02	[d]	.08	.09	.30	.62
Income over $15,000							
Renters							
1950	4.1	.02	.02	.11	[d]	[d]	
1960	[d]	.03	.01	.10	.03	.17	
1970	4.6	.01	[d]	.09	.15	.34	
Owner-Occupants							
1950	6.2	.01	.01	.04	[d]	[d]	.66
1960	[d]	.01	[e]	.06	.05	.19	.77
1970	6.5	.01	[d]	.06	.21	.31	.75

Source: de Leeuw, F.; Schnare, A.; and Struyk, R. "Housing." In *The Urban Predicament,* edited by William Gorham and N. Glazer. Washington, D.C.: The Urban Institute, 1976, p. 123.

[a] Data refer to real incomes in each interval 1950–70 for households with 1970 incomes in that interval. For example, 1950 and 1960 income equivalents for $5,000 are approximately $3,000 and $4,000, using GNP price deflator, 1967 = 100. Data are only for dwellings in metropolitan areas.

[b] Complete plumbing includes exclusive use of toilet and tub or shower, and hot and cold running water.

[c] Over one person per room.

[d] Data not available for this year.

[e] Less than 0.005.

Table 3–2. Housing Expense-to-Income Ratios, by Age and Household Type: 1950–1970[a]

	1950	1960	1970
All households	.20	.20	.19
Nonelderly Households			
Husband-wife families			
Head under age 45	.19	.17	.17
Head age 45–65	.17	.15	.14
Other families			
Male head	[b]	.18	.19
Female head	[b]	.25	.26
Single individuals	[b]	.29	.23
Elderly Households			
Husband-wife families	.23	.21	.21
Other families			
Male headed	[b]	.20	.19
Female headed	[b]	.25	.28
Single individuals	[b]	.51	.38

Source: de Leeuw, F.; Schnare, A.; and Struyk, R. "Housing." In *The Urban Predicament,* edited by William Gorham and N. Glazer. Washington, D.C.: The Urban Institute, 1976, p. 123.

[a] Data for metropolitan areas only. House values converted to rents using rent-value ratio of 0.008.

[b] For 1950, data for single individuals cannot be separated from non-husband/wife family data.

household size in urban and rural areas.[f] (The problems with using a simple poverty definition were described in Chapter 2.)

Another important characteristic of elderly households is the functional health and mobility status of household members. Unfortunately, neither the Annual Housing Survey nor other national data provide information on both health/mobility status and housing status. Although the correlation between the age and the extent of physical and mental impairments is only moderate (Shanas and Maddox 1976), age is often used as an indicator of health status and mobility constraints. Some of the tabulations, therefore, divide older households into two age groups: those sixty-five to seventy-four and those seventy-five years of age and older.

Finally, two geographic classifications are employed, including the four census regions and a metropolitan versus nonmetropolitan distinction. With these various disaggregations a picture of the current situation and recent trends in the housing of the elderly emerges.

[f] The poverty definitions are from U.S. Department of Health, Education and Welfare (1976: Table 2).

Table 3–3. Percentage Distribution of Elderly and Nonelderly Households, by Household Type, Race, and Location and Income, by Tenure Status: 1976

	Owner-Occupants		*Renters*	
	Elderly	*Nonelderly*	*Elderly*	*Nonelderly*
Household Types				
Husband-wife	53%	84%	25%	45%
Single individuals	34	6	64	27
Other	13	10	11	27
Race				
Black	7	7	12	17
Other	93	93	88	83
Household Type, by Race				
Husband-wife				
Black	6	6	11	12
Other	94	94	89	88
Single occupant				
Black	7	9	11	16
Other	93	91	89	84
Other				
Black	17	17	21	29
Other	83	83	79	71
Location				
Metropolitan	58	66	77	78
Nonmetropolitan	42	34	23	22
Income				
Below poverty	16	6	28	19
Poverty to twice poverty	35	15	43	27
Over twice poverty	49	79	29	54

Source: Unpublished tabulations from the Annual Housing Survey, 1976.

Table 3-3 contrasts various demographic and economic characteristics of elderly and nonelderly. The distinction between tenure forms is important since in 1973 about 73 percent of the elderly owned their homes compared with 65 percent for the nonelderly. The household composition of owner-occupants differs sharply between the elderly and nonelderly, with husband-wife households being much less important among the elderly. Most elderly renters are single-person households. In comparing the racial composition of the three household types, one sees that blacks account for a higher proportion of "other" households, that is, multiperson non-husband/wife households, for both the elderly and the nonelderly. Elderly homeowners are more evenly split between metropolitan and nonmetropolitan locations than the nonelderly; for renters the spatial distributions of the elderly and nonelderly are identical.

As expected from the discussion in the preceding chapter, the elderly are much more concentrated in the poverty class and the twice poverty income class, a pattern that holds for both homeowners and renters. Elderly homeowners, though, have substantially higher incomes than their renter counterparts.

Structural Characteristics

Traditionally, a discussion of housing conditions focused on the small set of deficiency measures collected in the decennial census because these data were available and because these indicators corresponded to widely held views about what constituted acceptable housing. Thus, three factors were (and still are) regarded as "the bottom line": (1) incomplete plumbing, that is, not having one or more of piped hot and cold water, a tub or shower, and a toilet for the exclusive use of the household available; (2) overcrowding, generally defined as more than one person per room; and (3) dilapidated condition of the structure. A dilapidated unit is defined by the Census Bureau as one that does not provide safe and adequate shelter and in its present condition, endangers the health, safety, or well-being of the occupants. Examples of defects that result in such a classification include holes, open cracks, or rotted, loose, or missing materials over large areas of the foundation, outside walls, roof, or inside walls, and so on, or substantial sagging of structural members. Shacks, huts, tents, and similar units can also be classified as dilapidated.

There was a high incidence of all of these three factors in the housing stock in 1950 when these data were first collected. With a decrease in their incidence, many housing professionals have come to take a broader view of the services provided by housing. On the structural side, in addition to the minimum health and safety requirements embodied in the old census definition, the flow of services yielded by the structure and component systems have become critical. Thus, in addition to having complete plumbing, it is equally important that it work dependably. Similarly, it is not only the number and size of the rooms in the dwelling that matter, but also the condition of the walls, ceilings, and floors. The more dependable the systems, the greater the structural integrity, and the better the physical condition, the greater the flow of services provided by the unit.

Each dwelling also has a set of neighborhood attributes associated with it including the condition of the neighbors' dwellings, the condition of the block front, and the public services provided in the area. If there is any doubt as to whether households value such neighborhood attributes, one need merely compare the sales prices of similar dwelling units in different school districts.

Unfortunately, no one has developed an index of factors that accurately measures service flows. As a consequence, one must examine a large number of indicators to piece together the overall situation for a given group or to compare the housing circumstances of one group with another. Table 3-4 describes the structural characteristics of the housing of the elderly by using a general description of the units occupied by households headed by a person over sixty-four years old. These data provide the background for examination of the question of the number of serious dwelling deficiencies experienced by the elderly, which will be taken up later in this chapter.

The data shown in Table 3-4 provide for a broad description of the housing of households headed by an individual sixty-five years of age and older compared with households headed by younger persons. Again, homeowners are distinguished from renters. The table provides information on tenure and on general physical characteristics of the dwelling units occupied: number of rooms, age of structure, and so on. A more detailed description of dwelling quality is in the next section.

Both elderly homeowners and renters reside longer in their units than their nonelderly counterparts. However, the differences are particularly great for owners: while 81 percent of younger households have lived in their home fifteen years or less, only 30 percent of the elderly are such "short time" residents.

In terms of the physical attributes, there is a consistent pattern of the elderly living in somewhat more modest units than other households. Among owner-occupants, the units occupied by the elderly have central heat less often, are smaller as measured by the count of rooms and bathrooms, have a lower incidence of air conditioning, are less well insulated and are substantially older. Additionally, about 5 percent more of the elderly than other owner-occupants live in multiunit structures, with the difference about evenly divided between two-to-four-unit and five-or-more-unit structures.

Among renters, substantially fewer of the elderly live in single-unit structures, probably because of the greater maintenance requirements of such units. Compared to younger renter households, the elderly live in much smaller apartments, units in somewhat older structures and in structures that are less well insulated. For many other characteristics, though, there is comparability between the aged and nonaged.

Dwelling Quality

While a broad description of the structural housing situation of the elderly is informative and important, it is also critical to know how many elderly fall below some standard of minimally acceptable housing. An attempt to calculate this number immediately raises the prob-

Table 3–4. Percentage Distribution of General Characteristics of Units Occupied by Elderly and Nonelderly, by Tenure: 1976

	Owner-Occupants		*Renters*	
	Elderly	*Non-elderly*	*Elderly*	*Non-elderly*
A. Tenure				
Year moved into dwelling unit				
Since 1970	15	48	55	87
1965–1970	13	20	20	8
1960–1964	12	13	11	3
1950–1959	24	14	8	2
before 1950	35	5	7	1
B. Physical Characteristics				
1. Units in structure				
1	90	95	22	33
2–4	7	4	28	29
5 or more	3	1	50	38
2. Number of complete bathrooms				
1	63	43	86	82
More than 1	34	56	7	14
None	3	1	7	4
3. Type of heating equipment				
Central heat	81	92	80	83
Room heaters	16	6	16	13
Fireplace, stove, other	2	2	3	2
None	1	1	1	1
4. Number of rooms				
1–2	...	...	18	9
3–4	21	8	65	56
5–6	60	56	16	30
7 or more	19	36	1	4
5. Year structure built				
Since 1970	3	16	12	16
1965–1970	6	13	11	12
1960–1964	7	14	8	9
1950–1959	21	25	11	12
1940–1949	16	10	11	10
Before 1940	46	22	48	41
6. Main water source				
Public or private system	86	85	96	93
Well	13	14	4	5
Other	1	1	1	1
7. Heating fuel used in winter				
Gas or oil	90	86	81	80
Electric	8	12	15	17
Wood or coal	2	1	2	1
Other or none	...	1	2	1
8. Unit is mobile home	6	6	1	2
9. Unit has full kitchen for private use	99	100	95	98

Table 3–4. continued

	Owner-Occupants		Renters	
	Elderly	Non-elderly	Elderly	Non-elderly
10. Unit has air conditioning	50	60	41	46
11. Leakage problems				
Basement	12	12	[a]	[a]
(percent of units having basement)	(53)	(51)	[a]	[a]
Roof leaks	5	4	[a]	[a]
12. Evidence of rats or mice	9	9	8	12
13. Electrical outlets present in every room	96	98	95	96
14. Must pass through one bedroom to reach another	6	5	9	8
15. Insulation				
Ceiling is insulated	71	85	7	14
All windows have storm windows	49	51	4	9
All doors have storm doors	55	52	5	9

Source: Unpublished tabulations from the Annual Housing Survey, 1976.
[a] Figures not computed because of potential sampling problems.

lem of defining "minimally acceptable housing," a formidable problem since there is no widespread agreement even on what should be included in such a standard,[g] or which set within the many that can be constructed using the Annual Housing Survey data is appropriate.

Three approaches to choosing a set of indicators are available. The first is to examine the results of various regression analyses that "explain" the variation in gross rents or house values in terms of the physical attributes of the unit (among other factors) and use those attributes the results show to have a statistically significant *negative* effect on rents or values. While this approach holds forth something of an ideal, the techniques used to develop data seem too crude to capture a number of important factors.[h]

The second approach is to rely on preferences of society at large. One begins with a cohort of households for whom it is reasonable to assume that current income is close to "long run" or normal income. When the housing of cohorts of households with successively higher incomes are contrasted, one observes a reduction in those "housing deficiencies" that society finds most objectionable. This particular method has been used previously in studying the housing of the elderly, fairly success-

[g] For a discussion of the distinction between indicators and standards of housing quality, see Baer (1976). Also see Rosenblatt (1971).
[h] For a discussion see Mendelsohn and Struyk (1976).

Table 3–5. Indicators of Housing Inadequacy

Variable Name	*Description*
Plumbing	Unit either lacks complete plumbing facilities or household must share their use.
Kitchen	Unit either lacks a complete kitchen or household must share their use.
Sewage	One or more of the following three services was unavailable or completely unusable for six or more hours at least three times during the past ninety days: (1) running water, (2) sewage system, (3) toilet.
Heat	The heating system was completely unusable for six or more hours at least three times during the past winter.
Maintenance	Two or more of the following four conditions exist: (1) leaking roof, (2) substantial cracks or holes in walls and ceilings, (3) holes in floors, (4) broken plaster or peeling paint in areas larger than 1 square foot.
Public Halls	The unit is in a building with public hallways and stairs, and two or more of the following three conditions exists: (1) missing light fixtures, (2) stair railings are missing or poorly attached, (3) missing, loose, or broken steps.

fully.[i] A problem with the method as applied in the past was that, in addition to deficiencies being eliminated as income rises, "luxury" items entered—for example, air conditioning. The result is a list too inclusive for a number of purposes.

The third approach, and the one followed in this study, is to include deficiencies that would disqualify the dwelling for assistance under the Housing Assistance Payments Program (commonly called the Section 8 program because it is Section 8 of the Housing Act of 1937 as amended in 1974), as administered by the Department of Housing and Urban Development.[j] The items included in the Section 8 standard certainly do not include luxury items. Use of these as quality indicators also has the benefit of pointing out what fraction of units could be brought into the nation's largest assisted housing program after some repair or rehabilitation work had been completed.

Table 3-5 defines six indicators used in this study. Note that some have several parts. Although these indicators do not exhaust the list of standards a unit would have to pass to participate in the program, they do include those that appear to measure best a low level of housing

[i] For a complete description of this procedure see Goedert and Goodman (1976). The procedure was applied to the elderly in Struyk (1977).

[j] The program is described in detail in Chapter 7. These standards are defined in U.S. Department of Housing and Urban Development (1978: 118–19).

services or chronic disruptions in services *and* that would require nontrivial investments to correct.

One way to judge the reasonableness of using these criteria is to look at how the flow of services provided by a dwelling is affected by the presence of one or more of the deficiencies. A crude measure for rental units is the level of gross rents.[k] These figures suggest that households place a lower value on rental units where services are made unavailable because of the deficiencies as defined in Table 3-5.[l]

Table 3-6 presents data on the quality of housing occupied by the elderly in 1976. The mass of figures may appear impenetrable, but when the data for specific groups are examined separately, a set of conclusions emerges.

Elderly versus Nonelderly. Panel A of Table 3-6 clearly shows that the elderly have a higher incidence of incomplete plumbing and kitchen facilities, a basic structural deficiency. Six percent of elderly renters have incomplete plumbing and 5 percent lack complete kitchens. Elderly and nonelderly are about evenly matched for heating system and sewage breakdowns; for maintenance deficiencies the results are clearly mixed, with elderly renters having fewer deficiencies than their nonelderly counterparts.

Household type. Among the three household types distinguished—husband-wife, single persons, and other—those in the "other" category have the greatest incidence of deficiencies for both homeowners and renters as shown in Table 3-6, panel B. Husband-wife households exhibit the lowest incidence, with single-person households the second lowest. The stronger economic position of "other" households makes this result somewhat surprising, but it could be explained by the joint income of the household—which may be two "partners" living together—and may not actually indicate the income available to the householder for meeting housing expenses.

Age. Panel C of the table shows the incidence of these deficiencies for households headed by the young-old (sixty-five to seventy-four) and old-old (seventy-five and older). The differences between these two groups is modest compared to those observed for the three household types. These figures indicate that age alone is not a good predictor of

[k] Value of dwelling figures are not used for owner-occupants because they represent the capitalization of the current and expected flow of services and hence embody both the flow of services and the estimate of the remaining useful life of the unit. Since the second varies in unknown ways, the value figure is a poor representation of flow of services.

[l] For further data on the quality rent relationship see Wieand, (1978).

housing quality despite its correlation with physical impairments and household type; that is, older persons are more likely to live in alternatives to the traditional husband-wife household.

Location. Two location breakouts are presented: the four census regions (panel D) and units located within and outside of metropolitan areas (panel E). The variation among regions is striking for the three deficiencies for which there is generally reliable data—plumbing, kitchen, and maintenance. The South has the greatest incidence of these deficiencies; the West has the least. For kitchens and plumbing, the incidence in the South is nearly twice that of the next worst region, with deficiency rates of 8 and 12 percent, respectively; for maintenance, the South and the Northeast have similar high rates compared to the North Central and West.

The incidence of deficiencies for elderly households living outside of metropolitan areas for plumbing and kitchens are several times the incidence of those living within metropolitan areas. Fourteen percent of nonmetropolitan elderly renters do not have complete plumbing facilities in their units; in metropolitan areas it is 4 percent. The differences for the other deficiencies are much more modest, but the problems of the nonmetropolitan South are pervasively evident.

Thus far, the data presented have provided few surprises to those generally familiar with housing conditions in the United States. In the following two sections the study will consider two additional and especially important characteristics of the elderly population: race and poverty status. In each case, the effect of the additional factor (race or poverty) is examined in relation to the differences in housing quality, after controlling for differences in tenure status and household types. This examination highlights the diversity of housing circumstances of particular elderly subpopulations.

Race. Elderly blacks exhibit a very high incidence of housing deficiencies among both homeowners and renters (panel F of Table 3-6). While black homeowners generally have lower deficiency rates than black renters, the differences are small compared to the differences between black and nonblack owners and renters. Sixteen percent of black single-person homeowners live in units not having complete plumbing facilities, 12 percent do not have fully equipped kitchens. The comparable rates for black single-person renters are 14 and 11 percent, respectively. The most poorly housed black group is "other" renters: one in five lives in a unit with plumbing deficiencies and one in seven lives in a unit with incomplete kitchen facilities or maintenance deficiencies. In 1976, there were only about 88,000

	Deficiencies[b]					
	Plumbing	Kitchen	Sewage	Heat	Maintenance	Public Hallways
A. *Elderly vs. Nonelderly*						
Owner						
Elderly	3.28	1.63	.29	.35	2.04	[d]
Nonelderly	1.08	.60	.32	.38	1.94	[d]
Renters						
Elderly	6.38	5.22	.57	2.01	6.26	.75
Nonelderly	3.28	2.72	.87	1.91	8.27	1.29
B. *Elderly, by Household Type*						
Owners						
Husband-wife	1.85	.84	.30	.24	1.19	[d]
Single persons	4.55	2.32	.25	.39	2.43	[d]
Other	5.94	3.10	.34[c]	.75[c]	4.61	[d]
Renters						
Husband-wife	4.17	2.03	.62[c]	2.60	6.25	.73[b]
Single persons	7.03	6.48	.57	1.87	5.86	.70
Other	7.76	5.26	.52	1.45[c]	8.67	1.08[b]
C. *Elderly, by Age*						
Owners						
Age 65–74	3.15	1.59	.29	.33	1.91	[d]
Age 75 and over	3.92	1.82	.28	.47[c]	2.65	[d]
Renters						
Age 65–74	6.19	5.32	.50	1.99	6.44	.77
Age 75 and over	7.13	4.79	.86[c]	2.01	5.56	.67[c]
D. *Elderly, by Region*						
Owners						
Northeast	2.15	.46[c]	.26[c]	.70	2.20	[d]
North Central	2.47	1.24	.39	.31	1.72	[d]
South	5.81	3.22	.30	.28	2.63	[d]
West	.69	.32[c]	.11[c]	.16[c]	1.14	[d]
Renters						
Northeast	4.22	4.60	1.20	4.34	7.36	1.02
North Central	5.94	3.60	.16[c]	.16[c]	4.27	.64[c]
South	11.88	8.54	.57[c]	1.58	9.00	1.01
West	2.81	3.55	.00[c]	.84[c]	2.87	.00[c]

Table 3–6. continued

	Deficiencies[b]					
	Plumbing	*Kitchen*	*Sewage*	*Heat*	*Maintenance*	*Public Hallways*
E. Elderly, by Location						
Owners						
Metropolitan	1.43	.59	.21	.24	1.67	[d]
Nonmetropolitan	5.88	3.08	.36	.50	2.55	[d]
Renters						
Metropolitan	3.92	4.29	.63[c]	2.28	5.80	.84
Nonmetropolitan	14.51	8.21	.33[c]	1.10	7.65	.33[c]
F. Elderly, by Race						
Owners						
Husband-wife						
Black	8.80	4.90	.96[c]	.24[c]	3.68	[d]
Nonblack	1.45	.68	.26	.24	1.05	[d]
Single persons						
Black	16.46	11.67	.64[c]	.65[c]	7.45	[d]
Nonblack	3.71	1.66	.23[c]	.37	2.07	[d]
Other						
Black	13.97	9.94	.40[c]	.77[c]	12.15	[d]
Nonblack	4.49	1.87	.00[c]	.75[c]	3.25	[d]
Renters						
Husband-wife						
Black	13.91	5.87[c]	1.39[c]	5.45[c]	19.64	1.35[c]
Nonblack	2.92	1.54	.52[c]	2.24	4.53	.66[c]
Single persons						
Black	13.64	11.18	.00[c]	3.93	13.62	1.12[c]
Nonblack	6.18	5.88	.74[c]	1.61	4.87	.64
Other						
Black	20.49	14.61	.00[c]	1.78[c]	15.50	1.78[c]
Nonblack	4.36	2.76[a]	.66[c]	1.36[c]	6.85	.89[c]

G. Elderly, by Income Status						
Owners						
Husband-wife						
Below poverty	9.01	4.01	.67[c]	.57[c]	3.05	[d]
Poverty to twice poverty	1.97	.85	.38[c]	.27[c]	1.27	[d]
Above twice poverty	.57	.28[c]	.19[c]	.16[c]	.83	[d]
Single person						
Below poverty	10.50	5.77	.24[c]	.82[c]	4.61	[d]
Poverty to twice poverty	3.50	1.45	.45[c]	.28[c]	1.69	[d]
Over twice poverty	1.23	.73[c]	.00[c]	.19[c]	1.65	[d]
Other						
Below poverty	11.65	6.10	.27[c]	.81[c]	9.20	[d]
Poverty to twice poverty	6.83	4.27	.38[c]	.94[c]	3.44	[d]
Over twice poverty	2.87	1.05[c]	.35[c]	.62[c]	3.34	[d]
Renters						
Husband-wife						
Below poverty	13.43	6.42	.52[c]	3.77[c]	11.46	1.85[c]
Poverty to twice poverty	4.14	1.66[c]	.83[c]	2.05[c]	6.74	.39[c]
Over twice poverty	.94[c]	.79[c]	.66[c]	2.64	4.02	.62[c]
Single persons						
Below poverty	11.86	7.60	.87[c]	1.91	7.53	.62[c]
Poverty to twice poverty	4.59	5.42	.47[c]	1.91	5.27	.55[c]
Over twice poverty	4.49	6.92	.28[c]	1.73[c]	4.44	1.12[c]
Other						
Below poverty	13.46	8.24[c]	1.33[c]	.00[c]	10.28	1.32[c]
Poverty to twice poverty	8.54	6.36	.40[c]	.82[c]	10.16	.83[c]
Over twice poverty	1.75[c]	1.12[c]	.00[c]	3.60[c]	5.18[c]	1.23[c]

Source: Special tabulations from the Annual Housing Survey, 1976.

[a] Rates per 100 households.

[b] Definitions are given in Table 3–5.

[c] Number in sample too small to be statistically reliable.

[d] Not computed for owner-occupied units.

households in this category, and it would indeed be a challenge to find the 20,000 most in need. On the other hand, the problems among elderly blacks are so pervasive that simply assisting them as a group would sacrifice little in terms of program efficiency.

Poverty Status. Panel G exhibits the anticipated pattern of decreases in the incidence of deficiencies as incomes rise. Not anticipated, however, is the consistency of the pattern across tenure and household types. For husband-wife homeowners, often taken to be stalwarts of the community, the incidence of plumbing, kitchen, and maintenance deficiencies for the group in poverty is several times higher when compared to the incidence for those with incomes between poverty and twice the poverty level. The implications of this pattern for defining those needing housing assistance are obvious, but one should not conclude that simply raising incomes will eliminate the housing deficiencies. Why this is the case is taken up in Chapters 5 and 7.

An important issue, which the data presented thus far do not permit to be addressed, is the extent to which deficiencies are concentrated. Is there a comparatively smaller number of units with multiple deficiencies, or is there a large number, each having only a single defect? If one is concerned with designing a program to assist households living in deficient units, the question is of considerable importance since the amount of resources to be allocated to each dwelling, and the way in which the program gives priorities to different dwellings, will be affected.

Data addressing this point are provided in Table 3-7. Overall, they show that deficiencies are not sharply concentrated in a few dwellings—but there are some important exceptions. First, note that 94 percent of elderly homeowners and 85 percent of the elderly renters live in units with none of the deficiencies considered here; further, only 2 and 5 percent, respectively, reside in units with more than one defect. Panels B and C of the table show that high incidences of multiple deficiencies are concentrated among blacks and among households with incomes below the poverty level. The incidence of multiple deficiencies is much higher among blacks, however, than among the poverty population. (Of course, a major portion of elderly blacks are poor.) Twelve percent of black single-person households—some 60,000 households—live in units with multiple deficiencies. Only one of the six black tenure-household type groups shown in the table has less than 10 percent of its members in multiple-deficiency units; by contrast, only one of the six similar poverty groups has as much as 10 percent of its members in multiple-deficiency units.

To place the idea of the quality of housing occupied by the elderly in

Table 3–7. Rates of the Total Number of Selected Housing Defects for Various Types of Households Headed by the Elderly: 1976[a]

	Owner-Occupants			*Renters*		
	None	*One*	*More than One*	*None*	*One*	*More than One*
A. *Elderly vs. Nonelderly*						
Elderly	94	4	2	85	10	5
Nonelderly	96	3	1	85	11	4
B. *Elderly, by Household Type and Race*						
Husband-wife	96	2	2	89	7	4
Black	86	8	6	71	15	14
Nonblack	97	2	1	91	6	3
Single persons	93	5	2	84	10	4
Black	90	8	12	73	15	12
Nonblack	94	4	6	86	10	4
Other	90	7	3	83	11	6
Black	78	10	12	68	16	16
Nonblack	92	6	2	87	9	4
C. *Elderly, by Household Type and Income*						
Husband-wife						
Below poverty	88	7	5	76	14	10
Poverty to twice poverty	96	3	1	89	7	4
Over twice poverty	98	1	1	93	5	2
Single persons						
Below poverty	85	8	7	80	13	7
Poverty to twice poverty	94	4	2	87	7	6
Over twice poverty	97	2	1	85	11	4
Other						
Below poverty	83	9	8	74	18	8
Poverty to twice poverty	89	7	4	83	9	8
Over twice poverty	93	6	1	91	7	2

Source: Special tabulations from the Annual Housing Survey, 1976.

[a] Rates per 100 households.

1976 in perspective requires an analysis of progress or decline compared with earlier years. As noted earlier, the limited data on deficiencies from the past three decennial censuses have been used to document very significant improvement in the housing quality of all groups in the postwar period. The data used in this chapter to compare the six deficiency measures were first available only in 1974, the first year that Annual Housing Survey records for individuals can be linked to those of later survey years.

Table 3-8 presents rates of deficiencies for 1974 and 1976 for the six household type and tenure group combinations. For each group two sets of figures are given. "Same households" are those headed by an elderly person in 1974 who did not relocate between 1974 and 1976. Since the Annual Housing Survey uses dwellings as the unit of observation, this is the only group of households that can be tracked over time. Seventy-nine percent of elderly owners and 49 percent of elderly renters in the 1974 file are in this set. The "all households" category includes all elderly households at the time of each survey.

The figures in the table show a widespread pattern of improvement, even over this short period. It is important to note that the pattern generally holds for "all households" and for "same households." There are, however, some exceptions that should be noted.

An increase in maintenance deficiencies is recorded among homeowners of all household types; and there is a slight increase in sewage breakdowns for husband-wife households, the only group for which reliable data on this item are available in both years. This pattern holds for both "same" and "all" households. These data are particularly disturbing for "same" households because they imply a reduction in maintenance/repair activities on the part of elderly homeowners as they age, with their dwellings gradually deteriorating. It is this process that can have sharply deleterious effects on potential investment in a neighborhood.

There is little progress overall among elderly renters and, in the areas of maintenance and heating system performance, some increases in deficiency rates. Hence, while there is improvement, it is uneven, with progress for some groups still proving elusive.

Neighborhood Conditions

Each dwelling unit, except those in truly rural areas, has a set of neighborhood attributes. In many locations, households pay considerable premiums for living where they wish; they also can obtain substantial discounts for residing in less desirable neighborhoods. In Table 3-9 the conditions in the neighborhoods in which the elderly reside are introduced.

Table 3–8. Rates of Dwelling Deficiencies for Households Headed by the Elderly, by Household Type and Tenure: 1974–1976[a]

	Deficiencies[b]									
	Owner-Occupants					*Renters*				
	Plumbing	*Kitchen*	*Sewage*	*Heat*	*Maintenance*	*Plumbing*	*Kitchen*	*Sewage*	*Heat*	*Maintenance*
Husband-wife										
Same households										
1974	2.94	1.21	.25	.20[c]	1.30	5.57	1.88[c]	.13[c]	4.33	9.73
1976	2.19	.99	.32	.27	1.39	5.19	2.90	.97[c]	4.16	9.00
All households										
1974	2.79	1.25	.24	.25	1.26	4.34	1.72	.62[c]	3.26	7.19
1976	1.85	.84	.30	.24	1.19	4.17	2.03	.62[c]	2.60	6.25
Single persons										
Same households										
1974	5.17	2.63	.21[c]	.29[c]	1.91	8.16	8.11	.67[c]	1.82	6.08
1976	4.92	2.46	.22[c]	.42	2.69	8.34	6.59	.92	2.80	8.34
All households										
1974	5.73	2.82	.18[c]	.27[c]	2.06	7.98	6.56	.55	1.47	5.06
1976	4.55	2.32	.25	.39	2.43	7.03	6.48	.57	1.87	5.86
Other households										
Same households										
1974	7.70	4.02	.52[c]	.61[c]	3.19	10.75	4.86	.30[c]	2.01[c]	12.88
1976	6.43	3.54	.49	.52[c]	5.13	8.02	5.65	.00[c]	2.39[c]	6.36
All households										
1974	7.10	3.57	.50[c]	.57[c]	3.60	9.39	4.08	1.02[c]	2.17[c]	12.95
1976	5.94	3.10	.34[c]	.75[c]	4.61	7.76	5.26	.52[c]	1.45	8.67

Source: Special tabulations from the Annual Housing Survey, 1976.

[a] Rates per 100 households.

[b] See Table 3–5 for definitions.

[c] Number of observations in this cell is too small to be statistically reliable.

The data presented in Table 3-9 are limited to three sets of opinion questions on neighborhood conditions included in the Annual Housing Survey. The first set asks the respondent about each of twelve separate objectionable conditions that may exist in his or her neighborhood. If the respondent says the condition exists, the respondent is asked if it is "bothersome"; if so, the respondent is asked if he "wants" to move to avoid it. For this analysis the "bothersome" answers have been tabulated. The second set of questions solicits the respondent's evaluation of six neighborhood services, ranging from shopping facilities (stores) to public transportation. If the services are termed "inadequate," the respondent is again asked if it is a problem of such importance that he wants to move. In the third set of questions, the respondent is asked to rate the neighborhood overall, from excellent to poor.

All of these opinion questions are potentially subject to measurement error; they do not take into account the respondents' expectations or experiences. To someone who has lived in marginal conditions all his life, a modest but somewhat shabby neighborhood might be rated "excellent." When large numbers of households are interviewed, it is hoped that such "background" factors cancel each other out so that the observed central tendency is generally unbiased. A more specific limitation concerns longitudinal analysis. It also seems likely that straight opinion questions are more subject to respondents "learning," that is, making systematically different, perhaps better, responses over time simply through having had the opportunity to formulate a response some time in the past. It is for this reason that only responses to the three sets of questions for the most recent year, 1976, were analyzed.

Table 3-9 summarizes the responses separately for homeowners and renters, and it permits comparisons of the elderly and nonelderly, and among the three types of households headed by an older person. The central conclusion from these figures is the similarity of the elderly and nonelderly and subgroups of the elderly.

The elderly overall found fewer bothersome conditions in their neighborhoods than did the nonelderly. The elderly complained most frequently about street noise and criminal activities in the neighborhood. The next most often voiced problems were the presence of excessive traffic and trash, litter, and junk. The pattern is similar for the nonelderly.

The level of dissatisfaction with neighborhood services was roughly the same for elderly and nonelderly. Both groups, and especially homeowners, viewed the lack of adequate public transportation as the greatest service inadequacy. This is somewhat surprising for the nonelderly who are generally thought of as being less dependent on public transportation. It is interesting to note that the elderly voiced a higher rate of dissatisfaction with the lack of shopping opportunities than the nonelderly. Again, there are no sharp distinctions among the various household types.

In an overall assessment of the neighborhood, the most important distinction is between homeowners and renters rather than the elderly and nonelderly. While 25 to 30 percent of renters rate their neighborhood as "fair" or "poor", only 12 to 13 percent of homeowners give such ratings. This conclusion agrees with other detailed information examined: the elderly view their neighborhoods much as their nonelderly counterparts do. If anything, their assessment is somewhat more positive.

Housing Expense Burden

What fraction of their incomes must the elderly devote to housing in order to enjoy the standard of housing described? It is an important question, one whose presumed answer—"too much"—has given birth to a series of programs to help the elderly, including real estate tax relief under so-called circuit breakers and emergency utility payments by the Community Services Administration.

Before the question can be addressed, the issue of the appropriate standard to be employed must be confronted. Should the same standard apply to the elderly as to other households? What is the relevant absolute standard? Likewise, a whole series of definitional problems must be resolved. These items are discussed in the appendix to this chapter. For now, the results of those considerations are given. A conservative definition of excessive housing expense—over 35 percent of income going to housing—has been adopted. The definition of out-of-pocket housing expense is quite broad, although it excludes maintenance expenditures, which is especially important for owner-occupants. A quite comprehensive income definition is also employed, but it does not encompass imputed rents from owner-occupants living in their own dwelling.

Using these definitions, the central finding is that in 1976 the average household headed by an elderly person devoted only slightly more of his income to housing than the average nonelderly household—23 percent versus 20 percent. The reason for the closeness between the two groups is that more of the elderly are homeowners with no mortgage debt on their property. The following data—for only those households for whom the census has the requisite information—document this point.

Table 3–9. Percentage Distribution of Resident Opinions of Neighborhood Conditions, by Age of Household Head, Type of Household Headed by the Elderly, and Tenure Status: 1976

Condition	*Renters*					*Owner-Occupants*				
			Elderly Household Type					*Elderly Household Type*		
	Non-elderly	*Elderly*	*Husband-wife*	*Single Persons*	*Other*	*Non-elderly*	*Elderly*	*Husband-wife*	*Single Persons*	*Other*
A. *Neighborhood Conditions Viewed as Bothersome*										
1. Street noise	15	12	13	12	11	12	12	12	9	13
2. Heavy traffic	12	9	10	9	7	10	9	9	8	11
3. Roads in poor condition	10	4	5	4	8	13	8	8	6	9
4. Roads impassible due to rain, snow	6	3	4	2	4	7	4	4	3	4
5. Inadequate street lighting	10	4	4	4	6	10	5	5	5	4

6. Neighborhood crime	16	13	15	13	12	13	12	9	7	10
7. Trash, litter, and junk	13	7	8	7	8	9	10	8	9	10
8. Abandoned buildings	4	2	2	2	2	2	2	1	3	2
9. Occupied housing in poor condition	7	3	4	2	4	6	3	3	4	3
10. Commercial or industrial activities	3	2	1	2	1	3	2	2	3	2
11. Odors, smoke, or gas	7	4	5	4	4	6	5	5	5	4
12. Noise from airplane traffic	6	6	7	6	6	6	6	6	5	5
B. *Inadequate Services*										
1. Public transport	23	20	22	14	23	41	37	38	36	34
2. Stores	12	16	12	13	10	14	17	14	19	20
3. Police protection	9	8	10	7	7	10	8	9	8	9
4. Fire protection	3	2	3	2	2	6	5	5	5	5
5. Hospitals	10	8	9	9	8	14	13	12	15	12
C. *Rating of Neighborhood*										
Excellent	20	28	27	29	22	41	41	43	40	34
Good	50	47	45	47	49	46	45	44	46	49
Fair	25	20	23	18	24	11	12	12	11	14
Poor	5	4	4	4	5	1	1	1	2	3

Source: Special tabulations from the Annual Housing Survey, 1976.

Distribution of Elderly and Nonelderly Households by Tenure Type (percent)

	Elderly	Nonelderly
Renters	35	41
Owners		
Without mortgage	56	15
With mortgage	9	44
	100%	100%

Among elderly homeowners, only one in six still has a mortgage; among the nonelderly, only one in four is *without* a mortgage.

The mortgage-free homeowner status of over half of all elderly households divides the elderly in two important ways: the first is in out-of-pocket housing expenses; the second is between those elderly in strong and those in weak asset positions, a very important point for policy discussions. While home equity is certainly not the exclusive asset holding of the elderly, it is the dominant one (Murray 1972).

Some idea of the asset position of mortgageless homeowners is given in Table 3-10. Over 3 million elderly homeowners have home equity in excess of $25,000. Eighty-seven percent of impoverished elderly homeowners own their homes free and clear, but of those, only 29 percent have units valued at over $25,000. The highest incidence of debtless ownership (94 percent) is among single persons, and two out of five households of this type have equity of over $25,000. This formidable diversity in economic status is recognized in the policy discussion in Chapter 9.

The basic information on the share of income devoted to housing by the elderly (using the definitions stated above) is presented in Table 3-11.[m] The table is divided into three panels, one each for renters, owners without mortgages, and owners with mortgages. In each panel, comparisons with the nonelderly and among subgroups of the elderly are provided.

The greatest differences in housing expense burdens are between those homeowners without mortgages and renters and other homeowners. Only 10 percent of elderly homeowners who do not have mortgage debt spend more than 35 percent of their incomes on housing, while 38 percent of renters and 30 percent of owners with mortgage debt do. There is a smaller percentage of nonelderly households in the over-35 percent category for each of these groups, an interesting figure

[m] Table 3-11 does not contain as detailed data for household types as do some other tables because of the large number of unreliable entries that result when further disaggregation is attempted.

Table 3–10. The Absolute and Relative Number of Houses Owned by the Elderly without Mortgage Debt and the Percentage Distribution of Mortgage-Free Property Values, by Household Type and Poverty Status: 1976

	Owners without Mortgage Debt		*Distribution of Property Values for Owners without Debt*				
Status	*Percentage of All Owners*	*Number*[a]	*Under $15,000*	*$15,000–24,999*	*$25,000–34,999*	*$35,000–50,000*	*Over $50,000*
All Households	84	6,393	25	27	22	17	10
Household Type							
Husband-wife	80	3,236	19	26	23	19	13
Single person	94	2,321	31	28	21	14	6
Other	76	836	28	28	22	13	9
Income Status							
Below poverty line	87	1,122	47	25	15	10	4
Poverty-twice poverty	86	2,340	29	32	22	12	5
Over twice poverty	81	2,930	13	23	25	23	16

Source: Special tabulations from the Annual Housing Survey, 1976.

[a] Numbers in thousands.

Table 3–11. Percentage Distribution of Housing Expense-to-Income Ratios, by Tenure Status: 1976

Tenure and Household Type	Housing Expense-to-Income Ratio[a]						
	Under .15	.16–.25	.26–.30	.31–.35	.36–.45	.46–.60	Above .60
A. *Renters*							
1. Elderly vs. nonelderly							
Elderly	13	27	12	10	15	13	10
Nonelderly	27	34	10	6	8	7	6
2. Elderly, by household type							
Husband-wife	21	27	13	10	14	9	6
Single persons	9	27	11	10	15	16	12
Other	20	26	12	7	16	10	9
3. Elderly, by income							
Below poverty	3	21	10	8	16	19	22
Poverty to twice poverty	6	25	13	11	18	16	10
Above twice poverty	33	34	12	8	9	4	1
4. Elderly, by race							
Black	13	31	12	11	16	10	7
Nonblack	14	26	12	10	14	13	10
5. Elderly, by location							
Metropolitan	13	27	12	9	15	13	11
Nonmetropolitan	16	27	12	11	15	12	7
B. *Owners without Mortgages*							
1. Elderly vs. nonelderly							
Elderly	53	27	6	4	5	3	2
Nonelderly	81	11	2	2	2	1	1
2. Elderly, by household type							
Husband-wife	65	24	4	2	3	1	1
Single person	36	32	9	7	8	5	3
Other	58	24	6	4	5	2	2

3. Elderly, by income							
Below poverty	16	30	12	9	13	10	9
Poverty to twice poverty	36	38	9	6	7	3	1
Above twice poverty	82	16	1	...	...	...	...
4. Elderly, by race							
Black	47	24	9	5	6	3	3
Nonblack	54	27	6	4	5	3	2
5. Elderly, by location							
Metropolitan	51	27	7	5	5	3	3
Nonmetropolitan	57	26	5	4	4	3	1
C. *Owners with Mortgages*							
1. Elderly vs. nonelderly							
Elderly	21	29	11	8	12	11	7
Nonelderly	39	39	9	5	4	2	1
2. Elderly, by household type							
Husband-wife	25	33	11	7	10	9	4
Single persons	12	17	11	11	18	17	15
Other	18	29	11	6[b]	12	13	10
3. Elderly, by income							
Below poverty	2[b]	4[b]	6[b]	5[b]	18	29	36
Poverty to twice poverty	1[b]	19	14	14	22	20	9
Above twice poverty	36	40	10	5	6	2	1[b]
4. Elderly, by race							
Black	8	22	14	5	17	20	14
Nonblack	24	30	10	8	12	10	6
5. Elderly, by location							
Metropolitan	23	28	11	8	12	10	7
Nonmetropolitan	16	32	10	10	14	14	11

Source: Special tabulations from the Annual Housing Survey, 1976.

[a] See definitions in text.

[b] Entry not statistically reliable.

in light of the extraordinary mortgage burdens of a number of recent home purchasers. Elderly renters and elderly owners with mortgage debt, as expected, have higher average housing expense ratios than the nonelderly in similar situations: 33 percent versus 24 percent, and 29 percent versus 20 percent, respectively. Not so obvious, though, is that the mortgage debt-free elderly owners also spend a larger share of income—17 versus 14 percent—than the nonelderly.

Among subgroups of the elderly, whether defined by race, income, or location, the broad patterns are remarkably similar across the three tenure groups. For this reason, we discuss the patterns for the three groups together. An examination of the figures in Table 3-11 leads to the following observations:

- Single persons living alone consistently devote more of their income to housing than other groups. Forty-three percent of single-person renters and half of single-person owners with mortgaged properties spend over 35 percent of their income on housing. Husband-wife households, by contrast, are in the most favorable position.
- Those elderly with incomes below the poverty line are often spending the majority of their income for housing. Almost three of every five poor renters spend over 35 percent of income for housing, and a full 83 percent of homeowners with mortgage debt are in this group. These latter households are certainly "housing poor," and it seems imperative to develop some method of assisting them to shift to a less burdensome situation.
- Black and white households exhibit similar expenditure burdens, in part because blacks live in consistently worse housing, as noted earlier. It is only black homeowners with mortgages who spend significantly more than their white counterparts.
- The differences in expense burdens between metropolitan and nonmetropolitan areas are modest overall, and do not display a great deal of regularity. The locational distinction for individual tenure groups does not seem especially important.

Although the data presented in the last table document the housing expense circumstances of the elderly, they do not provide much of an idea of the expenditure levels. For example, over half of the poor elderly renters spend over 35 percent of their income on housing, but how much rent do they pay? Expenditures are another measure of housing services consumed and are of interest. Table 3-12 displays the distributions of monthly housing expenditures for renters and owners without mortgages and for the three household types and three income groups used throughout this chapter.

Table 3–12. Percentage Distribution of Monthly Housing Expenses of the Elderly, by Tenure Status: 1976

	Housing Expenses						
	Under $50	*$51–$100*	*$101–$150*	*$151–$200*	*$201–$250*	*$251–$300*	*Over $300*
Renters							
Household type							
Husband-wife	2	18	24	24	15	8	8
Single person	14	33	24	17	6	3	2
Other	6	21	28	20	13	5	6
Income status							
Below poverty	24	38	22	11	4	1	1
Poverty to twice poverty	6	33	29	19	8	2	2
Over twice poverty	1	10	20	28	18	11	11
Owners without Mortgage							
Household type							
Husband-wife	13	49	27	8	3	1	[a]
Single person	29	50	16	4	1	[a]	[a]
Other	17	50	21	9	3	1	[a]
Income status							
Below poverty	43	44	9	2	1	[a]	[a]
Poverty to twice poverty	20	56	16	5	1	[a]	[a]
Over twice poverty	8	45	32	10	3	1	[a]

Source: Special tabulations from the Annual Housing Survey, 1976.

[a] Less than 0.5 percent.

The bulk of renters spend between $100 and $200 per month, including one-third of those with poverty-level incomes. What is even more striking is the large proportion who spend less than $100 per month: 47 percent of single persons and over 60 percent of those in poverty. Indeed, 24 percent of the impoverished elderly renters spend less than $50 per month. There is little doubt that the housing inhabited by those 64,000 households, or the 339,000 single-person renters (of all incomes) who spend the same, are of poor quality.

Among elderly homeowners without mortgages, almost half of all households spend between $50 and $100 per month, and only a small number spend over $150 per month. At the same time, there is a substantial percentage who spend less than $50. All together, there are about 117,000 households in this latter category, largely concentrated in the overlapping groups of single individuals and those with income below the poverty line. Even though these figures explicitly exclude maintenance expenditures, they strongly suggest that these units are being operated at the barest standard to permit habitation.

These figures, combined with those on expense burden, point to a cruel dilemma on the part of hundreds of thousands of the elderly: either to live in adequate housing and devote a major share of income to this purpose, or to be able to purchase other needed goods and services and spend only minimum amounts on housing. There is a second group in a more desperate situation: those for whom expenditure of only $50 per month represents a burden. This group includes anyone with an annual income of $1,714, or 63 percent of the official poverty-income level in 1976. As the data have shown, the majority of the elderly are neither impoverished nor devoting over 35 percent of their incomes to housing, but a significant number do have very serious income and housing problems.

The final question is whether the elderly are spending more of their incomes on housing today than they did previously. The progress in the postwar period in both housing quality and in the fraction of income spent on housing has already been noted. For the period for which the requisite data are available (1974–1976), some additional improvement in the condition of the units occupied by the elderly has been observed. The data in Table 3-12 indicate at least a temporary break in this progress in terms of housing expenditures.[n]

Table 3-13 provides information for all elderly households (disaggregated by tenure) in 1974 and 1976 and for "same" households, as defined earlier. For both groups there is a wide-based increase in

[n] This finding is consistent with evidence for all households. See, for example, Sternlieb, Burchell, and Listokin (1975).

expenditure ratios. For example, among nonmoving husband-wife renters, the percentage of those spending more than 35 percent of income on housing rose from 21 to 25. Only among single-person renters is there a decrease in the percentage with excessive expense burdens. This may be directly attributable to the improved economic position of this group through the Supplemental Security Income program. The trend is presently only of short duration and may be seen simply as an aberration a decade from now. Still, it deserves attention since it affects those continuing to live in the same unit for whom it can be presumed that the level of housing services consumed is held roughly constant, as well as for all elderly households.

SUMMARY

The definitions and figures presented in this chapter were designed to document three aspects of the housing status of households headed by elderly persons: the size, type, and quality of the dwelling units they inhabit; the perceived quality of the neighborhoods in which they reside; and the portion of incomes that are being used to consume these housing services. Some highlights from these materials are summarized below.

Structure Quality

Overall, the elderly live in units that could be characterized as somewhat smaller and more modest than those occupied by the nonelderly. Those subgroups of the elderly have been identified who have high rates of deficiencies in their units—deficiencies serious enough to prevent the unit from qualifying under Section 8 program standards currently employed by the Department of Housing and Urban Development without incurring significant costs. Very high deficiency rates are experienced by the black elderly and by the impoverished elderly. For blacks, these rates are shockingly high. For example, 162,000 of the 1.2 million elderly black households are living in units without complete plumbing facilities. Poverty status consistently predicts higher rates of such deficiencies for all household types and for both homeowners and renters.

There are a large number of elderly-occupied units with one or more of the six defects used in this analysis. About 388,000 renters and 303,000 homeowners live in units with one defect, and half as many of each tenure group live in dwellings with two or more. In total, 1.04 million elderly households live in such units—6 percent of homeowners and 15 percent of renters. Finally, the data show a widespread improvement in housing quality of the 1974–1976 period as measured by

Table 3–13. Percentage Distribution of Housing Expense-to-Income Ratios, by Household Type and Tenure Status: 1974 and 1976

	Under .15	*.16–.25*	*.26–.30*	*.31–.35*	*.36–.45*	*.46–.60*	*Over .60*
Husband-Wife							
Renters							
Same households							
1974	27	34	10	8	11	5	5
1976	28	29	6	11	14	8	3
All households							
1974	24	34	12	10	10	6	5
1976	21	27	13	10	14	9	6
Owners without mortgages							
Same households							
1974	70	19	5	2	2	1	[b]
1976	65	23	4	3	3	1	1
All households							
1974	71	19	4	2	2	1	[b]
1976	65	24	4	2	3	1	1
Single persons							
Renters							
Same households							
1974	10	23	11	11	18	13	14
1976	11	24	12	10	16	15	12
All households							
1974	9	24	12	9	17	15	13
1976	9	27	11	10	15	16	12

Owners without mortgages							
Same households							
1974	38	32	10	7	6	4	3
1976	37	32	9	7	8	4	3
All households							
1974	38	32	10	7	6	3	3
1976	36	32	9	7	8	5	3
Others Households							
Renters							
Same households							
1974	22	34	9	11	7	12	4[a]
1976	25	27	11	7	14	9	7
All households							
1974	20	31	11	11	10	11	6
1976	20	26	12	7	16	10	9
Owners without mortgages							
Same households							
1974	68	19	5	2	2	3	1[a]
1976	59	23	6	4	4	2	2
All households							
1974	67	20	5	2	3	3	1
1976	58	24	6	4	5	2	2

Source: Special tabulations from the Annual Housing Survey, 1974 and 1976.

[a] Entry too small to be statistically reliable.

[b] Less than 0.5 percent.

a reduction in deficiencies. One area of concern, though, is the increase in maintenance deficiencies among elderly owner-occupants.

Neighborhood Quality

There is close comparability in opinions on neighborhood conditions among the elderly and nonelderly and among different subgroups of the elderly. Examination of neighborhood conditions was limited to answers to a set of opinion questions. The consistency of the response pattern is striking, and the only real differences observed were among homeowners and renters, with homeowners giving their neighborhoods a higher overall satisfaction rating.

Housing Expense Burden

The average elderly household spent 23 percent of its income for out-of-pocket housing expenses in 1976, while the average nonelderly household spent 20 percent. It is important to distinguish among three tenure situations: renters, owners without mortgages, and owners with mortgages. The elderly spend a greater share of income on housing for all three groups, but they are much more heavily concentrated in the group with the lowest average expenditures—owners without mortgages—which keeps the overall difference between the elderly and nonelderly modest. There are about 2.3 million elderly households (or 22 percent of the total for whom the census has the necessary information) spending over 35 percent of their income on housing—an excessive burden. Again tenure differences are important: 38 percent of renters, 30 percent of owners with mortgages, and only 10 percent of owners with no mortgage debt. About one household in eight spending over 35 percent of income on housing is an owner with mortgage payments. Interestingly, the differences in housing expense-to-income ratios associated with race are much smaller than the quality differences observed earlier. In fact, the only real difference is for the numerically small category of owners with mortgage debt. For 1974–1976, the figures show the elderly devoting a somewhat greater share of income to housing in 1976 than in 1974. This is a reversal of the earlier pattern and one that deserves attention.

APPENDIX: DEFINING HOUSING EXPENSE BURDEN

Two types of guidance are available for judging what fraction of income devoted to housing is excessive for elderly households: the importance of housing in the budget of an elderly couple living at three different living standards as compiled by the U.S. Bureau of Labor Statistics

(1968) or the "25 percent rule-of-thumb" adjusted for the circumstances of the elderly.

The budget method calculates three budgets for couples living in urban areas and purports to reflect the full cost of living at a "low," "intermediate," and "high" standard of living. The type of housing included in these budgets is carefully defined and would, by most standards, be classified as a modest dwelling in a decent neighborhood.

The data displayed below show annual housing costs as a fraction of all expenditures for retired couples in 1969 in urban areas, contrasting the fractions for lower and intermediate-standard budgets. 1969 data were employed because the Bureau of Labor Statistics figures published currently are based on 1967–1968 survey results, updated using the Consumer Price Index. The farther from the data on which the base survey was conducted, the greater the possibility that the budget shares are inaccurate. Households are expected to consume less goods whose prices rise more rapidly than others; but, in updating the budgets, the definition of the group of goods consumed is held fixed.

Lower budget		Intermediate budget	
Renter	0.27	Renter	0.24
Homeowner	0.25	Homeowner	0.20

By these standards, renters should be spending about 25 percent of their income on housing, assuming that income and total expenditures are equivalent. The homeowner costs assume the home is owned mortgage free and that the imputed interest income on the owner's equity is not part of housing costs. For the homeowner, a little less than one-quarter of income should go for housing according to these figures.

The second form of guidance available to define what the elderly should spend on housing is obtained by adjusting the "25 percent rule-of-thumb" on the assumption that each dollar received by the elderly is worth more than the same dollar received by other households. The Bureau of Labor Statistics (1970) has estimated that, because of such factors as reduced expenses related to not working, lower income taxes resulting from Social Security payments being tax exempt and reduced real estate taxes in many places, a retired couple requires only 65–80 percent of preretirement earnings to have the same living standard as their nonretired counterpart. This widely used rule implies that the 25 percent housing expense standard should be increased to at least 30 percent—that is, twenty-five times (1/.8) (Munnell 1977). Thus, holding housing expenses fixed requires about 30 percent of income to be spent on housing after retirement, while maintaining the overall living standard at a preretirement level requires 25 percent of income.

The difference between the two types of guidance stems from whether the household adjusts its housing consumption after retirement or not. The budget data explicitly assume the household has shifted to the modest dwelling that the Bureau of Labor Statistics prices in its survey. The foregoing data assumes the opposite—a household spending one-quarter of its income on housing before retirement continues to live in the same house and now spends more. In this chapter we use a 35-percent rule of thumb. This choice is based on the low rates of mobility on the part of the elderly, which indicate most will remain in their preretirement dwellings for a number of years. Note that the 35 percent standard is conservative, as it corresponds to the elderly requiring a little over 70 percent of their preretirement income, toward the low end of the 65–80 percent range cited earlier. The tables presented in the body of this chapter display a range of housing expense-to-income ratios so that the reader may employ whatever standard he or she desires.

The definition of housing expenses and incomes, while straightforward conceptually, needs to be carefully specified empirically. Fortunately, the Annual Housing Survey provides data adequate to satisfy the conceptually meaningful definitions.

Only out-of-pocket housing expenses are included in the definition. This means that the foregone income from the homeowner's equity in his home is excluded. Thus, only the actual dollar expenditures are counted (similarly, on the income side, only actual income, exclusive of the potential income from equity holdings, is used). Other exclusions are the cost of maintenance activities for homeowners and the costs of housing-related services—such as chore services and shopping services for the physically impaired—for all households (Fein and White 1977).

For renter households, housing expenditures include the actual apartment rental payment and all utilities payments made separately, with the exception of the telephone. Separate questions are asked in the survey to determine if each utility (gas, electric, water, and so on) is included in the contract rent; if not, the separate cost is ascertained. It is also determined if the rent includes payment for furnishings or parking places; the payments for these items are excluded from the rental figures used in the computations.

For owner-occupant households, the task of obtaining the necessary information is somewhat more difficult when mortgage payments are being made (the term mortgage as defined here includes mortgages, deeds of trust, and land contracts). Difficulties arise where property tax and insurance payments, as well as some utility payments, may or may not be included in the mortgage payment. The Survey sorts through the possibilities, and ultimately, an amount is available that includes mortgage payments (if any), property tax and insurance payments, and all utility payments, including separate garbage collection costs where applicable. The only potentially serious problem is lumping together multiple mortgages, such as first and second mortgages; but this should be of minor importance among elderly households. Finally, the additional cost of site rental of mobile homes is included.

Costs for several classes of households are categorically excluded by the Census Bureau in doing the survey. Owner-occupied units are excluded if a commercial establishment or doctor's office is on the property, or if the home is on a lot of 10 acres or more. This restriction means most farmers will be excluded. Also, renter households paying no contract rent, whether or not they pay for utilities, have been omitted from the computations.

All sources of cash inflow are included in the definition of income. The hesitancy of households to divulge income information is legendary; and the Annual Housing Survey, like other surveys, is structured to make omissions difficult. Nevertheless, some underreporting seems likely.

The battery of income questions in the survey asks for the earnings of each person in the household related by blood, marriage, or adoption and for total family income from the following sources: private business, farm or ranch; Social Security and other retirement payments; veterans payments; interest on savings accounts and bonds, estates, and trusts; unemployment compensation; alimony or child support; and contributions from persons not living in the household. It is the total income from all of these sources that is used in the calculations. Incomes may be seriously understated when nonrelated persons are sharing a unit, since the income of only one of the persons will be recorded (when five or more unrelated persons live together, the unit is classified as "group quarters," and it is excluded by the Census Bureau from housing cost computations).

It is worth reiterating that, despite the seeming precision of the income figures used here, they provide only a rough measure of the actual economic resources available. The value of in-kind services from owner-occupied housing is omitted, and the data, being only for a single point in time, will inevitably catch some households in especially good or poor financial years.

REFERENCES

Baer, W.C. 1976. "The Evaluation of Housing Indicators and Housing Standards." *Public Policy* 24: 361–93.

Beyer, G.H. 1961. *Economic Aspects of Housing for the Aged.* Ithaca, N.Y.: Cornell University Center for Housing and Environmental Studies, Research Report No. 4.

Fein, J., and C.S. White, Jr. 1977. *The Ratio of Shelter Expenditures to Income: Definitional Issues, Typical Patterns, and Historical Trends.* Cambridge, Mass.: ABT Associates.

Follain, J.; J. Katz; and R. Struyk. 1979. "Programmatic Options to Encourage Homeownership." *Occasional Papers in Housing and Community Affairs.* Vol. 3.

Goedert, J.E., and J.L. Goodman, Jr. 1976. "Indicators of Housing Quality: An Exploration of the Annual Housing Survey." Washington, D.C.: The Urban Institute.

Mendelsohn, R., and R. Struyk. 1976. "The Flow of Housing Services in a Hedonic Index." Washington, D.C.: The Urban Institute.

Munnell, A.H. 1976. *The Future of Social Security.* Washington, D.C.: The Brookings Institution.

Murray, J. 1972. "Homeownership and Financial Assets: Findings from the 1968 Survey of the Aged." *Social Security Bulletin* (August): 3–22.

Rosenblatt, J.A. 1971. "Housing Code Enforcement and Administration: An Organizational and Political Analysis." Cambridge, Mass.: Ph.D. thesis, MIT.

Schieber, S.J. 1978. "Housing Conditions of Aged Welfare Recipients." Washington, D.C.: Social Security Administration. Unpublished.

Sternlieb, G.; R. W. Burchell; and D. Listokin. 1975. "The Private Sector's Role in the Provision of Reasonably Priced Housing." New Brunswick, N.J.: Rutgers University Center for Urban Policy Research.

Struyk, R. 1977. "The Housing Situation of Elderly Americans." *The Gerontologist* 17: 130–39.

Soldo, B.J. 1978. "Incomes of Black Aged: Their Determinants and Consequences." Paper Presented at the Conference on Blacks and Retirement: An Untapped National Resource, sponsored by the Council on Minority Planning and Strategy. Washington, D.C.: Center for Population Research. Mimeo.

U.S. Bureau of the Census. 1972. *Census of Housing: 1970 Metropolitan Housing Characteristics.* Final Report HC(2)-1, United States and Regions, Appendix. Washington, D.C.: U.S. Government Printing Office.

———. 1973. *Census of Housing: 1970 Subject Reports.* Final Report HC (7)-2, Housing of Senior Citizens. Washington, D.C.: U.S. Government Printing Office.

———. 1975. *Annual Housing Survey: 1973.* Part A, *General Characteristics for the United States and Regions.* Current Housing Reports Series H-150-73A. Washington, D.C.: U.S. Government Printing Office.

U.S. Bureau of Labor Statistics. 1968. "3 Budgets for a Retired Couple in Urban Areas of the United States, 1967–68." Bulletin 1570–2. Washington, D.C.: U.S. Government Printing Office.

———. 1970. "Revised Equivalence Scale for Estimating Incomes or Budget Costs for Family Type." 1970. Bulletin 1570–6. Washington, D.C.: U.S. Government Printing Office.

U.S. Department of Health, Education, and Welfare. 1976. *The Measure of Poverty*. Washington, D.C.: U.S. Government Printing Office.

U.S. Department of Housing and Urban Development. 1978. *Lower Income Housing Assistance Program (Section 8): Interim Findings of Evaluation Research*. Washington, D.C.: Office of Policy Development and Research.

Weicher, J. 1978. "The Affordability of New Homes." *AREUEA Journal* 5: 209–26.

Wieand, K. 1978. "Analysis of Multiple Defect Indicators of Housing Quality with Data from the 1976 Annual Housing Survey." Washington, D.C.: Office of Policy Development and Research, U.S. Department of Housing and Urban Development.

Chapter 4

Determinants of Dwelling Maintenance Activity by Owner-Occupants[a]

The previous chapters have documented the fact that the housing in which the elderly reside often has physical deficiencies and shows signs of deterioration. Dwelling maintenance requires that repairs be made in a timely fashion. This chapter and the next explore the factors that appear to be important determinants of dwelling maintenance. In this chapter the determinants are studied directly; in the next chapter the relation between dwelling quality (produced in part by maintenance activity) and the receipt of certain housing support services is studied. Both are attempts to understand the process that produces an observed quality of housing so that constructive intervention by government to improve deficient units might be efficiently organized.

The analysis of the determinants of dwelling maintenance and repair activity of elderly homeowners located in both urban and rural areas is especially important in view of proposals to foster greater dwelling maintenance by the elderly. The component of the Section 8 Housing Assistance Payments Program which leases units currently available, for example, implicitly assumes that one of the principal determinants is income.[b] No one knows with certainty that this is the critical factor; indeed, nothing is known of the relative importance of income compared to the importance of the proximity of children who can help make repairs, the role of physical impairments to the elderly,

[a] Written with Deborah Devine.

[b] The Section 8 program is discussed in detail in Chapter 7. It is currently restricted to renter households, but a proposal for including homeowners is presented in Chapter 9.

or the structure of the elderly households—for example, husband-wife household versus female individual. Clearly, formulation of efficient programs to encourage maintenance requires that the magnitude of these factors is established.

Prior work on dwelling maintenance by homeowners provides little assistance. While Sweeney (1974) and Dildine and Massey (1974) have done useful conceptual analyses on the level of maintenance activity which could most profitably be undertaken, only Mendelsohn (1973, 1977) has explored the probability of households making dwelling repairs. Mendelsohn employed the quarterly census micro data on maintenance, repair, and investment activity by homeowners to estimate reduced-form probability models. The results are highly suggestive, but the information on both the dwelling and the household is quite limited.[c]

Economists have yet to do much analysis of the demand for housing by the elderly. Typically, a dummy variable for the household over age sixty-five has been added to demand functions estimated with micro data. This procedure, given the hesitancy of the elderly to change dwellings when income falls at retirement, seems inadequate. In fact, as noted earlier, analyses using the Annual Housing Survey data have only recently been used to describe accurately the housing situation of the elderly in comparison to other households.

This chapter is clearly a first step in analyzing the housing maintenance and repair activities of the elderly. It is organized into two parts: census information on the level of repair activity of elderly homeowners and a model of repair and maintenance activity.

REPAIR ACTIVITY BY ELDERLY

The only source of detailed national information on this subject is a quarterly survey conducted by the Census Bureau of owner-occupied and rental-residential properties.[d] The data for owner-occupants in this survey—the Survey of Residential Repairs and Alterations—are employed in this analysis, both because of our specific interest and because of the greater reliability of these statistics compared to those for renters.

It is essential to point out a few details of the survey for the basic information to be properly interpreted. First, a dwelling is in the

[c] There have also been attempts to estimate supply functions for housing services; estimates using macro data are in deLeeuw and Ekanem (1971:814–26). Microbased estimates are in Ozanne and Struyk (1976).

[d] The Annual Housing Survey also provides some information, but the data is gathered in a much less careful way and is generally viewed as being much less reliable.

sample for six quarters, but a number of dwellings are added and deleted each quarter to provide a sample of constant size. The Census Bureau surveys the repairs made in each quarter. Thus, when data is used for more than one quarter, as is done in this study, a slightly different group of dwellings is represented in each. Second, from the data it can be ascertained if repairs were made, and if so, their cost; but there is no imputation possible for the value of contributed labor. Thus, the value of repairs made is understated. Finally, there is little information gathered about the occupant household and no information on dwelling condition prior to repairs, which limits more complete analyses.

With this in mind, it is possible to look at general patterns of activity. Table 4-1 displays the percentage of homeowners (elderly and nonelderly separately) who undertook repairs or improvements to their dwellings in the first and third quarter of 1977.[e]

At first glance, it is clear that the elderly are consistently less likely to undertake any of these activities than the nonelderly. While the difference is especially striking for improvements, it is also true for repairs as well.[f] Among households living inside metropolitan areas, for example, 29 percent of the nonelderly, but only 21 percent of the elderly reported repairs. There is a sharp distinction among the elderly between those with income of less than $5,000 per year and those with higher incomes. Repairs by the lower income group occur only about 60 percent as often as for those with higher incomes, and the poor also report very few improvements. This is a pattern both within and outside of metropolitan areas, although it is somewhat more pronounced in the latter. Generally, there is less activity for the low-income elderly: over a three-month period only about one in seven is likely to have made a repair involving some expenditure.

When expenditures are made, they tend to have a high reported mean value, as shown in Table 4-2. The table also shows the coefficient of variation for each reported mean. By any standard, the variance in expenditures—both total expenditures and repairs—is large. This indicates that the mean is being raised by a few very large expenditures.

[e] Data from two quarters are used to double the number of observations, which permits some tabulations that otherwise could not be made.

[f] Maintenance and repair expenditures are the current costs for the upkeep of the property rather than additional investment in the property. Examples of such activities include: repairs and maintenance of heating and central air conditioning systems; fixing plumbing stoppages and replacing faucets, traps, etc.; and repairing leaky roofs, caulking, and replacing shingles. Improvements are construction improvements and represent the kinds of outlays considered capital investments in the properties. Included here are additions, alterations, and major replacements. Complete definitions are provided in U.S. Bureau of Census (1976).

Table 4–1. Percentage of Homeowners Undertaking Repairs or Improvements to Their Dwellings, in a Quarter During the First and Third Quarters of 1977

	Head 65 Years or Older			*Heads under Age 65*		
	Any Expenditure	*Repairs*	*Improvements*	*Any Expenditure*	*Repairs*	*Improvements*
Income						
Under $5,000	15	14	1	23	18	6
$ 5,000–$9,999	32	24	11	32	24	12
$10,000–$14,999	34	27	9	37	29	16
$15,000 and over	32	28	9	42	31	20
Year Dwelling Built						
After 1960	22	18	6	38	28	17
1950–1959	28	20	8	38	28	17
1940–1949	29	23	8	31	24	13
Before 1940	23	20	6	36	27	16
Location						
Inside SMSA	27	21	8	38	29	17
Outside SMSA	22	19	5	34	25	16
Location by Income						
Inside SMSAs						
Under $5,000	18	[a]	[a]	21	[a]	[a]
$ 5,000–$9,999	31			34		
$10,000–$14,999	37			38		
$15,000 and over	31			42		
Outside SMSAs						
Under $5,000	14	[a]	[a]	24	[a]	[a]
$ 5,000–$9,999	34			30		
$10,000–$14,999	26			35		
$15,000 and over	36			41		

Source: Special tabulations from the U.S. Bureau of the Census, Survey of Residential Repairs and Alterations, Series C-50.

[a] Sample sizes too small for reliable calculations.

Table 4–2. Mean Expenditures and Coefficient of Variation of Mean Expenditures, of Homeowners Undertaking Repairs and Improvements to Their Dwellings, during the Quarter for the First and Third Quarters in 1977, by Age of Head

	Head 65 years or Older		*Head under Age 65*	
	Mean	*Coeff. of Variation*[a]	*Mean*	*Coeff. of Variation*[a]
Total Expenditures				
Income				
Under $5,000	$129	180	$332	235
$ 5,000–$9,999	235	152	251	208
$10,000–$14,999	331	170	357	273
$15,000 or more	486	300	451	318
Location				
Inside SMSAs	257	170	414	312
Outside SMSAs	263	327	366	241
Repairs				
Income				
Under $5,000	89	169	73	126
$ 5,000–$9,999	128	156	101	192
$10,000–$14,999	216	200	123	282
$15,000 or more	182	173	124	176
Location				
Inside SMSAs	149	187	127	224
Outside SMSAs	115	196	105	171

Source: Special tabulations from the U.S. Bureau of the Census, Survey of Residential Repairs and Alterations, Series C-50.

[a] Coefficient of variation is the (standard deviation/mean) *100.

Table 4-3 shows no more than 10 percent of households spending over $100 in a given calendar quarter on repairs.

The average repair expenditure for a calendar quarter reported by the elderly who had any expenditure was $136 compared to $121 for the nonelderly. Because the nonelderly are likely to make more of the repairs themselves, the difference in the repairs actually made is probably overstated by the expenditure figures. There is also reason to suspect bias in the opposite direction, however. There is evidence of households sustaining a high rate of repair and improvement activity in the first two or three years after moving into a house, with some of the work going to modify the dwelling to suit their preferences. Therefore, the dollar figures tend to understate the difference in genuine maintenance activity because of the much longer average tenure of elderly homeowners.

Table 4–3. Percentage Distribution of Homeowners Expenditures on Dwelling Repairs, by Income

	Head of House Age 65 or More Expenditure			*Head of House under Age 65 Expenditure*		
	None	*Under $100*	*Over $100*	*None*	*Under $100*	*Over $100*
Income						
Under $5,000	85	12	3	81	15	4
$ 5,000–$9,999	76	17	7	76	19	5
$10,000–$14,999	73	18	9	71	23	6
$15,000 or more	72	18	10	69	22	9

Source: Special tabulations from the U.S. Bureau of the Census, Survey of Residential Repairs and Alterations, Series C-50.

Perhaps more important than overall differences between the elderly and nonelderly is the pattern of expenditures with income. Those low-income elderly homeowners who undertook repairs spent some $89 in the quarter; those with incomes in the $5,000 to $10,000 range spent 44 percent more. Furthermore, if one takes into account the combination of lower frequency of repairs and lower average expenditures on repairs undertaken, the difference in the average expenditures for all elderly in the two income groups becomes even more remarkable. The average expenditure on repairs of all low-income elderly homeowners is $13 per quarter compared to $31 for those with $5,000 to $10,000 incomes, a 138 percent difference. It is difficult to imagine either figure being an adequate outlay, but it is clear that the $13 implies inadequate upkeep. Although nonelderly with similar incomes spend only slightly more ($16 per quarter) the position of the elderly compared to the nonelderly is driven home when one recalls that two-fifths of all elderly homeowners were in this lowest income group in 1976 compared to 12 percent of their younger counterparts.

THE DETERMINANT OF MAINTENANCE ACTIVITIES

The data in Table 4-2 raise the question of what causes the variance in frequency of repair and improvement activity and expenditures when such activity is undertaken. Of course, the elderly are a highly diverse group who are undergoing a series of life-cycle changes, many of which have implications for their demand for housing services and their ability to obtain them. Such changes may include alterations in the composition of the household as children move out or a spouse dies, reduction in income at retirement, and restrictions in physical capabilities. The elderly do, then, adjust their housing more frequently than one might suspect. Some make this adjustment by shifting dwellings,[g] but more frequently the adjustments are made by altering the current dwelling—by adding handrails and other special fixtures or, if economically necessary, by deferring certain types of maintenance.

CONCEPTUAL FRAMEWORK

Although it would be ideal to model the dynamics of the adjustment process, this study restricts itself to a simple static model of repair activity because the data available for estimation are cross-sectional. First the demand function is set out in the model, then the supply function, and then the two are combined.

The demand for repairs or repair activities, D, is derived from the demand for housing services. Therefore, the determinants of D closely parallel those for housing services.

$$D = D\ [Y, A, r, HH, C, N, P_1, P_2, P_3] \qquad (4\text{–}1)$$

Y is the household's current income and A are assets. Assets are especially important because: (1) they can be directly used to finance repairs; (2) they influence the household's judgment as to the fraction of income it feels it can devote to housing; and (3) they are indicative of the household's permanent income. The household's discount rate, r, can have a strong negative influence on D, as the household becomes increasingly aged; on the other hand, this may be offset by a strong bequest factor, so that r may have little effect on demand (Blinder 1976). Household composition, HH, influences D largely through the demand of individual members for a certain quantity of housing services, all things being equal (one spouse may be more sensitive to dwelling conditions than another). The condition of the dwelling, C, is an obvious determinant; in the extreme, repairs would have to be undertaken for the dwelling to remain habitable. N is the condition of the neighborhood; if it is declining, the return to maintenance activity would be sharply reduced.

Three price terms are included in the demand function, one for each of the relevant types of suppliers: P_1 is the price per unit of repairs if the household is making the repair itself; P_2 is the price if a friend or relative is making the repair, and P_3 is the price of employing someone else to make the repairs. Each source of supply involves a different

[g] See Newman (1977). A review of a number of studies is in Struyk (1976).

production technology and possibly different factor prices. The household chooses among the three different suppliers of repairs on the basis of price.

The determinants of these supply prices themselves are discussed in Chapter 5. For now, it is sufficient to note that they are in fact unobservable and that variables hypothesized to determine them—wage rates and so on—are substituted for the price terms and a reduced-form model derived in which the dependent variable is still the demand for repairs.

The formulation presented thus far tacitly assumes a "repair" to be a homogeneous good, regardless of who supplies it. It is quite conceivable, however, that the repairs are perceived to be differentiated goods depending on who supplies them. It is arguable that a job one does himself or herself is viewed as a superior good, since one knows "the job was done right." In recognition of the possible differentiation, "repairs" (and the demand for them) can be distinguished by their source of supply—D_1, D_2, D_3—in much the same way consumers distinguish among automobiles or cereals.[h]

In other words, if repairs were differentiated goods, in demand as well as supply, the demand function for D (eq. 4–1) would be replaced in a group of functions, one for each D_i type of repairs, distinguished by the main source of labor. One can easily write a reduced-form equation for each of the D_i as follows:

$$D_i = D_i\,[Y, A, r, N, HH, C, M, P_i, P_j, P_k, D_j, D_k \ldots]\; i \neq j. \qquad (4\text{–}2)$$

The levels of D_i are clearly determined jointly, since the P_j and hence the relative attractiveness of the jth type of repair depends on how much of the jth activity has been demanded in the relevant time period, except for contractors whose supply schedule to the individual household is flat, that is, contractors supply as much as demanded at a constant price. In other words, if self-made repairs are the most preferred, the demand for contractor repairs would depend on the relative price of self-repairs. This price would rise sharply as the household makes more repairs themselves. Assuming the demand for a repair activity—fixing a broken window, for example—the choice

[h] In recent years, economists have noted that housing in general is a differentiated good, in both demand and supply. The principal distinctions have to do with structural attributes of dwellings and the characteristics of the neighborhoods in which they are located. This is thoroughly exposited in Straszheim (1975:chap. 1), and Kain and Quigley (1975:chap. 2). The greatest experience with the demand for differentiated goods has been in the analysis of international trade of fairly specifically defined, but not identical goods. A very thorough discussion and empirical analysis of the differentiated goods issue is in Kravis and R.E. Lipsey (1971).

among the differentiated goods depends on the household's taste, other demand determinants, and the relative prices of the supply sources, which in turn are driven by the total demand for each repair type to date in the relevant time period.

This line of reasoning suggests that the mix of repair types observed over an extended time period, perhaps five years, would be sensitive to the time interval between individual repairs. If repairs were clustered, one would predict a higher fraction of contractor repairs; less bunching would imply a lower implicit wage rate of the householder and/or relative.

The data used in this analysis are from the 1975 "Survey of Maintenance and Repair Activity by Elderly Homeowners," a sample of 1,575 owner-occupied households.[i] The sample contained 225 elderly (sixty-two years of age and over) homeowners from each of seven areas, the areas selected to represent the location of elderly homeowners nationally. Of the seven areas, five are Standard Metropolitan Statistical Areas (SMSA), each one representing a different SMSA size category. These areas are: Philadelphia, San Francisco, Dayton, Tulsa, and Pittsfield, Massachusetts. The remaining two areas are a small city (New Ulm, Minnesota) and one rural area (Orangeburg County, North Carolina). The sample households within each area were selected by a stratified random sample, using median homeowner census tract income (or similar data) for stratification. The sample was restricted to dwellings built prior to 1961 in order to include properties more likely to require maintenance and repair activities. This analysis uses only the 1,367 observations for households aged sixty-five and over.[j]

While the survey gathered information on all of the areas critical to understanding the maintenance activity of elderly homeowners, an important question is the accuracy with which the survey data measured the factors hypothesized in the prior section as determinants of maintenance activity. Table 4-4 provides a succinct listing of the principal variables used in the analysis. The independent, or determining, variables are divided into seven groups: financial status, household type, dwelling condition, health, structure type, neighborhood charac-

[i] The survey was conducted by the Transcentury Corporation under HUD Contract H-2235R.

[j] For a more complete description of the sampling procedure see Jacobs and Rabushka (1976). We have compared several of the broad characteristics of the sample households with those of all elderly homeowners using data from the 1973 and 1974 Annual Housing Survey. In terms of household composition and income, there is close correspondence between our sample and the national population. On the other hand, the households in the sample have significantly higher ratios of housing expenses-to-income than the national, elderly homeowning population.

Table 4–4. Definition of Variables in the Analysis of Determinants of Dwelling Maintenance by Elderly Homeowners

Variable Name and Classification	*Description*
A. Independent Variables	
Financial Status	
TOTINC	Total household income in 1974. Sum of all earnings, income from professional practice, income from farming, dividends, interest, social security, supplementary security, other government sources, pension, rent on property, alimony.
ASSETS	Value of the sum of certificates of deposit, savings accounts, checking accounts, stocks, mutual fund shares, stock through investment clubs, U.S. Savings Bonds, other bonds, property value minus value owed on property, life insurance value.
COSTINC	Ratio of housing costs to average total family income per month. Housing cost defined as sum of monthly property tax, insurance, mortgage payment, electricity, natural gas, fuel oil, coal, other fuels, water, telephone, and other charges.
Household Type	
HT1	Household type 1 if respondent is married and living with spouse; 0 otherwise.
HT2	Household type 1 if respondent lives alone.
HT3	Household type 1 if respondent lives with others (relative or friend) but not with a spouse.
CH	1 if children of respondent live with respondent.
GCH	1 if grandchildren of respondent live with respondent.
Family Support	
VISITMON	Number of family members who visit monthly or more frequently.
TRAVEL2	Number of family members who travel two hours or less to reach the respondent.
Dwelling Condition	
HQSUM1	Sum of selected interior dwelling defects present in each room divided by the number of rooms (possible ten defects); includes absence of electrical outlets, defective electrical outlets, absence of light switches, defective light switches, absence of light fixtures, defective light fixtures, room lacks heating outlet, defective wall surface, defective ceiling surface, defective floor surface.
HQSUM2	Sum of selected major interior dwelling defects (possible six defects): lack complete bathroom, detached toilet facility; absence of complete kitchen facilities, lacks hot-cold running water, defective toilet facilities, no central heating system.
EHQSUM	Sum of exterior dwelling defects (possible nine items) include defective foundation, paint, exterior wall structure, exterior wall surface, roof surface, roof structure, chimney, entranceway, exterior stairs.
HR	1 if house has been remodeled since 1969.

Table 4–4. continued

Variable Name and Classification	*Description*
Household Health	
AGE	Age of respondent.
CANT	Count of the number of activities respondents found they cannot do (possible eight); includes go up and down stairs, leave home, walk around a room, do own laundry, get in and out of bed, clean own room, shop alone, change storm windows.
SFCANT	Takes on value of CANT for San Francisco households only. Defined because one activity—changing storm windows—is not applicable in the Bay area.
Structure Type	
ST1	1 if dwelling is a single-family detached unit.
ST2	1 if dwelling is a row house.
Neighborhood Characteristics	
TRTBLK	Percentage of households in the census tract headed by a black in 1970.
TRTINC	Median family income in the tract in 1970 (in $000)
SATIS	1 if household is generally happy with neighborhood as to location, etc.
NGHQAL	Rating of neighborhood quality by respondent, ranging from 4 (excellent) to 1 (very poor).
RACE	1 if the head of house is white, 0 if otherwise.
Control Variables	
C4 - C7	Dummy variables for Philadelphia, Pittsburgh, San Francisco, Tulsa (used only in the five urban cities sample).
REPAIRS	Total number of repairs made in last two years (maximum of five).
B. Dependent Variables	
Used in Analysis of Presence of Maintenance and Repair Activity	
RPR	1 if any repairs were made over last two years.
REP	Count of the number of repairs (maximum of five) made over last two years divided by 5.
Used in Analysis of how Repairs Made, Given Presence of Some Activity	
SELF	1 if respondent or persons living with respondent did any repairs.
FRIEND	1 if friend or relative not living with respondent did any repairs.
HIRE	1 if any repairs were done for hire, by individual or by contractor.
SLFRTIO	Fraction of all repairs done by self.
FRDRTIO	Fraction of all repairs done by friend.
HIRRTIO	Fraction of all repairs done by individual or contractor.

teristics, and controls. Most of these specifications are self-explanatory; a few require some explanation.

A set of four variables describe the condition of the dwelling unit. Of these, three—HQSUM1, HQSUM2, and HR—describe the interior condition of the unit. One part of the survey involved a detailed, room-by-room inventory of the dwelling. Taking advantage of this detail, the variable HQSUM1 is introduced; it is defined as the possible presence of each of ten defects for every room (excluding porches and similar spaces), with the sum divided by the number of rooms. Most of these defects could be remedied at modest expense. HQSUM2 totals several deficiencies, such as the absence of complete plumbing, which would be more costly to remedy. The final interior variable, HR, indicates that the unit was at least partially remodeled in the five years prior to the survey. Finally, EHQSUM totals nine exterior deficiencies. All four of the variables weight the included defects equally based on findings of other analyses of the insensitivity of house values to a set of deficiencies weighted in several alternative ways (Mendelsohn and Struyk 1975). CANT is defined as the sum of the number of activities out of a group of eight that the head-of-house reported he or she could not do without assistance. The activities in this list are similar to those in the Guttman scale, which has been found to be a reliable indicator of impairment (Rosow and Breslau 1975).

Two broad types of dependent variables are analyzed: (1) The presence and intensity of any repair activity over the two years prior to the interview and (2) who performed the repair. Although the survey explicitly asked that the respondent describe *any* repair or maintenance task completed and the amount of expenditure, the frequency of activity (reported in Table 4-5) suggests that households probably limited their response to fairly major tasks, such as painting, mending

Table 4–5. Number of Households with Repair Activity, by Number of Repairs

Number of Repairs	*Number*	*Frequency*
0	579	46
1	402	32
2	193	15
3	62	5
4	20	2
5	12	1
Total	1,268	100

Source: Special tabulation from the 1975 "Survey of Maintenance and Repair Activity by Elderly Homeowners."

a leaky roof, and so on. For example, only 54 percent of those surveyed reported any repairs being made. Furthermore, only about 15 percent of all repairs were made exclusively by the respondent. One would expect many small jobs to be undertaken by the household itself, and this low percentage may point to the larger jobs being reported. Yet, the low incidence of repair activity is generally consistent with the figures presented in Table 4-1 for a two calendar quarter period based on a national sample.

The number of repairs differ sharply by location. As noted previously, the sample areas contain five cities, one rural area, and one small town. Examination of household and housing characteristics for each of these locations showed that the cities form a relatively homogeneous group, whereas the small town and the rural areas are quite distinct. These differences are illustrated by the mean values of selected variables provided in Table 4-6. Differences in income, assets, household types, housing quality, and repair activity among the three locations are substantial. Because of these differences, it is more appropriate to analyze them separately.

The figures on the amount and type of repair activity shown at the bottom of Table 4-6 indicate that most repairs are being done by hired labor (HIRE); the smallest number of repairs are being performed by the elderly person himself (SELF). The average cost of repairs, given in the final three entries, are not out of line with the mean expenditures of owner-occupants reported by the census and reviewed earlier in this chapter. The cost of jobs performed by contractors (COST HIRE) does seem quite high, however. Several arguments might be proffered in support of only the largest expenditures being reported: only the major repairs were recalled or thought to be of sufficient importance,[k] the question itself may not have elicited the correct response;[l] the cost figures are simply in error. There is no basis to defend or reject these arguments. One guess is that the sample be biased toward major repair and maintenance activities, as is, then, the census data on repair expenditures.

With only about one-half the sample households reporting any repair activity over the observation period, there may be a strong bivariate relation between the presence of any repair activity and

[k] M. Powell Lawton (1978) has discussed problems of the elderly in responding to questions on current housing conditions.

[l] This explanation does not seem feasible. The general question on repair activity, which comes after a long series of queries on the condition of specific parts of the structure and major mechanical systems, was: "Within the past 2 years, have you done—or had anyone else do—any maintenance or repair work on either the inside or outside of your house?" If there was an affirmative answer, the specifics of up to five repairs were pursued.

Table 4–6. Mean Values of Selected Variables for Three Different Geographic Areas

	Small Town	*Rural*	*Five Cities*
TOTINC	4,250	2,899	6,633
ASSETS	17,509	4,911	21,418
COSTINC	.34	.44	.32
HT1	.39	.40	.51
HT2	.41	.25	.32
HT3	.20	.35	.17
CH	.12	.22	.15
GCH	.04	.15	.03
VISITMON	1.66	1.42	1.29
TRAVEL2	1.97	1.65	1.47
HQSUM1	.19	1.48	.25
HQSUM2	.35	1.25	.15
EHQSUM	.30	1.54	.42
HR	.17	.15	.16
AGE	74	74	74
CANT	.34	.66	.44
TRTBLK	[a]	[a]	6.67
TRTINC	[a]	[a]	11,493
SATIS	[a]	[a]	.91
NGHQAL	[a]	[a]	3.23
RACE	1.0	.58	.96
RPR	.44	.29	.62
REP	.14	.07	.20
SELF[c]	.21	.11	.18
FRIEND[c]	.30	.22	.18
HIRE[c]	.61	.70	.76
COSTSELF[b]	37.5	87.8	135.1
COSTFRIEND[b]	77.3	303.0	279.3
COSTHIRE[b]	622.2	975.0	851.9

Source: Special tabulation from the 1975 "Survey of Maintenance and Repair Activity by Elderly Homeowners."

[a] Variables only defined for cities.

[b] Average cost of repairs made by this type of supplier.

[c] Frequency of repairs, given *some* repair activity being done.

several of the hypothesized determinants. The figures on income shown in Table 4-7 are of special interest because of the disaggregation of households in the 0 to $5,000 income group. A positive association of repairs with income is evident. It would appear that the ratio of housing expenses to income has little discernible effect on repair activity, which calls into question the hypothesis that high housing expense burdens by themselves are a good indicator of the household's inability to make repairs. A similarly murky picture emerges when the pattern of repair activity with the three measures of dwelling unit condition is examined (Table 4-8). Both the rural area and small town generally

Table 4–7. Percentage of Households Making Some Repair, by Income Class and Location

Income Class	*Small Town*	*Rural*	*Five Cities*
No income reported	[a]	21	62
$1–$2,499	32	27	53
$2,500–$4,999	48	36	58
$5,000–$9,999	50	[a]	63
$10,000 and over	59	[a]	71

Source: Special tabulation from the 1975 "Survey of Maintenance and Repair Activity by Elderly Homeowners."

[a] Sample too small to be reliable.

show a slight increase in repair activity as the number of defects mounts, both for interior and exterior problems; but no pattern emerges from the data for five cities. Finally, regardless of the location, the extent of mobility impairment of the elderly household members (variable CANT) did not have a strong association with repair activity.

The differences in the extent of repair activity among location types and the weakness of the simple relation between repair activity and several prima facie important determinants suggest that the forces causing repair and maintenance work to be undertaken are quite

Table 4–8. Percentage of Households in Dwellings with Various Numbers and Types of Defects Making Repairs, by Location

Variable Range[b]	*Small Town*	*Rural*	*Five Cities*
	A. Minor Interior Defects (HQSUM1)		
0	40	22	60
0.01–0.99	52	30	64
1.00–1.99	[a]	31	58
2.00 or over	[a]	35	[a]
	B. Major Interior Defects (HQSUM2)		
0	42	29	63
1	56	33	51
2	[a]	20	61
3 or more	[a]	[a]	[a]
	C. External Defects (EHQSUM)		
0	39	28	63
1	60	26	60
2	[a]	41	59
3 or more	[a]	36	52

[a] Sample too small to be reliable.

[b] See Table 4–4 for variable definition.

complex. The multivariate analysis of the next section attempts to clarify some of the patterns observed thus far.

RESULTS OF STATISTICAL ANALYSIS

Because the estimated models are all reduced-form functions, it is frequently impossible to separate the influence of demand and supply factors; moreover, in some instances, countervailing demand and supply influences may cause a particular determinant to be statistically insignificant when it might be significant in a more complete structural model.

In establishing the determinants of the probability of the household undertaking any repair activity over the two-year observation period, the regressions were estimated separately for the three types of geographic areas. (They are reported in Appendix Table 4A-1.[m] There are two consistently significant variables: income and the number of family members visiting at least monthly. Elasticities based on the coefficients indicate that a 20 percent rise in income would cause a 1 percent increase in the probability of any repair activity in the five urban areas and about a 4 percent increase in the small town and rural area. (This is consistent with recent findings by Helbers (1979) for elderly households in two other cities.) A similar percentage increase in visitations by family members would, as an average, have about half the effect of the income increase. In the five cities, there are, in addition, two important neighborhood effects. First, the greater percentage of blacks in the area, the lower the probability of repairs. This might be due to the price of materials and contract labor being higher in black enclaves, as suggested by some researchers (Schafer et al. 1975), or to an adverse effect on expectations in transition neighborhoods.[n] Second, the affirmative influence of higher average income in the tract might reflect general social pressure to maintain one's unit.

As important as these significant coefficients is the inconsistency of the performance of variables indicating the household's ability to make repairs (CANT), the discount rate (AGE), the presence of children in the home, and household type. Further, the dwelling quality variables are of inconsistent sign, although sometimes significant. In fact, in

[m] All the models have been estimated using ordinary least squares, a procedure that is defensible for a dichotomous dependent variable when the mean value of the variable is between 0.30 and 0.70, as it is in these cases (Goodman 1976). Also, the significance criterion used for evaluating the regression coefficients shifts between a one-tail and a two-tail test depending on strength of the hypothesis on the net effect of each variable on the probability of repair activity.

[n] A more complete discussion of the types of neighborhoods in which the elderly are concentrated is provided in Chapter 6.

Table 4–9. Needed Repairs Perceived by Elderly Respondent and Expert Evaluator (Percent of Units Needing Repairs)

City	*Household Perception*[a]	*Expert Evaluation*[b]
Philadelphia	21	54
San Francisco	24	60
Dayton	27	70
Tulsa	25	44
Pittsfield	24	48
New Ulm	27	51
Orangeburg	57	99

[a] Respondent was specifically asked about twenty-eight items that might need repair. These included, for example, the water heater, toilet, wash basin, light switches, electrical outlets, furnace, radiator gutters, walls, ceilings, windows, storm windows.

[b] Includes, in effect, all of items described in footnote (a) plus a few additional items such as handrails and driveway needing repairs. But the two groups of indicator correspond fairly closely.

only two instances a dwelling condition variable is both significant and of the expected sign (HQSUM1 in the five cities model and EHQSUM in New U1m). There are several possible explanations for this inconsistency. Elderly homeowners may simply be unaware of some dwelling unit deficiencies, either from ignorance or because they have learned to live with them. This idea is supported by the data in Table 4-9 comparing perceptions and expert evaluations; the respondent was aware of only about half of the problems observed by the expert evaluator. Or, it is possible that a low number of deficiencies signals both good condition and little pressure for repairs *and* a proclivity of the household in the past to make repairs. Another factor at work is the way the data were assembled: whereas repairs were ascertained for the two years prior to the survey, condition of dwelling was recorded at the time of the survey. Thus, a dwelling's good condition at the survey might have been attributable to the repairs.[o]

Some of these results are amplified by the analysis of the probability of any repair activity being undertaken by the respondent (SELF), a friend or nonresident family member (FRIEND), or by a contractor or hired person (HIRE). (Estimated regression models, employing the data from the five cities are reported in Appendix Table 4A-2.) The neighborhood variables are excluded from these models, since expecta-

[o] Several variables—ASSETS, TRAVEL2, HR—have been omitted from the reported model because of their high correlation with other independent variables. Separate results for the intensity of activity (REP) are not reported as the determinants were generally similar to those for RPR.

tions should influence the decision to undertake a repair, not the way in which it is done. These models show several interesting patterns:

- An elderly homeowner is more likely to do the repair himself if it is a husband-wife household; a higher income also increases this probability. The likelihood *falls sharply* with advanced age and mobility limitations.
- The probability of a family member or friend making at least one repair increases as the number of persons visiting the elderly person/couple increases. The fact that this likelihood declines with increasing income suggests the elderly imposing on family and friends more often when financially constrained to do so.[p] Surprisingly, age and mobility impairments have little effect on repair activity when friends are making the repairs.
- Finally, the probability of the elderly hiring workmen or contractors to make repairs is positively related to income, being a non-husband/wife household, and being older. The housing quality coefficients suggest that hired labor is used more often when units are in good condition, a phenomenon possibly related to past household income.

The final set of regression (Appendix Table 4A-3) explores the determinants of the intensity with which the three methods of repair activity are employed by elderly homeowners. The dependent variable in each case is the number of repairs done by a particular method divided by the total number of repairs undertaken by the household. These models contain the same set of independent variables as those discussed, except that the total number of repairs has been added to account for increasing "wage rates" of the occupant or friends/relatives as the amount of repair activity increases.[q]

The results are generally very similar to those for the probability of using the given method just reported. The number of repairs variable (REPAIRS) does not have the anticipated effect. Looking across the three models, it indicates that over the range (and type) of repairs reported, the relevant wage rates are unaffected; indeed, SELF repairs increase as a fraction of all activity as total activity increases.[r] Another

[p] For a general discussion of the household support provided elderly persons by family members are Shanas et al. (1968), chap. 5.

[q] The addition of Q $(= Q_1 + Q_2 + Q_3)$ on the right-hand side means, of course, that the coefficients of the independent variables must be adjusted to obtain their true effect on, say Q_1/Q. In particular, if b is the coefficient of Q_1 then the coefficients must be divided by $[(1/Q) - b]$.

[r] Note that the causality in this instance probably runs in the opposite direction from that implied by the model. That is, as individuals are capable of and have the preference for repairing their own units, the total level of repair activity increases.

difference is that the dwelling quality variables are consistently positive in the self-equation—again pointing to the effect of good-quality units being more frequently repaired in response to the pressure of defects in causing greater repair activity.

TENTATIVE CONCLUSIONS

What are the implications of the results just presented? At the outset, it must be noted that definitive conclusions simply are not possible because of the limitations of the sample, and because of certain ambiguities arising from the nature of the estimated models. Even with this restriction, several statements are possible that have importance for formulation of policies to assist the elderly homeowner in maintaining his or her property.

First, the analyses make it clear that the decision to undertake repair activity is determined by a number of factors. Also, the determinants of this decision appear to vary with local housing conditions and social customs (for example, extent to which children provide support to their parents). There is a need for flexibility to be built into any program designed primarily to assist elderly homeowners maintain their dwellings.

Increased income is strongly associated statistically with repairs or maintenance activity being undertaken. On the other hand, the elasticity of such activity, with respect to income, is certainly modest. This low elasticity, combined with the sharp difference between the perception of the household of the need for specific repairs and the rating by an expert evaluator, suggest the earmarking of cash grants for repair activities. Such earmarking could take a variety of forms: inspection of the units with continued grants being dependent upon repairs being made, as is presently done in rental units under the Section 8 program;[s] or the full or partial cost of actual repairs reimbursed as is currently being done, e.g., under Boston's Housing Improvement Program (City of Boston Office of Housing 1977). The Section 312 Subsidized Loan Rehabilitation Program reviewed in Chapter 7 is another vehicle. This program has the advantage for the elderly of utilizing contractors but the disadvantage of being administratively complicated. These kinds of programs suggest that "circuit breaker" property tax relief for elderly households is a relatively inefficient way to maintain housing quality, although it may provide general income support.[t] Similarly, this applies to reverse annuity mortgages, although these do

[s] This program and a similar one, the Experimental Housing Allowance Program, are discussed in Chapter 7.

[t] A good description of "circuit breakers" is in Abt Associates (1975).

[u] Reverse annuity mortgages are also discussed in Chapter 9.

not involve a subsidy (Guttentag 1975).[u] Finally, the income responsiveness of repair activity highlights the desirability of making any assistance income conditional in order to achieve a reasonable degree of target efficiency.

Another set of implications can be derived from the information on how the repairs are actually made: husband/wife households make more repairs than others. This is true even with controls for differences in income probably because of the combination of mutual assistance in making the repairs and a reinforcement in the pressure to get them made when a deficiency occurs. In the same vein, repairs done by the household fall off sharply as physical impairments increase. These facts, combined with the general difficulty of hiring people to do small jobs, argue for the provision of chore services especially for non-husband-wife households and very old or the impaired couples. An alternative approach is to use a government-affiliated agency acting as a clearinghouse, arranging for work to be done, providing inspection and appraisal services, and helping to arrange financing.[v] This idea is buttressed by the finding that the elderly do not want to impose on friends or relatives for such activity even when their economic circumstances force them to do so.

Finally, the results suggest that conditions in the neighborhood surrounding the dwelling affect the probability of repairs being undertaken. These conditions have been crudely captured by the variables included in the present analysis, and the conclusion is far from definitive. One implication of the results is that increasing incomes in declining neighborhoods will produce less dwelling upkeep than in other areas; hence, it is particularly in the declining areas that the case is the strongest for placing a condition on the recipiency of assistance that the funds be spent on housing.

[v] Data on services of this type being provided under the Community Development Block Grant Program and Title XX funding are very scarce. Michael Gutowski (1978) presents fragmentary data on Title XX. Also see Chapter 8.

APPENDIX

Table 4A–1. Regression Analysis of Probability of Any Repair Activity (Dependent Variable Is RPR)

Independent Variable	*Small Town*		*Rural*		*Five Cities*	
	Coeff.	*T-stat*	*Coeff.*	*T-stat*	*Coeff.*	*T-stat*
CONSTANT	.915		.143		.543	
TOTINC	2.2×10^{-5}	2.2	1.9×10^{-5}	2.0	4.5×10^{-6}	2.8
COSTINC	.026	.5	.042	1.2	−.010	1.3
CH	−.068	.6	.168	2.0	−.063	1.3
GCH	.478	.9	.006	.5	.030	.3
VISITMON	.046	1.6	.043	1.5	.018	1.5
HQSUM1	−.115	.9	.035	.9	.060	1.5
HQSUM2	.062	.9	−.056	1.0	−.007	.2
EHQSUM	.099	1.6	−.013	.5	−.028	1.4
C4					.062	1.2
C5					.063	1.2
C6					.020	.3
C7					−.078	1.5
TRTBLK					−.002	2.0
TRTINC					.011	2.1
SATIS					−.083	1.3
NGHQAL					−.034	.8
RACE					−.057	.7
AGE	−.009	1.5	.0002	.5	.0005	.3
R^2	.078		.062		.048	
SEE	.489		.453		.480	
F	1.66		1.26		2.32	
df	176		171		881	

Table 4A–2. Regression Analysis of How Repairs Were Made, Given Some Repair Activity (Analysis Restricted to Five Cities)

Independent Variable	SELF		FRIEND		HIRE	
	Coeff.	T-stat	Coeff.	T-stat	Coeff.	T-stat
CONSTANT	.713		.140		.319	
TOTINC	2.7×10^{-6}	1.4	-5.8×10^{-6}	3.1	6.2×10^{-6}	3.3
COSTINC	.002	.2	−.004	.3	2.1×10^{-5}	[a]
AGE	−.009	4.5	.0001	.5	.007	3.5
CANT	−.023	1.4	.014	.8		
SFCANT	.033	1.0	.073	2.1		
HT1	.188	4.2			−.096	1.9
HT2	.025	.5			−.033	.6
VISITMON	.001	.1	.040	3.1	−.034	2.2
HQSUM1	.026	.7	.010	.2	−.001	.2
HQSUM2	.009	.2	.028	.8	−.085	2.0
EHQSUM	.022	1.0	.001	.1	−.038	1.5
R^2	.108		.041		.051	
SEE	.367		.379		.422	
F	5.85		2.61		3.19	
df	536		538		538	

[a] Less than 0.05.

Table 4A–3. Regression Analysis of Intensity of Repair Activity, by How Repair Was Made (Analysis Restricted to Five Cities)

Independent Variable	SLFRTIO		FRDRTIO		HIRRTIO	
	Coeff.	T-stat	Coeff.	T-stat	Coeff.	T-stat
CONSTANT	.542		.156		.279	
TOTINC	2.2×10^{-7}	.2	-6.2×10^{-6}	5.4	4.8×10^{-6}	2.1
COSTINC	.002	.2	−.002	.2	.002	1.1
AGE	−.007	3.5	−.0003	.1	.006	2.7
CANT	−.019	1.4	.016	1.1		
SFCANT	−.012	.4	.024	.7		
HT1	.167	4.4			−.106	2.0
HT2	.023	.6			−.043	.8
VISITMON	−.002	.5	.036	3.3	−.036	2.4
HQSUM1	.011	.3	−.0005	[a]	−.010	.2
HQSUM2	.027	.9	.042	1.4	−.063	1.5
EHQSUM	.036	2.0	.004	.2	−.039	1.6
REPAIRS	.022	1.6	−.006	.4	−.014	.7
R^2	.104		.043		.051	
SEE	.314		.325		.420	
F	5.24		2.49		2.91	
df	542		544		544	

[a] Less than 0.05.

REFERENCES

Abt Associates. 1975. *Property Tax Relief Programs for the Elderly*. Washington, D.C.: U.S. Government Printing Office.

Blinder, A.S. 1976. "Intergenerational Transfers and Life Cycle Consumption." *American Economic Review* 66 (May): 87–93.

City of Boston, Office of Housing. 1977. "Housing Improvement Program: Summary." Boston.

deLeeuw, F., and N.S. Ekanem. 1971. "The Supply of Rental Housing." *American Economic Review* 61 (December): 814–26.

Dildine, L.L., and F.A. Massey. 1974. "Dynamic Model of Private Incentives to Housing Maintenance." *Southern Economic Journal* 40 (April): 631–39.

Goodman, J.L., Jr. 1976. "Is Ordinary Least Squares Estimation with a Dichotomous Dependent Variable Really That Bad?" Washington, D.C.: Urban Institute Working Paper.

Gutowski, M. 1978. "Integrating Housing and Social Services Activities for the Elderly Household." *Occasional Papers in Housing and Community Affairs*. Vol 1.

Guttentag, J.M. 1975. *Creating New Financial Instruments for the Aged*. New York: New York University Center for Study of Financial Institutions.

Helbers, L. 1979. "Estimated Effects of Increased Income on Homeowner Repair Expenditures." Working Note Draft WN-197-HUD. Santa Monica: The Rand Corporation.

Jacobs, B., and A. Rabushka. 1976. "The Elderly Homeowner: A Proposal for Further Study Based on Preliminary Findings." Report to U.S. Department of Housing and Urban Development. Washington, D.C.: Transcentury Corp.

Kain, J.F., and J.M. Quigley. 1975. *Housing Markets and Racial Discrimination*. New York: Columbia University Press.

Kravis, L.B., and R.E. Lipsey. 1971. *Price Competitiveness in World Trade*. New York: National Bureau of Economic Research.

Lawton, M.P. 1978. "The Housing Problems of Community Resident Elderly." *Occasional Papers in Housing and Community Affairs*. Vol. 1.

Mendelsohn, R. 1973. "Housing Improvements of Single-Family Owner-Occupied Units in the United States." Senior Thesis, Harvard University.

———. 1977. "Empirical Evidence on Home Improvements." *Journal of Urban Economics* (October): 457–68.

Mendelsohn, R., and R. Struyk. 1975. "The Flow of Housing Services in a Hedonic Index." Washington, D.C.: Urban Institute Working Paper.

Newman, S. 1977. "Housing Adjustments of Older People, Part II." Ann Arbor: University of Michigan, Institute for Social Research.

Ozanne, I., and R. Struyk. 1976. *Housing from the Existing Stock: Comparative Economic Analysis of Owner-Occupants and Landlords*. Washington, D.C.: The Urban Institute.

Rosow, I., and N. Breslau. 1975. "A Guttman Health Scale for the Aged." *Journal of Gerontology* (October): 13–17.

Schafer, R.; W. Holshouser; K. Moore; and R. Santer. 1975. "Spatial Variations in the Operating Costs of Rental Housing." Cambridge, Mass.: Harvard University, Department of City and Regional Planning, Discussion Paper D 75-4.

Shanas, E., et al. 1968. *Old People in Three Industrial Societies*. New York: Atherton Press.

Straszheim, M. 1975. *An Econometric Analysis of the Urban Housing Market*. New York: Columbia University Press.

Struyk, R. 1976. "Housing for the Elderly: Research Needs for Informed Public Policy." Washington, D.C.: Urban Institute Working Paper 229-4.

Sweeney, J.L. 1974. "Housing Unit Maintenance and Mode of Tenure." *Journal of Economic Theory*, p. 111–38.

U.S. Bureau of the Census. 1976. *Residential Alterations and Repairs*. Washington, D.C.: Series C-50.

Chapter 5

Social Services and Housing Quality[a]

The focus of this chapter is on the role of housekeeping services, broadly defined and including public and private services, provided to elderly households by nonfamily members in assisting the elderly to maintain their dwelling units.[b] Housekeeping services as defined by the individual states under Title XX of the Social Security Act may encompass a host of activities, including shopping, personal care, and chore services, as well as the activities typically connoted by the word "housekeeping."[c]

Generally, the nexus between housing and housing-related services has been considered from the perspective of assisting the elderly to remain in their own homes.[d] The analysis in this chapter goes beyond this and focuses on the relation between a single housing-related service—housekeeping services—and dwelling quality. Two distinct but closely related matters are explored: (1) whether those receiving such services, especially from public agencies, have the greatest need for them, and (2) whether receipt of such services is correlated with an improved physical environment.

[a] Written with Deborah Devine.

[b] In some instances this definition could include family members when they are being paid by a public agency to provide the services, which is quite often the case.

[c] Gutowski (1977). Some states define chore services quite broadly; Michigan, for example, includes the following services: laundry, shopping errands, heavy cleaning, light cleaning, meal preparation, personal care, financial management, minor repairs, and yard work (Emling 1976). For a concise set of definitions of services provided to elderly households see U.S. Government Accounting Office (1977: Appendix V).

[d] See, for example, Shanas et al. (1978). Two reports of the U.S. General Accounting Office (1977, 1978) also have this focus.

Obtaining systematic information on both of these matters is increasingly important for a number of reasons. There is a desire to find ways of assisting the elderly in an economical way to remain in their own dwellings. There is a need for the housing occupied by elderly households to be adequately maintained so as not to discourage other housing investment in the neighborhoods in which the elderly live. The responsibility for providing housing services and fostering dwelling maintenance has been delegated to the Department of Housing and Urban Development, whereas housing-related services are the responsibility of the Department of Health, Education and Welfare. The latter services have the purpose of helping the elderly to remain in their own homes and are viewed from a health maintenance perspective.

The activities of the two agencies should be coordinated, and part of the basis for informed coordination is the knowledge of the degree to which their separate programs are partial substitutes for each other.[e] For example, if the provision of housekeeping services were found (for reasons to be amplified) to lead to improved housing conditions, then the limited HUD funds might well be directed to those not receiving such services. Similarly, it is quite possible (although not explored here) that living in assisted housing units or receiving rehabilitation funds from HUD improves the overall situation of some elderly sufficiently to reduce or to eliminate the need for the housekeeping services. Ultimately it would be useful to know the optimal mix of programs for individual households, but that is well beyond the present exploration.

The importance of coordination has risen with the dramatic increase in resources going both to housing and to support services. At the end of 1969, there were 279,000 households over age sixty-five in federally assisted dwellings; at the end of 1977, there were over 700,000—a 250 percent increase.[f] In addition, the elderly are receiving rehabilitation grants and loans under the $3.6 billion (1977) Community Block Grant Program, enacted in 1974. The main program to provide support

[e] HUD services are inventoried in Chapter 7; HEW services directly supportive of housing maintenance activities are described in Chapter 8; in Chapter 9 a proposal to minimize duplication of programs and foster HEW-HUD coordination is put forward.

[f] The figures for 1969 are from CEH Table 7 and LRPH Tables 20, 28, and 29 of the *1969 HUD Statistical Yearbook* (U.S. Department of Housing and Urban Development 1971). The 1977 figures are from Welfeld and Struyk (1979). The 1969 data are for units under the Section 202 program and Low Rent Public Housing; those for 1977 also include units under Section 236 and Section 8. These programs are described in Chapter 7. All figures have been adjusted to indicate the number of households with head of household over age sixty-five, as opposed to the definition of elderly used by HUD, which includes as well households with head of household ages sixty-two to sixty-four and the handicapped of all ages.

services—Title XX of the Social Security Act—was not enacted until 1975. The resources available under Title XX ($2.4 billion in 1977) dwarf those provided for all activities provided under the Older American Act of 1965 ($142 million in 1977).[g]

CONCEPTUAL FRAMEWORK

Recipients and Providers of Housekeeping Services

Given the cost of providing housekeeping services, it is important that they be utilized by those who most need them. In a market economy, those with economic power are able to purchase goods and services, regardless of their "need." It is important to know who receives housekeeping services and how the services are supplied—through the marketplace or through public action.

There are several potential sources of supply of housekeeping services for each elderly household, and it is essential to recognize the variety. Four types of suppliers are distinguished in Figure 5-1, which depicts a supply function for each type. In the four graphs, P is the price per unit for housekeeping services and Q is the quantity of the services provided in a specific time period, for example, one year. Panel (a) illustrates the provision of services by the household itself. The "price" here is an implicit one—the cost perceived by the household of doing various tasks for itself.[h] The supply schedule shows an upward slope. This is because the tasks of cleaning and making minor repairs become increasingly more difficult for members of the elderly household as more is done, because of their lack of stamina and possible physical impairments. The difference in the actual placement of the supply schedules with three levels of impairment (H/I) is suggested in the figure; the greater the level of impairment the more costly it is for the household to provide any quantity of services for themselves. Similar shifts in the schedules could be caused by either the presence or the absence of children or a spouse to help with various chores.

Panel (b) of Figure 5-1 depicts the provision of services by friends or family members not living with the elderly household. Again, the schedule is upward-sloping, this time because of the hypothesized aversion of these suppliers to providing services as the amount increases. Presumably this aversion begins after some level of services has been reached, but this discontinuity is not shown in the figure. The

[g] For succinct listing of major federal programs for the elderly see Case Reports (1977).

[h] The idea of the household producing housing services for itself is more fully discussed in Appendix G of Struyk and Ozanne (1976).

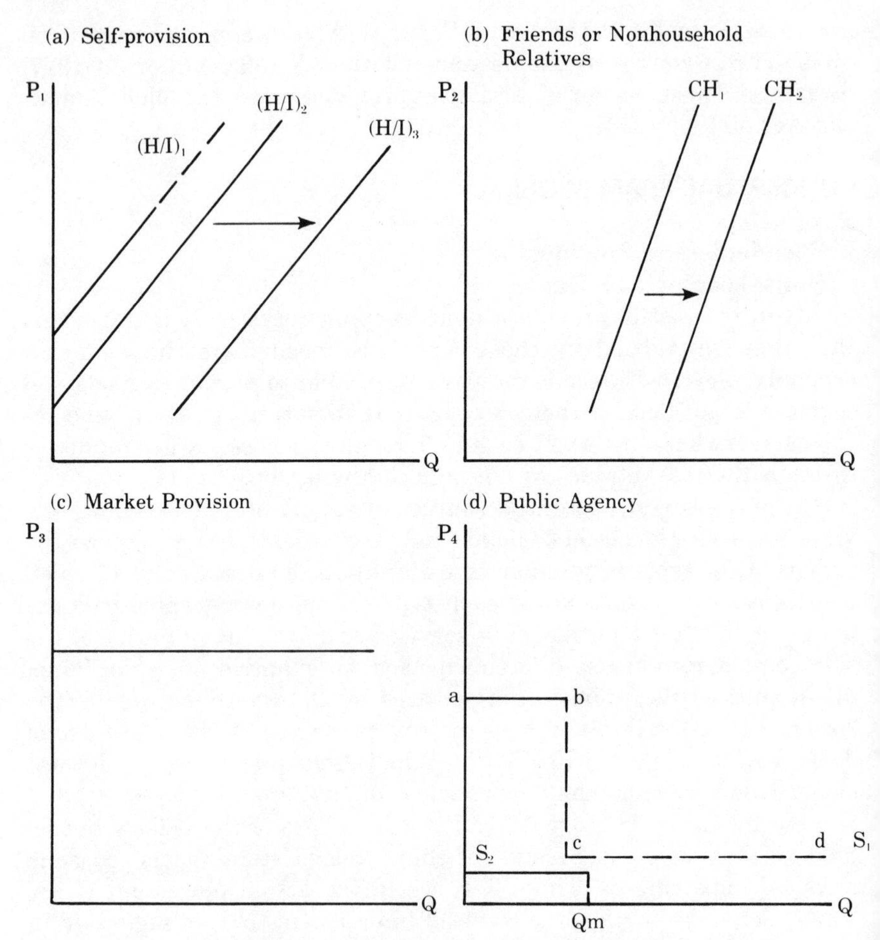

Figure 5–1. Alternative Suppliers of Housekeeping Services

steepness of the schedule is based on the observation in the previous chapter that the elderly homeowners seem to avoid asking friends or relatives for help in making repairs to their dwellings. Finally, note that the schedule is shown to shift out with more children (*CH*) residing within a short commuting distance of their parents' home.

Since the demand for housekeeping services by any individual household is slight compared to the total services available from commercial vendors, the elderly household is shown in Panel (c) as being able to purchase all desired services at the market price. On the other hand, public provision of services can be supplied under a variety of arrangements, two of which are illustrated in Panel (d). Note that this figure applies only to those households meeting the program requirements. The first schedule (S_1) is a program under which the household pays some price for the initial set of services in the year (line segment *ab*) and a negligible amount thereafter for as many services as it needs (*cd*). By contrast, S_2 is a program under which the only cost to the household is its time, but a fixed maximum amount of services (*Qm*) is available to it.

To clarify further the role of program provisions on the consumption of housekeeping services, it is useful to consider Figure 5-2, which is a standard indifference curve diagram. The diagram depicts the consumption of Q and all other goods. In the absence of the program, the household faces the budget constraint (*aa*), and its satisfaction is maximized at point *e*—the tangency of the budget constraint and the indifference curve I_1. The price of Q is reduced through the public program (for which this household qualified); and the budget line shifts to aa^1. Only a segment of aa^1 is, in fact, relevant (*fg*), because of the program's structure. That is, only Q up to Qmax will be subsidized. This causes the revised equilibrium to be at *g*. In this case, the household was forced to consume fewer housekeeping services than it would have in the absence of program constraints, but certainly more than without the program. Of course, the opposite case—one in which the household is required to overconsume to participate—can be drawn

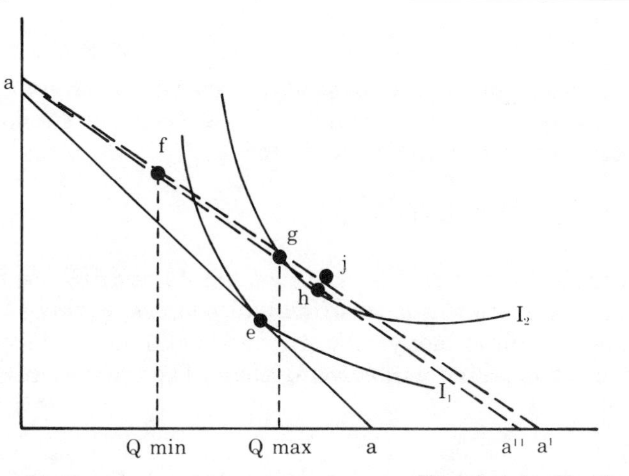

Figure 5–2. Effects of Program Provisions on Utilization of Housekeeping Services

just as easily. The important point is that local program regulations will clearly affect the level of housekeeping services actually consumed. Also, with hundreds of locally administered programs providing housekeeping services, the observations will be a composite; and nothing very precise about individual programs will be said. Turning to a standard demand–supply model, much like the one discussed in the last chapter, the quantity of services demanded depends on a number of factors: income (Y), assets (A), the fraction of income devoted to housing (R/Y), and its tenure status (T)—homeowner or renter. R/Y is included to provide a measure of the discretionary income available to the household, based on the fact that the variance among households in housing expenditures is greater than most other goods, such as food. The high variance in R/Y, in turn, is caused by the differential rates of adjustment in housing by the elderly—many continue to reside in homes where they raised families, whereas others either never had need for such a unit or have moved to smaller quarters as "empty nesters." This is relevant because of the greater array of tasks the homeowner, compared to the renter, must do for himself.[i]

Besides these factors, the demand for housekeeping services also depends on the price of these services. The elderly household looks across the alternative sources of supply—itself, friends or nonresident family, hired help and public agencies—and uses the prices (explicit or implicit) of these services to form its demand. Hence a demand function can be written as follows:

$$Q = Q(Y, A, R/Y, \quad T, P_1 \ldots P_4). \qquad (5\text{–}1)$$

Likewise, supply functions can be written, based on the considerations discussed in conjunction with Figure 5-1. The supply function for the household itself can be written as

$$P_1 = P_1(M, HH, CH, H/I, Q). \qquad (5\text{–}2)$$

M is the price per unit of nonlabor inputs and HH is the household type. The concept is that husband-wife couples, working together, may be able to perform many domestic duties at a more reasonable level of exertion than an individual living alone. The presence of children (CH)

[i] Note that the effects of the financial variables—income and assets—are somewhat ambiguous in this statement of the problem. Although it is evident that demand for market-provided services should be income-elastic, one might as well hypothesize that the demand for publicly provided services is income-inelastic. This suggests that chore services be modeled as differentiated goods by type of supplier for both demand and supply. Unfortunately, the available data will not permit estimation of such a rich model.

in the home is included on the same grounds. Health/impediments (H/I), of course, reflect the greater difficulty of those in less good health doing various domestic tasks. The function for friends and nonresident family members is the following:

$$P_2 = P_2[M, NCH, D]. \qquad (5\text{–}3)$$

NCH is the number of children within a reasonable distance of their parents' home and D is their actual proximity. The prices of market-provided (P_3) and publicly provided (P_4) services are exogenous. But the applicability of P_4 is conditioned on program eligibility requirements, which for simplicity are taken to be income alone. It is important to note that, in reality, the household faces a single supply curve composed of the relevant segments (the lowest price for a given Q) of each of the four schedules described. The resultant supply curve may be highly discontinuous. Since these intricacies cannot be determined, the simplification of including all four prices, without specifying the range over which each is "operable," has been adopted.

Further, because we cannot actually observe most of the prices, it is necessary to utilize a reduced-form model. So substituting equations (5–2) and (5–3) in equation (5–1), and relating the availability of publicly provided services to Y yields

$$Q = Q[Y, A, R/Y, H/I, T, NCH, D, HH, CH, P_3, M]. \qquad (5\text{–}4)$$

Working through the demand for and the supply of housekeeping services has made it abundantly clear that, in order to ascertain if the "appropriate" elderly are receiving such services when they are publicly provided, one must control for the availability of services from other sources, as is done in the reduced-form model. Equation (5–4) can be modified slightly for estimation purposes. The dependent variable is changed from Q, the quantity of services, to two binary variables describing the receipt of services: S_1, which takes on value of 1 if the household obtains housekeeping services from any source; 0 otherwise, and S_2, which takes on value of 1 if the household obtains housekeeping services through a public agency; 0 otherwise. It would be desirable, of course, to study the choice among additional sources of services—for example, nonresident family support, but the data used in this analysis do not allow such refinement.

Housekeeping Services Effects on Housing Quality

At first glance, housekeeping services might easily be defined as a person's assisting with cleaning duties. In fact, as noted earlier, the services included under this title have been heterogeneous indeed, including personal care, chore, and shopping services, among others.

A person providing assistance can effect the "supply of maintenance services" to the dwelling in several distinct ways. First, the assistance might be chore services, under which particular jobs might include holding a ladder or helping patch a crack in wall plaster preparatory to painting. A second effect is simply a direct substitution of labor: the elderly are able to expend their limited energy on maintenance, if other work is done for them. A third effect might result from a social worker's spotting problems of which the elderly are unaware. Finally, the assistance might be in arranging for work to be done either by a public agency or privately, the latter being the obvious solution in rental units.

The first two effects on the supply of maintenance services are illustrated in Figure 5-3. The initial supply curve (tt^1) is a composite of the supply of services available from the household itself, friends, nonresident family members, and commercial sources. The direct provision of services by a public agency shifts the curve outward to vv^1. If the household were purchasing the housekeeping services, however, the effect is less certain because there would be more likelihood of a substitution in demand between housekeeping and maintenance services. If the housekeeping services have an "efficiency effect," that is, assisting the elderly perform certain tasks, then a new supply curve might be uu^1t^1. At low levels of maintenance activity, such assistance can be remarkable; as the level of work rises, the amount the elderly can do diminishes (for the average person) so that the efficiency gain gradually diminishes until at u^1 the household is back on its original supply curve.

The kind of support being discussed in Figure 5-3 is probably quite modest. Hence, it could be hypothesized that the effects would be seen largely on the upkeep of interior and exterior areas (tidiness of the yard, condition of the paint and plaster on the walls, and so on). Such help would not remedy basic dwelling deficiencies (such as lack of complete plumbing or inadequate wiring or heating systems).

There is also a direct effect on the demand for maintenance activity that the public provision of assistance may produce. If the household purchases the services in the absence of public provision, its disposable income is increased by the substitution of public funds for its own, and demand will rise. Evidence from prior analysis of dwelling maintenance activity of the elderly suggests demand to be quite income inelastic. On the other hand, data reviewed in Chapter 7 indicate a somewhat greater responsiveness. Overall, the magnitude of the demand effect is unclear, but certainly moderate.

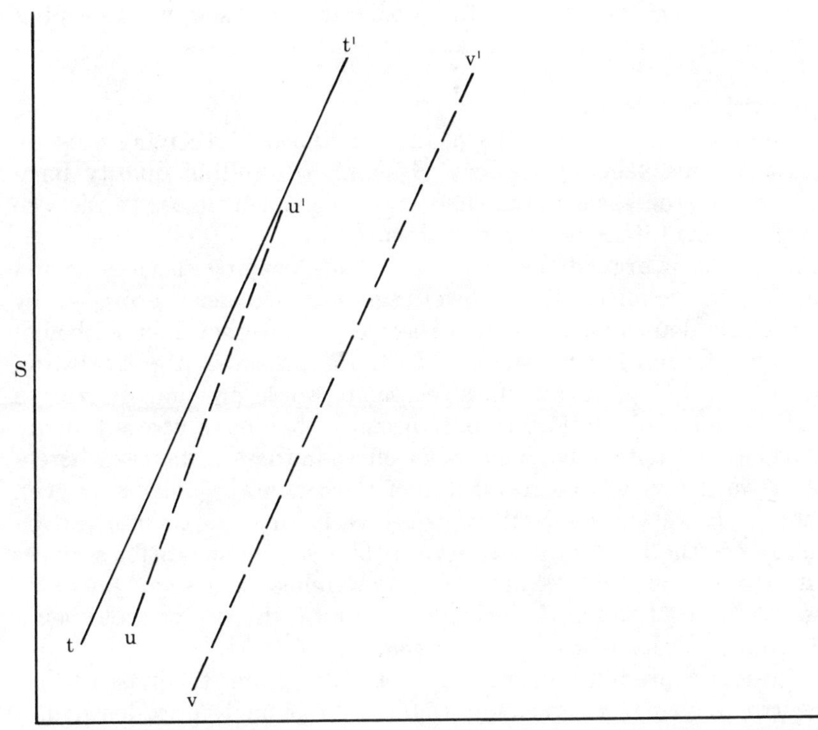

Figure 5–3. The Effect of Housekeeping Services on the Supply of Dwelling Maintenance

The appropriate model of the demand for and supply of housing quality closely parallels that developed to analyze maintenance and repair activity since both are derived from the demand for housing and involve multiple potential suppliers; and it is ultimately similar to the reduced-form model specified in equation (5–4) in this chapter. Demand for housing quality, defined as an index of the interior condition of the dwelling and the operating condition of basic mechanical systems, is a function of economic and demographic factors and the price of maintenance and repair activities. There are several potential suppliers of such activities; but, since the prices of the services from most sources are not observable, a reduced-form model is necessitated. The quantity of housekeeping services appears as a separate variable in the equation. It is included as a distinct factor because it is an input to the production of housing quality by the household; and, in deriving the supply schedule of the household as a supplier of housing quality (maximizing profits subject to the production function), housekeeping services appear as a separate determinant.

Joint Determination

Thus far, the determinants of the likelihood of receiving publicly provided housekeeping services (S_2) and of dwelling quality have been considered separately. These two phenomena may, in fact, be jointly, or simultaneously, determined.

It has been argued that receipt of housekeeping services should improve the condition of the dwelling. Now consider the process by which it is determined who will receive provided services. Although there are formal income rules and the like, there is a great deal of latitude in the system. Welfare recipients would presumably receive publicly provided services in part because they have access to more information. There may be a further effect in those instances where a social worker visits the residences of the welfare recipients or even where voluntary organizations assist recipients; judgments can be made as to the need for such services, and arrangements for services initiated. Presumably one of the factors weighed in these judgments is the condition of the unit, with those living in the worst units being determined to have the greatest need.

Without expressing the idea in a set of equations, the hypothesis is nevertheless clear: (1) recipiency status for publicly provided housekeeping services is determined in part by the condition of the dwelling unit; (2) condition of the unit is determined in part by whether the household receives these housekeeping services.

The hypothesis is simple conceptually, although the empirical difficulties appear formidable. Ideally, data over time on a group of households should be collected; that is, the condition of the unit should be known at the time recipiency status is determined and again at some later point in time. Since the available information is effectively cross-sectional, any estimates of the joint determination model will have to be interpreted cautiously.

THE SAMPLE AND VARIABLE DEFINITIONS

The SLIAD Sample

Empirical investigation of the questions discussed in the previous section requires an unusually rich body of data. The Survey of the Low-Income Aged and Disabled (SLIAD) provides a data set that is sufficiently rich to support the analysis. The SLIAD obtained information for each respondent household member in the following areas: (1) income and assets; (2) personal history; (3) household composition;

(4) health, health care, and capacity for self-maintenance; (5) standard of living, as indicated by diet and so forth; (6) housing quality and expenditures; and (7) attitudinal response to these conditions and circumstances.[j]

The SLIAD was designed to determine what effect the implementation of the Supplemental Security Income (SSI) program would have on the well-being of SSI recipients. The purpose affected the survey and sample design in two important ways: First, the SLIAD was cast as a two-stage, before-and-after survey based on large national samples. The surveys had to be on a tight schedule to follow the January 1974 implementation of SSI. Second, it was expected that the respondents were those likely eligible to receive SSI payments—a condition judged from the current welfare recipient rolls and from the 1973 responses to the Current Population Survey.

There was a total of 15,864 usable responses in the SLIAD—those for which data were obtained in both the 1973 and 1974 surveys. Of these, a much smaller number, 5,940, is available for the present analyses, since only households headed by those over age sixty-four are included.

The SLIAD's focus on low-income households is evident in Table 5-1. The figures compare several characteristics of the elderly households located in urban areas in the SLIAD with all urban elderly, as reported in the Annual Housing Survey (AHS).[k] The lower incomes of the SLIAD group are striking, as are the smaller rents paid by renters in the SLIAD sample compared to the AHS population. While there is little difference in the size of dwellings occupied, as measured by the number of rooms, there is a sharp difference in the composition of owner-occupant households. Specifically, there is a substantially greater fraction of single individuals living in owner-occupied units in the SLIAD sample than among all elderly.

The concentration of the SLIAD data on the low-income elderly has advantages and disadvantages for the present analysis. On the positive side, the analysis applies to the group that is the focus of the housing and household-support programs of the federal government. Hence, if interrelations of the type hypothesized earlier do exist, these data should certainly provide a reasonable test. On the negative side, the limited variation makes it difficult to determine whether assistance is targeted on the most needy. With about 70 percent of the sample having incomes of under $3,000 in 1973 (equivalent to $4,090 in 1977),

[j] This description draws heavily on Tissue (1977).

[k] These comparisons may be somewhat biased because the SLIAD data were not weighted for these computations, whereas the AHS were.

Table 5–1. Percentage Distribution of Selected Characteristics of Households Headed by Elderly, by Tenure Status from the SLIAD and the Annual Housing Survey

	A. Number of Rooms			
	Renters		*Owners*	
Number	*AHS*	*SLIAD*	*AHS*	*SLIAD*
1–2	18	20	1	2
3	35	36	5	10
4	27	27	21	30
5	13	12	30	28
6	5	3	25	20
7–10 or more	2	1	17	10
	B. Household Type			
	Renters		*Owners*	
	AHS	*SLIAD*	*AHS*	*SLIAD*
Husband-wife	28	21	53	42
Single individual	60	58	35	49
Other	12	20	12	9
	C. Income			
	Renters		*Owners*	
	AHS	*SLIAD*	*AHS*	*SLIAD*
Under $2,000	18	37	9	33
$2,000–$2,999	24	36	14	26
$3,000–$3,999	16	16	13	14
$4,000–$4,999	11	4	13	10
$5,000 and over	31	6	51	18
	D. Gross Rent			
	AHS	*SLIAD*		
Under $100	39	67		
$100–$200	53	30		
Over $200	8	3		

Source: Special tabulations from the 1974 Survey of Low Income Aged and Disabled (SLIAD) and the 1973 Annual Housing Survey (AHS). AHS tabulations were provided by the Philadelphia Geriatrics Center.

most of those receiving assistance would be classified as needy. Still, there is enough variation in income and other characteristics to provide a meaningful analysis of the targeting of housekeeping assistance.[l]

The data in Table 5-2 describe the economic, health, and housing circumstances of the sample households in greater detail. For clarity, four separate subgroups are shown: homeowners and renters in urban and rural locations. In both rural and urban areas about one-half the sample were welfare recipients at the time of the 1974 survey. Only a minority of each subgroup reported being in sufficiently robust health to be able to do all of eight tasks about which inquiries were made. In this regard, there is a wide variation in the physical capabilities of the sample households as indicated by "do with difficulty" and "cannot do" responses to the activity questions (see items 6 and 7 in the table).[m] Even though most households live in units without major structural defects, slightly under 50 percent have maintenance problems (items 8 and 9).[n] Similarly, most of the sample households devote a "reasonable" share of their income to housing; but about one in four allocates 40 percent or more to such expenditures.

Table 5-3 gives more exact definitions of most of the variables used in the descriptive and statistical analysis to be presented. The mean values for a few of these variables are shown in Table 5-4. The completeness of the financial information and the physical impairment measures are particularly noteworthy. Age is included under the impairment definitions because of the relation between age and increasing limitations on mobility. Also, note the definitions of the variable

[l] Throughout this analysis, the unweighted SLIAD sample is used. This means that some types of households, most notably welfare recipients, are heavily overrepresented and others are underrepresented. The decision to use the unweighted file was based mainly on our interest in the low-income segment of the elderly population, a population that can be amply described, as shown in the text. A secondary consideration was that the weights available in the SLIAD file are not very useful since the principle set of weights is structured to produce population estimates of persons, whereas our unit of observation is the household. There is a set of "unit" weights also included on the file; and, although these are closer to what is needed, the weights are still not exactly correct, by virtue of the inclusion of the elderly not in households headed by the elderly. But how significant are the differences in results between the unweighted and weighted files? The answer is "not very." Tests of differences in the coefficients of identical regression models (of the type discussed later in the text) using (1) an unweighted sample and (2) a weighted sample, both of which eliminate some double representation, show very infrequent significant differences. For the type of exploratory tests for differences in the mean values of a number of the key variables used in the multivariate analysis, treating the two samples as being independent shows no significant differences. See Dubois (1964:122–24); and DuMochel and Duncan (1977).

[m] These items are described more later in the chapter.

[n] A full description of the housing of the elderly in this sample is provided in Schieber (1978).

Table 5–2. Basic Characteristics of Sample Households and Their Housing in 1974, by Location and Tenure Status: 1974

	Urban Areas			*Rural Areas*		
	Total	*Homeowners*	*Renters*	*Total*	*Homeowners*	*Renters*
1. Monthly Housing Expenditures						
Under $100	74	83	67	90	91	88
$100–$199	22	14	30	9	8	11
$200 or over	4	3	3	1	1	1
2. Household Income Last Year						
Under $1,000	5	7	3	9	10	7
$1,000–$1,999	31	26	34	38	36	46
$2,000–$2,999	31	26	36	30	30	30
$3,000–$3,999	15	14	16	12	12	11
$4,000–$4,999	7	10	4	4	5	2
$5,000 or over	11	18	6	5	7	4
3. Housing Expense-Income Ratio						
Under 10%	9	17	2	17	20	7
10–20	20	34	8	28	32	16
20–29	23	20	25	22	22	24
30–39	16	10	21	11	9	19
40–49	11	6	16	7	5	14
4. Assets						
Under $1,000	58	24	88	52	40	95
$1,000–$9,999	18	29	9	25	31	3
$10,000–$19,999	10	18	2	9	11	0
Over $20,000	14	29	1	14	18	2
5. Received Welfare Last Year	50	36	62	54	51	66

Physical impairments						
6. A. No. of Tasks Done with Difficulty						
0	14	18	12	13	13	13
1	14	15	13	12	13	10
2	18	16	19	15	14	17
3	17	17	16	15	16	12
4	15	14	16	15	15	14
5	11	10	12	13	13	16
6 or more	11	10	12	17	16	19
B. No. of Activities "Can't Do"						
0	34	43	27	34	36	29
1	21	21	21	21	21	21
2	15	12	18	14	14	15
3	11	9	12	10	10	11
4	8	7	9	7	7	8
5 or more	11	8	13	14	12	16
Housing Condition						
7. A. Structural Defects						
0	88	90	87	62	67	46
1	6	4	7	6	6	7
2	2	2	3	4	4	4
3 or more	4	4	3	28	23	43
B. (Ratio Maintenance Problems to Possible Problems) 100						
0	68	70	65	50	53	42
1–10 percent	13	12	14	13	14	11
11–20 percent	8	8	8	12	12	13
Over 20 percent	11	10	13	24	21	36
8. Household composition						
Married	31	42	21	53	55	48
Single	53	49	58	38	37	39
Multiperson, non-husband-wife	26	9	20	9	8	13
Sample Size	4,690	2,240	2,450	1,250	962	273

Source: Special tabulations from the 1974 Survey of Low Income Aged and Disabled (SLIAD).

Table 5–3. Definitions of Variables in the Analysis of Housekeeping Services for the Elderly

Variable Name and Classification	*Descriptions*
INCOME	Includes all income received by sample respondent, spouse, and minor children, if applicable. Includes social security, SSI, earnings, workmen's compensation, private transfers, and sixteen other income sources. Variable expressed in thousands of dollars.
ASSETS	Sum of savings, checking account balance, net property value, stock, bonds, and other monetary resources available to the person. Expressed in thousands of dollars.
WELPAY	Value of 1 if household is receiving welfare payments from local, state, or federal agencies; 0 otherwise.
Household Composition and Location of Children	
MARRIED	Value of 1 if household has both husband-wife present; 0 otherwise.
SINGLE	Value of 1 if person lives alone or is a widow; 0 otherwise.
OTHER	Value of 1 if household is classified as neither MARRIED nor SINGLE; 0 otherwise.
CHLD	Value of 1 if children live at home; 0 otherwise.
CHLD10	Value of 1 if any children live within 10 minutes of respondent's home; 0 otherwise.
CHLDCTY	Value of 1 if any children live farther than 10 minutes away but within the same city or rural area; 0 otherwise.
Physical Limitation of Sample Respondent	
CANWDIF	Defined as the number of listed activities the respondent can perform but only with difficulty: washing; walking; using stairs; standing for long period; stooping, crouching or kneeling; lifting or carrying weights up to 10 pounds; lifting heavier weights; reaching; and, using fingers to grasp or handle.
CANNT	Defined as the number of activities enumerated under CANWDIF that respondent cannot do.
AGE	Age of head of household.
Housing and Other Costs	
HOUSMO	Monthly housing expense in month previous to the survey; not calculated for farmers or those operating business from residence. Includes all utilities of past month, mortgage payments, and one-twelfth of property taxes, insurance, etc., if reported on annual basis. Excludes maintenance and investment outlays.
NCHINC	Fraction of average monthly income devoted to housing, as defined by HOUSMO.
SERVRATE	Mean monthly earnings of state-employed social case workers and nursing assistants in 1974.
CARPRATE	Mean monthly earnings of state-employed carpenters in 1974.
Dwelling Condition	
HSYST	Measure of structural deficiencies count of the number of following deficiencies: lack of heating equipment, electricity, piped hot water, flush toilet, tub or shower, and kitchen or cooking equipment.

Table 5–3. continued

Variable Name and Classification	*Descriptions*
HMAIN	Measure of a unit's state of repair, based on the following 11 items: presence of (1) holes in floor, (2) wide cracks in wall or ceilings, (3) major areas of broken plaster or (4) peeling paint on walls or ceiling, (5) broken windows, and the following fixtures being out of order at the time of the interview: toilet, shower/tub, kitchen stove, kitchen sink, electricity, and heating system. Variable defined as such deficiencies.
Assistance with Housework	
RECDWRK	Value of 1 if household received paid-for help with housework, whether they paid for it, or not; 0 otherwise.[a]
RECDWEL	Value of 1 if household received help with housework paid for by a welfare agency; 0 otherwise
HOMEWRK	Value of 1 if household has received any other assistance in (1) finding a place to live, (2) home-delivered meals, (3) visiting nurse; 0 otherwise.

[a] The specific question asked was: "Now I would like to find out about the different kinds of advice or help that you may have gotten in the past year. During the past 12 months did you receive paid help with housework?" If the answer was yes, questions as to the source of the help were asked.

measuring the state-of-repair of the dwelling (HMAIN) and the variables describing the type of housekeeping services received by the household, if any (RECDWRK, RECDWEL, HOMEWRK).

An additional set of information gathered in the survey queried the respondents on their ability to do a number of daily activities. The answers to questions covering two of these areas are used extensively in this analysis: (1) light housework, such as dusting, making beds, washing dishes, and (2) heavy housework, such as moving furniture or scrubbing floors. For these activities the survey ascertained if the activity could be accomplished without assistance from others and if assistance were necessary, who assisted them.[o] Four choices for type of assistance were given: paid help, free help (others in household), free help (others not in household), and no one. The examination of the responses to the questions can provide a profile of how elderly households are coping with their needs.

WHO RECEIVES HOUSEKEEPING SERVICES?

Two approaches are taken to answer the question of who receives housekeeping services. In the first, the group of urban respondents who

[o] The other six activities are grocery shopping, preparing meals, washing clothes, dressing, bathing, and caring for one's self at home when sick in bed.

Table 5–4. Mean Values of Selected Variables for Owner-Occupants and Renters in Urban and Rural Areas

	Urban		*Rural*	
	Owner-Occupants	*Renters*	*Owner-Occupants*	*Renters*
HMAIN	.062	.073	.110	.172
RECDWEL	.027	.052	.036	.042
RECDWRK	.117	.121	.089	.089
HOMEWRK	.070	.149	.058	.095
INCOME	3.36	2.69	2.58	2.29
ASSETS	14.10	1.10	10.36	.60
MARRIED	.42	.22	.55	.48
SINGLE	.49	.58	.37	.40
CHLD	.13	.11	.18	.18
CHLD10	.37	.30	.48	.45

Source: Special tabulations from the 1974 Survey of Low Income Aged and Disabled (SLIAD).

identified themselves as being unable to do heavy housework, including tasks that contribute directly to the maintenance of the dwelling, are studied. The variation in the likelihood of receiving assistance from each of several sources is examined with respect to several factors, such as income, household composition, and proximity of children. In this analysis, the relation between receipt of services and each factor is considered separately, thus providing a good indication for who receives services, and why.

The second approach involves the estimation of the multivariate models described in the second section for RECDWEL and RECDWRK. For each of the included variables the results provide the answer to the question: What is the effect of this variable (for example, INCOME) on the likelihood of the household receiving housekeeping services *after* having accounted for the effects of other factors (for example, proximity of children) on this likelihood? The results of the second approach are more general than those of the first, both because of the statistical techniques employed and because it deals with all types of "housekeeping" services, whereas the first type is limited to assistance with heavy housework. Likewise, separate estimates are presented for urban and rural households. The results are less general, however, because they are restricted to paid assistance (whether privately or publicly provided) whereas the results for "heavy housework" include assistance from all sources.

Assistance with "Heavy Housework" from All Sources

About 60 percent of all respondents reported being unable to do heavy housework, such as scrubbing floors and moving furniture. Table 5-5 shows how these people coped with this inability. Comparison of the rural and urban samples suggests that the family support system is somewhat stronger in rural areas, where a smaller percentage of households in need of help fail to receive it and where a larger percentage of households than in the urban sample receive help free at home. From this point forward the analysis is confined to the urban portion of the sample. Comparisons between the two locales would be complicated by differences in service delivery mechanisms and the sheer volume of findings; analysis would be also restricted by the smaller rural sample size.

The variation in the receipt of assistance with several factors is considered below in detail. The factors, defined in Table 5-3, include financial condition, family proximity, health and housing quality variables.

Tenure. When the urban sample is divided into renters and owners, the main difference is that about 50 percent more renters than owners receive no help; but this difference is due almost exclusively to obtaining more assistance from others living in the home, which in turn is largely determined by differences in household composition.

Health Variables. One might expect that the poorer the *self-perception of health,* the greater the likelihood that a household head would seek assistance for heavy housework. One might also expect that, insofar as this perception is shared by others, the supply of free housework might expand to meet the need. However, the data do not show any significant increase in the proportion of household heads receiving help as self-perception of health worsens. It is true that on a range of self-perceived health from poor to good, the likelihood of needing, but doing without, heavy housework help slightly increases

Table 5–5. Source of Assistance for Those Reporting Inability to Do Heavy Housework (Percentages)

	Urban	*Rural*
None	13.5	9.4
Paid help	19.0	12.5
Free help from outside home	34.5	32.2
Free help from within the home	32.8	45.6

as self-perception goes from poor to good. The smallest proportion of those who do without help for heavy housework when a need is indicated for it, however, are those who perceive their health to be excellent, as seen in Figure 5-4.

It is hypothesized that an increase in the proportion of household heads receiving help when impairment exists above and beyond the functional inability to do heavy housework, then the *inability to lift weights over 10 pounds* should positively affect the receipt of heavy housework services. On the one hand, one would expect an increased impetus on the part of the household to seek such help and to make the necessary tradeoffs to secure it. On the other hand, there should be an increased social or family willingness to provide free help in response to aggravated need. The data in Figure 5-5 contradict the second hypothesis and show that more of those who are more severely impaired do without help than others. At the same time, the presence of aggravated disability (the double handicap of functional inability to do heavy housework and operational disability to lift weights over 10 pounds) is associated with a slightly greater proportion of those who pay for help from an outside source.

Housing Quality Variables. Since heavy housework is a form of *maintenance,* there could be a positive relation between the level of housing maintenance, as defined by HMAIN in Table 5-3 and the receipt of heavy housework. Actually there is very little apparent relation, as shown in Figure 5-6. Fourteen percent of households with over 30 percent of the specified deficiencies receive no help, while 12 percent of households with all systems working do not receive help. In the case of the *housing systems* variable (HSYST), the likelihood of receiving help for heavy housework could increase with an increase in the number of basic systems, such as plumbing and heating, which are present in the dwelling unit. There is an increase in the number of households doing without needed help as soon as one major system is absent. This levels off when two are absent, but the percentage doing without help again increases when three or more systems are absent (Figure 5-7).

Financial Ability Variables. Three financial ability variables are analyzed for their effect on the receipt or nonreceipt and the source of heavy housework services. In the case of the *housing cost-to-income ratio,* it could be anticipated that the lower the ratio, the greater the percentage of household heads receiving paid-for help with heavy housework. The data in Figure 5-8 show that as the ratio level increases, there is a fairly sharp decrease in the percent of households

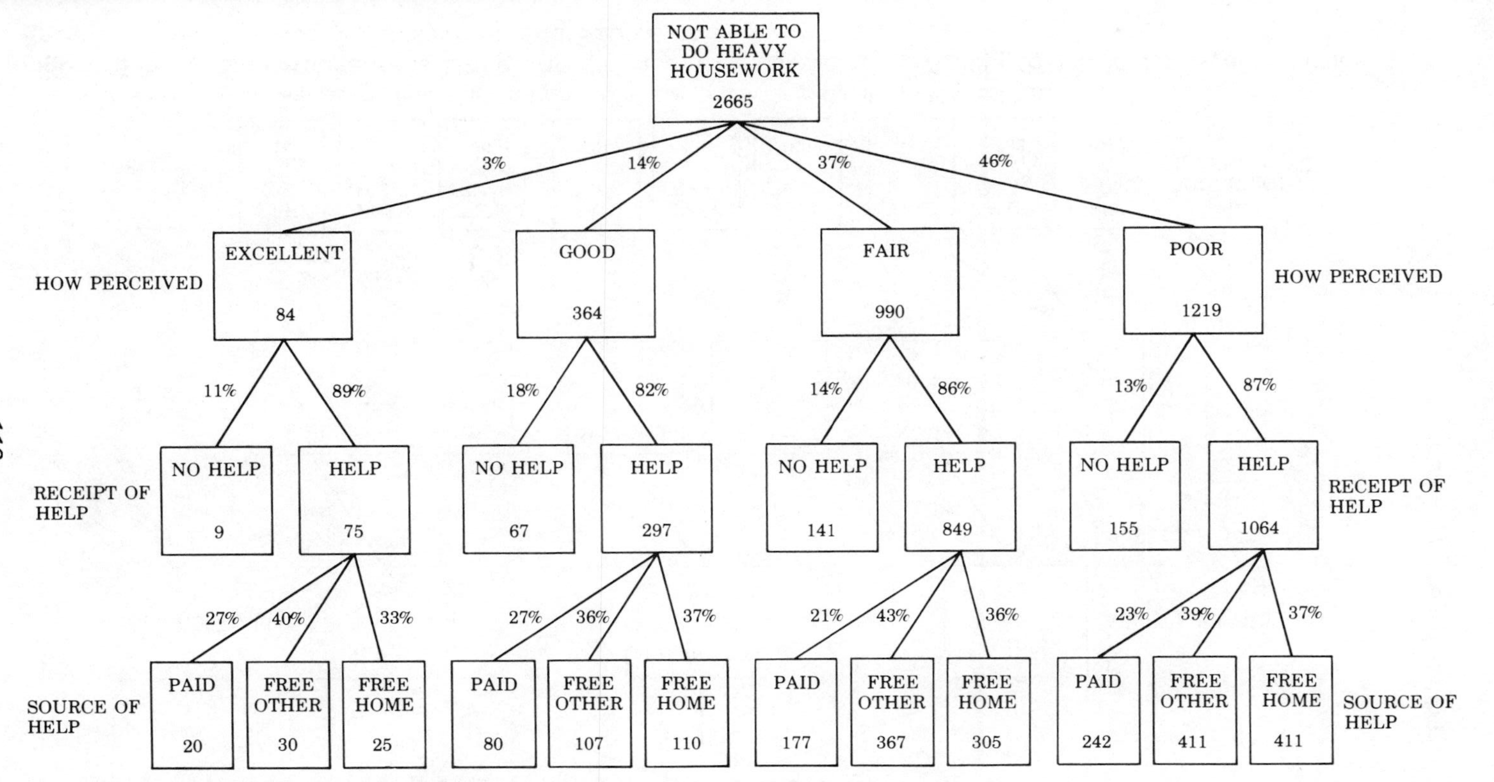

Source: Special tabulations from the 1974 Survey of Low Income Aged and Disabled (SLIAD).

Figure 5–4. Urban Households Unable to Do Heavy Housework, by Self-Perception of Health, Receipt of Help with Heavy Housework, and Source of Help

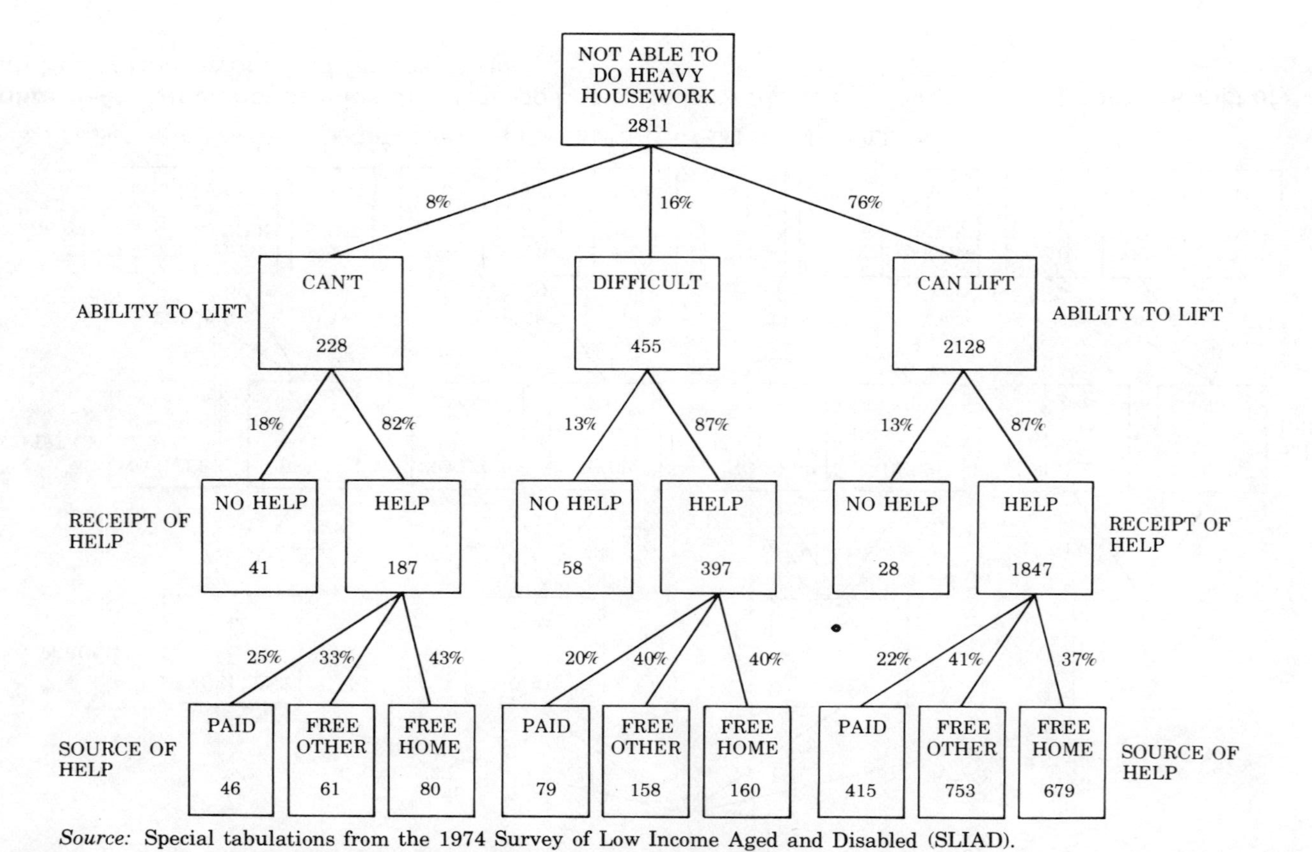

Source: Special tabulations from the 1974 Survey of Low Income Aged and Disabled (SLIAD).

Figure 5–5. Urban Households Unable to Do Heavy Housework, by Ability to Lift Weights over 10 lbs., Receipt of Help for Heavy Housework, and Source of Help

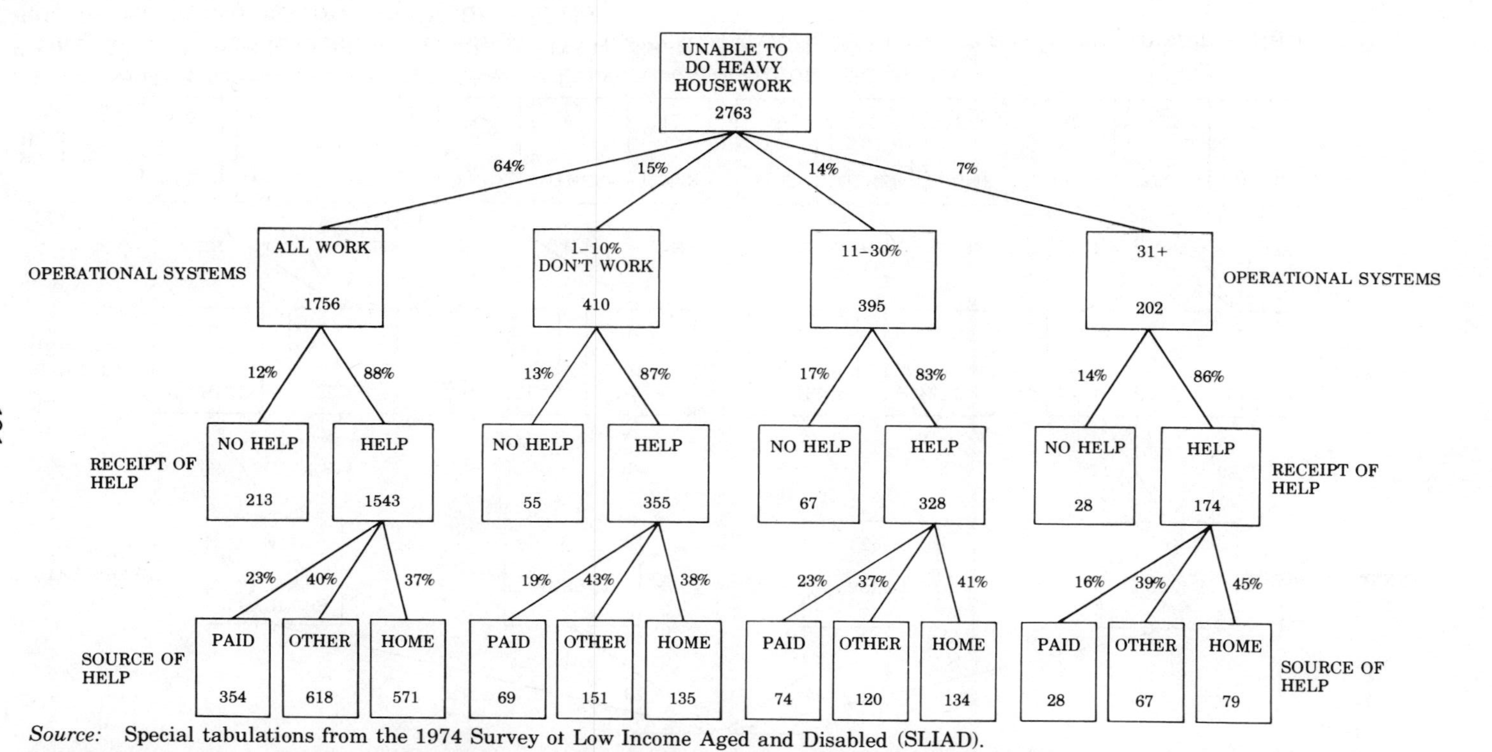

Source: Special tabulations from the 1974 Survey ot Low Income Aged and Disabled (SLIAD).

Figure 5–6. Urban Households Unable to Do Heavy Housework, by Housing Quality, Receipt of Help for Heavy Housework, and Source of Help

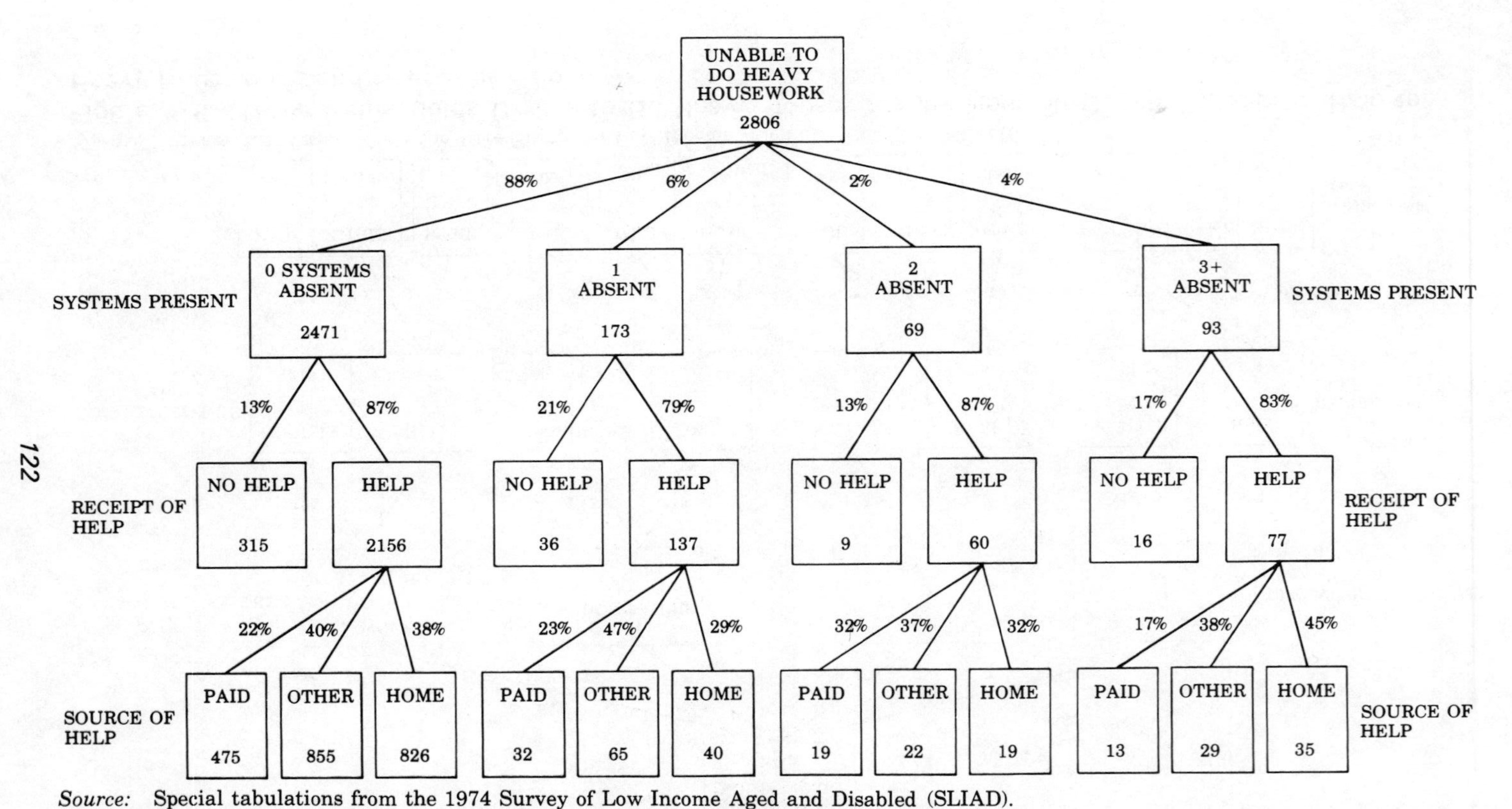

Source: Special tabulations from the 1974 Survey of Low Income Aged and Disabled (SLIAD).

Figure 5-7. Urban Households Unable to Do Heavy Housework, by Presence of Housing Systems, Receipt of Help for Heavy Housework, and Source of Help

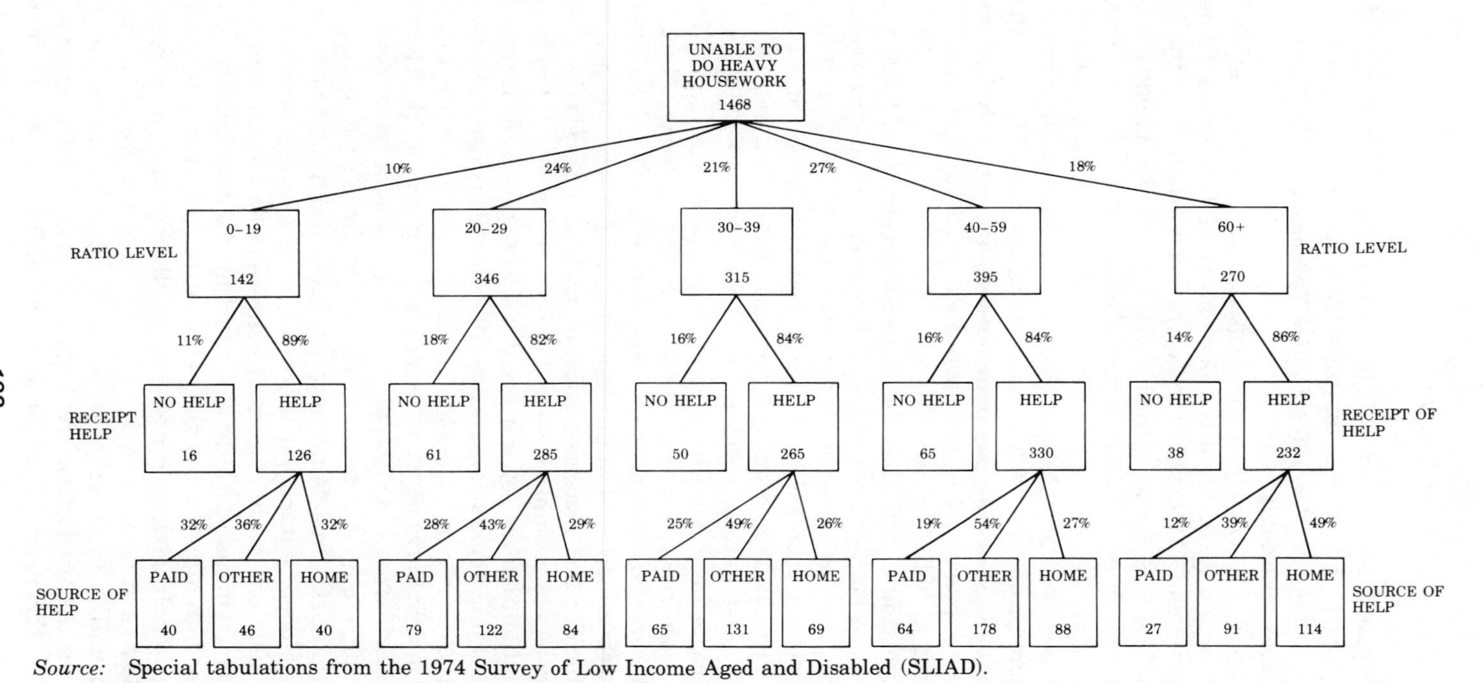

Source: Special tabulations from the 1974 Survey of Low Income Aged and Disabled (SLIAD).

Figure 5–8. Urban Households Unable to Do Heavy Housework, by Housing Cost-to-Income Ratio, Receipt of Help for Heavy Housework, and Source of Help

that receive paid-for-help—from 32 percent for those with a ratio of 10 percent or less to 12 percent for those devoting over 60 percent of income to housing. At the highest ratio levels, free help within the home increases noticeably.

In the case of *income,* one would expect a positive correlation between income and increase in the percentage of households in need who purchase help. At lower income intervals, there is actually a smaller likelihood of doing without help than in the $1,000–$3,999 income intervals (Figure 5-9). It is only after income reaches or exceeds $4,000 that there is a significant drop in the percentage of those in need who do without help. As hypothesized, there is a positive relation between increase in income and increase in the percentage of those who pay for help. Yet, the payment burden, at least in the $1,000–$3,999 income interval, does not reduce the percentage of those who must do without help.

It is interesting to note that the lowered percentage of those doing without help, at both the highest and the lowest income intervals, is not an effect that can be attributed to income directly. Rather, it can be associated with an increase in the proportion of help provided free at home or from other unpaid sources, an effect also evident in the case of the housing cost-to-income ratio. For example, at the $0–$999 and the $4,000+ income intervals this proportion is almost identical, 57–58 percent of those receiving help receiving it free at home. Thus, the effects of income are complex and are not captured in the simple relation between increased income and increased purchasing power or decreased income and increased subsidy, cash or otherwise.

Since the assets variable is so bound up whether or not the householders own their homes, separate analyses were conducted for renters and owners. First, there are striking differences between renters and owners in the distribution of assets: a full 70 percent of renters in this sample are in debt (have negative assets) as compared to only 5 percent of owners; furthermore, while 52 percent of owners have assets in excess of $5,000, only 3 percent of the renters have such assets. The data show that being in debt puts owners in as much risk of nonreceipt of help as it does renters. Furthermore, assets in excess of $5,000 provide no more of a cushion against nonreceipt for owners than they do for renters. This is partially explained by the nonliquidity of the assets. Indeed, in all asset categories, a greater percentage of renters than owners purchase the services. But, in all asset categories, renters get less help free at home than do owners. As suggested earlier, this is partially explained by differences in household composition. Yet, the differences in the proportion receiving free help at home cannot be attributed in the main to tenure and the differences in household

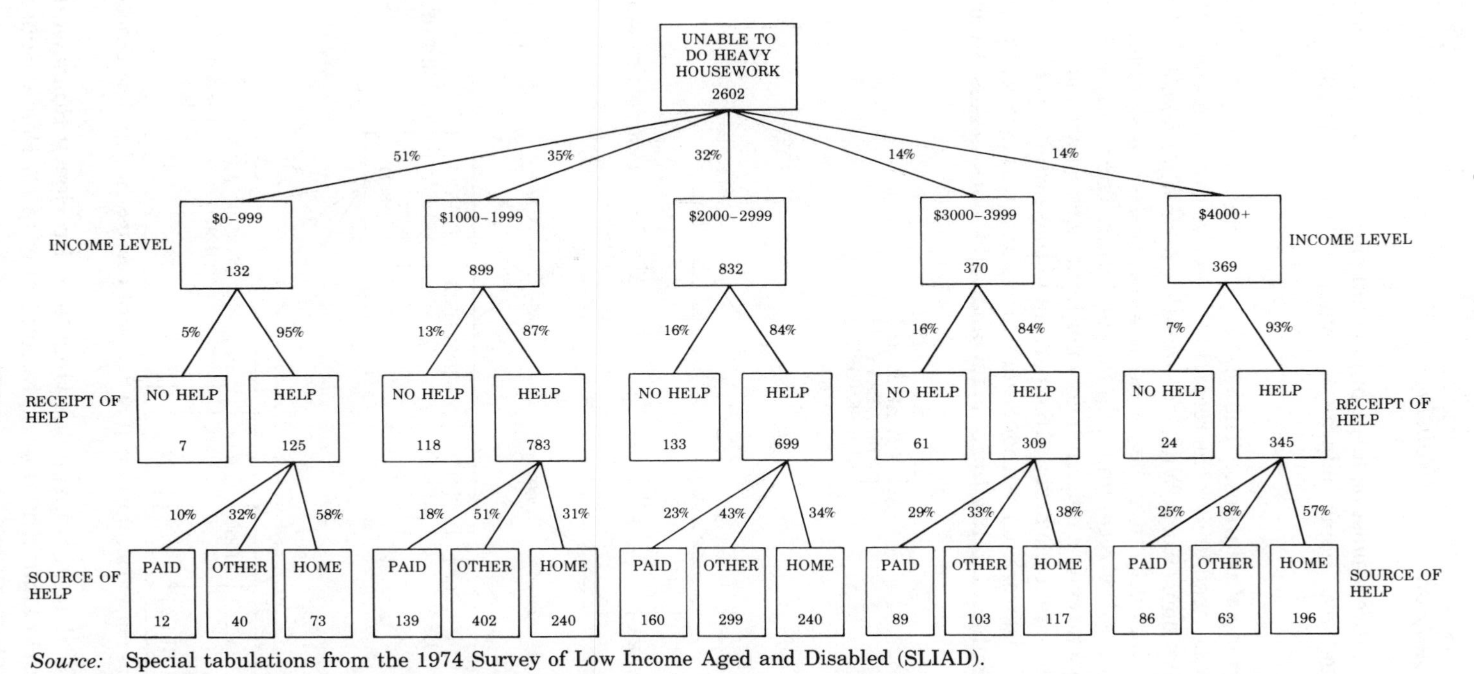

Source: Special tabulations from the 1974 Survey of Low Income Aged and Disabled (SLIAD).

Figure 5–9. Urban Households Unable to Do Heavy Housework, by Income, Receipt of Help for Heavy Housework, and Source of Help

composition, since almost as large proportion of renters at the $5000+ asset level get free home help as do owners at the 0–$4,999 assets interval.

Dual Service Variables. The next set of variables are those indicating a service need and/or the receipt of a service over and above the need for heavy housework. When the *inability to do light housework* is added to the inability to do heavy housework, there is a significantly greater likelihood of receiving help for the latter. Thus, only 3.8 percent of those who can do neither heavy nor light work go without heavy housework assistance, whereas 16.4 percent of those who are able to do only light housework do without help for heavy work. (See Figure 5-10.) The double inability to do heavy and light work makes it more

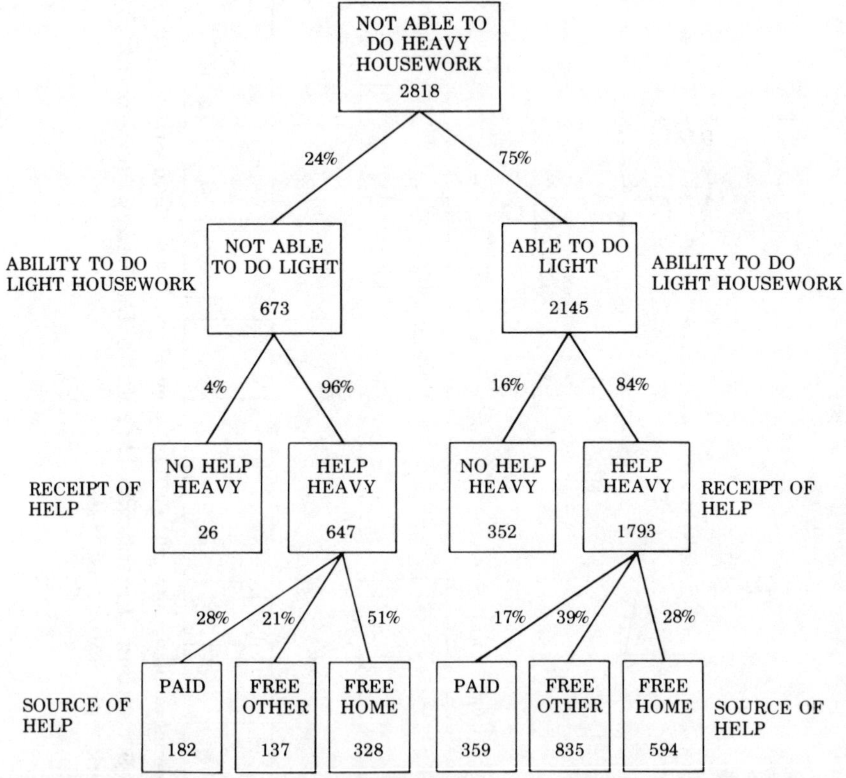

Source: Special tabulations from the 1974 Survey of Low Income Aged and Disabled (SLIAD).

Figure 5–10. Urban Households Unable to Do Heavy Housework, by Ability to Do Light Housework, Receipt of Help for Heavy Housework, and Source of Help

likely, among those ultimately receiving help, that the household head will need to purchase help to fulfill its need. Thus, whereas 28 percent of those who can do neither and who get help must pay for it, only 17 percent of those who are able to do light work must pay. In the case of those who can do neither heavy nor light housework, free help at home accounts for 51 percent of all help received, for those who can do light but not heavy work, the comparable figure is 28 percent. In short, there is sharp variance among all sources of services between these two groups.[p]

As with those who need both light and heavy housework, there are several possible outcomes that could be hypothesized in the case of those households who need help with both heavy housework and with *grocery shopping*. A demand explanation of consumption patterns, when more than one service need is involved as compared to a single service need, might show certain trade-off effects. That is, since grocery shopping is a life-support need and heavy housework is not, one would expect some attrition in the percentage of those who receive help with heavy housework when they also need help with grocery shopping. On the other hand, there may be tendency for the supply to expand to meet the increased need for both grocery shopping and heavy housework.

The data in Figure 5-11 show that for those household heads not able to do grocery shopping and also unable to do heavy housework, only 6 percent do without help for the latter. This rises to 19 percent for those who are able to do grocery shopping though unable to do heavy housework. Thus, some expansion in supply to meet the dual need is evident. But, while there is a high response level to both needs where they coexist, there is some attrition in the case of heavy housework.

[p] For those who are unable to do either heavy or light housework, the great majority (89 percent) of households received help for both heavy and for light work from the same source, while the remaining 11 percent did not receive help for heavy and for light work from the same source. Of this latter group, fifty more households were able to get free help at home for light but not for heavy work, eleven more households were able to get free help from another source for light housework while having either to pay or to forego help for heavy, and three households were able to pay for light work while foregoing help for heavy work. Thus, for those who can do neither light nor heavy housework, the receipt of light housework edges out the receipt of heavy housework and the free receipt of light housework (from home and outside sources) edges out the free receipt of heavy housework (from home and outside sources).

In the presence of double functional impairments, the survey data suggest that household composition adjustments may occur that show up in the increased proportion of help being provided free at home. Thus, while only 11 percent of households who can do light housework have children living at home, 28 percent of those who cannot do light housework have children living at home. The focus is on children rather than the spouse, since the former are not enjoined by the "in sickness and in health" disposition of marital living arrangements.

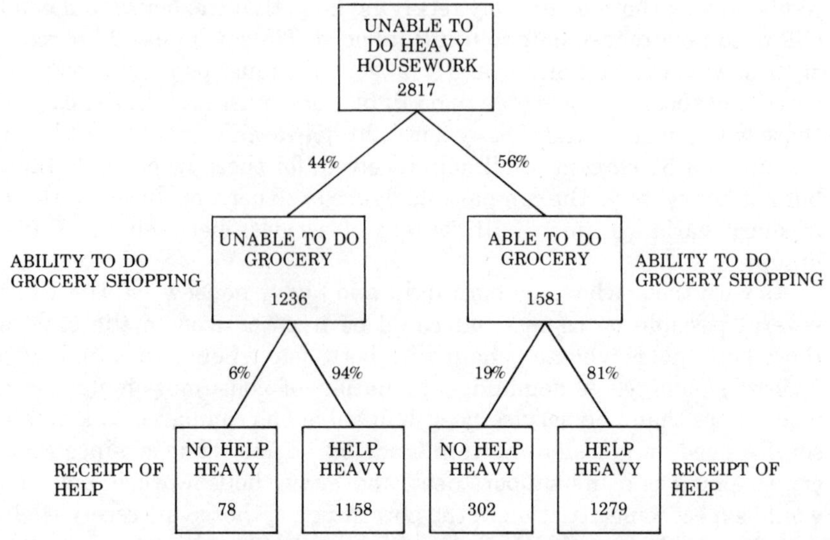

Source: Special tabulations from the 1974 Survey of Low Income Aged and Disabled (SLIAD).

Figure 5–11. Urban Households Unable to Do Heavy Housework, by Ability to Do Grocery Shopping and Receipt of Help for Heavy Housework

Less than 1 percent who can do neither do without help for grocery shopping, while 6 percent do without help for heavy housework.

In those households who received help for grocery shopping though not for heavy housework, the data show that both for those who depended on paid help and for those who depended on free help outside the home for grocery shopping, there was greater attrition in the receipt of help for heavy housework. Free home help is the help source that has the greatest likelihood of being available for heavy housework when it is available for grocery shopping. Furthermore, even when it is only available for grocery shopping but not for heavy housework, remaining service resources can be allocated with enough flexibility so that 99.2 percent of the households needing the service end up getting it, as shown in Figure 5-12.[q]

Proximity of Relatives. One would expect that for those urban elderly household heads living *with a spouse,* there would be a greater tendency to get help at home for heavy housework. This is, in fact, the

[q] One component of this flexibility is that the use of other service resources for heavy housework is free of competition from home-provided grocery shopping.

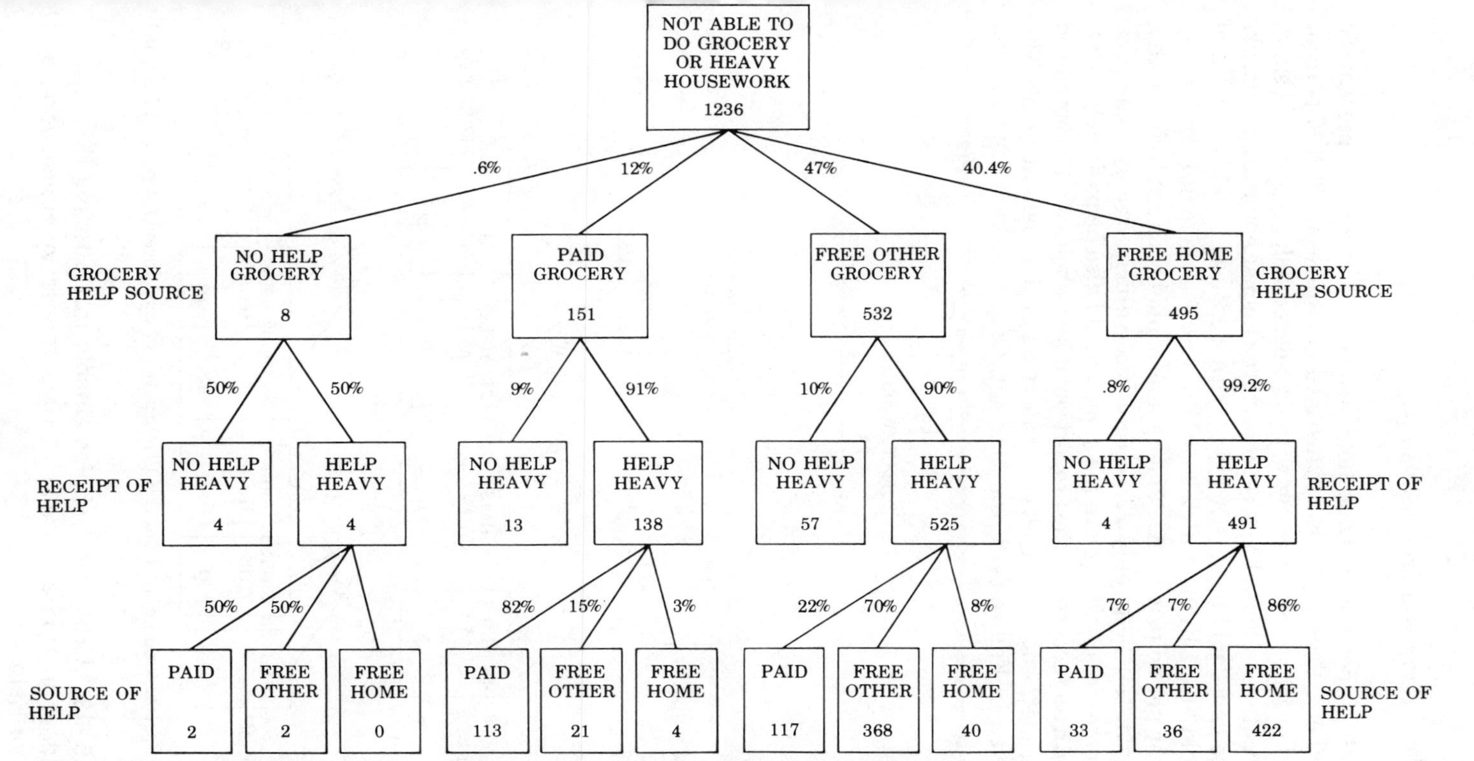

Source: Special tabulations from the 1974 Survey of Low Income Aged and Disabled (SLIAD).

Figure 5–12. Urban Households Unable to Do Heavy Housework, by Source of Help for Grocery Shopping, Receipt of Help for Heavy Housework, and Source of Help

case; only 6 percent of household heads with a spouse present do without help. Those who are not married are worse off, with 17 percent of such household heads doing without needed help. As hypothesized, the percentage of households receiving free help at home drops sharply for those household heads not living with a spouse. Seventy percent of household heads living with a spouse receive free help at home among those who get help, whereas, among household heads not living with a spouse who get help, only 22 percent receive help free at home.

The *presence of children in the home* should also be positively correlated with an increase in the proportion of household heads whose need is being met, and with a larger proportion of free help at home. The data given in Figure 5-13 bear this out. Only 3 percent of those who

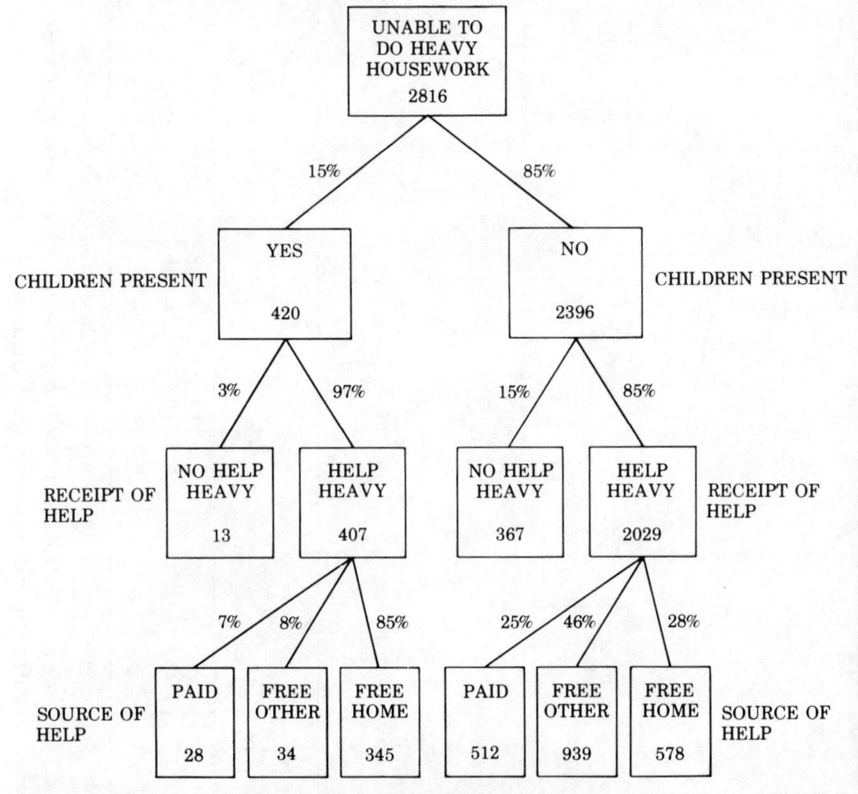

Source: Special tabulations from the 1974 Survey of Low Income Aged and Disabled (SLIAD).

Figure 5–13. Urban Households Unable to Do Heavy Housework, by Children in Home, Receipt of Help for Heavy Housework, and Source of Help

have children in the home do not receive needed help, while 15 percent of household heads without children do without such help. A much greater difference exists, however, in the proportion receiving help free in the home between household heads with children at home and those without children at home. Twenty-eight percent of those without children at home receive help free at home, whereas 85 percent of those with children at home receive help free at home. For those without children at home who do receive help, there is an increase in paid help and an even greater increase in the proportion of household heads getting free help from an outside source. Children in the vicinity (within 10 minutes or in the same city) surely contribute to this latter proportion.

The data support this last hypothesis. Eighteeen percent of those without children in the vicinity (within a 10 minute drive) do without help with heavy housework, whereas only 7 percent of those with children in the vicinity do without it. Furthermore, while 34 percent of those without children in the vicinity get free help from outside sources, 48 percent of those with children in the vicinity do so. As with children 10 minutes away, one would expect that having children elsewhere in the same city would be positively correlated, though more weakly, with an increase in the percentage of those in need who receive help and with an increase in the percentage who receive help from an outside source. There is such a correlation, which, as expected, is very weak.

Heavy Housework Assistance in Perspective

Of the eight services the survey covers, heavy housework is the service done without by the highest percentage of households in need. It is also the service with the lowest percentage of home provision and is one of three services, including clothes washing and light housework, that are purchased by over 20 percent of the population who receive it. In terms of rating the various sources of help as more or less "desirable," it seems fair to assume that in most cases paid help would be the source of last resort, although free help is not without its "costs." The percentage of those in need of either assistance with heavy housework or one of the other seven types of services are shown by source of assistance in Table 5-6.

The usage sequence—free help at home as the most frequently utilized, followed by free help other, followed by paid help, and, finally, by no help—is the most common one, representing as it does the usage pattern for five of the eight services listed. Heavy housework departs from this usage sequence in that the most frequently used source of help is free other, followed by free home, followed by paid. When free

Table 5–6. Sources of Assistance for Services

Rank	*Sources*	*Percentage Using Help*
	For services other than heavy housework	
First	Free help in home	51.0
Second	Free help from outside of home	34.5
Third	Paid help	11.0
Last	No help	3.5
	For heavy housework	
First	Free help from outside of home	34.5
Second	Free help in home	32.8
Third	Paid help	19.0
Last	No help	13.5

help at home is not as readily available, as is the case with heavy housework as compared to most other services, the household must fall back on alternative sources of help, which also happen to be subject to more stringent supply and demand forces than help at home.

Nevertheless, the data show that there is a strong tendency to compensate for the unavailability of one source of help by substituting another rather than doing without help altogether. For example, the difference between having children in the home and not having them in the home accounts for a difference of 12 percentage points in the proportion using help free at home (from any source) between those who have children at home and those who do not. This tendency to compensate is even more apparent in the case of grocery shopping, a life-support need, than it is in the case of heavy housework. Grocery shopping shares with heavy housework the distinction of being one of the two services with the lowest percentage of home provision. But, whereas of all services heavy housework has the highest percentage of no help, grocery shopping has the lowest. Free help from an outside source has become a significant substitute for the provision of help free at home for grocery shopping.

Scanning the impact on the receipt of help with heavy housework of the independent variables considered, as shown in Table 5-7, variation in housing quality variables, variables measuring proximity of kin, multiple service need variables, and financial ability variables are all to be found among those associated with a substantial variation in the percentage of persons in need of help who do not receive help with housework. The reader should be careful not to impute causality to the

Table 5–7. Distribution of Selected Variables for Respondents in Need of Assistance with Heavy Housework Who Do not Receive Such Assistance

	Range[a]		
Variable	*Qualitative*	*Numeric, %*	*Numeric Difference, %*
Martial status	Married–never married	6–24	18
Housing systems	0 Missing–4 missing	13–30	17
Grocery shopping	Can't do–Can do	6–19	13
Light housework	Can't do–Can do	4–16	12
Children at home	Yes to No	3–15	12
Income	$0–$999 to $2000–$2999	5–16	11
Children within 10 minutes	Yes to No	7–18	11
Perception of health	Excellent to Good	9–18	9
Assets	$5000–$999 to 0–$999	7–15	8
Housing cost-to-income ratio	0–19% to 20–29%	11–18	7
Weights to 10 lbs.	Can't do to Difficult to do	12–17	5
Weights over 10 lbs.	Difficult to Do	13–18	5
	to Can do	13–18	5
Housing maintenance	All work to 11–30% don't work	12–17	5

Source: Special tabulations from the 1974 Survey of Low Income Aged and Disabled (SLIAD).

[a] Definition of range, e.g., excellent-to-good vs. excellent-to-poor, chosen to give maximum numerical difference in receipt of assistance.

associations shown here; this type of analysis is the subject of the next section.

Determinants of Receipt of Paid-for Housekeeping Services

Recent analyses have established that there is substantial variation in access to and receipt of various housing-related support services, even within an individual metropolitan area (U.S. Government Accounting Office, 1977). The variation among locations is likely to be much greater. The volume of such services available in general is substantially larger today than was the case in 1974 when the SLIAD survey was conducted. This combined with program changes may make the distribution of services more rational today than in 1974. The purpose of this section is to investigate the characteristics of recipients and nonrecipients of paid-for housekeeping services in 1974 to provide guidance on what questions to ask about the current distribution of these services.

Two quite distinct analyses are presented. In the first, the determinants of being the recipient of housekeeping services provided by a public agency are studied. More precisely, the dependent variable in this analysis, RECDWEL, has a value of 1.0 if the household received some publicly provided services. It is 0 otherwise (see Table 5-4). Note, though, that the household may have spent some of its own funds in addition for these services. Households included were not limited to those receiving only publicly provided services because it has not been uncommon for agencies to require a nominal fee for initial services and/or cost-sharing for services beyond some threshold amount. This analysis focuses directly on the question of who is served by public funds. It may be that none of the characteristics hypothesized in the second section to effect recipiency status will be statistically significant. Such a finding would be extremely important as it would strongly suggest that recipiency status is randomly determined by the administrative agencies.

The second analysis takes a much broader perspective. The dependent variable, RECDWRK, has a value of 1.0 if the household received paid-for housekeeping services from any source; it has a value of 0 otherwise. Thus, commercially purchased services are included, as well as those provided through public agencies. The two analyses are presented together to provide contrasting results.

The analyses for RECDWEL and RECDWRK are quite similar. For each, regressions were estimated for the models specified in equation (5–4). These have the interpretation of probability estimates; one interprets the coefficient for a specific variable as giving the effect of it on the probability of receiving assistance. Separate regressions were estimated for four groups of households, based on the assumption that the determinants of recipiency status would vary systematically among them; the groups were urban homeowners, urban renters, rural homeowners, and rural renters. This assumption was supported by the estimates. Therefore, separate results are presented below for each group.

A final consideration concerns the well-known statistical problems that occur when the standard regression techniques are used to estimate models with a dichotomous (0–1) dependent variable, a problem that is aggravated when the fraction of the sample in one of the classes is small. All of the reported results are based on generalized least squares estimates, which overcome these problems (Goldberger 1965).

Table 5–8. Summary of Results of Regression Analyses on Receipt of Housekeeping Services

Independent Variables[d]	RECDWEL[b]				RECDWRK[b]			
	Homeowners		Renters		Homeowners		Renters	
	Urban	Rural	Urban	Rural	Urban	Rural	Urban	Rural
A. Elasticities								
INCOME	a	a	.02	.10	.32	.32	.31	a
AGE	−1.02	−1.63	−.46	a	−.34	−1.67	3.11	a
CANNT	.16	1.80	.32	a	.17	1.41	.53	a
B. Percentage Change in Mean Probability of Receiving Assistance								
WELPAY	15	36	7	a	a	a	a	a
MARRIED	a	26	a	a	a	a	a	a
SINGLE	7	a	a	a	a	a	a	a
CHLD	a	a	a	a	a	10	−43	a
CHLD10	a	22	a	a	a	17	−19	a
CHLDCTY	a	−16	a	a	a	12	a	a

[a] Regression coefficient not significant at 0.10 level or greater.
[b] Dependent variable for the four equations in this group.
[c] Full regression results reported in Appendix Table 5A–1.
[d] All variables defined in Table 5–3.

All of the results are also from single equation models, as opposed to multiple equation, joint determination models. The more complex models were estimated, but the joint determination was not supported.[r]

The main results of the regression estimates are given in Table 5-8. The entries in the table are based on regressions reported in Appendix Tables 5A-1; they have been converted to more readily comprehensible statistics for this presentation. The left-hand stub lists the nine independent variables included in the regressions.[s] For clarity, the same variables were included in all eight of the regressions reported; each column gives the results of a single regression. The two panels of the table present, respectively, (1) elasticities (evaluated at the means), that is, the percentage change in the probability of receiving services associated with a 1 percent change in the independent variable, for the continuous variables; and (2) for the dichotomous independent vari-

[r] In several cases the two-stage least squares models, in which RECDWEL and HMAIN were jointly determined, were highly statistically significant, but the variables were of the wrong sign. This incorrect result is attributed to having data only at one point in time, so that enrollment effects of HMAIN on RECDWEL are not being captured.

[s] A variety of other regression forms were run including the allowance for a number of nonlinearities. These provide some highly interesting additional results and often raised the explanatory power of the models significantly over those reported in the table. However, the results given in the table are sufficient to convey the general sense of the findings.

ables, the percentage change in the mean probability of receiving assistance associated with having a particular characteristic such as having children living in the home.

Turning first to the results for RECDWEL (columns 1–4), the probability of receiving publicly provided housekeeping services is:

Effectively unrelated to income,
Generally inversely related to age,
Positively related to having mobility limitations,
Strongly increased by being a welfare recipient; and
Generally unrelated to the presence of a spouse and the proximity of children.

These findings are striking and somewhat disturbing. They indicate, with controls for other factors, that in 1974, lower-income households were not being singled out for assistance. Also, older households were significantly less likely to be recipients, possibly because they were less able to confront the process of attaining recipiency status. On the other hand, especially for rural homeowners, respondents with mobility impairments were much more likely to receive housekeeping services.

It may be helpful to put in better perspective the trade-off between the effects of greater age, which lowers recipiency probability, and a greater degree of mobility impairment, which raises the probability. For a seventy-year-old person, a five-year increase in age is only a 7 percent change. For the same person increasing the number of impairments from two to three represents a 50 percent increase. Applying percentage changes like these to the elasticities in the table shows that the effects of increased physical impairments will more than offset the lowered probabilities associated with greater age.

Another effect worthy of comment is the "welfare effect." Being a welfare recipient clearly increases the likelihood of being a housekeeping service recipient. Once a household is in the system it is more likely to have the whole panoply of services made available. Although this works to the advantage of recipients, it heightens the inequities between recipients and nonrecipients.

The results for RECDWRK differ from those just discussed in one important dimension: among urban households, both owners and renters, the receipt of housekeeping services from all sources is clearly income-elastic. In fact, it appears to be about as responsive to income changes as is the overall demand for housing services.[t]

[t] For evidence on the demand for housing see Polinsky (1977).

Of equal interest to the results reviewed thus far is the absence of any generally significant pattern among types of households and proximity of children on the one hand and recipiency status on the other. In some other specifications of the regressions, these variables are highly significant; but the results are not very robust. This is contrary to expectation and results by others based on simple cross-tabulations, much like that presented earlier in this chapter. The results suggest that a few basic factors, especially health, are more important in determining recipiency status than previously thought and that support from children and spouse continues in the presence of such services. Since the data available do not allow one to look closely at substitution of family provided services for other services, no definitive statement can be given.

With these main results, some important limitations should be carefully noted. First, although separate models are estimated for urban and rural areas, it has not been possible to capture the effects of the economic, social, and institutional conditions in individual markets. As a consequence, these results should be taken only as broad indications of causal relations. A second point, related to the first, is that the explanatory power of the estimated models is quite low, even for models using individual households as the unit of observation. The models for rural renters are insignificant—there is simply no systematic pattern of recipient characteristics. Both of these factors argue strongly for considering these results as tentative, but they also call for a reexamination of the criteria actually being employed by local agencies in deciding which households are selected to receive publicly provided housekeeping services.

HOUSEKEEPING SERVICES AND HOUSING QUALITY

The previous section described in considerable detail what types of households receive paid-for housekeeping services. The next question to explore is the effect of purchased housekeeping services on dwelling quality. More specifically, we want to know whether the receipt of these services positively affects dwelling quality after one takes into account the influence of such factors as financial status, household composition, and health.

The measure of dwelling quality is the variable HMAIN, an index of some eleven possible deficiencies and service disruptions; the items included range from holes in the floor, to broken windows, to a stopped-up sink, to a broken heating system (see Table 5-3 for a full definition). The index is calculated as the sum of the defects divided by

Table 5–9. Summary of Regression Results on Determinants of Dwelling Unit Maintenance (HMAIN) for Owner-Occupants and Renters in Urban and Rural Areas (Signs of Independent Variables)

Independent Variables	Urban		Rural	
	Owners	Renters	Owners	Renters
INCOME	–	–	–	–
ASSETS	–	–	–	a
CANNT	+	a	+	a
MARRIED	–	a	–	a
SINGLE	–	–	–	a
CHLD	a	+	a	+
CHLD10	a	a	a	–
RECDWEL	a	–	a	a
RECDWRK	a	a	a	a
HOMEWRK	a	–	a	–

[a] Coefficient not significant at 0.05 level or higher.

[b] Sign of coefficient of independent variables.

the number of deficiencies possible. Hence, if the dwelling lacks a heating system, there is no possibility for it to be broken.[u] Major systems defects, such as lack of plumbing or heating, are not included, because it is unlikely that their correction would be influenced by the receipt of housekeeping services. Note that a larger value of HMAIN connotes a lower level of dwelling quality.

Three measures of housekeeping services are employed. RECDWEL and RECDWRK have been examined. The third measure is the variable HOMEWRK, which takes on the value of 1.0 if the respondent has, in the year preceding the survey, received the following assistance: (1) help in finding a place to live, (2) home-delivered meals, or (3) visiting nurse; otherwise it is 0.

Separate regression models, corresponding to the conceptual model described in the second section, were estimated owners and renters in urban and rural areas. Since the dependent variable in this case is continuous, ordinary least squares could be used.

The results for a "standard model" are summarized in Tables 5-9 and 5-10, and the full regressions are reported in Appendix Tables 5A-2 and 5A-3. Again, a variety of other models were estimated, but those summarized in these tables provide a good overview of the results.[v] In one sense the results are remarkably similar across the four

[u] An index in which all deficiencies have been weighted equally is used. Past analysis of the sensitivity of the market value or rent of units to a similar deficiency index gives results that were not sensitive to the weighting of the index. See Mendelsohn and Struyk (1975).

[v] Omitted from these models are the wage rate variables SERVRATE and CARP-

Table 5–10. Summary of Selected Quantitative Results for Regressions on Determining Dwelling Maintenance (HMAIN) for Renters and Owner-Occupants in Urban and Rural Areas

	Urban[b]		*Rural*[c]	
	Owner-Occupants	*Renters*	*Owner-Occupants*	*Renters*
	A. Elasticities Evaluated at the Mean			
INCOME	−.34	−.40	−.33	−.78
ASSETS	−.16	−.01	−.58	a
CANNT	.14	a	.17	a
B. Percentage Reduction in HMAIN Associated with Various Forms of Assistance				
RECDWEL	a	26	a	a
HOMEWRK	a	20	a	39
RECDWRK	a	a	30	a

[a] Variable not significant in regressions.

[b] Regressions reported in Table 5A–2.

[c] Regressions reported in Table 5A–3.

groups: whenever a variable is significant it is of the expected sign. On the other hand, a number of variables are only occasionally significant. Findings that stand out are the following:

Higher incomes and more assets are consistently associated with fewer dwelling defects.

Units occupied by a widow or a married couple will have fewer defects than units occupied by other types of households.

Physical impairments by homeowner respondents are associated with more dwelling defects.

Receipt of services included in HOMEWRK is associated with higher-quality units for urban and rural renters; by contrast RECDWEL improves dwelling quality only for urban renters.

For the purposes of this study, the most striking result is the lack of effect of RECDWEL and HOMEWRK on dwelling quality for owner-occupants. One possible explanation is that the public agents who come to a rental dwelling are more instrumental in getting the building owner or superintendent to make repairs than the agents are in actu-

RATE (defined in Table 5-3), which were to provide a measure of the cost of purchased services. These variables were highly significant but consistently of the wrong sign. These results are interpreted as again reflecting specification problems resulting from not having market-specific data for the analysis. The results for the coefficients of the variables reported in the tables were quite robust with alternative specifications, but the lack of market data should raise a caution to strictly interpreting the numerical results.

ally making repairs themselves or assisting with the repairs. The solution of having the superintendent make the repairs is, in a sense, the best; it involves no cash outlay by the elderly person and comparatively little effort. If this fails, relocation is always a possibility. The agent observing the same defect in an owner-occupied home is confronted with a more difficult situation. The agent can make the repair himself or assist, if it is among his responsibilities and within his competence *and* if the necessary materials are readily available. If this is not possible, he may have to suggest a contractor to the elderly person. Even if the agent is willing to follow up, the homeowner may not be enthusiastic—worries about the cost and having a stranger in his home may convince him to live with it as is. In any event, the results clearly indicate little change in dwelling quality, as measured here, is due to publicly funded housekeeping services. For rural homeowners, but not for the urban counterparts, there is evidence that privately financed housekeeping services reduce the number of defects.

Quantitatively, the effect of RECDWEL and HOMEWRK is substantial for renters. The overall effects shown in Table 5-10 suggest about a 40 percent reduction in HMAIN associated with receiving such services.

These broad results provide some food for thought for public policy. Consider four facts:

1. In 1974 only about half as many homeowners were recipients of services included in RECDWEL and HOMEWRK as renters. The differential in dwelling *quality* (as measured by HMAIN) was considerably smaller. (See Table 5-4.)
2. While some 700,000 elderly renter households live in HUD-assisted housing, very few owner-occupants do.[w]
3. Three-quarters of all elderly households are homeowners.
4. These results suggest that the housekeeping services provided through social service agencies have a positive effect on the physical environment of renters though no parallel effect is apparent for owner-occupants.

These facts, taken together, point to the growing need for the federal government to assist income-eligible elderly homeowners maintain their dwelling units. The best method to provide this assistance is debatable, but the growing inequity in the treatment of low-income elderly homeowners and renters is clearly evident.

[w] These few are the handful of homeowners receiving assistance under the Section 235 program. At the same time, it should be noted that a number of elderly are being assisted with dwelling rehabilitation through the Section 312 program and the Community Development Block Grant Program.

Independent Variables	RECDWEL[c]				RECDWRK[c]			
	Owners		Renters		Owners		Renters	
	Urban	*Rural*	*Urban*	*Rural*	*Urban*	*Rural*	*Urban*	*Rural*
CONSTANT	.120	.640	.147	.221	.310	−.715	−.357	.404
WELPAY	.0182	.0669	.0141	−.0364	.0135	.0017	.0133	−.0154
	(2.47)[d]	(3.30)	(2.30)	(1.13)	(1.17)	(.79)	(.97)	(.64)
INCOME	−.0002	.0316	.0031	.0150	.0085	.0081	0.40	.0043
	(.30)	(.48)	(1.59)	(1.45)	(2.00)	(1.39)	(3.73)	(.40)
AGE	−.0002	.0006	−.0002	−.0002	−.0004	.0016	.0050	−.0005
	(2.00)	(1.68)	(2.00)	(.25)	(1.78)	(2.01)	(4.76)	(1.00)
CANNT	.0023	.0348	.0079	−.0038	.0136	.0803	.0318	.0037
	(1.50)	(8.62)	(2.29)	(.79)	(3.09)	(8.07)	(9.19)	(.39)
MARRIED	.0068	.0479	.0076	.0107	.0003	−.0432	−.0207	.0112
	(1.12)	(2.10)	(.97)	(.24)	(.02)	(.90)	(.98)	(.36)
SINGLE	.0085	.0205	.0048	.0133	.0051	.0327	.0188	.0145
	(1.34)	(.86)	(.76)	(.30)	(.36)	(.67)	(1.10)	(.32)
CHLD	−.0056	−.0075	−.0059	−.0216	−.0133	.0319	−.0602	−.0132
	(1.10)	(.46)	(.75)	(.97)	(1.09)	(1.48)	(2.88)	(.44)
CHLD10	−.0039	.0424	−.0011	.0007	−.0013	.0880	−.0227	.0023
	(1.12)	(3.95)	(.19)	(.02)	(.14)	(3.25)	(1.62)	(.31)
CHLDCTY	.0008	−.0311	.0037	.0131	−.0150	.0410	−.0030	.0066
	(.21)	(2.70)	(.44)	(.68)	(1.54)	(1.60)	(.58)	(.24)
R^2	.005	.111	.003	.001	.037	.106	.057	.001
SEE	.799	1.37	1.02	1.05	1.05	1.56	3.17	.831
F	2.23	14.32	1.82	.72	10.62	18.59	17.50	.42
df	2230	952	2440	263	2230	952	2440	263
γ^b	.119	.184	.205	.210	.356	.332	1.21	.285
COMPLEX MODEL								
R^2	.009	.002	.013	.164	.051	.002	.014	.001
F	2.62	1.20	3.85	5.45	11.63	1.17	3.95	.61

[a] All models estimated using generalized least squares.

[b] This is the mean of the dependent variable when each observation is weighted by $(P(1 - P))^{-\frac{1}{2}}$, where P is the estimated value of the dependent variable from the comparable ordinary least squares regression.

[c] Dependent variable for this set of regressions.

[d] Student statistics are in parentheses beneath the coefficient.

Table 5A–2. Regression Results for Housing Maintenance for Urban Households (Dependent Variable is HMAIN)

	Renters						*Owners*			
	Equation 1		*Equation 2*		*Equation 3*		*Equation 4*		*Equation 5*	
	Coefficient	*t-stat*	*Coefficient*	*t-stat*	*Coefficient*	*t-stat*	*Coefficient*	*t-stat*	*Coefficient*	*t-stat*
CONSTANT	.098		.100		.098		.095		.096	
INCOME	−.011	4.41	−.011	4.43	−.011	4.41	−.006	4.76	−.006	4.65
INCOME**2	.0002	2.50	.0002	2.50	.0002	2.62	8×10^{-5}	4.00	8×10^{-5}	4.00
ASSETS	−.0009	2.02	−.0009	2.04	−.0009	1.95	−.0007	6.09	−.0007	6.00
WELPAY	.023	4.28	.023	4.25	.023	4.11				
CANNT	.012	.92	.001	1.08	.001	.85	.006	4.42	.006	4.32
MARRIED	−.005	.62	−.005	.63	−.005	.61	−.015	1.72	−.016	1.78
SINGLE	−.020	3.04	−.021	3.22	−.020	3.13	−.015	1.72	−.016	1.76
CHLD	.024	2.85	.023	2.85	.023	2.91	.003	.44	.003	.46
CHLD10	−.008	1.55	−.008	1.53	−.008	1.55	.0005	.09	.0005	.09
RECDWEL	−.019	1.60	−.016	1.33					.019	1.26
HOMEWRK			−.014	2.07					−.009	.87
RECDWRK					−.010	1.21	−.0014	.18		
R^2	.033		.035		.033		.055		.056	
$\bar{R}^2$	.030		.031		.029		.052		.052	
SEE	.124		.124		.124		.118		.113	
F	8.50		.813		8.39		14.50		13.26	
df	2439		2438		2439		2238		2229	

Table 5A–3. Regression Results for Housing Maintenance for Rural Households (Dependent Variable is HMAIN)

	Renters						*Homeowners*					
	Equation 1		*Equation 2*		*Equation 3*		*Equation 4*		*Equation 5*		*Equation 6*	
	Coef-ficient	*t-stat*	*Coef-ficient*	*t-stat*	*Coef-ficient*	*t-stat*	*Coef-ficient*	*t-stat*	*Coef-ficient*	*t-stat*	*Coef-ficient*	*t-stat*
CONSTANT	.344		.343				.196		.196		.197	
INCOME	−.0584	2.32	−.0603	2.36	−.0014	2.42	−.0143	2.73	−.0148	2.90	−.0141	2.74
INCOME**2	.0037	1.12	.0039	1.18	.0040	1.17	.0004	.99	.0004	1.01	.0003	.91
ASSETS	−.0037	1.00	−.0035	.96	−.0034	.94	−.0007	3.00	−.0006	2.95	−.0006	2.91
CANNT	−.0070	1.17	−.0069	1.15	−.0079	1.33	.0096	3.75	.0091	3.50	.0103	3.96
MARRIED	−.0098	.22	−.0085	.21	−.0070	.17	−.0779	3.90	−.0772	3.87	−.0789	3.90
SINGLE	−.0446	1.10	−.0435	1.07	−.0479	1.17	−.0603	3.02	−.0601	3.00	−.0595	2.95
CHLD	.0525	1.67	.0536	1.71	.0550	1.72	−.0013	.77	−.0011	.70	−.0011	.73
CHLD10	−.0536	2.25	−.0515	2.12	−.0520	2.13	−.0078	.82	.0080	.80	.0076	.84
RECDWEL	−.0637	.94			−.0773	1.32	−.0052	.19	−.0073	.03		
HOMEWRK	−.0626	1.51	−.0682	1.64					.0278	1.30		
RECDWRK			.0132	.30							−.0330	1.86
WELPAY												
R^2	.100		.096		.092		.072		.073		.074	
$\bar{R}^2$	.065		.063		.061		.063		.063		.066	
SEE	.196		.196		.196		.153		.153		.153	
F	2.90		2.79		2.96		8.15		7.50		8.55	
df	262		262		263		952		951		952	

REFERENCES

Case Reports. 1977. *Major Federal Programs to Assist the Elderly in Independent Living as of April, 1977*. Bethesda, Md.

Dubois, E.N. 1964. *Essential Methods in Business Statistics*. New York: McGraw-Hill.

DuMochel, W., and G. Duncan. 1977. "Using Sample Weights to Compare Various Repression Models." Ann Arbor: University of Michigan Department of Statistics, Technical Report No. 2.

Emling, D.C. 1976. *Adult Chore Services: A Profile of In-Home Assistance*. Lansing: Michigan Department of Social Services.

Goldberger, A.S. 1975. *Econometric Theory*. New York: John Wiley and Sons.

Gutowski, M. 1977. "Integrating Housing and Social Services Activities for the Elderly Household." Unpublished.

Mendelsohn, R., and R. Struyk. 1975. "The Flow of Housing Services in a Hedonic Index." Washington, D.C.: Urban Institute Working Paper.

Polinsky, A.M. 1977. "The Demand for Housing: A Study in Specification and Grouping." *Econometrica* 45, no. 2: 447–61.

Schieber, S.J. 1978. "Housing Conditions of Aged Welfare Recipients." Washington, D.C.: Social Security Administration. Processed.

Shanas, E.; P. Townsend; D. Wedderburn; et al. 1978. *Old People in Three Industrial Societies*. New York: Atherton Press.

Struyk, R., and L. Ozanne. 1976. *Housing from the Existing Stock: Comparative Economic Analyses of Owner-Occupants and Landlords*. Washington, D.C.: The Urban Institute.

Tissue, T. 1977. "The Survey of the Low-Income Aged and Disabled: An Introduction." *Social Security Bulletin* (February): 3–11.

U.S. Department of Housing and Urban Development. 1971. *1969 HUD Statistical Yearbook*. Washington, D.C.: U.S. Government Printing Office.

U.S. Government Accounting Office. 1977. *The Well-Being of Older People in Cleveland, Ohio*. Washington, D.C.: G.A.O. Publication HRD 77-70.

———. 1978. *Home Health—The Need for a National Policy to Better Provide for the Elderly*. Washington, D.C.: G.A.O. Publication HRD 78-19.

Welfeld, I., and R. Struyk. 1979. "Housing Options for the Elderly," *Occasional Papers in Housing and Community Development*. Vol. 2.

Chapter 6

Location and Neighborhood Conditions of the Elderly

In formulating housing policies for the elderly, it is necessary to know not only who the elderly are but also where they are. In Chapter 2 the former question was addressed; in this chapter the latter is answered. Typically, the question of where the elderly are located is asked in order to identify large concentrations of persons in the "target" population for purposes of planning service networks. That older persons are overrepresented in the central cities of older metropolitan areas, for example, suggests that senior centers are likely to reach a larger number of individuals in the appropriate target population by locating in downtown areas rather than in the suburbs.[a]

For purposes of this study, and apart from the logistics involved in service delivery, there are additional reasons for inquiring into the location of the elderly. By locating areas where the elderly are concentrated (as measured in either absolute or relative numbers), we have not necessarily located areas where the elderly have chronic housing problems. Climate, type of economic activity, attractiveness to inmigrants, and demographic factors all influence the supply, demand, cost, and mix of housing. As a result, the housing characteristics and consequent housing problems of the elderly vary from one area to the next. As we have seen, these subnational differences are masked if the

[a] This type of reasoning creates some problems as well. Results from a service utilization study conducted in Cleveland, Ohio, show that older persons living in the suburbs are underserviced in comparison to persons of comparable functional status who live in the center of Cleveland (U.S. Government 1977). Moreover, the suburban elderly who would benefit from select services face transportation problems unlike those confronting inner city elderly.

housing situation of older persons is studied only from a national perspective. Hence, in this chapter we examine the location of the elderly as a distinct but heterogeneous segment of the population, and the location of the elderly who, by virtue of income constraints or structural inadequacies, are likely to have "housing problems."

For purposes of analyzing spatial differences in the location of the elderly and in the quality of their housing, it is common to consider a number of different levels of aggregation. It is possible to make a case, at least theoretically, for examining the housing situation of the elderly in units ranging in size from multistate regions to individual cities. A state's ability to obtain federal housing moneys, for example, may influence the availability of certain types of units in the state. Even within states, there tends to be considerable diversity in supply-demand factors reflecting intrastate differences in geography, land costs, labor force composition, and property tax regulations. Still other important differences in the housing situation of the elderly may be observed with respect to units defined in terms of density (urban versus rural) or function (central city versus suburb).

Identifying differences in the characteristics of older persons at any of these levels of aggregation is but a descriptive exercise having only limited value for policy formulation. For this task, it is necessary to determine which level of geographic aggregation is most meaningful for the design and implementation of housing programs. Are regions in this country so similar with respect to the characteristics of their older residents that we need only to formulate a national housing policy, universally applicable? Or, alternatively, do the housing conditions and needs of rural elderly differ dramatically from those in metropolitan areas so that the problems of rural housing need to be singled out for special program attention? In this chapter we attempt not only to document differences among geographic and social units, but also to assess the relative homogeneity of these various units. Types of geographic areas are considered appropriate vehicles for policy implementation if it can be shown that (1) differences *between* regions, states or metropolitan areas are significant whereas (2) differences *within* the region, state or metropolitan area are minimal.

CONCEPTUAL MODEL

The organizing framework for the first part of this chapter is fairly consistent with that used in other research devoted to the topic of housing and the elderly. Housing problems are perceived from the standpoint of the older person. Expenditures on housing assistance programs are justified because poor housing conditions have an adverse effect on the physical, social, and psychological well-being of older persons. Most housing and social agency programs of the Department of Health, Education and Welfare reflect this perspective, which can be diagrammed simply as in Figure 6-1.

Housing assistance can assume many forms, and the various types of federally funded programs are described in Chapters 7 and 8. Regardless of the type of activity supported—relocation, rent supplements, or repair services—the logistics and approach are similar. Individuals in the target population are identified, assistance is rendered, and success is measured by the extent of positive impact on, or improvement in, the life-style of the recipient. Within this perspective, patterns of residential location are investigated in order to identify areas where potential program recipients are clustered. The effects of an intervention strategy, however, are assumed to be uniform as long as individuals having similar characteristics or occupying similar types of housing are the recipients. The broader aspects of residential location, so useful in locating the target population, often are ignored in the design or implementation of housing assistance programs.

In the last section of this chapter we investigate the housing situation of the elderly from a slightly different perspective. The model we use to guide this part of the analysis is an elaboration of the one shown in Figure 6-1 and can be represented as in Figure 6-2. This model broadens our perspective on the housing situation of older persons. Housing problems are redefined so as to include not only those emanating from structural conditions of the dwelling unit per se but also from the social and economic aspects of the immediate residential environment—the neighborhood setting. An older person living in a structurally sound unit in an unsafe neighborhood has a "housing problem" just as much as an older person whose home lacks adequate plumbing or heating.

Adoption of a broader perspective on housing alters our thinking about program planning and service delivery in rather significant ways. Knowledge of residential location patterns becomes a prerequisite, not only for planning the distribution of services, but also for anticipating the effect of a particular intervention strategy. Repair of particular structural problems is not likely to result in a marked improvement in the well-being of an older person if the neighborhood

HOUSING CONDITIONS OF OLDER PERSONS ⟶ OLDER PERSONS' WELL-BEING

Figure 6–1. Perspective of HEW Housing and Social Agency Programs

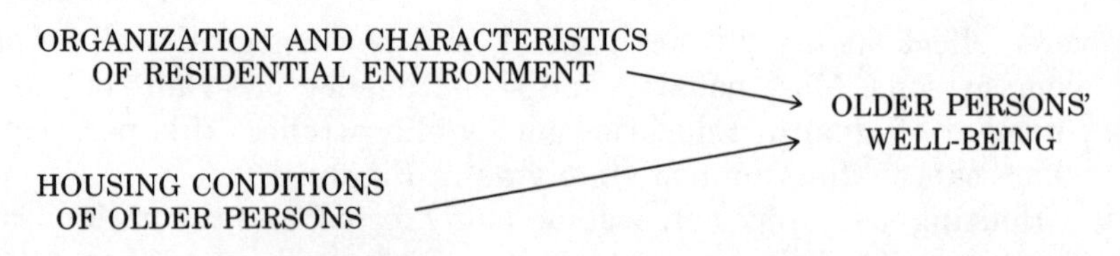

Figure 6–2. Model of Effects of Housing and Residential Environment on Well-Being of the Elderly

continues to be an unsafe one and trips to the grocery store are undertaken only with trepidation. The importance of the neighborhood context to the satisfaction and well-being of older persons is cited frequently in justifying the costs involved in relocating elderly to newly constructed housing in better neighborhoods.

Recognition of the fact that housing problems of older persons exist in a particular context also focuses attention on the reciprocal balance between individuals and their environment. Structurally inadequate housing, owned or rented by older individuals, both contributes to and reflects the general housing situation in the neighborhood. Along this line, Mathieu comments:

> Housing is unique in the degree to which its quality can enhance or diminish the well-being of individuals and families and in its impact on the structure and health of neighborhoods and communities. Unlike other essentials of living, inadequate housing cannot be hidden. Poor housing is apparent to any observer, *blighting not only the individual, but the community as well.* [Emphasis added.] (1976: p. 154)

One of the policy lessons embedded in almost fifty years of experience with large-scale social intervention programs is that the effects of a program are seldom confined only to the intended beneficiaries. At the policy formulation stage, it is prudent to consider the short- and long-range effects of a proposed strategy, as well as the possible repercussions of the program through the entire complex social structure. Thus, in specifying housing policies for the elderly, the intended effect on the older recipients must be balanced with the (perhaps) unintended effect on the area of residential location—the neighborhood.

LOCATION OF THE ELDERLY

One can discuss the residential location patterns of older persons in several different, but complementary, ways. The geographic distribution of the older population can be most easily expressed as the proportion of all older persons living in a particular region, state, or metropolitan area. For this calculation, the base (or denominator) is the total number of persons sixty or sixty-five years of age and over residing in the United States. For the most part, the geographic distribution of the elderly follows the spatial distribution of the population as a whole (U.S. Congress 1977). Table 6-1 shows the correlation between the relative concentration of the total population and the relative concentration of the elderly at different levels of aggregation. For regions, divisions, states, and metropolitan areas, these correlations are extremely high and indicate that the best predictor of where the elderly live is where people of all ages reside.

The residential location of the elderly also can be measured in terms of the *relative* concentration of older persons in a particular area. In this calculation, the number of elderly is expressed as a proportion of the total population. The elderly are said to be overrepresented, or concentrated, in those areas where the proportion of persons sixty-five years of age and over exceeds the national average—9.8 percent in 1970 and 10.5 percent in 1975. For policymaking and planning, this measure has the advantage of indexing the extent to which political and administrative units confront the problems associated with an aging population.

In fairly populous regions and states, there are more older people than in sparsely settled areas. In 1975, the six largest states and Florida (ranked eighth in population size) contained approximately 45 percent of all older persons, those sixty-five years of age and over. The

Table 6–1. Correlation Coefficient between Proportionate Distribution of Total Population and Proportionate Distribution of Population 65 Years of Age and Older, by Geographic Areas: 1975

Place or Residence	*Correlation Coefficient*
Regions[a]	.98
Divisions[b]	.99
States[c]	.98
Metro–nonmetro[d]	.92

[a] As defined by the U.S. Bureau of the Census: Northeast, South, North Central, and West.

[b] As defined by the U.S. Bureau of the Census: New England, Middle Atlantic, South Atlantic, East South Central, West South Central, East North Central, West North Central, Mountain, Pacific.

[c] Includes the District of Columbia.

[d] Defined by Metropolitan Areas of 1 million or more (In Central City–Outside of Central City), less than 1 million (In Central City–Outside of Central City) and Nonmetropolitan (Counties with no places of 2,500 or more, Counties with a place 2,500 to 24,999, and Counties with a place of 25,000 or more).

Northeast accounted for 23.1 percent of all individuals and 24.6 percent of the elderly. The Western states, including both the most and least populous states (California and Alaska), were the home of 17.8 percent of the population and 16.1 percent of the elderly. In sheer numbers, there are more elderly in the South than in any other region (7,018,000 out of 21,721,000 in 1975), although California is the state with the largest absolute number of older persons. New York, Florida, Pennsylvania, and Texas are ranked second through fifth, respectively.

Data permitting the comparison of the relative concentration of older persons in regions, divisions, and states with the national average are shown in Table 6-2. In 1975, slightly more than one of every ten Americans was sixty-five years of age and older. By this standard, three of the four major census regions—the Northeast, the South, and the West—had relative concentrations of older persons equal to or exceeding the national average. Only in the West did the proportion of older persons in the region fall below 10.3 percent, the national average in 1975.

For the most part, regional trends are replicated by their divisional components. All divisions and states in the densely settled Northeast region have consistently high concentrations of older persons. In the South, two of the three divisions have "older age structures"; in the North Central region one in two divisions has high concentrations of elderly and in the West, the proportion of elderly in two of the three divisions is less than the national average.

Only in the Northeast do state patterns follow regional or divisional ones. Each of the nine states in the Northeast can aptly be described as "aging" states. States in the South or North Central regions have a moderate degree of consistency with regional patterns. Approximately one-half of the states in either the Southern or North Central regions have proportions of older persons equal to or in excess of the national or regional average. The Sun Belt state of Florida has the largest concentration of older persons in the country (16.0 percent in 1975), while two of the Western states, Alaska and Hawaii, have the lowest (2.6 and 7.0 percent, respectively). Only one state in the West—Oregon—has a moderately large concentration of older persons.

Mid-decade population estimates by age and race are unavailable at the state level. The relative concentration of older nonwhites is shown in Table 6-2 for regions and divisions. The proportion of elderly in the nonwhite population is considerably smaller than in the total population. Approximately one in fourteen nonwhites was age sixty-five or older in 1975 in contrast to one in ten in the total population. Only in the South do we find an overrepresentation of older nonwhites, who are predominantly black. The South predominates as a nonwhite aging

Table 6–2. Percentage of Population Sixty-Five Years of Age and over and Percentage of the Elderly Population below Poverty Level, by Region, Division, and State: Percentage of the Nonwhite Population Sixty-Five Years of Age and over, and Percentage of the Elderly Nonwhite Population below Poverty Level, by Region and Division: 1975

Location	*Percent of the Population 65+*	*Poverty Rate of Persons 65+*	*Percent Nonwhite 65+*	*Poverty Rate of Nonwhite Persons 65+*
Northeast	11.0 (48,779)[a]	9.3 (5,351)[a]	6.3 (4,471)[a]	27.1 (282)[c]
New England	10.9 (12,060)	8.4 (1,312)	4.3 (437)	27.8 (19)
Maine	11.5 (1,054)	14.7 (121)		
New Hampshire	10.3 (818)	9.9 (84)		
Vermont	10.4 (469)	15.3 (49)		
Massachusetts	11.0 (5,746)	5.9 (634)		
Rhode Island	12.0 (912)	13.6 (109)		
Connecticut	10.3 (3,062)	7.8 (314)		
Middle Atlantic	11.0 (36,718)	9.6 (4,039)	6.5 (4,035)	27.1 (263)
New York	10.9 (17,815)	9.1 (1,948)		
New Jersey	10.3 (7,240)	8.2 (749)		
Pennsylvania	11.5 (11,663)	11.1 (1,342)		
South	10.3 (67,864)	21.9 (7,018)	8.5 (12,761)	42.7 (1,089)
South Atlantic	10.6 (33,573)	17.9 (3,566)	7.8 (6,960)	38.1 (542)
Delaware	8.5 (575)	12.6 (49)		
Maryland	8.2 (4,055)	11.4 (332)		
District of Columbia	9.8 (693)	13.6 (68)		
Virginia	8.5 (4,907)	18.2 (416)		
West Virginia	11.7 (1,792)	19.4 (209)		
North Carolina	9.1 (5,369)	24.7 (488)		
South Carolina	8.2 (2,781)	26.8 (227)		

(continued)

Table 6–2. continued

Location	*Percent of the Population 65+*	*Poverty Rate of Persons 65+*	*Percent Nonwhite 65+*	*Poverty Rate of Nonwhite Persons 65+*
Georgia	8.6 (4,908)	31.9 (421)		
Florida	16.0 (8,493)	11.3 (1,356)		
East South Central	10.3 (13,459)	28.5 (1,411)	10.1 (2,763)	40.2 (278)
Kentucky	10.6 (3,372)	22.6 (359)		
Tennessee	10.4 (4,178)	26.0 (436)		
Alabama	10.3 (3,585)	31.6 (370)		
Mississippi	10.6 (2,325)	37.0 (246)		
West South Central	9.8 (20,832)	24.4 (2,042)	8.8 (3,038)	45.5 (268)
Arkansas	12.4 (2,126)	29.1 (264)		
Louisiana	9.0 (3,739)	29.3 (336)		
Oklahoma	12.0 (2,680)	22.1 (321)		
Texas	9.1 (12,287)	22.5 (1,121)		
North Central	10.3 (56,979)	11.6 (5,864)	6.0 (5,022)	19.9 (303)
East North Central	9.7 (40,505)	10.2 (3,921)	5.5 (4,206)	21.4 (232)
Ohio	9.7 (10,632)	11.3 (1,028)		
Indiana	9.7 (5,258)	11.0 (511)		
Illinois	10.1 (10,983)	10.2 (1,108)		
Michigan	8.7 (9,063)	9.0 (787)		
Wisconsin	10.7 (4,569)	8.6 (487)		
West North Central	11.8 (16,474)	14.4 (1,943)	8.7 (817)	15.2 (71)
Minnesota	10.6 (3,888)	12.8 (414)		
Iowa	12.1 (2,836)	12.6 (343)		
Missouri	12.4 (4,704)	16.9 (582)		
North Dakota	11.1 (621)	15.4 (69)		
South Dakota	12.1 (672)	17.1 (81)		

Table 6–2. concluded

Location	Percent of the Population 65+	Poverty Rate of Persons 65+	Percent Nonwhite 65+	Poverty Rate of Nonwhite Persons 65+
Nebraska	12.0 (1,527)	15.4 (183)		
Kansas	12.2 (2,227)	12.2 (271)		
West	9.3 (37,686)	9.6 (3,488)	6.2 (1,989)	18.4 (124)
Mountain	8.5 (9,733)	13.7 (828)	4.5 (223)	50.0 (10)
Montana	9.7 (745)	13.3 (72)		
Idaho	9.3 (828)	15.1 (77)		
Wyoming	8.5 (376)	13.2 (32)		
Colorado	7.8 (2,536)	14.1 (197)		
New Mexico	7.8 (1,152)	19.5 (90)		
Arizona	9.9 (2,274)	12.2 (225)		
Utah	7.3 (1,221)	13.3 (89)		
Nevada	7.5 (601)	7.3 (45)		
Pacific	9.5 (27,953)	8.3 (2,660)	6.5 (1,766)	16.0 (114)
Washington	10.0 (3,496)	9.8 (351)		
Oregon	11.0 (2,290)	11.4 (251)		
California	9.5 (20,981)	7.6 (1,990)		
Alaska	2.6 (345)	5.0 (9)		
Hawaii	7.0 (842)	9.7 (59)		
Total United States:	10.3 (211,308)	14.0 (21,721)	7.4 (24,243)	34.8 (1,798)

Source: U.S. Bureau of the Census. "Consumer Income." *Current Population Reports.* Series P-60, Nos. 110, 111, 112, 113. Washington, D.C.: U.S. Government Printing Office, 1978, Table C.

[a] Base numbers in thousands shown in parentheses.

region because of the out-migration of younger nonwhites from the area.[b]

Table 6-2 also shows the poverty rate for all older persons by regions, divisions, states and, for the older nonwhite population, by regions and divisions. In 1975, 14.0 percent of all elderly had incomes below the poverty level.[c] In twenty-two states, the poverty rate of the elderly exceeds the national average; a majority of these (thirteen) are in the South.

Locating a region or state with a large proportion of elderly does not necessarily mean we have located an area with a large concentration of poor elderly. The correlation between the proportion of the state population sixty-five years of age and over and the proportion of the elderly state population in poverty is merely .10. The proportion of older persons with poverty-level incomes exceeds the national average in approximately one-half the states in which the elderly are overrepresented. In the Southern states, however, older citizens have excessively high poverty rates. This is particularly true for the nonwhite older population in the South, where the poverty rate is 23 percent higher than the already disturbingly high national poverty rate of 34.8 percent. Because the poverty rate is adjusted for urban–rural differences in the cost of living across the country, the excessively high rates of poverty among the elderly living in the southern states suggests that the cost of housing is a particular problem for a large number of older persons in the Sun Belt.

Consideration of a single variable and its geographic distribution, of course, is insufficient to assess the variations in the condition or status of the older population by regions or states. Do the poor or ill-housed elderly cluster in some regions or states and not in others? Chevan and O'Rourke's study (1972) of the twenty selected characteristics of the elderly across 48 states is useful in answering this question.[d]

Statistical techniques were used to determine if traditional regional groupings of states were homogeneous with respect to characteristics of older residents. Six state groupings were identified by a *Q*-analysis, but only one had any resemblance to a regional identity. With the exception of Florida, Maryland, Delaware, and Oklahoma, states in the third Q group duplicated the list of states in the Southern region as

[b] There is some recent evidence that the out-migration of young blacks to the urbanized areas of the North is abating (Long and Hansen 1975; Long 1978).

[c] See Chapter 2 for a definition of the poverty level and its derivation.

[d] Alaska, Hawaii, and the District of Columbia were excluded in the analysis. Their exclusion may bias the results since twenty-one of forty extreme values (highest or lowest on twenty variables) were observed in the excluded states. Indicators of housing quality or housing costs were not included, unfortunately, among the twenty variables.

defined by the U.S. Bureau of the Census and shown in Table 6-2. From this part of their analysis, Chevan and O'Rourke conclude, "the criterion of geographic continuity does not afford a reasonable foundation for grouping the older population of the United States . . . the concept of regionality takes on a characteristic of fluidity not previously attributed to it when it is extended through time and when it is defined in social rather than in geographic terms" (1972: 122, 125).[e] Using 1970 Census data, Kart and Manard (1976) updated the study of Chevan and O'Rourke. The objectives and methodology in a later study (1974) closely approximated those found in the earlier one. The conclusions also were similar: "aging regions," or groupings of states with sociodemographic homogeneous older populations, do not necessarily coincide with regions of contiguous states.

There is little reason to recommend formulation or support of programs for the elderly on a regional basis. Differences within regional populations overshadow differences between the elderly living in contiguous states. This is not a serious challenge to most existing programs because few use regional concepts in planning or delivering services.[f] Information on the homogeneity of the elderly within different states is lacking for the most part. In analyzing variations in living arrangements of the elderly by state, however, Myers and Soldo (1976) found that interstate differences were significantly reduced after controls were introduced for the urban–rural composition of the state's population. While states have intrinsic political and administrative utility for planning purposes, they do not necessarily possess innate social meaning (Chevan and O'Rourke 1974). Diversity within state boundaries reflects not only urban–rural differences, but also differences in city sizes, types, function, and age.

Urban-Rural Differences

The vast majority of the American population is urbanized, as is the elderly segment within it. The percentage distribution of those sixty-five years of age and over, by place of residence, is shown in the first column of Table 6-3. Six of ten older Americans live in metropoli-

[e] In a similar study of large metropolitan areas using 1970 census data, Beckham and Kart (1977) find some evidence for regionality in the ways in which cities cluster in a *Q*-analysis. They conclude, however, that "regionality may be less viable as an organizing principle than the ad hoc groupings of cities which emerged through the use of the factor-analytic scheme . . ." p. 240. The five factors that emerged were described as demographic, social-class, mobility-education, living arrangements, and ethnicity factors.

[f] An exception to this is the Administration on Aging (AoA), which coordinates activities in ten service regions. These regions, although comprising contiguous states, do not coincide with regions designated by the U.S. Bureau of the Census.

Table 6–3. Percentage of Total Population Sixty-Five Years of Age and Over, by Type of Residence: 1977

Type of Residence, by Population Size	*Percentage Distribution of the Population 65+*	*Percent 65+ in Total Population*
Metropolitan	62.7	9.7
In central cities	31.0	11.4
Of 1 million or more	17.0	11.8
Of less than 1 million	13.9	10.9
Outside central cities	31.7	8.4
Of 1 million or more	19.6	8.6
Of less than 1 million	12.1	8.2
Nonmetropolitan	37.3	11.9
Counties with place of 25,000+	4.6	11.4
Counties with place 2,500–24,999	23.7	12.1
Counties with no place of 2,500+	9.0	11.8
Total	100.0% (22,100)[a]	10.4% (212,566)

Source: U.S. Bureau of the Census. "Social and Economic Characteristics of the Metropolitan and Nonmetropolitan Population: 1977 and 1970." Current Population Reports. Series P-23, No. 75. Washington, D.C.: U.S. Government Printing Office, 1978, Table 1.

[a] Base numbers in parentheses in thousands.

tan areas; nearly 50 percent live in the central city, or core of the metropolitan area. The majority of the elderly living in nonmetropolitan areas lives in small towns, places with a population between 2,500 and 25,000.

The percentage of older persons in the population, by type of residence and size of place, is shown in the second column of Table 6-3. Older persons are overrepresented in the central cities of metropolitan areas and in rural places, particularly in small towns.

"Gray ghettos" exist in relatively new cities as well as in older cities, in the South as well as in the North. Gray ghettos are not a recent phenomenon. Large proportions of the elderly were noted in large central cities, such as Chicago, as early as 1910 (Newcomb 1951). Since that time a number of studies have examined patterns of age segregation in city centers. Using 1950 census data, Cowgill (1958) found high concentrations of the elderly near the center of almost all of the 57 cities he studied. Kennedy and DeJong (1977) used the dissimilarity index (Taeuber and Taeuber 1965) to measure and map trends in age segregation between 1960 and 1970. They found increases in the level of age segregation in only five of the ten cities they analyzed. Unlike earlier studies, Cowgill (1978) analyzed spatial patterns of age segregation between 1940 and 1970, using the entire metropolitan area, rather than the central cities only. In 1970, 241 metropolitan areas were analyzed and most showed moderately high levels of segregation by age. The degree to which the elderly were isolated in certain areas increased. Residential segregation of the elderly was found in cities that were growing rapidly, and had low proportions of elderly and increasing nonwhite populations.

Students of urban development patterns explain the more or less universal phenomenon of residential age segregation in terms of spatial differentiation and specialization processes. As communities grow, areas within them become differentiated by residential function, specializing in housing appropriate to different states in the family life cycle.[g] Cowgill notes further:

> Old people are concentrated toward the center of cities largely because they moved there years ago and have been "aging in place" (Golant 1972) while their children and other young families have gravitated toward the suburbs. Cities grow centrifugally and young families are on the growing edges while older persons stay behind in shrinking households and aging housing structures. (1978: 447)

A similar pattern of "inertia and attrition" explains the overconcentration of the elderly in small rural communities. Until recently, the population in rural areas was depleted continually by significant rates of out-migration.[h] Most of those leaving were the young, who sought better educational and employment opportunities in metropolitan areas; the older parents of the out-migrants were left behind. Cowgill (1970) speculates that older farmers may use nearby rural, but nonfarm communities, as a kind of "retirement center," thereby incrementing the proportion of elderly already living in such small towns.

Urban elderly differ in some major ways from those of comparable age living in nonmetropolitan areas. As noted in Chapter 2, older persons in rural areas have higher rates of poverty and lower incomes than their urban counterparts. As shown in Chapter 3, the rural elderly, particularly those in farm areas, are significantly less well housed than the urban elderly.

The housing stock in rural areas also is quite different from that found in urban areas. These differences are summarized in Table 6-4. The number of units in the urban housing stock is, of course, greater,

[g] This is essentially the theoretical argument underlying even the earliest work in "social area" analysis, including the works of Shevky and Williams (1949), Bell (1953, 1955, 1959), and Schmid (1950) and more recent studies by Golant (1972).

[h] Between 1970 and 1976, the population in nonmetropolitan areas grew at a faster rate than did metropolitan areas. Rural areas gained over 2 million migrants during the first six years of the decade (U.S. Department of Agriculture 1978).

Table 6–4. Characteristics of the Housing Stock, by Occupancy and Urban versus Rural Location: 1976

Location	*Owner-Occupied*				*Renter-Occupied*			
	No. Single Family Units	*No. of Multi Units*	*% Built[a] before 1939*	*Median No. of Rooms*	*No. Single-Family Units*	*No. of Multi Units*	*% Built[a] before 1939*	*Median No. of Rooms*
Urban	26,625	4,030	29.4 (31,615)[b]	5.8	4,274	17,002	42.0 (21,459)[b]	3.9
Inside SMSA	21,091	3,726	27.9 (25,608)	5.8	3,010	15,020	41.0 (18,149)	3.9
Outside SMSA	5,533	303	35.6 (6,007)	5.7	1,264	1,983	50.8 (3,101)	4.0
Rural	13,851	412	27.5 (16,289)	5.6	2,968	1,216	45.1 (4,642)	4.5
Farm	2,064	20	52.9 (2,193)	6.1	439	19	65.0 (477)	5.5
Nonfarm	11,787	392	23.6 (14,097)	5.5	2,529	1,197	42.9 (4,165)	4.4
U.S. Total	40,476	4,441	28.8 (47,904)	5.7	7,242	18,219	42.6 (26,101)	4.0

Source: U.S. Bureau of the Census. Annual Housing Survey: 1976. Volume E. Washington, D.C.: U.S. Government Printing Office, 1978, Table A1.

[a] Includes units vacant and seasonally occupied.

[b] Base numbers in parentheses, in thousands.

Table 6–5. Percentage of Housing Units Occupied by Person(s) Sixty-Five Years of Age and over, by Tenure and Place of Residence: 1976

	Units Occupied by Person(s) 65 and Over	
Place of Residence	*Owner-Occupied*	*Renter-Occupied*
Urban	25.2	18.4
Inside SMSAs	24.1	18.0
	(25,608)[a]	(18,149)
Outside SMSAs	30.2	20.3
	(6,007)	(3,310)
Rural		
Farm	31.6	16.6
	(2,193)	(477)
Nonfarm	23.5	16.5
	(14,097)	(4,165)
U.S. Total	25.0	15.6
	(47,904)	(26,101)

Source: U.S. Bureau of the Census. Annual Housing Survey: 1976. H-150-76, Volume, E, Washington, D.C.: U.S. Government Printing Office, 1977, Table A1.

[a] Base numbers in parentheses, in thousands.

and multiple-family units account for a much larger part of the total housing inventory in urban areas than in rural areas. Even the renter-occupied units in rural areas are more likely to be single-family units than multiple-family ones. In general, rural housing units, renter- or owner-occupied, are larger and older than dwelling units in urban areas.

The elderly's share of the housing stock by place of residence is shown in Table 6-5. Urban–rural differences are again evident. The elderly account for approximately 10 percent of the population nationally; they own one-quarter of all owner-occupied units. In rural farm areas, however, where the elderly represent 12 percent of the population, they own almost one-third of the housing stock.[i]

Similarities and differences among the rural elderly have not been analyzed systematically. It is reasonable, however, to speculate that the composition of the rural elderly population varies depending on proximity to a large metropolitan area, the dominance of farming in the community occupational structure, and the type of farming.

[i] Per capita federal housing expenditures in nonmetropolitan areas are significantly lower than in metropolitan areas. In the two areas where elderly are overrepresented, the per capita housing expenditure (in 1976) in central cities was $104 compared to $55 in small nonfarm areas. These data suggest that rural elderly whose housing is inadequate are not as likely as their counterparts in the core of metropolitan areas to receive housing assistance.

The homogeneity of urban elderly has been investigated in at least one previous study. Using techniques of multivariate analysis, Beckham and Kart (1977) analyzed 1970 Census data on the older population in thirty-three metropolitan areas with populations of one million or more. Seven Q groups were identified. Cities in the first group had a decidedly Southern orientation, although no other group of cities exhibited strong regional tendencies. Similarities in the racial composition of the elderly populations accounted for the clusterings of cities in the Southern group. Other groupings reflected similarities in social class variables, patterns of living arrangements, and the mobility or educational characteristics of the elderly. Although the elderly in large cities have a number of similarities, one cannot conclude that the elderly population is distributed in a homogenous fashion, even among large metropolitan areas.

These findings have significant implications for those charged with planning and formulating policies for the elderly. As the Beckham and Kart study advises:

> Clearly a program which is effective in one city or group of cities may be unsuccessful in other locations simply because the target populations differ. We urge that the general awareness of the differences among the elderly be supplemented explicitly by an awareness of how these differences are spatially manifested. (1977: 241)

Although the urban elderly and their housing differ significantly from the elderly in rural areas, the elderly in either setting are a heterogeneous group. Policy initiatives need to be targeted with more specificity than a simple urban–rural distinction allows. Low-income elderly homeowners in rural areas, for example, are likely to have general housing problems common to all persons with limited financial means (maintenance costs, for example) but may have housing problems distinct from those of their urban counterparts. In rural settings, housing problems often must be solved in the context of limited access to service centers, seasonal availability of construction workers and repair personnel, and larger home sites. Chapter 9 describes several new policy initiative for rural elderly that take into consideration these factors and the diversity of the elderly in rural areas.

PERSISTENCE OF LOCATION

Most older persons age in place. In 1973, one-third of those sixty years or older had lived in their present residence twenty years or more. Those living in nonmetropolitan areas are even more likely to age in

Table 6–6. General Mobility Rates per 1,000 Population for the Elderly Population, by Sex: 1975–1976

	Persons 65 Years of Age and Over		
Type of Move	*Both Sexes*	*Males*	*Females*
Interstate	9	10	9
Contiguous	2	2	2
Noncontiguous	7	7	6
Intrastate	47	45	48
Same county	35	33	37
Different county	11	12	11
From Abroad	57	56	58
	(21,662)[a]	(8,913)	(12,749)

Source: U.S. Bureau of the Census. "Geographical Mobility: March 1975–1976." Current Population Reports. Series P-20, No. 305. Washington, D.C.: U.S. Government Printing Office, 1977, Table 33.

[a] Base numbers in parentheses, in thousands.

place. Two of three farm families headed by an older person have maintained their current dwelling unit at least twenty years.

The older population is not completely sedentary, however. In one year time period (1975–1976), approximately 5 percent of those sixty-five years of age and over changed their place of residence. Most of the elderly (75 percent) who do undertake a move, relocate within the same area.[j] Approximately 12 percent of all elderly movers moved between metropolitan areas; four percent relocated from a nonmetropolitan area to an urban one, and an additional 8.5 percent move from metropolitan areas to rural locations. General mobility and metropolitan mobility rates for the older population are shown in Tables 6-6 and 6-7, respectively.

Older renters are more likely to move than older homeowners. Two-thirds of the households headed by an older person relocating between 1975 and 1976 rented their home prior to moving. For the most part, those elderly who do move are tenure-persistent. Eighty percent of premove homeowners continued to be homeowners after their move; three-quarters of premove renters also rented their new accommodations. Only one-fifth of all elderly-headed households changed their tenure status by moving.

Most older persons do not report housing related reasons as motivating their move. Data from Long and Hansen (1979) on the reason for

[j] This is not surprising since most persons searching for a new house or apartment conduct their search within a very limited geographical area, typically in the area they know (Goodman 1978).

Table 6–7. Metropolitan Mobility Rates per 1,000 Population, by Age, Race, and Type of Move: 1975–1976

	Persons Less than 65 Years of Age	*Persons 65 years of Age and Over*		
Type of Move	*All Races*	*All Races*	*White*	*Black*
Within same SMSAs	90	26	25	28
Between SMSAs	23	7	7	4
From outside to SMSAs	11	2	2	4
From SMSAs to outside	13	5	5	6
Outside SMSAs	48	16	16	17
From abroad	6	1	1	1
Total	191 (186,407)[a]	57 (21,662)	56 (19,654)	61 (1,795)

Source: U.S. Bureau of the Census. "Geographical Mobility: March 1975 to March 1976." Current Population Reports. Series P-20, No. 305. Washington, D.C.: U.S. Government Printing Office, 1977, Table 24.

[a] Base numbers in parentheses, in thousands.

moving by age and sex are shown in Table 6-8. Households headed by an older person (here defined as those fifty-five years of age and over) are more likely to move for family- or climate-related reasons than are households headed by younger adults. In Table 6-8, the category "all other reasons" includes households that moved because of dissatisfaction with their previous neighborhood, displacement by public or private acts, and the need for better or less expensive housing. Goodman (1978), using the same data (the Annual Housing Survey) from an earlier date (1973) tabulated reasons for within-metropolitan area mobility only. Among older metropolitan movers, 17 percent sought better housing, 9 percent moved because of neighborhood reasons, and another 9 percent moved to secure less expensive housing. Although comparable data are not available for nonmetropolitan mobility or mobility between urban and rural settings, such moves may be less motivated by housing needs since suitable alternatives are not as likely to be found in rural settings and those who do undertake within-rural area moves do so for other reasons. It is important to note that neither the volume of, nor reasons for, geographic mobility can be interpreted as indexing the number of older persons who would like to change location. The ability to move is largely dependent on financial resources and those who do move are a self-selected group, nonrepresentative of the elderly in general.

Of primary interest is the extent to which older persons who move secure better housing as a result of the move. For the total population, a change in residence typically involves a change and upgrading in

Table 6–8. Reasons for Moving, as Reported by Household Heads Who Moved between States in the Twelve Months Preceding the 1974, 1975, and 1976 Annual Housing Surveys, by Age and Sex

	Both Sexes			*Male*			*Female*		
Reasons for Moving— Total Heads and Workers	*20–34 years old*	*35–54 years old*	*55 and over*	*20–34 years old*	*35–54 years old*	*55 and over*	*20–34 years old*	*35–54 years old*	*55 and over*
All Heads	3,371	1,557	733	2,797	1,339	502	574	218	231
Reasons for moving									
Job transfer	25.4%	30.9%	6.0%	28.9%	34.0%	8.2%	8.2%	11.9%	1.3%
New job or looking for work	28.3	23.2	4.9	29.5	25.0	6.4	22.6	11.9	1.7
Other employment reason	2.0	3.1	2.6	2.1	3.4	3.2	1.4	1.4	0.9
Enter or leave Armed Forces	6.3	2.6	...	7.4	2.9	...	1.0	0.5	...
Attend school	7.5	1.2	0.4	7.1	1.0	0.6	9.6	2.3	...
Wanted change of climate	3.2	5.8	12.1	2.9	6.0	14.1	4.5	4.6	7.8
Retirement	0.0	3.3	19.8	0.0	3.2	25.7	...	3.7	6.9
To be closer to relatives	5.2	5.8	22.2	3.9	5.2	12.7	11.1	9.6	42.9
Other family reason	8.2	9.4	11.2	6.1	6.6	8.0	24.0	29.4	19.0
All other reasons	11.2	11.6	17.3	10.3	10.5	17.3	16.0	17.4	16.9
Not reported	1.7	2.6	3.3	1.8	2.0	3.6	1.2	6.0	2.6

Source: Long, L.H. and Hansen, K.A., "Reasons for Interstate Migration: Jobs, Retirement, Climate, and Other Influences," Current Population Reports. Series P-23, No. 81. Washington, D.C.: U.S. Government Printing Office, 1979, Table 2.

housing quality. Only 3 percent of those households moving during the period 1975–1976, and lacking plumbing prior to the move, failed to acquire this basic amenity in the process of moving. Nonmetropolitan moves, however, are less likely to result in improved housing than moves undertaken within metropolitan areas.

Struyk's analysis (1979) of pre- and postmove housing conditions of urban households headed by the elderly suggests that the net change in housing quality is quite small. Approximately four of five units occupied by older movers had no structural deficiency either before or after the relocation. About one-third of the households which, prior to moving, lived in substandard units improved their housing conditions by relocating. Almost an equal number of households, however, moved from standard to substandard units. As a result, the aggregate change in housing conditions was insignificant.

In summary, older persons do not relocate frequently. Geographic mobility is not a major force redistributing older persons. If one views housing as the means to an end—better quality of life—and not an end in itself, this finding has both positive and negative implications for housing policy. Generally low incomes and the persistence of older persons in the same dwelling units may account, in part, for the failure of older persons to identify major structural flaws and correct them. If a successful inexpensive solution to the problem can be found (like buckets to catch rain seeping in through a leaky roof), the structural flaw may no longer be perceived as an obstacle.

Dwelling units provide more than simply "shelter." Particularly for the very old, the household is the basis for social activity. Meeting one's nonhousing needs is predicated to a large extent on location. Older persons who have spent a good part of their adult lives in a particular neighborhood have access to a number of formal and informal support networks (Field 1972). Patterns of shopping, visiting, and mutual assistance are unique to each residential setting.

It is impossible to speculate on the trade-offs between housing quality and environmental stability as perceived by an older person.[k] Mathieu summarizes the quandry faced by social planners:

> Removal from these neighborhoods [of long-standing residence] is fraught with personal, social and cultural problems. Even if their housing is

[k] It would be misleading to interpret the relative value assigned to either housing quality or residential stability from existing data. Existing data refer to utilization, not need. Poorly housed older persons of long standing in the community are likely to be financially constrained. If the cost of better housing could be easily absorbed, residential stability might be downgraded in value. In such instances, the income to purchase needed services might be viewed as compensation for the loss of informally organized helping networks.

> substandard, it is nevertheless situated in an area of long-standing associations, familiarity and sometimes richness of resources, the values of which are attractive to the elderly. If the elderly must be relocated, the psychological cost must not be disregarded (1976: 162).

It is clear that improved housing has a significant and positive impact on the lives of poorly housed older persons (Carp 1977). The condition of the neighborhood also has been shown to be positively related to the morale (or life satisfaction) of older persons in a metropolitan area (Berghorn et al. 1978). Ideally, housing assistance programs for the elderly should not pit improved housing against residential stability. In the next section we consider the neighborhood as an appropriate arena for program strategies that seek to improve the housing situation of the elderly within familiar community settings.

OLDER NEIGHBORHOODS AND OLDER PERSONS

Considering the residential location of older persons as measured by large geographic units—regions, states, metropolitan areas—it is clear that the elderly are not distributed randomly across geographic units. In absolute numbers, the elderly are concentrated in areas having high population density; in relative numbers, the elderly are disproportionately concentrated in small rural towns and in the central cities of large metropolitan areas. This type of information is useful to those charged with planning for the elderly since it identifies the location of the "target population" in units having political or administrative meaning.

While a neighborhood lacks the clarity of geographic boundaries that characterize a state or city, it is perhaps the most meaningful unit of analysis from the perspective of the older person (Berghorn et al. 1978; Mathieu 1976).

Importance of the Neighborhood

Until fairly recently, housing for older persons was seen from a "mortar and bricks" perspective; the structural quality of the dwelling unit itself was the limited focus of urban planning efforts and federal housing policy. The relative simplicity of commonly accepted measures of housing adequacy such as the lack of complete plumbing facilities reflected this orientation. Indeed, this was the framework used in the previous analyses.

Contact among housing experts, psychologists, and sociologists in gerontological studies, however, has resulted in a rethinking and broadening of housing concepts as they pertain to older persons. The "mortar and bricks" perspective has been augmented by the addition of two new, interrelated concepts. The first concept, variously described as "goodness of fit" (Mathieu 1976) or "person-environment congruence" (Carp 1976), evaluates housing adequacy with reference to the capabilities, preferences, and limitations of the older occupants. Grounded in a transactional orientation, the goodness-of-fit principle introduces characteristics of older persons into the equation predicting housing adequacy: a third-floor dwelling unit in a building lacking an elevator may be evaluated as structurally sound, but for an older woman whose mobility is severely compromised by arthritis, the same unit may be "inadequate."

The goodness-of-fit concept also draws attention to the fact that there is no single ideal housing unit or plan appropriate for all older persons. The cultural, psychological, and functional diversity in the older population suggests that "adequate" housing can assume many forms: a well-designed high rise apartment building for older persons is not likely to be viewed as an ideal arrangement by an elderly couple retired from farming. Similarly, the distance of the hypothetical high rise from the home of a married daughter may undermine the idealness of the building for an older widow.

The goodness of fit between housing needs and housing characteristics is not static; housing needs and preferences change over the course of the life cycle. As families expand and contract with the entry and subsequent exit of children from the household, space requirements change. At the older ages, housing needs and preferences evolve still further as health declines, relatives move, or neighborhoods change.

The second concept, which broadens the meaning of housing, replaces the idea of physical space with one of social space. By virtue of their location, housing units serve more than the simple need for shelter. For persons of all ages, proximity to stores, recreational facilities, churches, and neighbors is predicated on residential location. For older persons, location vis-à-vis various facilities, including both commercial and service types, and relatives and friends assumes even greater importance. Hansen (1971) estimates that older persons spend 80 to 90 percent of their time in the immediate home environment. As job involvement ceases, work contacts dwindle, and physical and financial resources decline, the physical and social space occupied by older persons tends to contract. Montgomery (1972) suggests that the physical space occupied by older individuals is often circumscribed by the neighborhood grocery store, church, and dwelling unit. Exclusive reliance on public transportation may also reduce the distance traveled regularly by older persons in pursuit of food, clothing, social contacts, or needed services. For many older persons the immediate neighborhood is their world, particularly for those with long-standing residence in the neighborhood or limited access to transportation (Golant 1976).

In addition to location, other contextual factors affect the housing environment of older individuals. At the minimum, an adequate residential environment is one that allows for the safe conduct of accustomed social roles and activities. Carp (1976) lists as one of the main elements determining housing satisfaction "congeniality or threat in the surrounding environment." Threats to perceived safety can originate from physical aspects of the environment, such as unrepaired streets, poorly lit walkways, trash or rats, or from other individuals sharing the same environment (Havighurst 1969; Rainwater 1972). Because of functional limitations, older people may be particularly susceptible to the latter type of threat, including assaults, robberies, or verbal hostilities from neighbors. The importance of residential safety is highlighted by Rainwater's finding (1972) that poorly housed persons will express satisfaction with their dwelling *if* the unit affords security from the "most blatant threats." Only 3 percent of elderly homeowners and 4 percent of elderly renters who reported their neighborhoods had undesirable street conditions in the 1973 Annual Housing Survey also reported that they wanted to move.

Recognition of the importance of personal and environmental characteristics has clearly expanded the concept of housing. The adequacy of a dwelling unit is dependent upon not only the structural characteristics of the unit, but also how well those characteristics correspond to the needs and preferences of the inhabitant and the residential location of the unit. All three are important components of housing satisfaction, that is, adequacy as perceived by the inhabitant. Structural, personal, and environmental characteristics may be viewed as a tripod supporting housing satisfaction. The stability of this stand depends on all three legs and each may be adjusted to compensate for deficiencies in the other two. The stand will topple only if problems in one of the legs require adjustments in the other two that exceed their compensating capacity.

Perceived Satisfaction with Neighborhood

In Chapter 3 the satisfaction of most older persons with their neighborhood as a place in which to live was documented. Eighty-six percent of elderly homeowners and 75 percent of elderly renters evaluated the overall condition of their neighborhood as being either good or excellent, although a considerable number of older persons identified specific neighborhood problems.[1] The rural elderly, in general, have a more favorable impression of their neighborhood setting than do those who live in urban areas, and fewer rural elderly expressed interest in moving from their present location.

Data from a comprehensive survey of older persons in Rhode Island show that the elderly's evaluation of their neighborhood is fairly constant across age, sex, and income groups, although differences by race are significant (Rhode Island Department of Elderly Affairs 1978). Income differences became important when the elderly respondents in the Rhode Island survey were asked to assess their neighborhoods as a place for older persons to live. The median income of individuals who thought their neighborhood was a poor place to live was almost $1,000 lower than those who recommended their neighborhood as a good place for elderly persons. The authors of the Rhode Island report conclude that "median income level is indicative of overall neighborhood quality. It would appear that areas of concentrated low incomes are frequently characterized by physical and social attributes of a poor neighborhood" (1978: II-35).

Analysis Plans

In order to examine the "living environment" of older persons, let us focus on the neighborhood location of the elderly. If we identify neighborhoods with large concentrations of older persons and compare the characteristics of these neighborhoods with those of neighborhoods having younger age structures, we can develop a statistical profile of neighborhoods in which the elderly are disproportionately represented. Not surprisingly, the profile that emerges suggests that "older" neighborhoods tend to be those plagued by a mixture of social and housing problems. This initial finding suggests that improving the housing of older persons, either by relocation within the same neighborhood or by repair of single dwelling units, will not result in a qualitative improvement in the living environment of older persons. But to improve the overall environment upgrading individual housing *is* required.

In order to test the hypothesis of homogeneity of older neighborhoods with respect to housing characteristics, multiple discriminant techniques were applied to the data. The results from this multivariate

[1] Most respondents in a survey of the elderly in Kansas City also favorably evaluated neighborhood quality. Only 11 percent of the survey respondents rated their local environment as very poor in terms of both safety and attractiveness. Not surprisingly, persons in the latter group resided primarily in inner city neighborhoods that would be characterized as transitional, unstable, or even blighted (Berghorn et al. 1978: 117).

analysis show that older neighborhoods are quite distinct in terms of their housing characteristics.

The Data

Data for the neighborhood analyses are drawn from the Public Use Sample of Basic Records from the 1970 census.[m] The sample is a nationally representative microdata file containing household and individual information for approximately one-in-every-hundred sample units, i.e. households, vacant units, or individuals in group quarters (U.S. Bureau of the Census 1972, Public Use Samples). In order to protect the confidentiality of the respondents, no names, addresses, or detailed geographic information appear in the file. The 1970 files allow for three different levels of geographic specification: states, county groups, or neighborhoods.

The Neighborhood Characteristics File contains information not only on sampled households and individuals, but also on the area in which the household is located. "Neighborhood" is obviously an ambiguous concept. Even individuals living in the same area will disagree as to where "the neighborhood" begins and ends. The concept of neighborhood was introduced into the terminology of the Bureau of the Census with the 1970 census and was made operational using computer-generated geocodes. Neighborhoods were not designated with reference to maps, nor was socioeconomic or demographic homogeneity necessarily a criterion for grouping smaller units (blocks or enumeration districts) into neighborhoods; moreover it is not possible to distinguish between urban and rural neighborhoods. For the most part neighborhoods do not coincide with census tracts or other minor civil divisions for which data are published. Census-defined neighborhoods do not cross county lines.[n]

In general, only contiguous areas were grouped together to form neighborhoods. Despite this, neighborhoods "may straddle a meaningful social boundary such as an urban freeway" (U.S. Bureau of the Census, 1972, Supplement No. 1). Neighborhoods also tend to be relatively compact areas, with the average population size in the range of 4,000 to 5,000 people.

The definition of neighborhood employed by Bureau of the Census is not, perhaps, an ideal one. Because areal units were grounded into

[m] For a general description of the data base consult U.S. Bureau of the Census (1972). Additional technical information for the Neighborhood Characteristics File is contained in Supplement 1 to this document and supercedes it.

[n] Technical documentation of the Neighborhood Characteristics File indicates that in rare instances of adjacent counties with "extremely low population density" county lines may be crossed.

neighborhoods without reference to social boundaries and do not necessarily reflect a consensus of residents' perceptions, a desirable dimension of social space or territory is not operationalized completely. Despite these limitations, the Neighborhood Characteristics File is adequate for our present purposes. Because data are available on a large number of neighborhoods (42,950), random biases in boundary designation are likely to be cancelled out. The richness of descriptive detail on the neighborhood also recommends the use of the 1970 Neighborhood Characteristics File in the following analyses. Problems in the data base are sufficient to warrant caution in interpretation, but not the complete dismissal of the data base.

The data descriptive of neighborhoods are ecological variables—that is, data gathered at the level of a geographic unit. Additional caution, therefore, must be used in interpreting findings lest one lapse into the "ecological fallacy" (Robinson 1950). Data pertaining to one level of analysis cannot be used correctly to describe relations operating at a lower level. It would be incorrect, for example, to surmise the relation between age and the probability of homeownership from the correlation between the proportion of neighborhood residents sixty-five years of age and over and the proportion of homeowners in the neighborhood. Ecological data are used appropriately to describe only characteristics of the geographic area (however defined) and not the individuals residing in the area under study (Langbein and Lichtman 1978).

Older Neighborhoods

The chronological age of an individual has obvious and immediate meaning. A person's age is simply the number of years elapsed since birth; the "age" of a geographic unit is a somewhat more obtuse concept. The "age" of a geographic unit is measured with reference to the area's age structure.[0] Areas with relatively high proportions of persons sixty-five years of age and over are considered "aged"; areas with low proportions of older persons are considered "young" (Coale 1964). (At the time of the 1970–1971 censuses, the German Democratic Republic, with 15.6 percent of its population sixty-five years of age and over, was the "oldest" country in the world. The United States, was slightly less than 10 percent of its population in the older age groups also was

[0] The age structure of a population is simply the distribution of members of the population by age. Frequently the age structure of a population is displayed graphically as a population pyramid. The proportion of the population in each age group (usually five-year intervals) is calculated and each proportion is represented by a horizontal bar graph. Stacked one on top of another, the sequence of bar graphs resemble a pyramid. "Young" age structures are broad at the base, indicating large proportions of children; "old" age structures have population pyramids that are top-heavy or resemble hourglasses.

considered to be an "aged" country. The youngest country was Mali, in which only 1.6 percent of the people were elderly. In a worldwide sample of 81 countries, the median concentration of older persons was 5.0 percent.)[p]

The 1970 Public Use Sample Neighborhood Characteristics File contains data descriptive of 42,950 neighborhoods. In this sample, the percentage of elderly in the population of a neighborhood ranges from 0 (199 neighborhoods) to 87 percent (one neighborhood). The mean percent of older persons in a neighborhood is 10.05; the median, 9.48. Seventy-five percent of the neighborhoods contain less than 13 percent elderly. The distribution is obviously skewed to the lower end of the scale. On the basis of the percentage of elderly in a neighborhood population, the age structure of each area is classified into one of four categories: (1) neighborhoods in which the elderly accounted for more than 14 percent of the local population are considered "aged"; (2) neighborhoods with "mature" age structures are those having between 10 and 13 percent elderly in their total population; (3) those areas with 7 to 9 percent elderly are labeled "adolescent"; and (4) "young" neighborhoods are defined as those containing less than 7 percent elderly. The cut-off points were chosen to create categories of approximately equal size. (See Table 6-9.)

Table 6–9. Classification of Neighborhoods by Age Structure

Type of Neighborhood	*Number of Neighborhoods*	*% of Sample*
Aged	9,522	22.2
Mature	11,893	27.7
Adolescent	9,811	22.8
Young	11,724	27.3
Total	42,950	100.0

CHARACTERISTICS OF NEIGHBORHOODS

The immediate housing environment, broadly defined, is shaped both by people (neighbors) and the pervasive housing conditions of the neighborhood. The Neighborhood Characteristics File contains

[p] Various typologies exist for classifying the age structure of countries. The United Nations considers countries "aged" if more than 7 percent of the population is sixty-five and over, "mature" if the percent of elderly is between 4 and 7 and "young" if the percent is less than 4. Cowgill (1970), citing problems with the size of the open-ended "aged" category, has suggested modifications in the UN typology. He expands the typology into four categories—"young" (under 4 percent), "adolescent" (4–7 percent), "mature (7–10 percent), and "aged" (over 10 percent). Thus between 1970 and 1975, the United States evolved from a mature to an aged nation.

data descriptive of both aspects of the residential environment. Population-based characteristics index the demographic, social, and economic composition of the neighborhood population; housing characteristics summarize the quality of the dwelling units in the local area. Of particular interest to this study is the extent to which housing in "old neighborhoods" is different.

In Table 6-10 the ecological variables used in the analysis are defined. With few exceptions (for example, the average number of persons per household), each of these variables was originally computed as a ratio with a range of .00 to .99.[q] To facilitate interpretation, each ratio was read and analyzed as a percentage.

Table 6-11 shows the mean value for each variable by type of neighborhood age structure. Column 1 in Table 6-11 shows the grand mean—the average value of the variable across all types of neighborhoods. The means within types of neighborhoods, shown in columns 2–5, can be regarded as deviations from the overall grand mean. Because of the large sample size, even very small mean differences are statistically significant. Hence, standard statistical tests for evaluating differences between samples are of little use in guiding the interpretation of the results.

Population Characteristics

For the most part, differences between neighborhoods with a relatively high concentration of elderly and neighborhoods with younger age structures are in the expected direction. As shown in the first panel of Table 6-11, the population of old neighborhoods contain proportionately fewer minors but more individuals living alone than other types of neighborhoods.[r] Whereas only one in ten individuals living in neighborhoods with a "young" age structure head a nonfamily household, approximately one of every three individuals in "old neighborhoods" lives alone or as a nonrelative. The increased concentration of primary individuals (most of whom live alone) in "old neighborhoods," also is reflected in the relatively low person-per-household ratio in such neighborhoods. The older the age structure of an area, the smaller the average household size. This pattern is caused, in part, by the high proportion of elderly persons living either alone or with a spouse only.

[q] Ratios of 1.00 were coded as 0.99 on the file prepared by the U.S. Bureau of the Census.

[r] Note that the percentage of individuals aged zero to seventeen decreases in a linear fashion as the proportion of elderly increases. Although this trend is intuitively reasonable, it illustrates the demographic fact that most areas, whether countries or neighborhoods, age because of a narrowing at the base of the population pyramid. In general, the proportion of middle-aged persons is relatively constant in a population. Populations become "young" or "aged" because of a trade-off in the relative concentration of older persons vis-à-vis children and adolescents.

Table 6–10. Ecological Variables Used in the Analysis of Aging Neighborhoods

I. Population	
A. General Population Characteristics	
% 0–17	Percentage of the total neighborhood population *less than* eighteen years of age.
AV PER/HH	Average number of persons per neighborhood household.
% PRIMARY IND	Percentage of the total neighborhood population enumerated as primary individuals; i.e., heads of nonfamily households living alone or with nonrelatives.
% GROUP QUARTERS	Percentage of the total neighborhood population living in group quarters.
B. Family and Fertility Characteristics	
% FEMALE HD	Percentage of the total neighborhood families headed by a female.
% H-W FAMILIES	Percentage of those zero to seventeen years of age in the neighborhood who reside in husband-wife families.
% DIVORCED	Percentage separated or divorced in the total ever-married neighborhood population.
CEB	The number of children ever born to ever married females thirty-five to fourty-four years of age in the neighborhood.
C. Ethnic-Racial Composition	
% BLACK	Percentage of the total neighborhood population that is black.
% SPANISH	Percentage of the total neighborhood that is of Spanish heritage. In New York, New Jersey, and Pennsylvania "Spanish heritage" refers to those of Puerto Rican birth or heritage; in Texas, Colorado, New Mexico, Arizona and California, "Spanish heritage" includes those of Spanish language or Spanish surname. In all other states, people speaking Spanish are identified as being of "Spanish heritage."
% Foreign	Percentage of the total neighborhood population that is either foreign born or of foreign or mixed parentage.
D. Educational Characteristics	
% Incomplete	Percentage of the neighborhood population sixteen to twenty-one years of age who are not in school and are not HS grads.
% 16–21	Percentage of the total neighborhood population sixteen to twenty-one years of age.
% IN COLLEGE	Ratio of the number of neighborhood residents three to thirty-four years of age enrolled in college to the total number of neighborhood residents eighteen to twenty-one years of age.[a]

(continued)

Table 6–10. continued

D. Educational Characteristics—continued	
% PRIMARY SCH.	Percentage of the neighborhood population twenty-five to fifty-four years of age with zero to seven years of school completed.
% HS GRAD	Percentage of the neighborhood population twenty-five to fifty-four years of age with twelve or more years of school completed.
% COLLEGE	Percentage of the neighborhood population twenty-five to fifty-four with four or more years of college completed.
MEDIAN ED	Median number of school years completed for the neighborhood population twenty-five to fifty-fo
E. Mobility Characteristics	
% STAYERS	Percentage of those five years of age and over who lived in the same house in the neighborhood five years ago.
% MOVER	Percentage of those five years of age and over who lived in a different county five years ago.
F. Employment Characteristics	
% MCLF	The percentage of civilian males sixteen years of age and over participating in the civilian labor force.
% FCLF	Percentage of civilian females sixteen years of age and over participating in the civilian labor force.
% UNEMPLOYED 16–21	Percent unemployed in the neighborhood population sixteen to twenty-one years of age not enrolled in school.
% UNEMPLOYED	Percentage of the total civilian neighborhood labor force sixteen years of age and over who are unemployed.
G. Occupation and Industry Characteristics	
% PROF	Percentage of the total number of employed civilians, sixteen years of age and over, employed as professionals, technical workers, managers, or administrators. Excludes farm managers.
% FARM	Percentage of the total number of employed civilians, sixteen years of age and over, working as farmers, farm managers, farm laborers, or farm foremen.
% BL COLLAR	Percentage of the total number of employed civilians, sixteen years of age and over, working in blue collar jobs. Includes craftsmen, operatives, and laborers except farm laborers.
H. Income Characteristics	
% < $5,000	Percentage of total neighborhood families with less than $5,000 annual family income. Refers to the annual income for the calendar year prior to the census, 1969.

Table 6–10. continued

% $15,000+	Percentage of total neighborhood families with $15,000 or more in annual family income in 1969.
MEDIAN INC	Median family income of the neighborhood in thousands of dollars.
INDEX	The Gini index of income concentration for the neighborhood. Index ranges from 0.01 to 0.99; the higher the index the greater the inequality of the income distribution in the neighborhood.
% FAM POV	Percentage of total families in neighborhoods with incomes below the 1970 poverty level.
% PER POV	Percentage of total population for which poverty status was determined with incomes below the 1970 poverty level. Poverty status was not determined for individuals living in institutions or unrelated individuals less than fourteen years of age.
II. Housing	
A. General Housing Characteristics	
% OWNER OCC	Percentage of all occupied neighborhood units occupied by owner.
% CROWDED	Percentage of all occupied neighborhood units with an average of 1.01 or more persons per room.
% CROWDED-STD	Percentage of all occupied units with complete plumbing facilities and 1.01 or more persons per room.
% SUBSTD	Percentage of all occupied units lacking some or complete plumbing facilities.
B. Value/Rent Characteristics	
% < $10,000	Percentage of owner-occupied units valued at less than $10,000 (1970 prices).
% $25,000+	Percentage of owner-occupied units valued at $25,000 or more (1970 prices).
% RENT < $40	Percentage of renter-occupied units with gross monthly rent less than $40 (1970 prices).[b]
% RENT < $60	Percentage of renter-occupied units with gross monthly rent less than $60 (1970 prices).[b]
% RENT $150+	Percentage of renter-occupied units with gross monthly rents of $150 or more (1970 prices).[b]
% RENT/INC .25	Percentage of renter-occupied units with gross rent-income ratios of 0.25 or more.[c]
% RENT/INC .35	Percentage of renter-occupied units with gross rent-income ratios in excess of 0.35.[c]
C. Vacancy Characteristics	
% Vacant	Percentage of all-year-round units that are vacant.
% RENT/SALE	Percentage of all-year-round units vacant for rent and/or sale.

(*continued*)

Table 6–10. concluded

D. Structural Characteristics	
% 1-UNIT	Percentage of all-year-round units in one-unit structures.
% 5+ UNITS	Percentage of all-year-round units in structures with five or more units.
% < 2 ROOMS	Percentage of all-year-round units that contain less than two rooms.
AV. # RMS.	Average number of rooms per unit.
% 1960+	Percentage of all-year-round units built in 1960 or later.
% < 1939	Percentage of all-year-round units built in 1939 or earlier.
% HEATED	Percentage of all-year-round units with steam or hot water; central warm air furnaces, built-in electric units and floor, wall, or pipeless furnace.

[a] A value of 1.00 or more is recorded as 0.99.

[b] Denominator excludes units for which no cash rent is tendered.

[c] Units where family income is zero or negative and units for which no cash rent is paid are excluded from tabulation of rent-income ratios.

With respect to family characteristics, old neighborhoods differ only minimally from those with younger age structures. Cumulative fertility rates, in particular, are invariant by type of neighborhood age structure. The percentage of female-headed households and divorced persons in older neighborhoods is somewhat above the national average, although the difference is not great. The excess of divorced persons in older neighborhoods may seem at first paradoxical. While the cohorts in the older age groups in 1970 had very low lifetime divorce rates, neighborhoods in which older persons are overrepresented tend also to be those areas with disproportionately high concentrations of divorced individuals. It is reasonable to speculate that older persons and divorced individuals, particularly the childless, have similar housing needs.

The populations of older neighborhoods are quite distinct racially. Black and Hispanic individuals are underrepresented proportionately in old neighborhoods while the proportion of the foreign born in old neighborhoods is 30 percent above the national average and 56 percent higher than the mean in young neighborhoods. This finding may seem puzzling. Previously in this chapter, we noted that the elderly are significantly overrepresented in central cities. These areas frequently are not only "gray ghettoes" but also black ones. Why then is there an inverse relation between the percentage of blacks (or Hispanics) and the percentage sixty-five years of age and older? The explanation is both technical and demographic. In earlier sections of this chapter, the residential location of older persons was assessed by calculating the percentage of all older persons who live in a particular geographic unit. The base for these calculations was the number of persons sixty-five years of age and over. In this section the unit of analysis is neighborhoods. Distinctions were made between neighborhoods in terms of their age structure. Those areas with a high *proportionate* concentration of older persons were deemed "old neighborhoods." The base for this calculation is the total neighborhood population. Thus an area could contain a large absolute number of older persons and still be labeled a "young" neighborhood if the ratio of old to young is low. Areas with large minority-group concentrations tend to have young age structures because the fertility of black and Hispanic women is higher than that of white women. These neighborhoods have age structures that are broad at the base and narrow at the apex.[s] Older persons living in neighborhoods with above-average proportions of blacks or Hispanics (neighborhoods with "adolescent" or "mature" age structures) live in areas having less age-race homogeneity than those elderly living in "old" neighborhoods.

Neighborhoods in which blacks and Spanish-speaking individuals are underrepresented—neighborhoods with young and old age structures—have higher proportions of high school graduates and college-educated persons than neighborhoods with adolescent or mature age distributions. Similarly, the median educational level is slightly above average in neighborhoods with either very low or very high concentrations of elderly persons.[t]

Although the populations in "young" and "old" neighborhoods are quite similar racially and educationally, they differ with respect to the degree of population turnover. The population residing in old neighborhoods is relatively stable. The proportion of individuals in old

[s] For similar reasons, the black population is considered to be "younger" than the white population. Because of racial differentials in fertility, only 7 percent of the black population in 1970 was sixty-five years of age or over in contrast to 9.9 percent in the white population. By 1977, the number of elderly in the black population had increased by 25 percent, raising the proportion of elderly blacks to 8 percent; the increase in the number of older whites was somewhat smaller—a 17 percent increase—resulting in a proportionate increase to 11 percent.

[t] In interpreting these data, it is important to note that the educational statistics were calculated using the number of persons twenty-five to fifty-four years of age as the denominator. If the educational attainment of older persons had been included in these calculations, the results shown in Table 6-11 may have been reversed since older persons, and the foreign born in particular, tend to have accumulated fewer years of formal schooling than those middle-aged. As calculated, however, it is reasonable to conclude only that the middle-aged population in neighborhoods where the elderly are overrepresented have educational backgrounds slightly above average.

Table 6–11. Mean Value of Neighborhood Characteristics, by Type of Neighborhood Age Structure

		Type of Neighborhood Age Structure			
Variable[a]	*All Neighborhoods*	*Young (< 6 percent 65+)*	*Adolescent (7–9 percent 65+)*	*Mature (10–13 percent 65+)*	Old *(> 14 percent 65+)*
General Population Characteristics					
% 0–17	34.4	39.7	36.2	33.3	27.3
AV PER/HH	3.2	3.7	3.3	3.1	2.7
% PRIMARY IND	18.3	11.2	15.8	20.0	27.7
% GROUP QUARTERS	7.6	11.0	5.9	4.7	6.5
Family and Fertility Characteristics					
% FEMALE HD	11.1	9.2	10.8	12.0	12.7
% H-W FAMILIES	82.3	84.7	82.5	81.3	80.2
% DIVORCED	7.1	6.3	6.7	7.2	8.2
CEB	3.1	3.1	3.2	3.2	3.1
Ethnic-Racial Composition					
% BLACK	10.9	10.6	13.2	11.7	7.9
% SPANISH	4.5	6.1	5.0	3.7	3.3
% FOREIGN	16.5	13.8	14.5	16.8	21.5
Educational Characteristics					
% INCOMPLETE	15.5	13.4	16.4	17.0	15.4
% 16–21	10.5	11.6	10.9	10.3	9.2
% IN COLLEGE	37.9	42.0	36.1	34.3	38.9
% PRIMARY SCH	9.7	7.7	11.3	11.2	8.7
% HS GRAD	61.5	67.1	58.8	57.5	62.6
% COLLEGE	12.4	15.0	11.4	10.3	12.6
MEDIAN ED	11.7	11.9	11.5	11.5	11.8
Mobility Characteristics					
% STAYERS	53.1	46.3	54.8	57.1	54.7
% MOVERS	18.3	24.6	16.6	14.7	16.6
Employment Characteristics					
% MCLF	76.2	81.3	77.5	74.6	70.4
% FCLF	41.0	42.3	41.6	40.6	39.5
% UNEMPLOY 16–21	39.3	37.7	39.8	40.4	39.2
% UNEMPLOY	4.5	4.2	4.5	4.8	4.6

% PROF	22.4	25.9	21.2	19.9	22.7
% FARM	3.5	1.4	3.6	4.6	4.4
% BL COLLAR	36.5	33.9	39.5	39.5	33.1
Income Characteristics					
% < $5,000	20.8	14.0	20.3	24.1	25.7
% $15,000+	20.1	26.1	19.9	16.7	17.3
MEDIAN INC	$ 9,800	$11,200	$ 9,900	$ 9,000	$ 8,900
INDEX	.33	.29	.33	.34	.36
% FAM POV	11.1	8.1	11.5	13.1	12.1
% PER POV	13.9	10.0	14.1	16.1	16.0
General Housing Characteristics					
% OWNER OCC	64.3	69.0	67.3	63.3	56.4
% CROWDED	8.4	9.6	9.5	8.3	5.8
% CROWDED – STD	7.1	8.8	7.9	6.6	5.0
% SUBSTD	5.8	2.6	6.6	7.9	6.2
Value/Rent Characteristics					
% < $10,000	23.3	10.9	23.2	30.5	29.6
% $25,500+	20.8	29.2	20.9	15.8	16.7
% RENT < $40	4.7	1.7	5.0	6.7	5.4
% RENT < $60	13.7	5.7	14.2	18.1	17.4
% RENT $150+	23.0	37.9	21.3	15.0	16.4
% RENT/INC .25	35.7	35.5	33.5	34.9	39.2
% RENT/INC .35	22.1	20.3	20.7	22.3	25.7
Vacancy Characteristics					
% VACANT	5.9	4.4	5.5	6.5	7.4
% RENT/SALE	3.0	2.9	2.8	3.0	3.5
Structural Characteristics					
% 1-UNIT	69.6	71.5	74.7	70.5	60.8
% 5+ UNITS	12.8	12.3	9.7	10.6	19.4
% < 2 ROOMS	4.6	2.8	3.6	4.6	7.9
AV # RMS	5.1	5.4	5.2	5.1	4.8
% 1960+	25.5	42.0	25.4	17.2	15.7
% < 1939	39.4	14.9	35.4	51.8	57.9
% HEATED	74.5	79.5	73.4	71.3	73.4

Source: Authors' tabulations, Public Use Sample, Neighborhood Characteristics File from the U.S. Bureau of the Census 1970 Census of Population and Housing.

[a] Consult Table 6–10 for definitions of variables.

neighborhoods who maintained their place of residence in the five years preceding the last census is slightly above the national average; the proportion moving into old neighborhoods from outside the county between 1965 and 1970 is below the national average. The most residentially stable neighborhoods, however, are not those with old age structures but those with mature age structures. Only the neighborhoods classified as young have a high degree of population turnover.

Not surprisingly, the populations in old neighborhoods have relatively low levels of labor force participation, for both males and females. Undoubtedly the retirement of elderly residents contributes to the relatively low levels of economic activity in "old" neighborhoods. The slightly above average unemployment rate in these neighborhoods is an additional explanatory factor. Still, seven of ten adult males and four of ten adult females are employed in neighborhoods having high proportions of older persons.

The occupational profiles of "old neighborhoods" are consistent with the educational characteristics of such areas. The population in both "young" and "old" neighborhoods is underrepresented disproportionately in the blue-collar occupations. Of the four types of neighborhoods examined here, aged neighborhoods, in fact, have the lowest proportion of blue-collar workers in the area's civilian labor force. The proportion of professionals in the population of aged neighborhoods is extremely close to the national average. Only in neighborhoods having young age structures, are professionally employed persons overrepresented in the civilian labor force.

Of perhaps most interest in the occupational data are those on the farm population. In general, the older the age structure of a neighborhood, the higher the proportionate average of farmers in the employed population. Because of out-migration by the young, rural farming areas tend to have extremely high concentrations of elderly in their population.

Income characteristics complete the survey of population characteristics by type of neighborhood. The interpretation of these data is straightforward; regardless of the measure used (median income, poverty ratios, or percent of the population above or below certain levels), the population of old neighborhoods has comparatively low levels of money income.[u] The median income in old neighborhoods, for example, is only 79 percent of the median average in young neighborhoods; the average proportion of individuals living below poverty is 60

[u] The U.S. Bureau of the Census classifies as low-income neighborhoods those with poverty rates in excess of 20 percent. None of the four types of neighborhoods considered here meet this criterion. Data on "low-income neighborhoods" are available in the PC(S) series of reports from the 1970 census.

percent higher than the average in young neighborhoods and 15 percent higher than the national average.

Of equal importance to our understanding of neighborhoods with old age structures is the data on the Gini index of income concentration. As noted in Table 6-10, this index ranges between 0.0 and 0.99. The higher the index, the less homogeneous the area's income distribution. Of the neighborhood types considered here, old neighborhoods are the least homogenous. In statistical terms, this is akin to saying that there is a greater dispersion around the mean. From the data, it is not possible to determine unequivocally whether this disparity is because of extremely low or because of extremely high incomes in the neighborhood population, although the relatively high rates of poverty in old neighborhoods suggest it is the former.

The emerging picture of population characteristics in old neighborhoods is fairly complex demographically. The average household size tends to be small; an excessive number of households are headed by women or individuals living alone; relatively few of the residents in old neighborhoods are black or Spanish-speaking, while the foreign born are substantially overrepresented. Residents of neighborhoods with old age structures also evidence moderately high levels of residential stability.

Old neighborhoods are most distinct economically. The excessively low labor force participation rates, particularly for males, and above-average unemployment rates suggest that residents in old neighborhoods rely on nonearned income sources to a greater extent than residents in younger neighborhoods. The income data shown in Table 6-11 support this hypothesis. Aged neighborhoods are characterized by comparatively high rates of poverty and low median incomes. As low-income areas, neighborhoods with large concentrations of older persons also are likely to have problems with crime, availability of community services, and physical deterioration—environmental factors not conducive to life satisfaction.

Housing Characteristics

The housing profile of older neighborhoods is consistent with the image of such neighborhoods as low income areas. Data referring to the housing situation of various types of neighborhoods are shown in the bottom half of Table 6-11.

Older persons are overrepresented in neighborhoods with low rates of owner occupancy. Although the majority of older persons own their dwelling units, the average owner occupancy rate in old neighborhoods is almost eight percentage points below the national average of 64.3 percent. In a study by Sclar (1976) of Boston communities from

1930–1970, the author found a similar pattern.[v] He noted, however, that elderly living near the central city frequently live in areas in which a large percentage of the dwellings are rental units.

The data are not sufficiently detailed to test the hypothesis that the elderly are in fact the owner-occupants in neighborhoods dominated by rental property. The information available, however, does lend strong support to this hypothesis.

As noted above, the average number of persons per household is lowest in neighborhoods with old age structures. It is not surprising then, that on the average, there are fewer crowded dwelling units in old neighborhoods than in any other type of community. For the most part, those few units that are crowded do not lack complete plumbing facilities and are considered of standard quality. The difference between the mean percent of crowded units (% CROWDED) and the mean percent of crowded but standard units (% CROWDED-STD), is less than 1 percent in old neighborhoods. This is the lowest mean difference for any type of neighborhood. Approximately 14 percent of the *crowded* units in old neighborhoods are substandard in contrast to a national average of 15.5 percent. In neighborhoods with large concentrations of elderly, however, a majority of the substandard units may not be crowded.

The owner-occupied housing stock in old neighborhoods contains a disproportionate number of low-value dwelling units. Whereas approximately one in five owner-occupied units nationwide, and one in ten units in young neighborhoods, was valued below $10,000 in 1970, an average of one in three units in old neighborhoods was of such low value. The reverse is true of units with high market value—units valued at $25,500 and over in 1970 are under-represented in neighborhoods with large concentrations of elderly. Rental property duplicates this pattern as well; low and moderately priced rental units dominate the market in old neighborhoods. Despite the low average rent of units, a large proportion of renters in old neighborhoods have excessive housing burdens if one accepts the rule of thumb that housing costs should not exceed 25 percent of household income. An average of four in ten rental households in old neighborhood spends 25 percent or more on housing. Even under a stricter definition of overconsumption (a rent-income rate of 35 percent or more), one in four renters in old neighborhoods has excessive housing costs. Given the low income status of old neighborhoods, this finding is not surprising—the poor are much more likely to spend excessive amounts for rent than are those of even middle-class standing (Soldo 1978).

[v] It should be noted that Boston, compared to other cities of comparable size, has a very low rate of homeownership in general.

The vacancy rate in old neighborhoods is 25 percent above the national average of 5.9 per 100 units. Regardless of neighborhood type, approximately one-half the vacant units are for rent or sale. Only in old neighborhoods, however, does the proportion of vacant units for rent or sale exceed the national average, suggesting that units may remain on the real estate market a longer time in old neighborhoods.

Structurally, the housing in old neighborhoods closely resembles the profile of inner city housing. On the average, old neighborhoods contain proportionately fewer single family units than does any other type of neighborhood considered here. In contrast to a national average of almost 70 percent, the housing stock in old neighborhoods is only 61 percent single-family units. Multiunit buildings, however, are over-represented in the housing stock of old neighborhoods. The average number of multiunit buildings in old neighborhoods is twice the average in neighborhoods with adolescent or mature age structures. Unlike many of the other neighborhood characteristics considered in this analysis, the mix of housing in old neighborhoods is quite distinct from the housing stock in mature neighborhoods. In general, neighborhoods with mature and old age structures have similar population characteristics and dissimilar housing characteristics.

The size of the housing units in old neighborhoods is consistent with the fact that old neighborhoods contain proportionately fewer large or crowded households than other types of communities. The average number of units containing two or fewer rooms in old neighborhoods is 71 percent higher than the national average; the average number of rooms per unit is lowest in neighborhoods with large concentrations of older persons. In contrast to units in young neighborhoods, the average household in old neighborhoods contains one-half room less.

The majority of the dwelling units in old neighborhoods also are old (having been built prior to 1940); the proportion is 47 percent higher than the national average and almost four times the average in young neighborhoods. In itself, the age of a dwelling unit is a limited indicator of quality. Older renovated housing can often compete qualitatively with housing of more recent construction. The data on the proportion of substandard units indicate that this is not the case in old neighborhoods, however. The comparatively low proportion of centrally heated units in old neighborhoods also suggests that the predominantly old units in aged neighborhoods have not been properly maintained or upgraded.

The housing profile of aged neighborhoods is much more cohesive than the population profile. In neighborhoods with excessively high proportions of older persons, the housing itself tends to be old, and of rather low quality. On the average, the value of property in aged neighborhoods is relatively low, but nonetheless expensive compared to the incomes of the residents. Although the units are, on the average, small, overcrowded units are underrepresented in the housing stock of old neighborhoods. Above-average vacancy rates indicate that aged neighborhoods are those with either (excessively) high rates of building abandonment or sluggish real estate markets. This fact, coupled with low property values in old neighborhoods, suggests that residents living in even mortgage-free homes would find it financially burdensome to sell their units and compete in the housing market for more desirable neighborhoods.

The preceding analysis of neighborhoods is primarily a descriptive one. It was undertaken to identify the environmental characteristics of neighborhoods in which older persons are overconcentrated. The environmental profiles of aged neighborhoods that were sketched obviously do not pertain to the residential milieu in which all older persons reside. Older persons are represented, to varying degrees, in almost all of the neighborhoods analyzed. Less than 1 percent of the sample of 42,950 neighborhoods is totally devoid of persons sixty-five years of age and over.

In general, the analysis indicates that neighborhoods in which the elderly are overrepresented are more likely to have a number of environmental problems, including those associated with deteriorating housing, than are more age-integrated neighborhoods. Many of these problems—low incomes, inferior housing, and excessive housing expenses—undoubtably affect older persons living in other types of neighborhoods, even those with comparatively good housing profiles. The analysis demonstrates, however, that these problems tend to cluster in neighborhoods with large concentrations of elderly. Regardless of their own individual situations, residents of such neighborhoods, young or old, are likely to experience an environment that is socially or physically inhospitable.

Housing problems in neighborhoods with relatively young age structures are more the exception than the rule. Inadequate housing for the elderly in these neighborhoods may be remedied by direct assistance to the older person. In aged neighborhoods, however, merely improving the physical space occupied by older individuals will not solve the problems of the social space surrounding the household. Renovation of a single unit in an aged neighborhood will not change the overall housing profile of the area. Is large-scale relocation the only solution to the housing problem of the elderly currently residing in aged neighborhoods?

Even if such a solution were feasible, and assuming that older residents were willing to move, it does not address questions concerning the quality of life in the abandoned neighborhood, such as the continual deterioration of the housing stock in aged neighborhoods. In the short run, relocation programs are expensive; in the long run, there are additional hidden costs. Lacking coordinated housing assistance programs, aged neighborhoods are likely to decline still further. The scenario of decaying neighborhoods is a familiar one in the older metropolitan centers; crime rates escalate, additional buildings are abandoned, businesses relocate or fail, unemployment increases, and property values fall. As a result, public monies are increasingly funneled into aged neighborhoods.

Poor housing is not simply a problem of older persons; in communities with large concentrations of elderly, it is often a neighborhood problem. An appropriate housing policy for the elderly must respond to the needs of both individuals and neighborhoods. In aged neighborhoods, older residents are clearly part of the housing problem, particularly older homeowners who do not maintain their dwelling units sufficiently. Older residents in aged neighborhoods also may be an important part of the solution. Because the elderly are likely to be owner-occupants in neighborhoods dominated by rental property, coordinated repair-renovation assistance to older residents is a key to preserving the housing stock and quality of life in aged neighborhoods. A systematic program to upgrade housing occupied by elderly in problem-ridden aged neighborhoods may be sufficient to brake the process of neighborhood decay. The cost of such a program is likely to be high initially, but if it initiates neighborhood revitalization, long-run, hidden costs are likely to be low.

The success of such a program depends, in part, on the soundness of targeting housing repair-renovation programs at aged neighborhoods. The data we have presented suggest that aged neighborhoods exist in both rural and urban settings. Because of the high concentration of farmers in aged neighborhoods, at least some of the aged neighborhoods are likely to be in rural areas. However, the preponderance of multifamily units in aged neighborhoods indicates that perhaps a majority are located in city centers. Considering the diversity of settings, it is necessary to ask if housing characteristics are a common denominator in areas with larger concentrations of elderly regardless of location. This question is examined in the following section.

HOMOGENEITY OF AGED NEIGHBORHOODS

In order to determine the extent of homogeneity in aged neighborhoods with respect to housing characteristics, the sample of neighborhoods was analyzed using a multiple discriminant procedure. This multivariate technique provides for an assessment of the distinctiveness of the housing stock in aged neighborhoods.

Multiple discriminant analysis is a procedure in which the "dependent variable" is a set of dummy variables defining group membership (Eisenbeis and Avery 1972). In this case, groups are defined by type of neighborhood age structure. Four groups—corresponding to young, adolescent, mature, and aged neighborhoods—comprise the dependent variable. The independent variables are the twenty housing characteristics defined at the bottom of Table 6-10 (% OWNER OCC to % HEATED).

In discriminant analysis, linear combinations of the independent variables, or discriminant functions, are chosen so as to maximize the discriminant criteria defined as the ratio of the between to the within sums of squares in the cross-product matrices. This ratio takes the place of "variance explained" as the criterion for determining the significance of each successive function (Van de Geer 1971). The dimensions, or the unmeasured variables, so derived are orthogonal; that is, successive functions are determined so as to maximize relative separation after the effects of preceding functions are "partialed out" (Huberty 1975).

Two significant discriminant functions were extracted from the data on neighborhood housing characteristics. The two functions accounted for 95 percent of the discriminating ability present in the set of independent variables.

The standardized discriminant function coefficients on the two significant functions are shown in Table 6-12. Of the twenty variables initially considered, only the seven variables listed in the table made a significant contribution to either function. The discriminant coefficients can be interpreted in a manner analogous to regression coefficients. They indicate the relative contribution of each variable to the unobserved variable described by the function and are actually partial coefficients of effects showing the importance of each variable net of the others. Although it is tempting to lend a substantive meaning to each function, as is common in factor analysis, discriminant coefficients as partials, do not pertain to the common aspects among the discriminator variables.[w]

On the first function, three variables—AV. # ROOMS, % CROWDED, and % < 1939—account for 75.8 percent of the separation between neighborhood types. The first two variables have a negative sign, the last a positive one. Of the three, the variable measuring

[w] Huberty has noted "two discriminators having large positive coefficients would not necessarily have anything in common that contributed to group separation" (1975: 552).

Table 6–12. Standardized Discriminant Function Coefficients (N = 42,000)[a,b]

Variable[c]	*Function 1*	*Function 2*
% OWNER OCC		− .40
AV. # ROOMS	− .66	−1.29
% CROWDED[d]	− .65	.94
% 5+ UNITS[d]		− .62
% < 2 ROOMS[d]		− .57
% 1960+		− .54
% < 1939	.46	− .88
Canonical r	.77	.53
Relative %	75.81	19.92
Cumulative %	75.81	95.10

[a] Functions shown are significant at p = 0.001.

[b] Only coefficients greater than ± 0.4 are shown.

[c] For definition of variables consult Table 6–10.

[d] Because of the skew in the distribution, variable was logged prior to entry into discriminant equation.

average number of rooms makes the largest relative contribution to the function. All seven variables load on the second function, which accounts for an additional 20 percent of the discriminating ability in the independent variables. The three variables having large coefficients on the first function also score highly on the second function, although in the case of two variables (% CROWDED and % < 1939) there is a sign change.

Group centroids are the average score of each type of neighborhood on the two discriminant functions. The extent to which housing characteristics distinguish among types of neighborhood age structures can be demonstrated by plotting the group centroids for the two significant functions. This type of plot is shown in Figure 6-3. The first function distinguishes mature and aged neighborhoods from the two with younger age structures; the second function separates young and aged neighborhoods from the middle-aged neighborhoods. Aged neighborhoods are isolated by positive scores on both functions.

The discriminant functions based on housing characteristics are quite successful in correctly classifying neighborhoods by type of age structure. Overall, 60 percent of the neighborhoods were identified correctly based on their score on the two functions we have described. Approximately 65 percent of the aged neighborhoods were classified as such. Complete classification results are shown in Appendix Table 6A-1.[x]

[x] An appropriate way to measure the success of a discriminant procedure is to examine the classification results in the smallest group. In this analysis, aged neighbor-

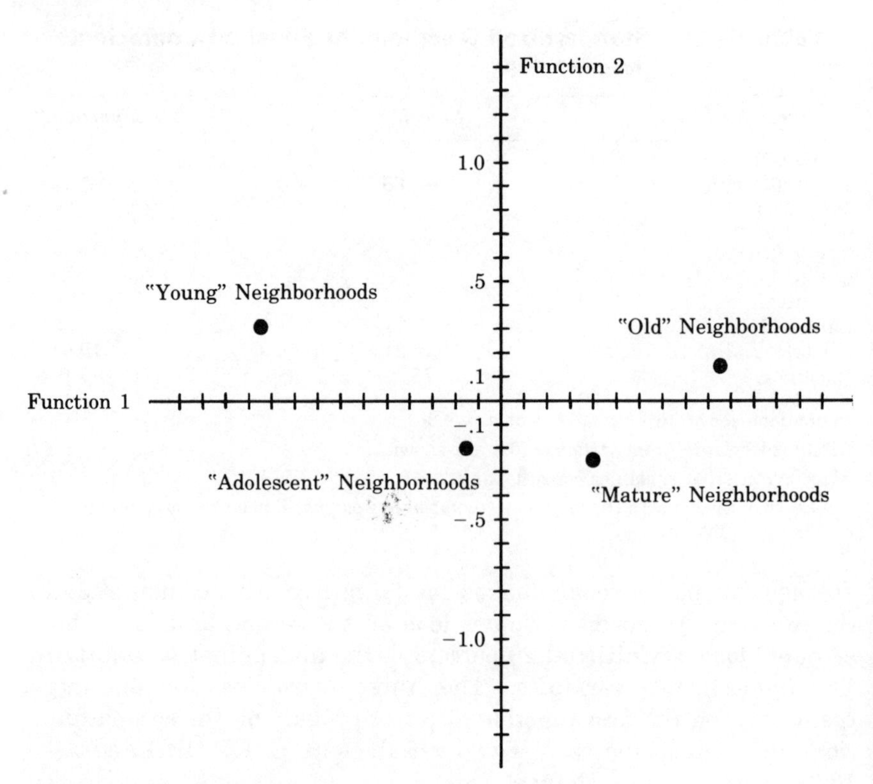

Figure 6–3. Plot of Average Neighborhood Scores on the Two Significant Discriminant Functions

The discriminant analysis of neighborhoods shows that (1) aged neighborhoods are distinct from other types of neighborhoods in terms of their housing stock characteristics and (2) differences between neighborhood types are greater than within group differences. Thus, it is reasonable to single out neighborhoods with large concentrations of the elderly as communities for comprehensive and coordinated housing assistance programs, which emphasize housing stock preservation strategies.

---

hoods contain the fewest cases (9,522). Predicting type of neighborhood on the basis of a simple proportionate marginal model, one would "guess" correctly 22.2 percent of the aged neighborhoods. In the discriminant classification, 10,302 were identified as aged neighborhoods. Of these, 6,165 or 59.8 percent were assigned the correct classification. This translates into a 37.6 percent improvement in prediction under the discriminant classification scheme.

SUMMARY

In formulating housing policy, an important factor to be considered is the location of the elderly. Nationally, one in ten Americans are age sixty-five or older, and their geographical distribution reflects the spatial distribution of the population as a whole. The elderly tend to concentrate in areas where people of all ages typically reside—in the more populous states and in the urban centers of the country. Housing needs and housing quality, however, vary between urban and rural locations.

Although the geographic characteristics of older populations are diverse, neighborhoods with large concentrations of the elderly tend to be more homogenous. Demographically "old" neighborhoods have a high proportion of households headed by women or individuals living alone, and the households tend to be smaller in size. Environmentally "old" neighborhoods are associated with substandard and defective housing, as well as with deteriorating neighborhood conditions.

Because the elderly show a low propensity to move, there is a need to channel program support into areas containing a large proportion of elderly. Such a strategy will not only improve the housing conditions for the older population but will serve to benefit their neighborhoods by preserving the housing stock and deterring neighborhood blight.

APPENDIX

Table 6A–1. Classification Results from Discriminant Analysis of Neighborhoods, by Type of Age Structure (percent)

Actual Type of Neighborhood Age Structure	*Predicted Type of Neighborhood Age Structure*				
	Young	*Adolescent*	*Mature*	*Aged*	*Total*
Young	69.0 (8,091)	25.4 (2,980)	2.7 (314)	2.9 (339)	100.0 (11,724)
Adolescent	14.2 (1,396)	55.9 (5,481)	21.4 (2,099)	8.5 (835)	100.0 (9,811)
Mature	3.4 (399)	24.7 (2,939)	47.0 (5,592)	24.9 (2,963)	100.0 (11,893)
Aged	2.8 (270)	5.1 (485)	27.3 (2,602)	64.7 (6,165)	100.0 (9,522)
Total	23.6 (10,156)	27.7 (11,885)	24.7 (10,607)	24.0 (10,302)	100.0 (42,950)

REFERENCES

Beckham, B.L., and C.S. Kart. 1977. "Heterogeneity of the Elderly in Large Metropolitan Areas." *Urban Affairs Quarterly* 13, no. 2: 233–42.

Bell, W. 1953. "The Social Areas of the San Francisco Bay Region." *American Sociological Review* 18: 39–47.

———. 1955. "Economic, Family and Ethnic Status: An Empirical Test." *American Sociological Review* 20: 45–52.

———. 1959. "Social Areas: Typology of Neighborhoods." In M.B. Sussman, ed., *Community Structure and Analysis*, pp. 61–92. New York: Thomas Y. Crowell Company.

Berghorn, F.J.; D.E. Schafer; G.H. Steere; and R.F. Wiseman. 1978. *The Urban Elderly: A Study of Life Satisfaction*. New York: Universe Books.

Carp, F.M. 1976. "Housing and Living Environments of Older People." In R.H. Binstock and E. Shanas, eds., *Handbook of Aging and the Social Sciences*, pp. 244–71. New York: Van Nostrand Reinhold Company.

———. 1977. "Impact of Improved Living Environment on Health and Life Expectancy." *The Gerontologist* 17, no. 3: 242–49.

Chevan, A., and J.F. O'Rourke. 1972. "Aging Regions of the United States." *Journal of Gerontology* 27: 119–26.

———. 1974. "A Factorial Ecology of Age Groups in the U.S., 1960." In J. Gubrium, ed., *Late Life*. Springfield, Ill.: Charles C Thomas.

Coale, A.J. 1964. "How a Population Ages or Grows Younger." In R. Freedman, ed., *Population: The Vital Revolution*, pp. 47–58. Garden City, N.Y.: Anchor Books.

Cowgill, D.O. 1958. "Ecological Patterns of the Aged in American Cities." *The Midwest Sociologist* 20: 78–83.

———. 1970. "The Demography of Aging." In A. Hoffman, ed., *The Daily Needs and Interests of Older People*, pp. 27–70. Springfield, Ill.: C.C Thomas Publishers.

———. 1978. "Residential Segregation by Age in American Metropolitan Areas." *Journal of Gerontology* 33, no. 3: 446–53.

Eisenbeis, R.A., and R.B. Avery. 1972. *Discriminant Analysis and Classification Procedures*. Lexington, Mass.: D.C. Heath.

Field, M. 1972. *The Aged, the Family and the Community*. New York: Columbia University Press.

Golant, S.M. 1972. "The Residential Location and Spatial Behavior of the Elderly." Chicago: University of Chicago Department of Geography, Research Paper, No. 143.

———. 1976. "Intraurban Transportation Needs and Problems of the Elderly." In M.P. Lawton, R.J. Newcomer, and T.O. Byerts, eds., *Community Planning for an Aging Society: Designing Services and Facilities*, pp. 282–308. Stroudsburg, Pa.: Dowden, Hutchinson and Ross, Inc.

Goodman, J.L., Jr. 1978. "Urban Residential Mobility: Places, People and Policy." Washington, D.C.: The Urban Institute.

Hansen, G.D. 1971. "Meeting Housing Challenges: Involvement—The Elderly." In *Housing Issues*. Proceedings of the Fifth Annual Meeting,

American Association of Housing Educators. Lincoln: University of Nebraska Press.
Havighurst, R.J. 1969. "Research and Development Goals in Social Gerontology: A Report of a Special Committee of the Gerontological Society." *Gerontologist* 9: 1–90.
Huberty, C.J. 1975. "Discriminant Analysis." *Review of Educational Research* 45, no. 4: 543–98.
Kart, C.S., and B. Manard. 1976. "Aging Regions of the U.S.: 1970." In C. Kart and B. Manard, eds., *Aging in America*. Port Washington, N.Y.: Alfred.
Kennedy, J.M., and G.F. DeJong. 1977. "Aged in Cities: Residential Segregation in 10 U.S.A. Central Cities." *Journal of Gerontology* 32: 97–102.
Langbein, L.I., and A.J. Lichtman. 1978. *Ecological Inference*. Beverly Hills, Ca.: Sage Publications, Inc.
Long, L.H. 1978. "Interregional Migration of the Poor: Some Recent Changes." Current Population Reports, Series P-23, No. 73. Washington, D.C.: Government Printing Office.
Long, L.H., and K.A. Hansen. 1975. "Trends in Return Migration to the South." *Demography* 12: 601–14.
———. 1979. "Reasons for Interstate Migration: Jobs, Retirement, Climate and Other Influences." Current Population Reports, Series P-23, No. 81. Washington, D.C.: Government Printing Office.
Mathieu, J.T. 1976. "Housing Preferences and Satisfactions." In M.P. Lawton, R.J. Newcomer, and T.O. Byerts, eds., *Community Planning for an Aging Society: Designing Services and Facilities*, pp. 154–72. Stroudsburg, Pa.: Dowden, Hutchinson and Ross, Inc.
Montgomery, J.E. 1972. "The Housing Patterns of Older Families." *The Family Coordinator* 21: 37–46.
Myers, G.C., and B.J. Soldo. 1976. "Variations in Living Arrangements Among the Elderly." Final project report prepared for the Administration on Aging. Department of Health, Education and Welfare, AoA Grant No. 90-A-313/02.
Newcomb, C. 1951. "Graphic Presentation of Age and Sex Distribution of Population in the City." In P. Hatt and A.J. Reiss, Jr., eds., *Cities and Society*. New York: Free Press.
Rainwater, L. 1972. "Fear and the House-as-a-Haven in the Lower Class." In J. Palen and K. Flaming, eds., *Urban America: Conflict and Change*. New York: Holt, Rinehart and Winston.
Rhode Island Department of Elderly Affairs. 1978. *An Analysis of Social Data Affecting the Lives of Rhode Island's Older Population*. Providence: Rhode Island Department of Elderly Affairs.
Robinson, W.S. 1950. "Ecological Correlations and the Behavior of Individuals." *American Sociological Review* 15: 351–57.
Schmid, C.F. 1950. "Generalizations Concerning the Ecology of the American City." *American Sociological Review* 15: 264–81.
Sclar, E.D. 1976. "Aging and Residential Location." In M.P. Lawton, R.J. Newcomer, and T.O. Byerts, eds., *Community Planning for an Aging Society: Designing Services and Facilities*, pp. 266–81. Stroudsburg, Pa.: Dowden, Hutchinson and Ross, Inc.

Shevky, E., and M. Williams. 1949. *The Social Areas of Los Angeles*. Berkeley: University of California Press.

Soldo, B.J. 1978. "The Housing and Characteristics of Independent Elderly: A Demographic Overview." In R.P. Boynton, ed., *Occasional Papers in Housing and Community Affairs*, pp. 7–38. Publication No. HUD-497-PDR. Washington, D.C.: Government Printing Office.

Struyk, R.J. 1979. "Housing Adjustments of Relocating Elderly Households." Unpublished.

Taeuber, K.E., and A.F. Taeuber. 1965. *Negroes in Cities*. Chicago: Aldine Publishing Company.

United Nations. 1956. "Aging Populations: Economic and Social Implications." United Nations Manual No. 26. New York.

U.S. Bureau of the Census. 1972a. *Public Use Samples of Basic Records from the 1970 Census: Description and Technical Documentation*. Washington, D.C.: Government Printing Office.

———. 1972b. *Supplement No. 1 to Public Use Sample of Basic Records from the 1970 Census: Description and Technical Documentation*. Washington, D.C.: Government Printing Office.

U.S. Department of Agriculture. 1978. *Rural Development Perspectives*. RDP No. 1 (November). Washington, D.C.: Government Printing Office.

U.S. Government Accounting Office. 1977. *The Well-Being of Older People in Cleveland, Ohio*. Report prepared for the Congress of the United States. HRD 77-70. Washington, D.C.: Government Printing Office.

U.S. Senate Special Committee on Aging. 1977. *Developments in Aging: 1976*. Washington, D.C.: Government Printing Office.

Van de Geer, J.P. 1971. *Introduction to Multivariate Analysis for the Social Sciences*. San Francisco: W.H. Freeman and Company.

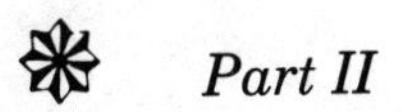

Part II

Public Policy

Chapter 7

Existing Housing and Neighborhood Preservation Programs: A Critical Review

The federal government currently provides a large number of households headed by the elderly with housing assistance. Indeed over 700,000 elderly renters live in units that are directly subsidized by the U.S. Department of Housing and Urban Development. Others are receiving assistance through subsidies passed through local governments under the Community Development Block Grant (CDBG) program. In fact, it is often argued that the balance in the use of limited resources between the elderly and nonelderly has swung too far in favor of the elderly.

This chapter provides an overview of the major subsidy programs presently operating and funded through HUD. The companion chapter, which follows, describes the housing assistance provided by other federal agencies, including the Department of Health, Education and Welfare and the Farmers Home Administration. In this chapter, each program is evaluated using six criteria, to the extent that the available data permit. This information on the strengths and weaknesses of the present programs—as well as their omissions in coverage of needy groups of households—forms the basis for the policy options set forth in Chapter 9.

Even though only a few programs are reviewed, a simple classification system, based on how the assistance is designed to improve the housing situation of the recipient, is used in this analysis. So defined, the programs fall into three broad classes: the first group consists of those directly improving quality of housing available to the recipient and usually lowering the rent of the dwelling below market rates. An example is the traditional public housing program under which solid, moderate-quality housing has been built explicitly to house low-income persons. Rents are based on the tenants' ability to pay, and the subsidy, which the tenant never sees, is the difference between the rent paid and the actual cost of providing the housing. Programs of this type, which augment the availability of units of acceptable quality that the target population can afford, are termed "supply" housing programs. This review takes up three such programs besides public housing: the Section 202 program, created by the Housing Act of 1959, under which new units for the elderly and handicapped are produced; the Section 312 rehabilitation loan program, created by the Housing Act of 1964, under which loans below market rate are made to eligible households; and third, the locally administered rehabilitation loan and grant programs operated with funds provided through CDBG.

The complement to the supply housing programs is the "demand" group. The strategy here is to increase the purchasing power of the recipients so that they will be able to buy additional housing services in the marketplace; at the limit, such assistance is simply an unrestricted cash grant for the household to spend as it wishes, possibly devoting none of it to improving housing while continuing to occupy a substandard unit. Housing programs place some restriction on the use of the cash: typically the dwelling occupied must meet a set of minimum physical standards. HUD now operates the Housing Assistance Payments Program (Section 8), one portion of which is of this type. Income-eligible households who occupy "standard quality" units (either initially or after they relocate) are given a subsidy determined by the approximate difference between the cost of such a unit and 25 percent of their income.

The Section 8 program has two other elements that are structured to increase the supply of available units—either through new construction or substantial rehabilitation—by entering into long-term lease agreements with developers. Although the actual subsidy payment is channeled through the recipient household who occupies one of these units, the effective guarantee of the subsidy is the ultimate incentive for the developer to participate in the program. Thus, although these elements of Section 8 could be classified as a demand program, there are strong supply elements involved.

The third element is activity to improve the general physical environment in residential neighborhoods. Much of this activity is funded through the Community Development Block Grant program. Attention is restricted to the subset of these activities that involves comprehensive strategies to upgrade neighborhoods, which often include dwelling rehabilitation as a key element.

In the following discussion, each program is described briefly and then evaluated against a set of six criteria derived in large part from the goals which HUD has set for itself.

1. *Efficient targeting*. Housing assistance resources being limited, they should be reserved for those low- to moderate-income groups living in the worst housing and devoting a disproportionately large share of their income to housing.
2. *Housing improvement*. Programs should, at a minimum, ensure no further reduction in the quality of housing occupied by recipients, and all recipients should reside in dwellings meeting minimum physical standards.
3. *Equal opportunity*. The programs should foster the equal opportunity objectives stated in the law. Accomplishing this goal is extremely difficult since success in reaching minority groups and promoting integration depends heavily on the preferences of minority households as well as on the structure of the program. Data are presented, to the extent available, on minority participation and the extent of project and neighborhood integration.
4. *Preservation of housing stock*. Programs should be designed *and* administered to make maximum use of the existing stock of housing in order to promote preservation of the stock and neighborhood stability. Clearly, in housing markets characterized by high vacancy rates and/or long vacancy durations for moderate- to low-quality dwellings, construction of new units to house some of the current occupants of these units will result in even higher vacancy rates or housing abandonment. Similarly, in markets with the opposite characteristics, total reliance on demand-augmenting programs may produce little improvement in the housing of recipients.[a] The question of the proper mix of new construction and stock utilization programs has been addressed by the Congress and HUD in determining the requirements for housing assistance plans from local governments as part of the application process for block grants.[b] Since the indirect program effects are often important, and very difficult to measure, it is difficult to apply these criteria quantitatively.
5. *Cost minimization*. Housing objectives should be reached at the lowest possible cost. From the foregoing, it is evident that, since no

[a] For a further discussion of the local market-program mix question, see Struyk (1977).

[b] More is said about the housing assistance plans in the discussion of the Section 8 housing program.

single program can universally meet the conditions in local markets, no single program should be selected for implementation on the basis of cost alone. Nevertheless, the relative costs of different approaches should influence the determination of the "best" mix in specific markets. Obviously, more households can be assisted by a cheaper program.

6. *Administrative simplicity.* This is the preferred relationship within the administrating agency, between the central government and local agencies, and between local agencies and recipients.

Some evaluations of the current programs are more effectively made program by program; others by applying a single criterion to all the programs at the same time. Accordingly, the comparisons of cost and efficient targeting are made after each program has been discussed.

SUPPLY PROGRAMS

The following four programs are considered in turn: low-rent public housing, the Section 202 direct loan construction program, the Section 312 rehabilitation loan program, and rehabilitation grants and loans under the block grant program.

Low-Rent Public Housing

Program Description.[c] The major federally supported housing support program intended solely for low-income persons has been low-rent public housing. State and local governments have been cooperating in this federal program for more than three decades. In 1976, there were over 1.2 million federally supported units.

While earlier fledgling programs were attempted, the 1937 U.S. Housing Act served to cement the involvement of the federal government in low-rent public housing. The act authorized the use of federal funds and credit to alleviate present and recurring unemployment and to remedy the unsafe and unsanitary housing conditions and the acute shortage of decent, safe, and sanitary dwellings for families of low income.

Under the 1937 Act, federal assistance was limited to assistance in the development, acquisition, or administration of low-rent housing as slum clearance projects. Before any construction began, the federal

[c] The initial portion of this description draws heavily on an internal paper by Julie Pastor of the Office of Policy Development and Research in the U.S. Department of Housing and Urban Development.

government (now HUD) would enter into an annual contributions contract with the local housing authority, not to exceed forty years. The federal grant or subsidy would cover interest and amortization on long-term bonds to be issued by the local housing authority after construction was completed. In turn, the local housing authority would pledge annual contributions from its rent collections toward full payment of the debt in the annual contributions contract.

While the federal government provided for development costs, the local housing authorities were required to meet operating expenses out of rents and utility charges collected from tenants. Any excess over current operating expenses was to be immediately remitted to the federal government. This regulation was later softened by allowing local housing authorities to maintain reserves for six months to meet future operating expenses. (Thus, most local housing authorities would keep rents low so that they could avoid paying back a surplus.) More than 84 percent of the annual contributions were offset by such remissions in 1948 and 1949, but only about 2 percent in 1971. Today, in light of the increasing deficit of most local housing authorities, this provision has been rendered virtually meaningless.

The policy for rents and admission was also addressed by the 1937 Act. It imposed a minimum rent-to-income ratio at admission of 20 percent and established that incomes could not be in excess of five times the annual rental for the unit. By 1959, however, there was a growing pressure for greater local control of the public housing program. This led to substantial changes that year in the statute, which took the form of a local autonomy amendment. The major change was the ability of local housing authorities to assume control over setting rent and income limits. There was very little federal or state guidance given for rent determination to the local housing authorities. Thus, most localities adopted rent systems in which rent was based on a portion of income and units were assigned to tenants based on need.

Tenant composition in public housing has changed rapidly throughout the duration of the program, from the early 1930s to the present. As the displaced working class exceeded the income limits for continued occupancy, they were often replaced by unemployed, fixed-income, minority-group families who viewed public housing as a permanent residence (perhaps because they anticipated a lifetime of inability to pay for housing in the private market). Coupled with this dramatic change in tenant composition, operating expenses per unit per year increased from $37.79 to $96.13 (from 1966 to 1976).

During the 1965–1970 period, many local housing authorities instituted rent increases, even though incomes of the tenants were not rising. The financial and social pressures building up in the program led to rent strikes, tenant dissent, and eventually, congressional action.

The Brooke amendments in the Housing Act of 1969 stipulated that the annual rent payment of a tenant could not exceed one-fourth of the tenant's income. The Brooke amendments also enabled the secretary of HUD to make, and contract to make, annual operating subsidy payments to public housing agencies so that they could provide housing within the means of families of very low income and provide improved operating and maintenance services. Administrative policy of HUD interpreted the provisions by restricting operating subsidy payments to meet operating deficits and to allow some maintenance of financial reserves. The expansion of services to tenants under the subsidy has been limited.

Table 7-1 gives some basic information on the elderly occupants of public housing, for households reexamined for continued occupancy in the twelve months ending September 30, 1976. The elderly included may be in either "elderly only" or "mixed" projects. Since the elderly, as defined in the program, include the handicapped of all ages and all households headed by someone sixty-two years of age or older, the figures in the table are not totally accurate. Overall, about 25 percent of those classified as elderly are under age sixty-five. Applying this rate to *all* elderly public housing occupants means that about one-third or 342,000 of the 1.036 million occupied units were occupied by the elderly.

The figures show a low mean (and a lower median) income of elderly tenants, and nearly universal recipiency of welfare or social security payments. They also show that the blacks constitute 36 percent of elderly occupants; Hispanic Americans are 6 percent of the total.[d]

Evaluation

Housing improvement. Three types of information reflect on the average housing improvement experienced by elderly public housing occupants. The first simply compares the physical characteristics of public housing with the characteristics of units occupied by elderly renters in general. Public housing will, at a minimum, provide complete cooking and sanitary facilities to a household, and should be free from the other defects examined in Chapter 3. On this basis, it would appear that, at a minimum, about one in five or six elderly public housing occupants should experience substantial improvement in his or her housing by moving into a project.

[d] A more complete description of the evolution of public housing is Chapters 1 and 2 of Rabushka and Weissert (1977).

A second indicator of improvement can be obtained from public housing authority records on the quality of housing occupied by program applicants prior to admission to the program. The reliability of these data is likely to vary considerably among authorities, but should be reasonably reliable for questions about gross defects, gathered at the time the application is taken, in the applicant's present housing—one criterion for receiving a priority position on the authority's waiting list. Among the 25,000 elderly-headed households (defined here as over age sixty-two) admitted to public housing in the fiscal year ending September 1976, 28 percent were classified as moving from substandard housing (HUD 1976). This is a plausible figure in light of the data on deficiencies of impoverished aged households reviewed in Chapter 3.

Third, there is a group of statistical analyses that compares quantity of housing services consumed by households in public housing with the quantity of housing services it is expected the same households would consume if they were given, in cash, a subsidy equivalent to the public housing subsidy. These analyses, based on careful economic logic, have consistently shown that public housing tenants are better housed than they would be if they were given their housing subsidy in cash. They also show, however, that the households could attain a level of general satisfaction they experience as public housing tenants for fewer subsidy dollars, if they were given cash directly. These results are consistent with the fact that the households appear to value the additional housing services at less than it costs the government to provide them.[e]

In the aggregate this information indicates convincingly that public housing tenants are better housed than similar households not in public housing. Furthermore, they are better housed than they would be if given an equivalent cash subsidy to spend as they wished.

Equal opportunity. While the broad question of the participation of elderly minority group members in HUD programs is addressed in a separate section, a few salient facts on the extent of project integration are examined here. In total, 53 percent of all public housing tenants are black; among the elderly, 35 percent are black. Data on the extent of racial integration of individual projects are available only for the thirty housing authorities with 5,000 or more units, which, combined, account for 43 percent of all public housing. Table 7-2 gives separate data for elderly and family projects. The family projects are sharply segregated, with only 14 percent of the projects having a tenancy that

[e] Two studies drawing this conclusion are Barton and Olsen (1976) and Adams (1972). Both of these analyses use the method developed by Joseph de Salvo (1971).

Table 7–1. Low-Income Housing: Summary of Characteristics of Elderly Families Reexamined for Continued Occupancy during the Twelve Months Ended 9/30/76, by Minority-Group Category

Characteristics	*Elderly Families*[a]	*White/ Nonminority*	*Negro/ Black*	*Spanish-American*
Number reexamined	158,357	89,288	56,464	10,582
Percent	100	100	100	100
Receiving assistance and/or benefits	97	98	97	94
Assistance with/without benefits	30	20	41	57
Benefits only	67	78	56	37
Not receiving assistance or benefits	3	2	3	6
No workers	92	95	88	85
One worker	7	4	11	13
Two or more workers	1	c	1	2
Age of family head, all[b]	156,891	88,315	56,195	10,557
Under 25	c	c	c	c
25–34	1	1	2	2
35–44	3	1	4	5
45–54	6	3	10	11
55–61	7	5	11	12
62–64	8	6	10	12
65–69	18	17	19	20
70–74	20	22	18	17
75 and over	36	45	26	19

Median age	72	74	68	67
Elderly, as a % of all families	41	68	28	24
Under $25.00 gross rent	1	1	2	1
$25.00–34.99	6	5	7	5
$35.00–44.99	27	26	32	20
$45.00–54.99	21	22	20	24
$55.00–64.99	16	19	12	12
$65.00–74.99	9	9	8	7
$75.00–84.99	6	6	6	5
$85.00–99.99	5	5	5	6
$100.00 and over	8	6	9	20
Median gross rent	$52.25	$53.15	$49.85	$55.30
Mean gross rent	58.70	57.70	58.09	69.08
Median income	$2,833	$2,894	$2,668	$3,114
Mean income	3,437	3,293	3,503	4,163

Source: U.S. Department of Housing and Urban Development, *1976 Statistical Yearbook*, p. 179, Table 121.

[a] Includes families for whom data by minority-group category are not available.

[b] Based on data for families reporting sex of head of household.

[c] Less than 0.5 percent.

Table 7–2. Racial Composition of Projects in Major Public Housing Authorities[a]

	Distribution					
	Percentage Minority Occupancy in Projects[b]					
Type of Project	0–5	6–25	26–50	51–75	76–95	96–100
Family	1	3	6	8	21	61
Elderly	19	19	16	15	14	17

Source: Special tabulations provided by the Office of Housing, U.S. Department of Housing and Urban Development.

[a] These are the 1 percent of authorities with 5,000 or more units under management; they account for 43 percent of all public housing units.

[b] Figures are not weighted by the number of units in a project.

is 25 to 75 percent black. Among the elderly projects, 31 percent are in this category; and one project in five has between 6 and 25 percent black occupancy. These figures indicate a much greater degree of integration in elderly public housing projects than exists in private residential accommodations.

Preservation of housing stock. Essentially, public housing is a program of new construction. Although there are some notable examples of public housing authorities using their construction funds to rehabilitate units, as was done in Baltimore, these are exceptional cases. As new construction, the program's effects on the preservation of the existing stock depend critically on the local balance between the demand for and supply of moderate-quality housing. Where suitable units are in short supply—both currently and in the foreseeable future (as might be the case in rapidly growing areas)—new construction is warranted. In other situations, the case is more difficult to make, but still feasible. Use of modest-scale new construction to fill-in undeveloped sites or sites cleared through public action like urban renewal could be especially effective in helping to stabilize or to anchor a neighborhood. In general, though, the softer the market for moderate-quality housing, that is, the greater the excess of supply to demand for such units, the less useful the creation of more housing—housing explicitly designed to draw tenants out of existing moderate- to low-quality units. In such cases, a strong argument can be made for greater use of rehabilitation of housing, although it is necessary to be careful that the housing is being set aside explicitly for elderly occupancy. The cost of widening doorways or passageways to accommodate walkers and wheelchairs may make rehabilitation excessively costly for some units. This would have to be evaluated in light of the specific units available for rehabilitation, but the general principle is clear.

A separate dimension of housing stock preservation concerns the maintenance and external appearance and the deportment of tenants in already existing public housing, which can have dramatic effects on the quality of life in an entire neighborhood. Such neighborhood problems fostered the growth of "elderly only" projects in the public housing program.[f]

This observation, although often made, has induced remarkably little action on the part of local or federal government. Local jurisdictions devote little of their own funds, including block grant allocations, to improve key projects. Similarly, the allocation of public housing modernization and other funds rarely shows that this factor has been considered. One recent, and important, exception was the funding of the rehabilitation of the Cochran Gardens project in St. Louis as part of a broader strategy to revitalize a key neighborhood. Likewise, the Urban Initiatives program announced in the summer of 1978 may be helpful; but it is far too early to tell.

Administrative simplicity. In principle, the public housing program need not be terribly difficult to administer. For those public authorities blessed with units built in the past ten to fifteen years and able to pay their operating expenses from revenues they generate themselves, the program is not administratively demanding. In fact, it is probably only slightly more demanding than private housing because of tenant screening, local politics, regulations on wage rates, maintenance policies, and various HUD reporting requirements.

For other authorities, administration is more difficult. For example, the older projects are in need of funds for modernization. The funds appropriated by the Congress have been small compared to the need, and they have been allocated on criteria that shift from year to year, resulting in sharp inequities among authorities. Each authority must apply for its funds and prepare detailed plans for their use, plans that often must be revised each year to meet the new HUD priorities.

For those authorities who require operating subsidies (about 1,900 of the 2,700), there are additional reporting requirements and directions from HUD. The necessity of much of this cannot be argued against, if accountability is to be maintained. Some of the current reporting goes to feed the operation of the Performance Funding System, the system devised to allocate operating subsidies against some criteria of what an authority with a given set of characteristics *should* need (Sadacca, Isler, and DeWitt 1975). Although there are sharp

[f] Of course, neighborhood conditions likewise influence the ability of the projects to deliver satisfactory services. See Sadacca and Loux (1978:26).

arguments about how "should" is defined, the principle is clearly correct: there must be some standard; otherwise authorities would have an open line to the federal treasury.

In adding together these various elements—regular operations, modernization, operating subsidies—the administration of the public housing system appears labyrinthine. It is, and it is unlikely to improve significantly in the near term.

New Construction— The Section 202 Program[g]

Program Description. Although the Section 202 program has undergone a number of administrative and legal modifications since its creation by the Housing Act of 1959, it remains clearly distinguishable from most other new construction programs by three criteria:

1. The projects are financed by a direct federal loan to a private, nonprofit sponsor. Thus, the sponsor need not seek out private financing, and the government, as mortgagee, can exercise options private mortgagees might not.
2. The program is restricted to the elderly and to the nonelderly handicapped.
3. It is the only program relying exclusively on nonprofit sponsors to develop and operate projects.

The initial program provided forty-year loans at 0.5 percent interest above the U.S. Treasury borrowing rate. In 1964, it was modified to provide loans to sponsors at 3 percent interest, and the sponsors were responsible for all operating expenses. Later, it was felt that this resulted in the exclusion of some low-income households because the rent levels were set too high.[h]

In response to this problem, two changes were made in the 1974 Housing and Community Development Act: (1) the applicable interest rate was defined as the U.S. Treasury's long-term borrowing rate, and (2) a Section 8 subsidy was set aside for each unit to be built under the Section 202 program in order to assure that at least 20 percent of all participants were low-income households. Given the long lead time for new construction under a revised subsidy program, the information on occupancy patterns and so forth are for the projects built prior to the 1974 modifications.

[g] The initial part of this section draws heavily on U.S. Department of Housing and Urban Development (1978).

[h] Income limits are 135 percent of public housing admission limits or 80 percent of median income, whichever is greater.

The Section 202 projects are expected to provide more than shelter. The HUD handbook states:

> The housing projects shall be designed to provide, and management plans also shall include, an assured range of necessary services for the occupants, such as, among others, health, continuing education, welfare, informational, recreational, homemaker, counseling and referral services, as well as transportation where necessary to facilitate convenient access to such services and also to employment opportunities and participation in religious activities. (HUD 1978: 3)

At the same time, however, there are sharp limits on the health care facilities and services to be provided in the project. Furthermore, designs of moderate cost in low-rise structures are clearly encouraged. Loan limits are established on a per unit basis.

The Section 202 program had, by 1977, produced 335 projects containing 45,275 units. For the 1975–1977 fiscal years, an additional 46,000 units of the combined Section 202/Section 8 units have obtained fund reservations from HUD. This compares with about 1 million subsidized units under all programs in the same period. Thus, compared to the public housing and Section 8 programs, it is a modest activity. However, the program has been popular with the Congress and with elderly groups, which has resulted in the continuation of Section 202 as a separate activity instead of its being subsumed by other broader purpose programs like Section 8.

Evaluation

Housing improvement. Although it is expected that Section 202 units will pass minimum physical standards based on their initial cost and on an evaluation of project condition since construction, it is difficult to know whether moving into Section 202 projects resulted in a significant improvement in housing quality. The program had no asset limitations on eligibility and most tenants have had moderate incomes. Hence, significant improvements for this group seem dubious. Still, at the time of an evaluation, about one-quarter of Section 202 tenants were lower-income households receiving housing subsidy payments from some HUD program (such as rent supplements); and for this group housing quality improvement would certainly be possible (HUD 1978, "Section 202": 43, 43a). There is, however, no explicit evidence on this point.

Equal opportunity. The Section 202 program can only be given low marks in this area. Both the HUD evaluation and a 1973 study show only about 3 percent of project occupants to be members of minority groups (HUD 1978, "Section 202": 43, 43a; Lawton and Klaussen 1973: 68). Furthermore, minority individuals are concentrated in a few projects located in predominantly or almost exclusively black neighborhoods (HUD 1978, "Section 202": 43, 43a).

Housing stock preservation. The low marks accorded public housing apply here with equal force. It should be noted that, like public housing, Section 202 can finance the substantial rehabilitation of existing structures for use in the program. This option has, however, been used infrequently.

Administrative simplicity. One of the hallmarks of the original Section 202 program was its informal administrative structure and comparatively simple set of rules and regulations. Special staff members were assigned to the program in HUD field offices. With the introduction of the Section 8 feature, administration of the program has, by necessity, become more complicated although it is still less complicated, for both sponsors and for the central HUD staff, than the public housing program. Even though income certifications and management plans must be reviewed and a physical inspection of the project made, there are less detailed management concerns than with most other programs.

Rehabilitation Loans—Section 312

Program Description. Created by the Housing Act of 1964, this program provides federal funds directly to finance rehabilitation needed to bring properties at least into conformance with local housing codes.[i] It is operative only in Community Development Block Grants or other federally assisted projects such as homesteading or urban renewal. The program provides a 3 percent interest rate rehabilitation loan, with a maximum repayment period of twenty years. Applications are locally reviewed and funded using funds distributed to applicant communities by HUD.

The purpose of the program is to provide financing to households who could not obtain rehabilitation financing through private financial institutions. This emphasis has resulted in high default rates compared to the rates for loans made by private institutions.[j] Since Section

[i] An excellent discussion of the Section 312 program (and its former companion grant program S. 115, which has been terminated) is in Gressel (1976).

[j] Gressel describes the underwriting process by explaining that a Section 312 loan can be made only if the loan represents "an acceptable risk, taking into consideration the

Table 7–3. Section 312 Loans, by Income of Recipient: 1967–1977

Income Interval[a]	*Percentage Distribution*	*Cumulative Percentage*
Under $2,992	10.8	10.8
$2,992–$4,488	9.9	20.7
$4,489–$7,480	20.8	41.5
$7,481–$10,472	20.8	62.3
$10,473–$11,968	8.6	70.9
$11,969–$13,464	7.1	78.0
$13,465–$14,960	5.6	83.6
$14,961–$16,456	4.3	87.9
Over $16,456	12.1	100.0

Source: Section 312 Information System, Office of Community Planning and Development, U.S. Department of Housing and Urban Development.

[a] All incomes refer to income recorded at the time of the loan.

312 loans are supplemental, they need not be secured by a first mortgage on the property. In fact, for small loans no lien is required.

Section 312 loans are available to both owner-occupants and investors, but about 80 percent of all loans have gone to owner-occupants. The law requires that priority be given under the program to low- and moderate-income families. (The income definition is roughly equivalent to that of the Section 8 program, 80 percent of the metropolitan median family income for a family of four being considered the criterion for moderate income.)

Table 7-3 presents data on the incomes of loan recipients over the 1967–1977 period. The incomes are those recorded at the time of the loan, with no adjustment for inflation over the period. Thus, the data as presented are only suggestive and will sharply overstate the fraction of low-income households receiving loans. According to these figures, even with the substantial bias present, 40 percent of recipients had incomes of over $10,500. The program has, though, reached blacks, with 45 percent of all loans going to such households.

The program has not been large in the past. In fact, through fiscal 1976, only about 47,500 loans had been made to assist the rehabilitation of some 75,000 units. Funds for expansion of the program have been appropriated for fiscal 1979 as part of the Carter administration's urban strategy, and a major portion is slated for use in multifamily properties.

---

need for the rehabilitation, the security available for the loan, and the ability of the applicant to repay the loan" (1976:16). It is the first consideration—the consideration of need—that really distinguishes the Section 312 standards from those of the private lender.

There is only suggestive information on the extent to which elderly headed households participate in the program. Data for 1975–1976, taken from a sample of performance reports under the Community Development Block Grant program, show around 20 percent of the committed loans going to elderly and handicapped households. It is not possible, however, to say whether this is an appropriate share, since the age composition of eligible households is unknown in the geographic areas where Section 312 loans can be made.[k]

Evaluation

Housing improvement. By definition, dwelling quality is improved at the time the rehabilitation work is completed. Two questions, unanswerable at present, deserve attention: (1) In the case of renter-occupied units, is there a change in tenancy so that higher income households benefit from the subsidy? (2) Is the dwelling improvement maintained over time—that is, if demand was insufficient to maintain a unit previously, will one-time assistance create an increased demand sufficient for the household or investor to maintain a unit at a higher level?[l]

Equal opportunity. As noted earlier, blacks have constituted 45 percent of loan recipients. Although it seems likely that blacks are receiving a fair share of such loans, it is impossible to know from the data available. To be certain, it is necessary to know the racial and income mix of the neighborhoods designated for Section 312 loans *and* whether there had been any discrimination in selecting these neighborhoods.

Two additional points concerning equal opportunity stem from two administrative features of the program. First, it is a loan program that requires that recipients have sufficient income to pay it back. This clearly limits the class of recipients. Whereas initially the Section 115 grant program was used in tandem with Section 312 to permit lower-income households to participate, now CDBG funds are to be used for this purpose; and the extent to which this is occurring is not clear. Second, the regulations require that work be done by contractors, a feature that may discourage Section 312 use by some households who might do the work more cheaply themselves; but the households still have the option of participating.

[k] For more on participation see Mayer's (1979) recent analysis.

[l] An impact evaluation of this question is now underway by HUD. In addition, some highly interesting results based on simulations are reported in Ozanne and Vanski (1977).

Housing stock preservation. The program clearly receives high marks, if the results of the rehabilitation are sustained, as noted previously.

Administrative simplicity. As administered until the middle of 1978, the program rates a low score. The multitude of forms, checks, inspections, and estimates are legend.[m] Modifications were introduced in 1978 to streamline the program, but the ultimate effects of these changes remain to be seen (HUD 1978, "Revisions in Section 312").

Rehabilitation Loans and Grants under CDBG

Program Description. The Community Development Block Grant Program, enacted as part of the 1974 Housing and Community Development Act, was designed to provide local communities greater flexibility in dealing with blight and neighborhood decay than the set of categorical grant programs it replaced. Under CDBG, major cities and other populous urban jurisdictions apply for an annual grant that is determined by a formula specified in the law and the total amount of funds appropriated. In contrast to these "entitlement communities," other jurisdictions receive their funds on a discretionary basis; the rules for these grants are broadly established in the law. Applicants compete with others within the same state, and winning applications are selected by HUD. The total program is large, about $3.5 billion in fiscal 1977; of this, about 70 percent is distributed to entitlement communities.

While housing and rehabilitation was regarded as a secondary element in CDBG in the 1974 legislation, it was upgraded by the Congress in 1977, following the clear pattern of use of CDBG funds.[n] A group at the Brookings Institution, which has been monitoring CDBG expenditures in sixty-one entitlement jurisdictions since the program's initiation, estimates that 23 percent of the CDBG funds in these jurisdictions went to housing rehabilitation in the second program year (fiscal 1976), the latest year for which data are available (Dommel et

[m] For an outline of the administrative process, see Gressel (1976:18–19).

[n] The objectives of the CDBG program, as enumerated in the 1977 act, are (1) elimination and prevention of slums and blight; (2) elimination of conditions detrimental to health, safety, and the public welfare; (3) conservation and expansion of the housing stock; (4) expansion and improvement of community services for persons of low and moderate income; (5) more rational use of land and other natural resources; (6) increased diversity and vitality of neighborhoods; (7) restoration and preservation of properties having special value; and (8) alleviation of physical and economic distress by stimulating private investment and community revitalization in areas with population out-migration or stagnating or declining tax bases.

al. 1978; chap. 5; HUD 1978, "3rd Annual Report"). This means that block grants were by far the largest federal funding source for housing rehabilitation in 1976.[o]

Communities are adopting a broad range of rehabilitation programs, with four key design elements in common:

Rehabilitation standards. Most communities can require that code violations be abated; they may also specify that only code violations be covered. Higher standards might be used or other types of improvements permitted.

Geographic concentration. Although all block grant funds must be used predominantly to assist low- to moderate-income households, communities may use these funds throughout all eligible areas or the funds may be targeted to badly deteriorated areas or areas of incipient decline.

Subsidy depth. The community can provide outright grants, grant/loan combinations, loans with a fixed degree of interest subsidy, or it may vary the subsidy terms with the incomes of recipients.

Bank involvement. Inducing financial institutions to use their funds through "leveraging" techniques such as guarantees by the city of private bank loans, with the guarantees backed by CDBG funds; interest subsidies, with the city using its funds only for the subsidy; and combining city grants with market-rate loans.

With the range of combinations implied by these four design elements, it is difficult to classify accurately how cities are spending their rehabilitation funds.[p]

At present, little information about the recipients of these rehabilitation grants and loans is available at the national level. Although the law stipulates that block grant funds predominantly assist low- and moderate-income households, compliance with this requirement has been monitored using data on the incomes of the households in the census tracts in which the funds are spent rather than on the compilation of data for individual recipients. HUD now has an evaluation of the impacts of the block grant program underway that will provide information on recipients of rehabilitation assistance, but these data are not yet available. As in the Section 312 program, the only information now available is from a sample of early performance reports. These show elderly-occupied units accounting for about one-third of all

[o] This pattern was probably sustained through fiscal year 1978. It will likely still hold in FY 1979 despite the major expansion of the Section 312 program we noted.

[p] One compilation has been made of program types. See U.S. Department of Housing and Urban Development (1977).

units receiving rehabilitation assistance, with five out of six elderly recipients being homeowners. Again, this information cannot be translated into judgments about whether the elderly are adequately served, since the household composition of target neighborhoods is unknown.

When the focus is shifted to smaller communities (under 50,000 population), it is important to note that a recent survey of small cities outside of metropolitan areas found city officials ranking improved housing for low- and moderate-income families no less than fifth among eighteen high-priority needs. In 1977, 35 percent of the applications from such communities included housing rehabilitation as an activity to be funded under CDBG funds (HUD 1978, "Developmental Needs of Small Cities": chaps. 3, 6).

Evaluation

Housing improvement. For households remaining in an improved unit, improvement in housing quality through rehabilitation is assured. For those displaced directly (forced out during the repairs) or indirectly (by the improved dwelling attracting more affluent households willing to pay higher rents or dwelling prices), the final answer is much less certain. The issue of displacement and its ultimate consequences is a very complicated one and, at present, there is little solid evidence available on its nature and extent.[q]

Equal opportunity. Like other federal housing and community preservation programs, the CDBG statute has strong language mandating equal opportunity. Because of the complementary citizen participation provisions, the visibility of spatial expenditure patterns within each participating community, and the enforcement efforts on the part of the Department of Housing and Urban Development, equal opportunity within entitlement jurisdictions is likely to be good, although again, hard data are lacking.

The equality of treatment of those in entitlement jurisdictions compared to those in the smaller communities in the discretionary portion of the program is a much greater problem. Most discretionary grants have been for a single purpose and have been concentrated among infrastructure investments, especially water and sewerage facilities. The role of block grants for rehabilitation has been less significant here, but has shifted toward this activity recently. While the question of equality of treatment under CDBG is far too broad to be adequately

[q] For an excellent review of current information and a discussion of the issues see Sumka (1979) and Myers (1978).

addressed here, the basic facts suggest that little improvement in physical housing conditions has resulted from the program in most nonmetropolitan areas—the areas where the need is greatest.

The funds allocated under the block grant program to entitlement communities are targeted on the basis of need (Dommel et al. 1978; chap. 2). One estimate shows entitlement areas in the highest quartile of need—as measured by indices of poverty, unemployment and growth lag—receiving about three times the per capita grants of those in the lowest quartile (HUD 1978, "Distressed Cities"). No comparable analysis of the targeting of discretionary grants has been done.

Housing stock preservation. There is no question that CDBG grants and loans for rehabilitation are preserving the existing stock of housing.

Administrative simplicity. The grant and loan procedures instituted by individual communities are typically much less complicated than those under many other programs. One example is the Boston Housing Improvement Program, in which a city inspector estimates the cost of program-qualifying repairs. Once the repairs have been made, the household is given a rebate based on a percentage of the estimated cost. The work can be done either by the household or by a contractor. The degree of the rebate depends on the type of household (elderly versus nonelderly) and the level of distress in the neighborhood in which the dwelling is located (City of Boston 1977). This type of procedure is less cumbersome than that of the traditional Section 312 program.

At the same time, though, federal regulations are being added to the CDBG program that may eventually limit this flexibility and simplicity for rehabilitation. Some of the areas of actual, or potential, regulations are the following: removal of lead base paint hazards, applicability of union wage scales for labor employed in block grant-financed projects (so-called Davis-Bacon requirements), and payments of relocation fees to households displaced by rehabilitation. Enforcement of these and other requirements could restrict the use of CDBG funds to large projects ("gut rehab"), where their cost would be a smaller share of the full job; this, in turn, could work against the participation of some groups of households.

In the area of the relations between HUD and local jurisdictions, CDBG probably represents an improvement for most jurisdictions. On the one hand, the law does require more systematic planning for meeting the housing and community development needs on the part of entitlement communities. On the other hand, there is a single application process instead of multiple, and the flexibility in fund use is impressive.[r]

DEMAND PROGRAMS

As noted earlier, the demand approach involves increasing the purchasing power of households with the expectation that at least a share of this purchasing power will be used to improve housing. This section describes two demand programs: one, housing allowances, has been only experimental to date; the other, the Section 8 Housing Assistance Payments Program, is presently the largest program operated by the Department of Housing and Urban Development. Although wide-ranging evaluations of both programs have been completed, much more is known about the effects of housing allowances.

The two programs are similar in many ways. To participate in either, an income-eligible household must live in a unit that meets minimum quality standards. If this condition is met, the household receives a subsidy equal approximately to the difference between the rent of the unit and its specified contribution to the rental payment, usually 25 percent of income. The programs are administered by local authorities. The details of the programs differ somewhat, but the general principle is clear.

One difference that should be highlighted, however, concerns the range of activities under each program. Once the Experimental Housing Allowance Program (EHAP) certifies households as eligible, the recipients find their own units, and then the units are inspected. The program uses the existing stock of housing. Under Section 8 there are two distinct program elements. The first, the "existing program," is very similar to EHAP. In the second, long-term assistance payments contracts are signed with developers or landlords who will then build, or substantially rehabilitate, units for occupancy by low- to moderate-income households. The subsidy is through a guaranteed subsidized demand. Thus, the Section 8 program is flexible enough to meet diverse market conditions.

The remainder of this section details how these programs operate and describes how the elderly fare under them, based on the completed evaluations.

Housing Allowances

Program Description. Since the congressional authorization of EHAP in 1971, housing allowance payments have been made in twelve

[r] For an overall program assessment see Dommel et al. (1978).

areas under three separate experimental elements. Most of the information used here is from the "supply experiment" which is still going on in the Green Bay, Wisconsin (Brown County), and South Bend, Indiana (St. Joseph County), metropolitan areas. This element is designed to determine whether a national program with universal eligibility of income-eligible households will adversely affect the housing market. Because of funding limitations, no current housing programs are run on an entitlement basis; that is, by virtue of the ability to meet an income or other test, a person is "entitled" to the subsidy. Hence, the Housing Allowance Supply Experiment (HASE) provides especially valuable data on program participation. Allowance payments will be made for ten years in each site to ensure that experimental biases from shorter payment periods are overcome.

The second element of EHAP, the "demand experiment," was a careful study of the types of expenditures several hundred recipients made using the additional income from their allowance payments. These data were contrasted with two other groups, one that received cash payments with no restriction that they be used for housing, and one that received no subsidy at all but only small payments for agreeing to be interviewed periodically. It is data of this type, gathered in Pittsburgh and Phoenix, which allow a determination of the extent to which allowances cause households to consume better housing than they would otherwise. This experiment involved payments to households for three years; the field stage is past and the analysis is virtually finished.

To clarify the mechanics of an allowance program, an outline of how the supply experiment program operates follows.[s] The assistance offered to an eligible household is designed to permit the household to live in a safe, decent, but modest unit. The actual payment is the difference between the cost of a modest unit (as determined by the program administrators) and one-fourth of the recipient's income. The assistance payment cannot exceed the actual cost of housing.

Virtually all households who meet the income and asset requirements are eligible. Income cannot exceed four times the standard cost of adequate housing for a given household size; that is, allowance payments are geared to the size of the unit, which in turn depends on household size.[t] The asset limit has been set at $32,500 for an elderly-

[s] The description relies heavily on material in (The RAND 1978). For succinct overview of all the experimental components, see (U.S. Department of Housing and Urban Development 1978, A Summary Report).

[t] Household income is adjusted for work expenses and for elderly persons and dependents, generally paralleling adjustments made under the public housing programs.

headed household and $20,000 for others. This asset ceiling is relatively high to permit homeowners with low income to participate. But gross income is determined so as to include imputed income from home equity and real property that does not yield a cash flow.

The household, whether owner or renter, seeks its own unit, with some assistance if requested. The unit selected must meet the physical standards of the program, and the household must spend at least an amount equal to its subsidy payment for housing. In practice, the first condition is much more important than the second. Households can relocate as often as they want, but each unit must pass the program standards. Income eligibility is periodically verified, and those no longer income-eligible leave the program; but if income is again reduced, the household can reenroll in the program.

Some idea of the magnitude of the program is provided by the data in Table 7-4, which record the total number of applicants, the number eligible, those authorized for payments, and those currently receiving payments. Even though the program in St. Joseph's County was begun about six months later (January 1975), the number of applicants and participants has been larger than in Brown County. However, the major point is the sheer volume of participants—8,000 households receiving payments in the two sites in September 1976.

Of equal importance is the amount of assistance received by recipients. Table 7-5 shows that the average annual payments received by various household groups is clearly important to participants. For elderly renters, such aid is equivalent to about 17 percent of gross income; for elderly homeowners, about 12 percent. Aside from the improvement in housing, which is detailed in the following sections, it

Table 7–4. Selected Statistics on Housing Allowance Program Size in the Supply Experiment, through September 1977

	Brown County		*St. Joseph County*	
	Number of cases	*Percent of total*	*Number of cases*	*Percent of total*
All applicants	12,745	100	21,943	100
Eligible and enrolled	6,782	53	10,026	46
Authorized for payment	5,562	44	7,490	34
Currently receiving payments	3,148	25	4,913	22

Source: Fourth Annual Report of the Housing Assistance Supply Experiment. R-2302-HUD. Santa Monica, Calif.; The RAND Corporation, 1978, Table 2.1.

Table 7–5. Participants' Incomes and Alowances: Housing Allowance Programs in Brown and St. Joseph Counties, End of Year 2[a]

Age of Head and Household Type	Average Annual Amount ($)					
	Renter			Owner		
	Gross Income	Adjusted Gross Income	Allowance Payment	Gross Income	Adjusted Gross Income	Allowance Payment
	Brown County					
Nonelderly	4,676	3,835	887	5,464	4,030	906
Young couple, young children	5,446	4,452	1,009	5,566	3,912	1,030
Single head with children	4,763	3,852	878	6,244	4,921	794
Other	3,866	3,293	803	4,712	3,362	901
Elderly	3,655	3,051	592	4,399	3,638	504
Elderly couple	4,801	3,927	642	5,382	4,359	539
Elderly single	3,385	2,845	581	3,887	3,263	485
All types	4,393	3,618	805	4,916	3,828	699
	St. Joseph County					
Nonelderly	3,510	2,634	1,114	4,916	3,703	850
Young couple, young children	4,861	3,777	1,115	5,813	4,437	860
Single head with children	3,325	2,389	1,180	4,898	3,573	928
Other	3,438	2,880	883	4,589	3,597	738
Elderly	3,315	2,764	632	4,105	3,334	526
Elderly couple	4,745	3,873	639	5,265	4,184	515
Elderly single	3,121	2,614	631	3,649	2,999	530
All types	3,465	2,664	1,004	4,428	3,481	655

Source: Tabulated by the Housing Assistance Supply Experiment staff from Housing Assistance Office records through June 1976 for Brown County and December 1976 for St. Joseph County.

[a] Entries are based on records for 1,572 renters and 1,209 homeowners in Brown County and for 1,584 renters and 2,369 homeowners in St. Joseph County who were receiving payments at the end of year 2. Those counts exclude 33 renters and 2 homeowners in Brown County and 107 renters and 15 homeowners in St. Joseph County whose rent records were defective or who were living rent-free. Entries are based on the participants' last recorded incomes and payment amounts.

is clear that the allowance payments provide substantial budgetary relief.[u]

Evaluation

Housing improvement and stock preservation. In a demand program, improvement for those who become recipients while remaining in the same dwelling unit, the effect on their housing and stock are identical. Because of this overlap for part of the recipient population, these two criteria are treated together.

Two types of information are presented to measure housing improvement: (1) changes in housing expenditures of renters and (2) the level of maintenance and repair activity induced by the program for owner-occupants and, to a lesser extent, for renters. For both it is essential to have some type of control group against which to compare the behavior of recipients.

As noted earlier, the demand experiment was structured specifically to determine whether housing allowances (with their minimum housing requirements) induced greater housing expenditures compared with unrestricted cash grants or with the expenditures of households who received no income supplements. This analysis assumes a close correspondence between rents and the quantity of housing services a dwelling provides, an assumption that was shown in Chapter 3 to have general validity.[v] The sample sizes in the demand experiment were relatively modest, and analysis has not been done separately for households headed by the elderly. Hence, the results are summarized for all types of households.

Table 7-6 displays the increase in housing expenditures induced by the allowance program. These were determined by subtracting the increase in housing expenditures of households similar to allowance recipients who received no payment from the housing expenditure increase of recipients. Three groups of recipients are distinguished in the table on the basis of their initial housing quality and whether they moved to meet program standards. Renters whose initial units passed inspection and who remained in the units increased their expenditure by only 2 percent more than nonrecipients; those who met the requirements, either after repairs to the initial unit or after moving to an acceptable unit, increased theirs by 19 percent over nonrecipients; and

[u] Appendix Tables 7A-1 and 7A-2 display the preprogram housing expense-to-income ratios of program participants, renters, and homeowners. Most households have what is usually defined as excessive housing burdens.

[v] Analyses of the experimental data include examination of the physical characteristics of units occupied by recipients and nonrecipients.

Table 7–6. Program-Induced Increases in Housing Expenditures of Allowance Recipients Compared to Nonrecipients (Percentage Change in Housing Expenditures)

	Pittsburgh	*Phoenix*	*Average*
Allowance recipients who only met housing requirements after enrollment[a]	12	26	19
Allowance recipients who met requirements at enrollment[a]	2	2	2
Mover households who became allowance recipients	16	30	22

Source: Wallace, J.E. *Preliminary Findings from the Housing Allowance Demand Experiment.* Cambridge, Mass.: ABT Associates, 1978, Figures 2 and 4.
[a] For recipients of allowances under the "housing gap" plan only.

those who moved increased theirs by 22 percent, on the average, over nonrecipients. Thus, allowances do induce increased housing expenditures, but the extent depends heavily on the initial housing status of the recipient, and the average overall increase is modest.

But, do allowances induce greater expenditures on housing than would an unrestricted cash transfer? The answer, as documented in Table 7-7, is yes: allowance recipients devoted about three times as much of their transfer payments to housing as recipients of unconstrained grants. The housing requirement does indeed make a difference.

In examining the data available from the supply experiment on repairs and improvements, it is important to distinguish between initial repairs, repairs that were necessary for a unit to meet the program's minimum physical standards, and annual repairs, those undertaken following the acceptance of the unit (and its occupant) into the

Table 7–7. Comparison of Change in Program-Induced Housing Expenditures as a Percentage of Payment for Allowance Recipients and Recipients of Unconstrained Cash Grants

Program	*Pittsburgh*	*Phoenix*	*Average*
Housing Allowance[a]	26	32	29
Unconstrained cash transfers	0	19	10

Source: Wallace, J.E., *Preliminary Findings from the Housing Allowance Demand Experiment.* Cambridge, Mass.: ABT Associates, 1978, Figures 2 and 4.
[a] Recipients of allowances under the "housing gap" allowance plan only.

program. Some annual repairs may have been required as a result of the annual reinspection of units in order for the dwelling to continue to meet program standards. Also, note that initial repairs include those made to units occupied by eligible households who stayed in the unit and eventually qualified it, as well as repairs required to units for relocating households.

The basic information on repair activity is presented in Table 7-8, which gives data on both initial repairs (top panel) and annual repairs (lower panel).

In examining the data on initial repairs, although it is clear that the median cost of such repairs was modest, it is noteworthy that the large difference between the median and average cost of repairs indicates that some major repairs were undertaken. Among owner-occupants who made repairs, the elderly spent more than their more youthful counterparts at both sites—$59 versus $54 in Brown County and $93 versus $67 in St. Joseph County. This may reflect a generally poorer initial state of repair of the elderly-occupied units. No clear pattern is evident among rental properties. Furthermore, both elderly renters and homeowners are more likely to repair their initial unit rather than move or terminate.[w]

The average cost of annual repairs is several times the cost of initial repairs, with the expenses reported by homeowners being about twice those reported for rental units.[x] There is no consistently different expenditure pattern for the elderly.[y]

The foregoing data are informative, but they do not confront directly the question of program-induced repairs. By contrast, the data in Table 7-9 do, by comparing the annual repair and improvement expenditures of homeowner allowance recipients and similar homeowners who are not recipients. Recipients spent about 80 percent more in Brown County and 30 percent more in St. Joseph County than nonrecipients, with elderly households being roughly similar to the nonelderly in both sites. These are major and significant differences. This early evidence suggests a genuine efficacy of allowances for housing stock preservation, although this should be interpreted with caution. A

[w] See Appendix Table 7A-3 and the discussion of paths to enrollment in the section on equal opportunity.

[x] Expenditures on rental units are those reported by tenants, which could easily be biased downward, since the tenant questioned may be unaware of general improvements made to the property that only indirectly affect the unit occupied by the respondent.

[y] A full description of expenditures for repairs requires data on both the cost and frequency of such repairs. Frequency data for owners and renters, disaggregated by site and age of head of house, are reported in Appendix Table 7A-4. Elderly households are consistently required to make fewer repairs as a condition for program participation than the nonelderly.

Table 7–8. Cash Outlays for Repairs to Clients' Dwellings, by Tenure by Household Type: Housing Allowance Programs in Brown and St. Joseph Counties, 1976–1977

Site, Tenure, And Household Type	*Cash Outlay ($) per Dwelling*[a]			
	All Evaluated Dwellings		*Repaired Dwellings Only*	
	Median	*Average*	*Median*	*Average*
	Initial Repairs			
Brown County				
Renter				
Elderly	8	55	9	58
Nonelderly	7	35	7	36
Owner				
Elderly	10	58	10	59
Nonelderly	10	53	10	54
St. Joseph County				
Renter				
Elderly	10	21	10	22
Nonelderly	10	37	11	39
Owner				
Elderly	10	89	12	93
Nonelderly	10	65	10	67
	Annual Repairs			
Brown County				
Renter				
Elderly	[b]	95	87	235
Nonelderly	[b]	85	60	186
Owner				
Elderly	104	273	206	369
Nonelderly	105	400	215	540
St. Joseph County				
Renter				
Elderly	[b]	136	110	320
Nonelderly	[b]	109	58	251
Owner				
Elderly	153	358	275	468
Nonelderly	80	326	186	466

Source: Tabulated by the Housing Assistance Supply Experiment staff from Housing Assistance Office records for January 1976 through June 1977.

[a] Entries include cash outlays for labor and materials insofar as they were known to the dwelling's occupant or could be estimated by the HAO's evaluator. Repairs made by landlords and their costs were not always known to tenants, so entries for renters are probably underestimates.

[b] Less than half of all renters reported any repairs during the preceding year.

Table 7–9. Homeowners' Annual Cash Outlays for Repairs and Improvements: Allowance Recipients versus Low-Income Households[a]

	Brown County			*St. Joseph County*		
		Cash Outlay ($)			*Cash Outlay ($)*	
Program Status and Age of Head	*Number of Records*	*Median*	*Mean*	*Number of Records*	*Median*	*Mean*
Allowance Recipient						
Nonelderly	522	105	400	737	80	326
Elderly	788	104	273	1,356	153	358
All cases	1,310	105	324	2,093	125	347
Low-Income Households (Not Enrolled)						
Nonelderly	59	151	241	37	26	287
Elderly	116	40	143	74	55	257
All cases	175	56	182	111	50	268

Source: Tabulated by the Housing Assistance Supply Experiment staff from Housing Assistance Office records for January 1976 through June 1977, and records of the baseline survey of homeowners in each site.

[a] For allowance recipients, entries are based on cash outlays for the preceding year, as reported by each recipient homeowner whose dwelling had an annual evaluation during the indicated eighteen month period. Low-income households (not enrolled) are those reporting incomes under $7,000 for the year preceding the baseline survey (1973 in Brown County, 1974 in St. Joseph County). Many of these households subsequently enrolled.

Entries have not been adjusted to reflect changes in incomes, allowance entitlements, or the prices of repair materials and labor; the latter were rising at annual rates of 7 to 10 percent annually, 1973–1977. Medians and means for low-income households are based on the samples indicated, but records were weighted to reflect sampling probabilities.

more sophisticated analysis, along the lines presented in Chapter 5, needs to be done: controlling for differences in household type, health, and assistance provided by relatives and friends may alter these results significantly. Still, the simple statistics presented here deserve serious attention.

Equal opportunity. The question of equal opportunity in a conditional cash transfer program, such as a housing allowance, is especially complex because of the great number of points at which the would-be participant can fail to fulfill the conditions necessary to attain recipiency status. Data comparing the participation rates of various groups do provide basic indicators; in order to judge the program intelligently, it is also essential to know something about how participation rates change at the several steps an applicant must go through to become a participant. For example, a large number of minority-group individuals may enroll in the program, but there may also be a disproportionate number unable to find housing that meets the program standards. This combination of factors yields a low recipiency rate.

The basic information on enrollment and recipiency status is provided in Table 7-10. The general structure of this table is based on the number of eligible households estimated through a baseline survey; not all narrowly defined household groups were adequately represented in the survey to permit reliable counts of eligibles. Thus, for some groups reliable enrollment rate estimates (the ratio of enrollees to eligible households) are not available. Enrollment data are for the end of the second program year, so that there is a two-year gap between the baseline eligibility figures and the enrollment figures. As a consequence, all of the figures in the table are approximations. Separate data for minorities are presented for St. Joseph County only, because of the small number of minorities in Brown County.

The table is organized to give three figures for each household group specified: (1) enrollment rates, that is, the percentage of eligible households who actually fill out the application forms and are told that if they find program-acceptable housing they will receive payments; (2) the rate at which enrollees become recipients, that is, the rate at which they find and lease acceptable housing; and (3) the rate at which eligible households become recipients, that is, the product of (2) and (1). It is the last set of rates that answers the question usually posed about program participation. The summary results are reviewed first. (See the final column in each trio of columns.)

Note that these rates vary sharply among the household types distinguished. Ultimately, about one elderly household in three receives payments, whereas among the nonelderly the rate is about two in five. These low recipiency rates for the elderly resulted even after extensive outreach efforts in both sites. Note too, that the recipiency rates of specific groups of the elderly and nonelderly overlap, so that broad generalizations about the elderly rates may be inaccurate.

Elderly renters receive payments at slightly higher rates than owners, and among both owners and renters, elderly couples receive payments at lower rates than elderly single persons. It is anticipated that participation is influenced by the size of the subsidy, and, because single persons have lower incomes than couples, a higher participation rate is expected.

Unfortunately, the only reliable data on black households are limited to three of the renter household types, and none are available for owner-occupant types in St. Joseph County. Among the three for which such data are available, nonelderly blacks are becoming recipients at rates at least as high as their white counterparts. For elderly single persons, though, blacks achieve recipiency status at a lower rate than similar white households (31 versus 24 percent). Based on a single city and early in the program, these figures must be considered cautiously.

Other columns in the table reveal systematic differences between the elderly and nonelderly in the composition of the recipiency rates. Among both renters and owner-occupants in St. Joseph County, the elderly enroll at lower rates than the nonelderly; but they move from enrollment to recipiency status at significantly higher rates than the nonelderly. In Brown County the picture is similar, but the rates for some nonelderly and elderly household types overlap. In both sites elderly renters enroll at higher rates than owner-occupants, but homeowners are more likely to occupy (or find) an acceptable unit.

In St. Joseph County black renters enroll at higher rates than whites in similar household types. (Data are not available for owners.) But blacks, both among homeowners and renters and among the elderly and nonelderly, consistently move from enrollment to recipiency status at lower rates.

Clearly, the causes for these differential rates are important; and the data in Table 7-11 allow us some insight by disaggregating the various steps in the process of becoming a recipient, or terminating from the program. Comparing black and white households in St. Joseph County, blacks live in units at enrollment that initially, or ultimately, meet program standards less often than do whites. For owner-occupants, 85 percent of whites live in "ultimately passing" units at enrollment compared to 74 percent of blacks; for renters it is 61 versus 42 percent. There are two potential consequences of this "first step" in qualifying a unit: more blacks must move to acceptable housing or not participate, that is, terminate their enrollment. In fact, blacks do both. Among program-enrolled black renters, for example, 19 percent move from an unacceptable unit to a qualifying unit (compared to 19 percent of whites) and 26 percent terminate (compared with 19 percent of whites). These results are consistent with the observations in Chapter 3 on the lower quality of housing occupied by blacks relative to whites. They also have an important implication for program design: the more stringent the standard for acceptable units established by the program, the more likely blacks will be differentially excluded from program participation.

The final equal opportunity question to be addressed is to what extent does receipt of allowance payments result in increased residential integration by permitting blacks to move into less dominantly black neighborhoods than those in which they originally lived? This is

Table 7–10. Participation Rates in an Entitlement Allowance Program, End of Year 2[a] (Percent)

	Renters			*Owner-Occupants*		
	Eligible Households Enrolled[b]	*Enrollees Becoming Recipients*	*Eligibles Becoming Recipients*	*Eligible Households Enrolled*[b]	*Enrollees Becoming Recipients*	*Eligibles Becoming Recipients*
St. Joseph County						
White households						
Nonelderly						
Young couple, young children	32	63	20	c	75	c
Single head with children	63	75	47	31	84	26
Other	48	73	35	28	83	23
Elderly						
Elderly couple	20	80	16	14	93	13
Elderly single person	38	82	31	26	90	23
Minority households						
Nonelderly						
Young couple, young children	37	61	23	c	71	c
Single head with children	c	67	c	c	74	c
Other	68	67	45	c	79	c
Elderly						
Elderly couple	c	58	c	c	87	c
Elderly single person	33	73	24	c	84	c

Brown County						
All households						
Nonelderly						
Young couple, young children	40	73	29	22	82	18
Single head, with children	69	84	54	52	88	46
Other	70	81	57	35	83	29
Elderly						
Elderly couple	30	82	25	22	90	20
Elderly single person	46	89	41	43	91	39
White households						
Nonelderly	50	71	36	26	81	21
Elderly	34	81	28	21	91	19
Elderly couple	20	80	16	14	93	13
Elderly single	38	82	31	26	90	23
Minority households						
Nonelderly	87	66	57	40	75	30
Elderly	34	70	24	[c]	85	[c]
Elderly couple	[c]	58	[c]	[c]	87	[c]
Elderly single	33	73	24	[c]	84	[c]

Source: Unpublished tabulations prepared by staff of the Housing Allowance Supply Experiment (HASE).

[a] Includes only those enrolling at least six months before the end of year 2, so as to exclude most of those still repairing their dwellings or looking for alternatives.

[b] The observation dates for eligibility and enrollment differ by about two years, during which the number of eligibles may have changed. About one-third of all enrollees terminated enrollment before the end of year; they are not counted in the enrollment rate.

[c] Based on less than ten survey records, to establish the eligible population; or too few enrollers for reliable estimate.

Table 7–11. Major Paths to First Housing Certification in Housing Allowance Supply Experiment in First Two Years[a] (Percentage of Enrollees)

			St. Joseph's County							
			All Households				*Elderly Households*			
	Brown County		*Whites*		*Blacks*		*Whites*		*Blacks*	
Outcome	*Owners*	*Renters*	*Owners*	*Renters*	*Owners*	*Renters*	*Owners*	*Renters*	*Owners*	*Renters*
Preenrollment dwelling certified										
Without repair	49	46	50	37	40	21	52	49	43	37
After repair	36	25	35	24	34	21	37	29	39	29
Moved before certification										
From acceptable dwelling	[c]	1	[b]	1	[c]	3	[b]	[c]	[c]	2
From unacceptable dwelling	2	10	3	12	5	19	2	5	3	9
No dwelling ever certified										
Enrollment terminated	11	14	9	19	17	26	6	10	10	14
Still enrolled	2	2	3	7	4	10	3	7	5	9
All outcomes	100	100	100	100	100	100	100	100	100	100

Source: Fourth Annual Report of the Housing Assistance Supply Experiment. R-2302-HUD. Santa Monica, Calif.: The Rand Corporation, 1978, Table 4.7. Also special tabulations by the HASE staff.

[a] Data base includes only records for households enrolling at least six months before the end of year 2, so as to exclude most of those still repairing their dwelling or looking at alternatives.

[b] Less than 0.5 percent.

[c] Zero.

an especially important question because higher quality units (those meeting program standards) are often more readily available outside black areas, and this availability can affect recipiency rates.

There are two elements to this question. First, do allowance recipients move more often than similar nonrecipient households? The data from the demand experiment do not provide a clear "yes" or "no," but they do indicate that if there is an effect, it is a modest one. For practical purposes, therefore, essentially no additional movement is generated (Weinberg 1977).

The second element concerns where relocating minority households go. Here the result is fairly clear: little additional integration occurs (Atkinson and Phipps 1977). However, it is important to note that the current pattern of black search behavior (defined to include method of search as well as places searched)—rather than actually encountering discrimination—is the reason for this result (Vidal 1978). Thus, efforts to disseminate information on available units outside of predominantly black areas could be quite effective. Of course, it is possible that once blacks begin searching for housing in predominantly white areas, they will encounter discrimination (Wienk et al. 1979). Still, the potential of demand programs seems substantial.

Administrative simplicity. There is no doubt that, compared to the new construction programs, an allowance type program is easier to administer. Yet it is far from simple. The rents of modest dwellings must be established, incomes must be certified and dwellings inspected. In addition, outreach efforts must be directed to both landlords and households. Two broad types of information are available on allowance program administration: (1) the general experience of those administering the program and (2) detailed comparisons of the cost of operating the supply experiment field offices and those of typical income maintenance field operations. The latter provides a benchmark for what is often considered a fairly simple welfare administration activity; and it answers the question: What is the additional administrative cost associated with the imposition of housing standards?

In addition to the supply and demand experiments, there was a third element in the experimental allowance program, the Administrative Agency Experiment (AAE). Under this element, small allowance programs were established in eight diverse communities using different types of administrative agents. The eight agents consisted of two local housing authorities, two county agencies, a city department, and three state agencies.[z] While the experiment was designed to give

[z] The agencies and the experimental sites were the Housing Authority of Salem

Table 7–12. Administrative Cost of Housing Allowances versus Aid to Families with Dependent Children (AFDC)[a]

Program and Jurisdiction	Annual Cost per Case ($)		
	Income Transfer	*Housing Requirements*	*Total*
Housing Allowance Program			
Brown County	149	58	207
St. Joseph County	144	81	225
Average	146	70	216
AFDC[b]			
New York (highest cost)	582	...	582
California	441	...	441
Indiana	226	...	226
Wisconsin	145	...	145
Mississippi (lowest cost)	77	...	77
National average	295	...	295

Source: Fourth Annual Report of the Housing Assistance Supply Experiment. R-2302-HUD. Santa Monica, Calif.: The Rand Corporation, 1978, p. 150, Table 6.4.

[a] Housing allowance costs per case are based on a postulated three-year average duration of recipiency, as in Table 6–3. AFDC costs per case are based on amounts spent during fiscal year 1976 for determining eligibility and administering payments, divided by the average monthly caseload during that year; costs of social services to recipients are excluded from the table.

[b] Entries are shown for selected states; the national average (fifty states) weights each state's costs by its caseload.

each agency considerable latitude, it is impressive that all these different agencies were able to establish and to operate the program successfully. This experience speaks well for the ease of administration, as does the early experience of local sponsors under the Section 8 program.[aa]

The Housing Allowance Offices in the supply experiment provide excellent data on the cost of administering the allowance program. The figures in Table 7-12 make two important points. First, the cost of enforcing the housing requirement in the allowance program is modest, about $70 per recipient. This constitutes about one-third of the total administration cost. Second, the administrative cost of the allow-

(Oregon); Housing Authority of Tulsa (Oklahoma), Commonwealth of Massachusetts Department of Community Affairs (Springfield); Illinois Department of Local Government Affairs, Office of Housing and Buildings (Peoria); San Bernardino County Board of Supervisors (San Bernardino, California); Social Services Board of North Dakota (Bismark); Jacksonville Department of Housing and Community Development (Florida); Durham County Department of Social Services (North Carolina).

[aa] For an overall description of the experiment see Hamilton, Budding, and Holshousers (1977).

ance program overall compares favorably with the costs of administering Aid to Families with Dependent Children (AFDC). In fact, only six states have recipient costs less than the allowance program as administered at these two sites.[bb]

Overall allowances—or their close cousin the Section 8 existing program—get high marks on administrative simplicity at the local level. Furthermore, the administrative problems at the level of the federal department are minimal compared with those for new construction programs, especially when supplemental operating subsidies have been added to initial capital subsidies.

Section 8

Program Description. The Housing and Community Development Act of 1974 created the Housing Assistance Payments Program, commonly referred to as the Section 8 program (Title II, Section 8; 43 USC 1437f). The program was designed to supplement or supplant a number of other programs serving low- to moderate-income households. The federal government assists eligible households in paying their monthly rents through a direct cash payment to landlords, hopefully inducing developers, builders, and financial institutions to provide decent housing.

The program affords local jurisdictions substantially more flexibility in meeting their housing needs than did the former capital subsidy programs, which it displaced. Importantly, the program permits variety in a mix of construction of new units, substantial rehabilitation of substandard units, and the use of standard existing units to meet the needs of the lower-income population. The variations should depend, in part, on the condition of localities' housing stock. Once the mix of new, rehabilitated, and existing housing is determined, the local agency (often a public housing authority) enters into lease agreements with suppliers and uses federal funds to make the subsidy payments.[cc]

The local flexibility embodied in the Section 8 program is truly innovative. For the first time it effectively permits a community to design a housing program best suited to its own needs. Large communities ("entitlement communities") applying for community development block grants must prepare housing assistance plans that (1)

[bb] An excellent discussion of administrative costs in the allowance program is Rand Corporation (1978).

[cc] In practice, the local authority administers that portion of the program dealing with the existing stock. Developers generally deal with the HUD area offices or state housing finance agencies on commitments for new and substantial rehabilitated units, although some authorities are involved in new construction under Section 11(b) provisions.

survey the condition of existing housing, (2) establish present and future housing needs, and (3) design a strategy for meeting the needs, including a justification for building new units, if such construction is included in the plan. The present discussion will not deal further with the "macro" aspects of the program but will turn to the operation of the individual components and the experience of the elderly under each.

As noted in the introduction to the demand programs, Section 8 is quite similar in structure to the Housing Allowance Program just reviewed. For this reason, and because the data on allowances are much richer, the Section 8 program is less thoroughly evaluated than were housing allowances.

There are, however, several important distinctions in the details of the two programs which should be kept in mind:

1. In Section 8, the household cannot spend more than the fair market rent (FMR) for a unit and still participate. In EHAP there is no limitation, but the government will pay only the difference between the FMR and 25 percent of income. Thus, Section 8 households search within a smaller segment of the housing stock.
2. Under Section 8, landlords receive two payments: the subsidy payment directly from the government agency and the household's share from the tenant. In EHAP, by contrast, the agency pays the participant household, who deals directly with the landlord.
3. While EHAP includes both owners and renters, Section 8 is currently limited to renters. While EHAP does not exclude households renting new units, it does not directly promote new construction. Section 8 does so by entering into long-term lease agreements with developers.
4. In Section 8, the income eligibility for the program is determined with reference to the median family income of the area: A family of four can have no more than 80 percent of the reference income. In EHAP, the income cut-off was four times the fair market rent.

An important commonality between the two programs is that in both the potential recipient must take the initiative to apply for the program and frequently must also take the initiative to repair its current unit or find a dwelling that will meet the minimum quality standards of the program. Hence, it is interesting to see how the elderly are faring in the program compared to their younger, and possibly more energetic, counterparts.

There are two sources of information available for describing the experience of the elderly. The first is from an early evaluation of the experience (1975 and 1976) of households, landlords, and administrative agencies under the program. Because of the much longer time required for the new construction portion of the program to become operative and for new units to become occupied compared to the time necessary to execute initial lease agreements on already existing units, this evaluation deals almost exclusively with the "existing segment" of Section 8.[dd] The second source is the records maintained in HUD's Management Information System (MIS). While the MIS data are less comprehensive, they provide relatively current information on the participation of the elderly in all portions of the program.

Experience in the Existing Program

Some statistics relevant to the participation by the elderly are given in Table 7-13. They point to a number of noteworthy facts: First, the *average* income of elderly recipients is quite low—lower in fact than the mean income of all single-person, elderly renters in 1976. Note, however, that this result is not produced by program income cut-offs per se; the income limits for one- and two-person elderly households are, in fact, quite generous. A one-person elderly household can have an adjusted income of up to 56 percent of the family median income in its area and still qualify. The national median family income was about $16,000 in 1976, so a single elderly person could have an adjusted income of $8,960—or a money income of about $10,000—and still qualify. At the same time, because the subsidy payment is calculated as the difference between the FMR and 25 percent of income, the qualifying income could often be lower. If the FMR for an efficiency apartment were $170 per month, the household's income at the point at which subsidy ceases would be $6,120, ignoring adjustments. The adjustment for household size employed by Section 8, a reduction in the 80 percent figure by 10 percent for each person in the household less than four, is, on balance, considerably less stringent than that used in the poverty or standard-of-living definition. For more on this point, see Welfeld and Struyk (1979).

There is a smaller proportion of husband-wife participants than in the renter population as a whole, but significantly more black participants than in the renter population (18 percent versus 11 percent based on AHS data).

As in the allowance program, most of the elderly remain in their pre-Section 8 unit, and very few of those who did not relocate bothered to look for a different unit. Interestingly, no greater portion of elderly

[dd] The two summary reports of this evaluation are U.S. Department of Housing and Urban Development 1978, *Lower Income Housing Assistance Program (Section 8): Interim Findings and Lower Income Housing Assistance Program (Section 8): Nationwide Evaluation.*

Table 7–13. Selected Statistics on the Participation of Households Headed by Elderly in the Section 8 Program as of 1976

	Elderly			
	Total	*Nonminority*	*Minority*	*Nonelderly*
Characteristics of Participants				
Annual income ($)				
All recipients	3155	3128	3224	3719
Movers	3075	2969	3837	3590
Stayers	3210	3241	2915	3878
Nonrecipients	3511	3555	3295	4715
Proportion receiving income assistance[a]	.93	.96	.89	.30
Proportion who are minority	.18	0	1.00	.46
Proportion with male head of household	.25	.22	.32	.20
Proportion who are husband-wife households	.14	.11	.28	.17
Unit Selection Process				
Proportion who stayed in pre-Section 8 unit	.65	.66	.57	.47
Proportion who searched for a unit				
All recipients	.30	.30	.40	.48
Movers	.80[b]	.77[b]	.94[b]	.85[b]
Stayers	.04	.04	0	.10
Nonrecipients	.39	.43	.17	.48
Proportion indicating they wanted to move	.37	.36	.45	.52
Proportion who gave program-related reasons for moving	.36	.32	.73	.45
Proportion of stayer recipients who said they faced constraints in moving[c]	.59	.61	.54	.67
Agency assistance				
Proportion who said agency gave at least enough help looking for a unit	.93	.94	.88	.91
Proportion who said they made a better choice of unit because of agency help	.42	.42	.42	.61
Proportion of movers who found new unit through the agency	.33	.39	.20	.14

Proportion saying "finding an available unit" was a major problem	.43	.41	.54	.49
Housing Expenditure and Condition				
Mean monthly pre-Section 8 expenditures[d] ($)				
All recipients	109	108	118	129
Movers	105	101	119	122
Stayers	111	112	106	135
Mean monthly expenditure under Section 8 ($)				
All recipients	147	146	155	180
Movers	156	156	156	186
Stayers	143	142	146	174
Mean monthly subsidy under Section 8 ($)				
All recipients	84	83	90	111
Movers	95	95	94	120
Stayers	79	78	85	102
Mean ratio: Preprogram expenditures as a proportion of income				
All recipients	.40	.40	.44	.38
Movers	.37	.37	.37	.36
Stayers	.41	.41	.43	.41
Nonrecipients	.38	.40	.28	.30
Proportion of dwellings requiring repairs to qualify for program				
Movers	.29	.36	.36	.45
Stayers	.21	.27	.18	.39
Proportion of movers who said conditions were better in the Section 8 assisted unit	.56	.51	.78	.61

Source: Lower Income Housing Assistance Program (Section 4): Nationwide Evaluation of the Existing Housing Program, Technical Supplement. Washington, D.C.: U.S. Department of Housing and Urban Development, 1979.

[a] Includes Social Security, Supplemental Security Income, and similar payments.

[b] Not all movers are reported as having searched for a unit because of inconsistencies in questionnaires used by two contractors, who performed parts of the evaluation.

[c] Respondent thought he could not find a better unit because of family size or lease requirement, or thought move was too expensive or difficult.

[d] Only for households with positive pre-Section 8 rents.

than nonelderly felt they were constrained from moving by the program's lease requirement or by the expense or difficulty moving entailed (row B.5 in table). Also, the vast majority thought the local administering agency was helpful.

In program outcomes, the elderly become recipients at a higher rate than the nonelderly, once they enroll in the program. The elderly constitute 35 percent of all recipients, but only 18 percent of nonrecipients (HUD 1978, "Nationwide Evaluation"). Likewise, there is a reduction in the average ratio of housing expense to income for recipients from 40 to 23 percent.

It is more difficult to judge the improvement in the quality of housing occupied but, for several reasons, it would appear to be modest, at least in the first year. Only one-fifth of elderly nonmovers needed to make any repairs to qualify a unit; this contrasts with two-fifths of nonelderly nonmovers making repairs. Also, although a higher proportion of movers occupy repaired units and movers increase their housing expenditures by 48 percent on the average, only one elderly participant in three relocated. Among all nonmovers, rents rose 28 percent, a surprisingly large increase. This was produced in large part by very large rent increases for units with preprogram rents of $50 or less, although units with initial rents of $50–150 also had sizable increases. These increases may imply an increase in services received, but it is more likely caused by landlords using the opportunity to pass along deferred rent increases. This seems a more feasible explanation, because recipients have little incentive to hold back rent increases and because the direct relationship between the administering agency and the landlord may increase the landlord's ability to bargain for higher rents as a condition for participation. In the early days of the program, when there was pressure to get households enrolled into suitable units, administering agencies may have acceded fairly readily to such requests. In this same vein, there has been little rent rise for nonmovers in supply experiment EHAP where tenants maintain an interest in low rents because they get to keep the difference between the FMR and 25 percent of income.[ee]

But the program should not be judged solely on the initial period of operation. If deferred rent increases have been made current, improvements in the level of services should be forthcoming. Also, if a landlord's expectations have been altered (for example, by having a unit under lease when there was formerly no lease), one would expect to see units maintained at least at the current level of services, and

[ee] Under Section 8 there has been a complicated and poorly understood shopping incentive that was designed to split any savings between the household and the government. For a thorough discussion of this point see Khadduri (1978).

possibly increased. More complete information on these points will be discussed in the second evaluation of Section 8, which will be completed in 1980.

Elderly Participation in the Full Program. Although the burden of participation is on the recipient in both the new and existing segments of the program, the administration of the two segments has pervasive differential effects on participation. Section 8 is not an entitlement program, and the number of units for which there is budget authority appropriated by the Congress must be allocated to the individual communities. The communities, in turn, are to use their allocation of units to meet the goals they have established in their Housing Assistance Plan (HAP). The local public housing agency (usually a traditional housing authority) administers the existing portion of the program.

Units to be constructed are administered by the HUD area office, state housing finance agencies, and in some cases, even a local authority. The mix of new units between elderly and family units in each jurisdiction is supposed to follow the local HAP. The agency advertises the availability of funds for building new units and waits for developers to apply. In theory, the number of elderly units should correspond to the HAP. However, a number of factors can, and have, intervened to change the mix. Often, developers do not apply for funds where available; local communities seek priority status for elderly housing; Congress acts to channel more units to the elderly, thus making it virtually impossible to fulfill the HAPs; and, finally, the elderly occupy some family units. This combination of factors has resulted in the elderly being overrepresented in the Section 8 program.

Table 7-14 gives occupancy data through the end of 1977. The elderly constitute half of all Section 8 occupants. There is an especially high fraction of newly built units designated for the elderly. It is clear from the more recent statistics on starts and reservations of units—that is, units likely to be built but not yet started—that the elderly's share of new units will be reduced; but in the foreseeable future, it will probably be at least 60 percent.

WHO IS SERVED?

Defining who is served by the various housing programs has been postponed until all existing programs had been explored and could be discussed at once. As noted previously, there is little reliable information on recipients of subsidized rehabilitation loans (either Section 312 or CDBG financed) and, for this reason, discussion is restricted to the

Table 7–14. Section 8 Units Occupied in Total and by the Elderly: 1977[a]

Segment of Program	Total Units	Elderly Occupied	Elderly as a Percentage of the Total
New construction	25,636	22,548	87.9
Substantial rehabilitation	4,341	3,233	74.5
Existing	232,505	110,621	47.6
Loan management[b]	95,292	44,015	46.2
Total	357,774	180,417	50.4

Source: Special tabulations, Office of Research, U.S. Department of Housing and Urban Development.

[a] Includes disabled, handicapped, and persons sixty-two to sixty-five years old; data as of January 1, 1978.

[b] Section 8 assistance provided to qualifying tenants in HUD multifamily projects whose capital cost was subsidized under another program.

recipients of assistance in rental units. While it would be preferable to have data on the rehabilitation loan recipients as well, this group, at least to date, would be small compared to the number of elderly receiving rental assistance. Thus, the figures presented below give a good picture for all the elderly.

The first question is, do the elderly receive their fair share of the housing subsidies? Specifically, are they served in proportion to their eligibility to the programs? The answer is yes. Table 7-15 summarizes the participation of the elderly in each of the rent subsidy programs. Three programs are included in the table that have not been previously

Table 7–15. Elderly Occupancy in HUD-Subsidized Rental Housing Programs as of the End of 1977 (65 and over)

Housing Programs	Total[a]	Number of Elderly[a]	Percentage Elderly
Public housing	1,036	342	33.0
Section 236	550	171	31.1
Rent supplement	110	5	10.0
Section 221(d)(3)	180	18	10.0
Section 202	45	36	80.0
Section 8	358[b]	180[b]	50.2
Total	2,279[b]	752[b]	33.0

Source: Special tabulations, Office of Research, U.S. Department of Housing and Urban Development.

[a] Numbers in thousands.

[b] Totals are overstated because some residents receive assistance from more than one program.

discussed. All these are currently inactive, in the sense that they are not being expanded. Two of the programs, Section 221(d)(3) and Section 236, subsidized new construction through low interest rates; rent supplements provided Section 8-like payments to eligible households living in FHA-insured housing projects. Elderly representation is highest in the Section 202 program, as would be expected; it is next highest in Section 8. The representation of the elderly is the lowest in the rent supplement and Section 221(d)(3) programs. Overall, those sixty-five years of age and older constitute about 33 percent of all recipients.

To calculate the number of eligible households, the Section 8 income limits were applied, household by household, to the 70,000 households in the 1976 Annual Housing Survey. In this application, separate income limits were used for each census region, and the appropriate adjustments were made for household size. The aggregate result was that those households headed by a person sixty-five or older represent 31.7 percent of all those eligible.

The elderly are currently being served by rental programs in proportion to their numbers in the eligible population. Having said that, it should be noted that eligible households include those who are currently owners as well as renters. This means that elderly renters are heavily overrepresented in comparison to all eligible renters, since a greater share of the elderly are homeowners than are the nonelderly. This would seem to call for a shift in assistance away from elderly renters to elderly homeowners.[ff]

The second question concerns the variation in program participation among subgroups of elderly households. Three types of subgroups are examined: income, race, and location.

In terms of income, are program resources being concentrated on the neediest? Because income-eligibility definitions make it possible for moderate-income households to participate in these programs, how large a share of recipients do such households constitute? Basic information on this point is presented in Table 7-16. Unfortunately, the comparison between the incomes of recipients and eligible households is not very precise because the data are only available for two years—1976 for eligibility and 1978 for recipients. Furthermore, the data on recipients include those aged 62–65 and the nonelderly handicapped. Because of inflation, use of the 1978 figures has the effect of understating the extent to which low-income households are participating.

For simplicity, a $5,000 income limit is used to define those who are clearly in need. This is a generous figure, given the high proportion of

[ff] For a separate analysis of public housing, see Gutowski and Kosel (1977).

Table 7–16. Percentage Distributions of Elderly Income-Eligible and HUD Program Participant Households

Income	All Households		Blacks		Whites	
	Eligible Households[a]	Program Participants[b]	Eligible Households[a]	Program Participants[b]	Eligible Households[a]	Program Participants
Less than $1,000	1	[c]	2	[c]	1	[c]
$1,000–$1,999	6	7	12	14	6	8
$2,000–$2,999	17	38	28	42	16	36
$3,000–$3,999	16	25	18	19	16	27
$4,000–$4,999	12	13	14	9	12	12
$5,000–$5,999	11	7	8	6	11	8
$6,000–$6,999	8	5	6	4	8	5
$7,000–$7,999	7	2	4	2	7	2
$8,000–$8,999	6	1	2	1	6	1
$9,000–$9,999	4	1	2	1	5	[c]
$10,000 and over	11	1	3	2	12	1

Source: Special tabulations, Office of Research, U.S. Department of Housing and Urban Development.

[a] Households with head sixty-five years and older, determined to be income eligible in 1976 using 1975 income data. *Source:* 1976 Annual Housing Survey, special tabulations.

[b] Households with head sixty-two years old and older and all handicapped occupying HUD-assisted housing—low rent public housing, rent supplements, Sections 8, 202, 235, 236—in 1978. *Source:* Division of Special Studies, Office of Policy Development and Research, U.S. Department of Housing and Urban Development, 1977; figures are projections to end of 1978.

[c] Less than 0.5 percent.

Table 7-17. Participation Rates of Selected Groups of Elderly Households

	Number of Households (in thousands)		
	Eligible[a]	*Occupants of Subsidized Housing*[b]	*Ratio Col. 2 to Col. 1*
Race[c]			
Whites	10,530	830	.079
Blacks	1,340	286	.213
Location			
Inside metro areas	7,620	891	.117
Outside of metro areas	4,250	224	.053

[a] Households with head sixty-five years and older; determined to be income eligible in 1976 using 1975 income. *Source:* Special tabulations from the Annual Housing Survey, 1976.

[b] Households sixty-two years and older, and all handicapped, occupying HUD-assisted housing—low rent public housing, rent supplements, Sections 8, 202, 221 BMIH, 235, 236—in 1978. *Source:* Division of Special Studies, Office of Policy Development and Research, U.S. Department of Housing and Urban Development, 1977; data are projections to end of 1978.

[c] Whites include all nonblacks.

the elderly who are single-person households. Eighty-three percent of program participants and 52 percent of eligible households have incomes of $5,000 or below. In addition, those with income under $3,000 constitute 45 percent of recipients. These figures imply that those in need—as measured by income—are predominantly being served, though some low-income households may have substantial assets. Also, 17 percent—or some 121,000 households—with higher incomes are being served, suggesting that even more should be done to assist those most in need.[gg]

Finally, the participation rates of black households and households located in rural areas are considered. The data used to make these calculations involve the same imprecision as those used previously. Participation rates, defined as the ratio of recipient households to those income-eligible by race and location, are shown in the last column of Table 7-17. Even allowing for a reasonable margin of error, it is clear that black households are *overrepresented* compared to white households; households outside of metropolitan areas are *underrepresented*

[gg] For a discussion of the treatment of assets under HUD programs for the elderly, see Welfeld and Struyk (1979).

compared to those within metropolitan areas. Caution should be used with the latter figure because the Farmers Home Administration serves the elderly in rural areas, the majority of which are outside of SMSAs.

COMPARATIVE PROGRAM COSTS

The cost of providing housing assistance is an important consideration, not only in comparing programs, but in an absolute sense as well, since the cost per recipient determines the number of households that can be served. Only those housing programs involving a long-term federal commitment are considered; therefore, the Section 312 loan program and various rehabilitation grant and loan programs funded through the CDBG program are excluded here.

Both direct and indirect subsidy costs for all programs under which new housing is constructed are displayed in Table 7-18. Four programs are included: the standard Section 8 new construction program (with the Section 221(d)(4) insurance); the Section 202 program, shown with and without an accompanying Section 8 subsidy to the household; and

Table 7–18. Comparison of Housing Program Costs[a]

		Program			
Household Income	*Year*	*Section 8 with S.221(d)(4)*	*Section 202 with Section 8*	*Section 202 without Section 8*	*Conventional Public Housing*
		Efficiency Unit			
$5,200	1st	$ 2,812	$ 2,440	$ 398	$ 2,712
	15-yr run-out	27,956	25,133	3,739	28,232
	40-yr run-out	50,495	45,129	4,975	49,945
$6,800	1st	2,442	2,069	398	2,429
	15-yr run-out	22,737	19,919	3,739	23,545
	40-yr run-out	38,051	32,684	4,975	38,764
		One-Bedroom Unit			
$6,500	1st	3,004	2,594	449	2,975
	15-yr run-out	29,145	26,157	4,232	29,792
	40-yr run-out	51,385	45,706	5,630	51,245
$8,500	1st	2,541	2,122	449	2,558
	15-yr run-out	22,580	19,633	4,232	23,932
	40-yr run-out	35,793	30,159	5,630	37,259

Source: A Comparison of Subsidy Costs for Multi-Family Housing Programs for the Elderly. Washington, D.C.: U.S. Department of Housing and Urban Development, Office of Economic Affairs, Division of Housing and Demographic Analysis, 1978.

[a] Data include total program subsidy costs, including direct and indirect subsidies, in 1978 dollars, discounted to present values.

conventional public housing. Section 202 without the accompanying Section 8 assistance is by far the least expensive. As noted earlier, even though it costs less, most low-income households could not live in these projects without some other form of assistance.

The other three programs are characterized by high total subsidy costs. An efficiency apartment occupied by a relatively well-off person who receives income of $5,200 per year still requires at least a $2,400 subsidy—a subsidy equivalent to 46 percent of income. For a household with $2,500 in annual income, the subsidy of $3,075 represents 123 percent of its income.

The subsidy costs for conventional public housing and Section 8 with Section 221(d)(4) insurance are effectively equivalent. The Section 202/Section 8 program, by contrast, is about 10 percent cheaper. The difference, compared to the regular Section 8 program, stems from lower annual loan amortization and the absence of a return on owner equity for Section 202 projects; these savings are partially offset, though, by higher indirect costs under Section 202.[hh]

Compared to these new construction programs, the cost of the component of the Section 8 program, which uses the existing stock, appears small. The simplest comparison is of the average Fair Market Rents for new and existing units. These are as follows for 1977:

Type of Unit	*Existing*	*New*
Efficiency	$150	$236
One-bedroom	$170	$275

Obviously, the same budget appropriation will serve many more households if the existing portion of the Section 8 program is emphasized. The wisdom of such emphasis, as noted, depends on the conditions in the local housing market and the current and projected needs of the elderly.

COMPREHENSIVE NEIGHBORHOOD PRESERVATION PROGRAMS

Discussion of individual housing programs has shown that each has important consequences, whether intended or not, on preserving the existing stock of housing and, therefore, neighborhoods. Furthermore, the CDBG program has stock and neighborhood preservation as an explicit objective. In this section, the four federally assisted programs

[hh] For details see U.S. Department of Housing and Urban Development (1978, A Comparison of Subsidy Costs).

designed to deal with residential neighborhood decline are described. Most of these—Neighborhood Strategy Areas, Neighborhood Housing Services, the geographical allocation of CDBG, and the Urban Homesteading Program—build on the programs already reviewed. A description of each program's intent and mechanics is followed by a description of the type of neighborhoods in which the program is operating. A comparison among the programs is given at the end.

Neighborhood Strategy Area (NSA)

The NSA Program is young; indeed, the first awards of assistance were made by HUD in the closing days of fiscal 1978. Hence, there is little documentation beyond press releases and regulations.[ii]

Program Description. The main components of the NSA program are (1) the development of a strategy for a given neighborhood by the local government, who may use a planned resource of its own, or those provided under the Community Development Block Grant program plus additional rehabilitation resources from HUD; (2) the allocation of funds to rehabilitate rental housing from HUD through the Section 8 program;[jj] and (3) the demonstration of interest by residents and local financial institutions, the latter being expected to provide loans for the HUD subsidized rehabilitation. The neighborhoods selected must be areas in which concentrated housing and community development activities are expected to result in significant neighborhood revitalization within a 5-year period. The program is especially attractive to local governments because it allows them to perform most of the processing of the Section 8 applications, thus tightening the relationship between the city and the landlord and making it easy for the city to help the small landlords participate. This is viewed by HUD to be of special importance in light of the predominance of such owners among rental property owners and their low participation in federal

[ii] An unusually good program description is provided in (U.S. Conference of Mayors and National Community Development Association 1978).

[jj] As explained earlier, the Section 8 program is a rental assistance program for low- and moderate-income families. It does not provide mortgage insurance or mortgage financing, although it may facilitate the owner's task of obtaining financing. Under the Section 8 program, HUD enters into an agreement with owners who have been selected to participate in the program. The owner agrees to rehabilitate a property and to rent it to low- and moderate-income families. When the rehabilitation is completed and low- and moderate-income families are occupying the units, HUD will pay the difference between what the families can afford to pay (not to exceed 25 percent of income) and the agreed-upon (contract) rent. The owner retains all responsibility for managing the property, subject to HUD review to ensure that the owner is keeping units in decent, safe, and sanitary condition and is fulfilling his responsibilities under the contract with HUD. The term of the contract with HUD may be for twenty, thirty, or forty years, depending upon specific circumstances.

rehabilitation programs in the past. Finally, it is HUD's intention that its resources be used as a catalyst to encourage private investment in the area.

In September 1978, HUD made awards to 155 neighborhoods based on a review of some 173 applications. A commitment of almost 38,000 units of substantial rehabilitation under Section 8 was involved in these awards, or about 250 units per neighborhood. HUD has committed an average of about $41 million to each of these areas over the thirty-year life of the Section 8 contract.

The guidelines prepared by HUD use the phrase "not too big, not too bad, and not too many properties" to define a suitable neighborhood. In doing so, they build directly on the experience of the Urban Reinvestment Task Force. (See the description of Neighborhood Housing Services below.) However, the areas must be deteriorated enough to qualify for CDBG assistance.

Community Development Block Grants

Program Description. The structure and purpose of the CDBG program has been discussed already. Presently, little is known about how the block grant resources have been used to promote neighborhood revitalization. According to the Brookings Institution's monitoring study, housing and neighborhood conservation[kk] accounted for $168 million or 37 percent of block grant expenditures by central cities in the second program year. Furthermore, about 55 percent of these funds financed rehabilitation projects, 28 percent went to public improvements (street, sidewalks, and so on) and the remainder to recreation facilities (Dommel et al. 1978:chap. 5).

We also know from the Brookings Institution that most of the rehabilitation funds were spent in declining, but not severely deteriorated, areas (Dommel et al. 1978:chap. 6). But there is no national data yet available on block grant communities or the mix of strategies being used in them.

Homesteading

The homesteading program began as a demonstration with twenty-three participating cities in 1975. In 1977, some sixteen additional cities were added, and later in the same year the Congress decided to convert from demonstration to program status. This description is

[kk] In this accounting, only those improvements indicated by associates to have been used to target neighborhoods for the specific purpose of upgrading the area are included; similar activities for communitywide use or a single activity to serve part of the community are excluded.

based on the experience of the original twenty-three demonstration cities.

Program Description.[11] The Housing and Community Development Act of 1974 authorized HUD to transfer one- to four-family properties in its inventory to local governments for use in local homesteading programs. HUD area offices were to inform local governments of the available properties, and upon local government selection, these properties would be transferred to them. Acting with this authority, HUD designed the Urban Homesteading Demonstration Program as a cooperative venture between HUD and local governments. The 1974 act defined broad guidelines for the demonstration, but key decisions on program design and goals were left to local governments, thus providing program flexibility and allowing the demonstration cities to test a number of approaches to homesteading. The basic requirements for a demonstration program were as follows:

1. The authorized homesteading agency must make conditional conveyance of homestead properties without any substantial consideration.
2. The local program administrators must develop an "equitable procedure for selecting homesteaders, giving special consideration to the recipient's need for housing and his capacity to make, or cause to be made, necessary improvements to the homestead property."
3. The selected homesteader must agree to repair the property to minimum health and safety standards before occupying the property; repair the property to applicable local standards for decent, safe, and sanitary property within eighteen months after occupancy; occupy the property for at least three years; and permit periodic inspections to ensure compliance with these conditions.
4. The authorized homesteading agency must transfer "fee simple" title to the property to the homesteader without additional consideration, upon completion of his obligations.
5. The homesteading program must be part of a coordinated approach toward neighborhood improvement and upgrading community services and facilities.

Homesteading is clearly viewed as one tool in stabilizing and improving what might be termed "fragile" or downward transitional neighborhoods. The applications to HUD for participation in the dem-

[11] This description is almost a direct quotation from Urban Systems Research and Engineering (1978).

onstration (and presumably in the actual program, although regulations are not yet final) have to detail the complementary activities the city would undertake and an overall strategy. One manifestation of these strategies has been the use of the Section 312 rehabilitation loan funds (which HUD allocates to the cities along with funds for property purchase) for nonhomesteaded properties in the same neighborhoods.

There is enormous local variation in the administration of the program in the demonstration cities, and, as a consequence, in the rate at which the program has developed and the characteristics of participating households and neighborhoods. The first cohort of participating heads of households are young (age thirty-four), of moderate annual income ($12,300) and about equally divided between single- and two-parent households. Based on the experience of early homesteaders, the mean value of contracted repairs was about $4,200 with the homesteader purchasing about $1,500 in materials and achieving about $1,500 in labor and materials savings through his own efforts (Urban Systems Research and Engineering 1978, "Baseline Analysis"). The total size of the program in the original twenty-three cities as of April 1978 was small, but growing: 1,045 properties had been conveyed to the cities, 700 had been conveyed by the cities to homesteaders and 518 homesteaders were occupying their units.

Since an evaluation of the homesteading program has been underway for almost two years, there is documentation of the forty neighborhoods involved in the twenty-three demonstration cities. Several points stand out in Tables 7-19–7-21, which provide evidence on three key indicators—income, racial composition, and extent of homeownership—of neighborhood structure in 1970 and 1977:

1. The average income in these areas in 1970 was 88 percent of the national household median; by January 1977 it had declined to 72 percent of the national figure. Only four neighborhoods rose relative to the national median. The mean 1977 income, in fifteen of the forty areas, was less than 90 percent of the *1970* SMSA average.
2. Racial composition has been dynamic: the aggregate percentage of black households increased from 45 to 65 percent from 1970 to 1977. Only thirteen neighborhoods had increases of less than five percentage points; in six the change was over 40 percent.
3. Surprisingly, the rate of homeownership rose over the 1970–1977 period, from 54 to 65 percent. An increase occurred in twenty-five of the forty neighborhoods.

This picture is one of phenomenal variety. Various neighborhoods can be classified by these three characteristics to get an idea of the

Table 7–19. Classification of Neighborhoods in Terms of 1970 and 1977 Mean Household Income as a Percentage of SMSA Mean Household Income (1970 Neighborhood and SMSA Income Data from 1970 Census; 1977 Neighborhood Income Data from Household Interview Survey on Urban Homesteading Neighborhoods)

1970 Mean Household Income as Percentage of 1970 SMSA Mean Household Income		*1977 Mean Household Income as Percentage of 1970 SMSA Mean Household Income*			
		Less than 80 Percent	*80–90 Percent*	*90–110 Percent*	*More than 110 Percent*
	More than 100 Percent			Freeport Philadelphia-E. Mt. Airy	Gary-Horace Mann Jersey City-Greenville South Bend-Riverside Manor
	80–100 Percent		Chicago-Roseland New York-New Brighton	Decatur-South Decatur Indianapolis-Forest Manor New York-Baisley Park Philadelphia-Wynnefield	Islip-Old Central Islip Kansas City-Blue Hills South Bend-Lasalle Park Tacoma-Tract 621 Wilmington-Price's Run
	70–80 Percent	Atlanta-Oakland City Chicago-Austin Oakland/Elmhurst #4	Indianapolis-Brookside Oakland-Elmhurst #1 South Bend-Run Village Tacoma-Tract 613	Baltimore-Park Heights Cincinnati-Madisonville Columbus-Near South Side Dallas-Trinity Lisbon Kansas City-49-63 Area Milwaukee-Northwest Side New York-South Ozone Park Rockford-Westside	
	Less than 70 Percent	Wilmington-Westside	Minneapolis-Northside Oakland-Fruitvale Oakland-Central East Oakland-Elmhurst #3 Tacoma-Tract 617	Milwaukee-Eastside Oakland-Elmhurst #2 Wilmington-Baynard Blvd.	

Source: "Baseline Analysis of the Urban Homesteading Demonstration." Draft: Report to U.S. Department of Housing and Urban Development. Cambridge, Mass.: Urban Systems Research and Engineering, 1978.

Table 7–20. Classification of Neighborhoods by Percentage of Black Households 1970 and 1977 (1970 Data from 1970 Census; 1977 Data from Household Interim Survey in Urban Homesteading Neighborhoods)

Percentage of Black Households 1970	Percentage of Black Households 1977: 0–25 Percent	25–50 Percent	50–75 Percent	75–100 Percent
0–25 Percent	Indianapolis-Brookside Islip-Old Central Islip Kansas City-Blue Hills South Bend-Riverside South Bend-Rum Village	New York-New Brighton Minneapolis-Northside Oakland-Fruitvale Tacoma-Tract 621		Chicago-Austin Milwaukee-Eastside
25–50 Percent		South Bend-Lasalle Park Tacoma-Tract 613 Rockford-Westside	Cincinnati-Madisonville Freeport-Area #1 Jersey City-Greenville Wilmington-Westside	Atlanta-Oakland City Chicago-Roseland Gary-Horace Mann Oakland-Elmhurst #2 Wilmington-Price's Run
50–75 Percent			Columbus-Near South Side New York-South Ozone Park Philadelphia-Wynnefield Tacoma-Tract 617	Dallas-Trinity-Lisbon Decatur-South Decatur Indianapolis-Forest Manor Kansas City-49-63 Area Milwaukee-Northwest Side Philadelphia-E. Mt. Airy Oakland-Elmhurst #1 Oakland-Central East
75–100 Percent			Wilmington-Baynard Blvd.	Baltimore-Park Heights New York-Baisley Park Oakland-Elmhurst #1 Oakland-Elmhurst #4

Source: "Baseline Analysis of the Urban Homesteading Demonstration." Draft: Report to U.S. Department of Housing and Urban Development. Cambridge, Mass.: Urban Systems Research and Engineering, 1978.

Table 7–21. Classification of Neighborhoods by Homeownership Rates 1970 and 1977 (1970 Tenure Data from 1970 Census; 1977 Data from Household Interim Surveys in Urban Homesteading Neighborhoods)

1970	Less than 50 Percent	50–60 Percent	60–70 Percent	More than 70 Percent
More than 70 Percent			Indianapolis-Forest Manor Tacoma-Tract 621	Islip-Old Central Islip Kansas City-49-63 Area New York-South Ozone Park New York-Baisley Park Philadelphia-Wynnefield South Bend-Lasalle Park South Bend-Riverside Manor South Bend-Rum Village
60–70 Percent		Tacoma-Tract 617	Wilmington-Price's Run	Atlanta-Oakland City Dallas-Trinity-Lisbon Decatur-South Decatur Kansas City-Blue Hills Oakland-Elmhurst #4 Philadelphia-E. Mt. Airy Wilmington-Baynard Blvd.
50–60 Percent	Cincinnati-Madisonville Oakland-Cent. E. Oakland Oakland-Elmhurst #1 Oakland-Elmhurst #2		Freeport-Area #1 Minneapolis-Northside Wilmington-Westside	Chicago-Roseland Gary-Horace Mann Indianapolis-Brookside Tacoma-Tract 613
Less than 50 Percent	Baltimore-Park Heights Jersey City-Greenville New York-New Brighton Oakland-Elmhurst #3	Columbus-Near South Side Milwaukee-Northwest Side Oakland-Fruitvale	Milwaukee-Eastside Rockford-Westside	Chicago-Austin

Source: Baseline Analysis of the Urban Homesteading Demonstration." Draft Report to U.S. Department of Housing and Urban Development. Cambridge, Mass.: Urban Systems Research and Engineering, 1978.

range. Still, an overall, if crude, composite does emerge: these are areas that have declined generally in economic status in the 1970s but which frequently have the seeds of increased stability through higher rates of homeownership.

Neighborhood Housing Services (NHS)

Program Description. The NHS program performs a series of remarkably straightforward (and essential) functions in a specific neighborhood to facilitate the upgrading of the housing stock. It is derived from what appears to be a very complex partnership among four partners. The premise underlying the NHS is that the availability of financing is critical to housing improvement, and, even with financing present, there must be a commitment from the residents if any improvement in an area is to occur. The four partners are as follows:

1. The residents of the target neighborhood. For an NHS to be established, the residents must be formally organized, be somewhat active and clearly want to participate in the NHS.
2. Local financial institutions. These institutions must be willing to participate in several ways: by contributing substantially to the administrative expenses of the NHS, by making rehabilitation loans in the area when applications meet their lending standards, and by helping staff the NHS's loan committee, which makes recommendations on loans in effect applied for by residents through the NHS.
3. The local community. The city must commit itself to providing improved services and/or some capital improvements in the NHS and to operating a housing code enforcement program.
4. The NHS. It is the glue that holds the enterprise together (after being requested by the city to come in), helps in the selection of the neighborhood and, once the NHS is established, places and staffs an office in the neighborhood.

Briefly, the NHS process is one of applying pressure to make housing improvements and then providing help in their accomplishment. The pressure comes both from the code enforcement program and from members of the neighborhood organization who talk to others, often those living on their own block. The assistance is available once the household (usually an owner-occupant) decides to make necessary repairs and improvements. The NHS will make a cost estimate and will frequently have a list of reputable contractors. If necessary, it also helps with financing by arranging for a local financial institution to

Table 7–22. Selected Neighborhood Statistics[a]

City	*Percent Change Population 1960–1970 City/NHS*	*Percent Black Population in NHS 1970/1960*	*Median Family Income in NHS 1970*	*Percent of City Median*	*Percent Owner-occupied in NHS Structures/Unit*	*Percent of Total Units in 1–4-Unit Structures in NHS*
Albuquerque	21.1/6.0%	2.1/1.6%	$5,653	58.6%	n.a./39.9%	85.4%
Atlanta	1.9/−10.9	29.9/1.6	$6,698	85.0	50.0/30.7	89.8
Baltimore	−3.5/−11.1	10.8/3.5	$8,083	91.6	67.0/53.6	98.4
Boston						
Mission Hill[b]	−8.0/−13.1	16.8/2.3	$7,394	80.9	67.0/07.2	32.7
Savin Hill	−8.0/−9.8	12.6/3.5	$8,562	93.7	85.0/23.5	71.7
Buffalo	−13.1/−12.1	3.1/0.8	$8,824	100.2	n.a./59.0	94.4
Chicago						
Heart of Chicago	−5.2/−10.7	2.1/0	$9,116	89.0	75.0/27.3	73.2
Austin	−5.2/−6.4	2.1/0.1	$10,318	100.7	85.0/28.7	56.7
North West	−5.2/−9.3	2.3/1.6	$9,670	94.7	77.0/28.5	75.1
Cincinnati	−9.9/−0.1	39.7/26.6	$8,872	99.7	60.0/54.8	98.0
Cleveland						
West Side	−14.2/−12.2	0.1/. . .	$8,394	92.1	53.0/32.2	89.3
Buckeye	−14.2/−10.0	51.9/36.8	$9,096	99.8	n.a./45.1	87.4
Dallas	24.2/12.5	76.5/34.8	$7,969	79.5	60.0/55.0	77.2

Jamaica, New York Queens County	9.7/50.8	94.5/83.1	$10,000	86.5	67.4/67.4	99.8
Kansas City	−6.6/−2.2	19.1/0	$9,530	96.1	60.0/59.8	90.0
Nashville	. . .	29.2/. . .	$8,210	86.6	45.0/37.3	77.2
Oakland	−1.6/17.3	64.1/12.2	$8,193	85.1	60.0/55.4	93.1
Philadelphia						
#1 (Tract 171, 172)	−2.6/3.2%	84.8/4.1%	$7,769	82.9	n.a./70.6	99.6
#2 (Tract 294, 300)	−2.6/−9.6	20.6/15.5	$8,523	90.9	n.a./55.9	90.6
Plainfield	3.3/10.0	81.0/35.0	$9,176	83.7	90.0/53.6	91.3
St. Louis	−17.0/−44.8	0.5/0.5	$6,676	81.5	50.1/19.1	90.6
San Antonio	11.3/22.5	0.4/0[c]	$4,386	56.7	55.0/40.8	92.0
Washington, D.C.	−0.9/3.0	91.3/48.9	$7,679	80.1	n.a./10.8	52.8

Source: *The Neighborhood Housing Services Model: A Progress Assessment of the Related Activities of the Urban Reinvestment Task Force.* Washington, D.C.: Office of Policy Development and Research, U.S. Department of Housing and Urban Development, 1975.

[a] The following is the estimated number of structures in each neighborhood for which data were available. Atlanta 2,700; Baltimore 4,000; Boston, Mission Hill 1,000; Chicago, heart of Chicago 2,800; Chicago, Austin 2,300; Chicago, North West 2,600; Cincinnati 5,000; Cleveland, West Side 2,000 to 2,500; Dallas 1,750; Jamaica 2,100; Kansas City 1,400; Nashville 1,200; Oakland 4,000; Plainfield 252; and St. Louis 2,800.

[b] Figures skewed due to presence of two public housing projects.

[c] The Mexican-American population in 1970 in the NHS neighborhoods was 70.3%, 39.2%, and 98.0%, respectively, of the total NHS population in Albuquerque, heart of Chicago, and San Antonio.

n.a. Not available

make the loan or, if the applicant does not meet the institution's underwriting standards, by making the loan from a national pool for "high risk" loans. Rehabilitation grants and subsidized loans are available sometimes from the city. While this is the main activity of the NHS, the small, local staff dispenses a variety of real estate advice and often acts as a real estate agent in effect, since regular brokers have often quit the neighborhood. A final, very important point is that an NHS will not be established unless all of the local participants clearly support the program.

The establishment and management of NHS is the principal program of the Urban Reinvestment Corporation (URC), an independent federal agency whose board of directors includes the heads of the Federal Home Loan Bank Board, other financial regulatory agencies, and the Department of Housing and Urban Development. In 1978, there were about sixty-five NHSs operating in some fifty cities with about half again as many under development.

The rapid expansion in the number of NHSs in the past two years has made it difficult to keep a careful accounting of the neighborhoods. Furthermore, most of the available data are from the 1970 census. Table 7-22 presents a few characteristics for the NHSs in eighteen cities that participated early. The neighborhoods have a substantial rate of owner-occupancy (including an owner occupying one unit of a multiunit structure) and the vast majority of structures contain one to four units. Most neighborhoods suffered some population decline during the 1960s. Also, most had 1970 median family incomes of 80–95 percent of the city's median family income, although there is some variance. Racial composition is highly variable. Although not shown in the table, the NHS areas tend to be modest in size, averaging perhaps 9,000–11,000 people or 2,800–3,700 dwelling units.

While no uniform characterization is possible, it seems fair to say that these areas are ones that have undergone some downward transition by the time the NHS arrives; indeed the deterioration of the housing stock is one of the prime reasons for NHS presence. They are inhabited by households of modest means, the majority of whom live in owner-occupied units.

Some Common Elements

The diversity of activities and neighborhoods in which the activities are being implemented gives one pause in searching for common elements among the four intervention strategies—homesteading, NSA, CDBG, and NHS. Still, there are some unifying characteristics: All are designed to leverage a modest investment in technical assistance and in physical improvements into a greater degree of private investment.

All involve local government: in homesteading, NSA, and CDBG, the city is a primary partner in both planning and execution; in NHS it is a less dominant partner. All are being used in a small neighborhood area, in places that have experienced some decline but are still potentially capable of stabilizing and improving themselves. These areas are *not* characterized by an extremely low-income population, extensive abandonment and physical destruction, or any of the worst social pathologies. None of them accord elderly residents a special role as a general matter. This is particularly troublesome in light of the findings of the last chapter that elderly-headed households tend to be concentrated in exactly the types of neighborhoods being treated by these programs.

Finally, none are part of SMSA-wide strategies for the promotion of housing stock preservation, racial integration, and improved housing. This is a central flaw since it is possible for public programs to work at cross purposes within the same metropolitan area.

There are notable differences: While NHS and the CDBG programs are founded on citizen participation, this is less the case with homesteading and possibly with the NSA program. Only the CDBG serves a broader range of areas, but generally not as a strategy in target areas. The NHS is differentiated by its reliance on the private financial community (facilitated by its close connection with the FHLBB) and its lack of reliance on subsidized repairs for its "seed investments." Finally, only the NSA program uses a federal housing program (as distinct from block grants or Section 312) as a primary tool; and it will be the only one to tackle the deteriorated multifamily stock systematically.

SOME LESSONS

It would appear that the elderly are receiving at least their fair share of the subsidized housing resources; they are represented among recipients in proportion to other income-eligible households. Furthermore, since elderly households have, on the average, fewer persons in them, the per capita subsidy rates are higher for the elderly than for others. Similarly, a disproportionate share of expensive new housing built under the Section 8 program has been for elderly households.

The distribution of aid among the elderly, however, leaves something to be desired. While the housing programs are directed reasonably well to the lowest income households, there is room for improvement, especially in the treatment of assets. The elderly outside of metropolitan areas are underserved by HUD programs, but the combined effect of HUD and FmHA assistance is unclear. Most importantly, the subsidized housing programs serve only renters, whereas eligibility figures include homeowners as well. Thus, elderly renters are being greatly overserved while homeowners receive no direct housing subsidies.[mm] Elderly owner-occupants do receive state and local assistance through reduced property taxes but this is a poor way to encourage housing maintenance. Moreover, the elderly are assisted to an unknown extent with rehabilitation loans and grants, but the fragmentary evidence available suggests the imbalance of all housing assistance in favor of renters is nevertheless formidable. The much higher rate of homeownership of elderly households compared to nonelderly income-eligible households makes the exclusion of elderly homeowners from housing programs especially inequitable.

Housing subsidies for newly built units are expensive—about $2,500 in the first year for a typical efficiency occupied by an elderly person with a $5,200 annual income. Renting existing units that meet certain physical standards is much cheaper but only makes sense in markets where an adequate supply of moderate-quality housing is available.

There is substantial evidence that the housing programs—both those that cause the construction of new units and those that use existing housing stock—improve, on the average, the quality of housing occupied by the subsidy recipient. The supporting data are strong for public housing, housing allowances and Section 8. The situation for the old Section 202 program, with its higher income participants, is much less clear.

Under the rehabilitation programs, the postrehabilitation housing quality for initial occupants of the units depends critically on whether the original tenant remains in the unit. If forced to move, either because repairs need to be made or because of higher postrehabilitation rents, there is no guarantee of improved housing. For homeowners, where there is coincidence of tenant and landlord, the improvement going to the initial occupant is assured.

Table 7-23 provides an evaluation of the five main programs discussed in detail in this chapter. The qualitative entries in the table range from "high"—meaning superior average performance for a particular criteria—to "low." Public housing, for example, gets high marks for the average improvement in recipients' housing but low marks in the subsidy cost per dwelling. Note that the cost is on a per-dwelling basis; there is not sufficient information to rate the programs on the preferred basis of cost per unit of service of incremental

[mm] Actually, a handful of elderly do receive assistance from HUD's Section 235 program.

Table 7–23. Summary of Effectiveness of Current Programs in Meeting Housing Objectives[a]

Program	*Improvement in Participants' Housing*	*Equal Opportunity*	*Stock Preservation*	*Administrative Simplicity*	*Cost per Occupied[a,c] Dwelling*
Public housing	high	moderate	moderate/ low	low	low
Nonprofit sponsor New construction (Section 202)[b]	not known	low	moderate/ low	moderate	high
Rehabilitation loans (Section 312)	moderate/ high	not known	high	low	high/ moderate
Rehabilitation grants and loans (community development block grants)	low/ moderate	not known	high	high	high/ moderate
Demand subsidies (housing allowances; Section 8 existing and substantial rehabilitation)	moderate/ high	moderate/ high	high	high/ moderate	high/ moderate

[a] A "high" rating means the program performs well in terms of this criteria; "low" means the opposite.

[b] This is the Section 202 program without Section 8.

[c] This is the gross average subsidy cost per assisted dwelling, not the cost per unit of incremental housing services procured with the subsidy.

housing services provided to the recipient by the program. The fact that many entries read "moderate/high" suggests the difficulty of even making these qualitative rankings. The specific entries reinforce comments made earlier. The broad lesson is obvious: no single program excels in all dimensions, and the desired mix of programs depends on local conditions.

The comprehensive strategies for neighborhood preservation are not included in the comparison table, because of the lack of solid information on any of them. A major omission from these programs as a group, though, is in any general reference to the elderly. Given the type of neighborhoods in which these programs are operating and the information presented in Chapter 6, it appears that the elderly are a very important segment of the resident population. By implication, these programs have assumed that the same tactics used to upgrade the housing of the nonelderly will work for the elderly—in particular, elderly homeowners. No awareness of the need for specially tailored programs is evident in these programs nor is the importance of keeping the elderly homeowner in the neighborhood appreciated. All too often, homes in a neighborhood characterized by incipient decline will be purchased by absentee landlords who, intentionally or not, contribute to further decline by higher occupant turnover and, in many instances, a lower level of dwelling maintenance. Chapter 9 examines how the existing arsenal of programs could be supplemented to foster greater efficiency in attaining the goals of housing improvement, housing stock preservation, and equity of treatment.

Payments at the End of Year 2[a]

Age of Head and Household Type	Number of Records	Percentage Distribution by Housing Expense/Income Ratio[b]						
		Negative Ratio[c]	.00–.15	.16–.25	.26–.40	.41–.60	.61 or more	Total
			Brown County					
Nonelderly	1,133	4	[d]	2	19	38	37	100
Young couple, young children	255	9	...	2	35	29	25	100
Single head with children	576	2	[d]	1	11	42	44	100
Other	302	3	...	4	20	37	36	100
Elderly	419	1	1	4	24	36	34	100
Elderly couple	79	2	...	4	43	34	16	100
Elderly single	340	...	1	5	20	37	38	100
All Types	1,552	3	[d]	3	20	37	36	100
			St. Joseph County					
Nonelderly	1,265	7	[d]	2	12	19	60	100
Young couple, young children	150	19	...	3	24	21	33	100
Single head with children	846	6	[d]	2	8	16	67	100
Other	269	5	[d]	2	17	26	51	100
Elderly	349	...	...	5	19	32	45	100
Elderly couple	42	...	...	7	31	48	14	100
Elderly single	307	...	...	4	17	30	49	100
All Types	1,614	6	[d]	2	13	22	56	100

Source: Tabulated by the Housing Assistance Supply Experiment staff from Housing Assistance Office records through June 1976 for Brown County and December 1976 for St. Joseph County.

[a] Entries are based on records for 1,552 renters in Brown County and 1,614 in St. Joseph County who were receiving payments at the end of year 2, but describe their circumstances when they enrolled. Forty-four renters in Brown County and 108 in St. Joseph County are excluded because they were then living rent-free in dwellings owned by others. Percentages may not add up to 100 because of rounding. Ellipsis (...) stands for zero.

[b] Annualized monthly gross rent, divided by annual adjusted gross income.

[c] Adjusted gross income is negative because of deductions and exclusions.

[d] Less than 0.5 percent.

Table 7A–2. Ratio of Housing Expense to Income at the Time of Enrollment: Homeowners Receiving Payments at the End of Year 2[a]

Age of Head and Household Type	*Number of Records*	*Percentage Distribution by Housing Expense/Income Ratio[b]*						
		Negative Ratio[c]	*.00–.15*	*.16–.25*	*.26–.40*	*.41–.60*	*.61 or more*	*Total*
Brown County								
Nonelderly	585	9	1	11	25	27	26	100
Young couple, young children	172	16	2	7	18	30	27	100
Single head with children	196	2	[d]	10	28	34	27	100
Other	217	11	1	14	29	20	25	100
Elderly	635	[d]	[d]	22	58	14	5	100
Elderly couple	217	1	1	48	38	8	5	100
Elderly single	418	[d]	[d]	9	69	17	5	100
All Types	1,220	5	1	17	42	20	15	100
St. Joseph County								
Nonelderly	917	6	[d]	11	29	24	29	100
Young couple, young children	131	8	1	5	34	24	28	100
Single head with children	444	5	...	7	27	23	38	100
Other	342	6	1	19	30	26	18	100
Elderly	1,436	[d]	1	24	48	21	6	100
Elderly couple	403	[d]	1	53	34	9	2	100
Elderly single	1,033	[d]	[d]	13	53	26	8	100
All Types	2,353	2	1	19	40	22	15	100

Source: Tabulated by the Housing Assistance Supply Experiment staff from Housing Assistance Office records through June 1976 for Brown County and December 1976 for St. Joseph County.

[a] Entries are based on records for 1,220 homeowners in Brown County and 2,353 in St. Joseph County who were receiving payments at the end of year 2, but describe their circumstances when they enrolled. Percentages may not add exactly to 100 because of rounding. Ellipsis (. . .) stands for zero.

[b] Annual housing expense as calculated by the HAO (it excludes the opportunity cost of the owner's equity in his home), divided by annual adjusted gross income.

[c] Adjusted gross income is negative because of deductions and exclusions.

Table 7A–3. Client Responses to Initial Evaluation Failures, by Tenure and Age of Head: Housing Allowance Programs in Brown and St. Joseph Counties through Year 2[a]

Tenure and Age of Household Head	*Number of Records*[b]	*Percentage Distribution by Action Taken*			
		Move	*Repair*	*Terminate*	*Total*
		Brown County			
Renter					
Nonelderly	862	19	57	23	100
Elderly	171	12	71	18	100
Owner					
Nonelderly	519	1	76	23	100
Elderly	305	[c]	85	15	100
		St. Joseph County			
Renter					
Nonelderly	1,062	18	55	27	100
Elderly	181	6	80	14	100
Owner					
Nonelderly	709	1	71	28	100
Elderly	747	[c]	86	13	100

Source: Tabulated by the Housing Assistance Supply Experiment staff from Housing Assistance Office records through June 1976 for Brown County and December 1976 for St. Joseph County.

[a] Percentages may not add exactly to 100 because of rounding.

[b] All enrollees with complete records whose preenrollment dwellings were evaluated and failed, and who had subsequently taken one of the indicated actions. In Brown County, 2,073 enrollees failed, 188 had yet to act following failure, and 28 records were excluded because of missing data or tenure or age of head. In St. Joseph County, the corresponding numbers are 3,148, 406 and 43.

[c] Less than 0.5 percent.

Table 7A–4. Results of Housing Evaluations in the Supply Experiment, through Year 2 (Percent of Units Acceptable)[a]

	Renters			Owners		
	Initial Evaluation			*Initial Evaluation*		
	Pre-enrollment Unit	*Other Enrollee Nominated Unit*	*Reevaluation of Failed Unit*	*Pre-enrollment Unit*	*Other Enrollee Nominated Unit*	*Reevaluation of Failed Unit*
Brown County						
Nonelderly	50	38	92	44	61	91
Elderly	65	71	96	57	77	95
Couples	51	71	97	54	[b]	95
Singles	68	71	96	58	[b]	95
St. Joseph County						
Nonelderly	37	34	73	44	48	86
Elderly	51	42	90	50	[b]	94
Couples	55	[b]	88	54	[b]	93
Singles	51	[b]	90	49	[b]	94

Source: Tabulated by the Housing Assistance Supply Experiment staff from Housing Assistance Office records through December 1976.

[a] If feasible, each enrollee's preenrollment residence is evaluated even though the enrollee may plan to move. Prospective residences are evaluated only at the enrollee's request; often, several such evaluations are conducted on behalf of the same enrollee. Households reinstated after an earlier termination of enrollment must have their dwellings reevaluated as though they were new enrollees. Failed units are evaluated (after repair) at the enrollee's request.

[b] Number of cases too small to be reliable.

REFERENCES

Adams, J.E. 1972. "The Performance of Public Housing in Small Cities: Net Tenant Benefits and Federal Expenditures." *Nebraska Journal of Economics and Business* 15, no. 3: 59–71.

Atkinson, R., and A. Phipps. 1977. *Locational Choice, Part II; Neighborhood Change in the Housing Allowance Demand Experiment.* Cambridge: Abt Associates.

Barton, D.M., and E.O. Olsen. 1976. "The Benefits and Costs of Public Housing in New York City." Madison, Wisc.: Institute for Research on Poverty, Paper 372–76.

City of Boston. 1977. *Housing Improvement Program: Summary.* Boston: Office of Housing.

Dommel, P.R., et al. 1978. *Decentralizing Community Development.* Washington, D.C.: The Brookings Institution.

de Salvo, J. 1971. "A Methodology for Evaluating Housing Programs." *Journal of Regional Science* 11: 172–86.

Gressel, D. 1976. *Financing Techniques for Local Rehabilitation Programs.* Washington, D.C.: National Association of Housing and Redevelopment Officials.

Gutowski, M., and J. Kosel. 1977. *Methods for Assessing Age Discrimination in Federal Programs.* Washington, D.C.: The Urban Institute.

Khadduri, J. 1978. "The Rent Reduction Credit Feature of the Section 8 Existing Housing Program." Washington, D.C.: Office of Policy Development, U.S. Department of Housing and Urban Development.

Hamilton, W.; D.W. Budding; and W.L. Holshousers, Jr. 1977. *Administrative Procedures in a Housing Allowance Program: The Administrative Agency Experiment.* Cambridge, Mass.: Abt Associates.

Lawton, M.P., and E. Klassen. 1973. "Federally Subsidized Housing, Not for the Elderly Black." *Journal of Social Behavioral Science* 19 (Summer-Fall).

Mayer, N. 1979. "The Effectiveness of Federal Home Repair and Improvement Programs in Meeting Elderly Homeowner Needs." Washington, D.C.: Urban Institute Working Paper 1283-1.

Myers, P. 1978. *Neighborhood Conservation and the Elderly.* Washington, D.C.: The Conservation Foundation.

Ozanne, L., and J.E. Vanski. 1977. "Rehabilitating Central City Housing: Simulations with the Urban Institute Housing Model" (Washington, D.C.: Urban Institute Report).

Rabushka, A., and W.G. Weissert. 1977. *Caseworkers or Police? How Tenants See Public Housing.* Stanford: Hoover Institution Press, 1977.

The Rand Corporation. 1978. *Fourth Annual Report of the Housing Assistance Supply Experiment.* Santa Monica: R-2302-HUD.

Sadacca, R., and S.B. Loux. 1978. "Improving Public Housing Management: A Technical Report." Washington, D.C.: Urban Institute Working Paper 255-2.

Sadacca, R.; M. Isler; and J. DeWitt. 1975. *The Development of a Prototype Equation for Public Housing Operating Expenses*. Washington, D.C.: The Urban Institute.

Struyk, R. 1977. "The Need for Local Flexibility in U.S. Housing Policy." *Policy Analysis* (Fall): 471–84.

Sumka, H.J. 1979. "Displacement in Revitalizing Neighborhoods: A Review and a Research Strategy." *Occasional Papers in Housing and Community Affairs*. No. 2.

Vidal, A. 1978. "Draft Report on the Search Behavior of Black Households in Pittsburgh in the Housing Allowance Demand Experiment." Cambridge, Mass.: Abt Associates.

Weinberg, D., et al. 1977. *Locational Choice, Part I: Search and Mobility in the Housing Allowance Demand Experiment*. Cambridge, Mass.: Abt Associates.

Welfeld, I., and R. Struyk. 1979. "Housing Options for the Elderly," *Occasional Papers in Housing and Community Affairs* 3: 1–143.

Wienk, R.; C. Reid; J. Simonson; and F. Egger. 1979. *Measuring Racial Discrimination in American Housing Markets: The Housing Market Practices Survey*. Washington, D.C.: Department of Housing and Urban Development.

Chapter 8

The Scope of Existing Social Programs

The Department of Housing and Urban Development has a legislative mandate to initiate and direct federal programs affecting the size, composition, quality, and location of the national housing stock. Residential repair, renovation, and maintenance programs are clearly within the purview of HUD. The mandate given the Department of Health, Education and Welfare is much more complex and broadly defined than that given HUD. HEW is charged with coordinating and administering programs that improve the quality of life and the life chances of individual citizens. Because efforts to improve housing conditions benefit individual recipients as well as the national housing inventory, programs to upgrade the housing units occupied by older persons also are of legitimate concern to HEW.

In the preceding chapter, the discussion and evaluation of housing assistance programs was confined to those administered by HUD; in this chapter programs emanating from federal departments other than HUD are reviewed. At the federal level, responsibility for housing programs is allocated primarily to HUD and HEW. Unlike HUD's programs, those administered by HEW are predicated on a social service perspective; in order to promote adequate housing among the elderly, services, not housing units, are provided. In addition to reviewing HEW policies for housing assistance, we also will examine briefly programs originating from the Farmers Home Administration, within the Department of Agriculture.

The task of identifying those social services that support residential maintenance is a complicated one. A basic problem of definition is encountered at the very beginning of this task: what constitutes a social service supportive of residential maintenance activities? As noted in Chapter 4, there are multiple determinants of home maintenance activities for older homeowners. Such activities are a function of income, neighborhood conditions, the cost of purchased services, the extent of donated services, the availability of family or friends, the feasibility of self-repair, and the nature of the repair activity itself. Thus, programs that modify any of the determinants of housing repair activity in the desired direction are indirectly supportive of home maintenance. Consider for example the potential effects of two nonhousing programs administered by HEW. The Supplemental Security Income program provides additional monthly income to qualifying low-income aged and disabled persons. To the extent that SSI increments discretionary income and that such income is expended for needed housing repairs, SSI can be viewed as a program having an indirect and positive effect on home maintenance services. Similarly, health care costs absorbed by Medicare may protect or increase income allocated for the purchase of repair and maintenance services. Medicare coverage also may encourage preventive health care behavior and extend the ability of the older homeowner to make his own needed repairs. Clearly, any number of nonhousing social services may influence indirectly the home maintenance patterns of older persons. In the following sections only select nonhousing social service programs are discussed. In part, the decision to limit the discussion reflects the need to establish realistic guidelines for closure. A complete description of all social programs, even those originating at the federal level, far exceeds the scope or purpose of this book. In addition, the effects of such programs on home maintenance activities are tenuous and nearly impossible to quantify.[a] As a result, programs directly supportive of housing maintenance activities are emphasized at the expense of indirectly supportive programs.

Social programs directly supportive of housing maintenance services can assume many forms. Some programs provide cash grants or loans to qualifying older homeowners, others provide repair services per se from a pool of workers maintained for that express purpose. Still others reimburse workers from the private sector. Frequently, the payment schedule operates on a sliding scale, with older homeowners above a certain income level covering a portion of the repair costs.

The availability and structure of social service home maintenance

[a] The research findings in Chapter 4 are an obvious exception. Data from the Survey of Maintenance and Repair Activity by Elderly Homeowners show that a small portion of supplemental income is voluntarily allocated to home maintenance or repair. Despite the limitations of the data, the analysis strongly suggests that the indirect effect of income maintenance programs is, at best, weak.

programs varies widely because of the funding intrastructure. With few exceptions, the responsibility for housing maintenance programs is shared by the federal and state governments and, in some cases, by social service agencies at the county or municipal level. Typically, funds are provided to the state to implement the broadly defined objectives of federal legislation, such as Title XX of the Social Security Act. The states assume the responsibility for planning and operating programs that are compatible with the objectives of the legislation. Although the initiating legislation usually imposes guidelines regarding program activities and eligibility, the states have the flexibility to determine what specific services are offered, to whom they are offered and where. Thus, it is impossible to speak of Title XX housing service programs as a single, unified program initiative. Rather, there may be as many as fifty-one Title XX housing programs, one operating in each state and the District of Columbia.

The states' role in delivering housing maintenance services for the elderly also is expanded by the federal revenue sharing program. Under this program, a percentage of the federal tax money collected from the residents is returned to the state or local government based on factors such as population size, poverty rates, and state and local tax efforts. Expenditure of this money is at the states' discretion.[b] Individual states may elect, for example, to allocate some proportion of these funds to housing maintenance programs. In such instances, the design, implementation, and structure of the program are totally at the state's discretion. A state could decide to make housing repair assistance available to all homeowners in a certain income group or to design programs only for the elderly.

Because of the importance of the states' role in delivering housing services for the elderly, a comprehensive national perspective on social service housing programs is nearly impossible to develop and is of limited analytic utility. In the following sections a disaggregated approach is used.

PROGRAMS DIRECTLY SUPPORTIVE OF HOUSING MAINTENANCE

Programs directly supportive of housing maintenance are those that provide either the services of trained workers for the express purpose of home repair, renovation, maintenance, or reimbursement of the

[b] Typically, the states have allocated very little of General Revenue Sharing funds to social services, including those for the elderly. The General Revenue Sharing Amendments of 1976 repealed priority spending categories, one of which was social services for the poor and aged.

homeowner for the cost of such services purchased through a private or semiprivate contract. A survey of non-HUD federal service programs indicates that at least three programs provide some type of housing maintenance assistance. These are (1) Title XX of the Social Security Act, (2) Title III of the Older Americans Act, and (3) Sections 502 and 504 of the 1949 Housing Act, administered by the Department of Agriculture. Most of the non-HUD programs providing housing maintenance are social service programs funded through Title XX and Title III. These funding sources are emphasized in the following review.

Title XX

Title XX of the Social Security Act (Grants to States for Services, Public Law 93-647) was enacted in 1974 and took effect October 1, 1975. Although a relatively new program initiative, Title XX is heir to a twenty-year history of federal cost-sharing programs for the provision of social services. Since 1956, the federal contribution for such services has increased from 50 to 75 percent.[c] Federal expenditures have reached $2.5 billion for fiscal year 1977.

Under Title XX, money is allocated to the states strictly on the basis of population for the purposes of planning and providing social service programs directed towards five goals:

1. Achieving or maintaining economic self-support to prevent, reduce or eliminate dependency;
2. Achieving or maintaining self-sufficiency including reduction or prevention of dependency;
3. Preventing or remedying neglect, abuse, or exploitation of children and adults unable to protect their own interests or preserving, rehabilitating, or reuniting families;
4. Preventing or reducing inappropriate institutional care by providing for community-based care, home-based care, or other forms of less intensive care;
5. Securing referral or admission for institutional care when other forms of care are not appropriate or providing services to individuals in institutions.

Most of the services provided to older persons "tend to be those closely related to strengthening their capability to function independently in their housing environment." (Gutowski 1978: 120).

[c] Under Title XX, the federal government reimburses the state an amount equal to 90 percent of expenditures for family planning services and 75 percent for the expenditures incurred in meeting the five goals specified in Section 202 of the Social Security Act, as amended.

Title XX continues the federal social service commitment to low-income individuals and households. Programs are designed to service three categories of recipients: (1) persons qualifying for income-tested programs may participate in programs such as Supplemental Security Income, Aid to Families with Dependent Children, or Medicaid; (2) persons with income not in excess of 15 percent above the state median income (adjusted for family size) may receive all services subsidized by Title XX; and (3) any individual, regardless of income, may obtain information, referral, family planning, or protective services provided under Title XX auspices.

Within these constraints, individual states have a great deal of flexibility in planning and delivering a social service package that is tailored to the unique needs of state residents. Under previous social service programs, HEW had the authority to mandate the provision of certain services; under Title XX, each state determines which services are offered, as long as at least one service addresses each of the five goals of the legislation and at least three services are provided to recipients of Supplemental Security Income. Through Title XX, states also acquired the authority to adapt their service delivery approach to meet the varying demands of different areas within the state. Under Titles IV-A and VI of the Social Security Act, the predecessors of Title XX, any service offered had to be provided on a statewide basis regardless of the need for such a service throughout the state. All but sixteen states have opted for disaggregating service delivery among substate areas.

Because states bear the responsibility for identifying and delivering needed services, the legislation establishing Title XX also requires states to develop and publish a Comprehensive Annual Services Program Plan (CASP). Each state report must:

> describe[s] program objectives, services to be provided, categories of individuals to be served, availability of services by geographic area, sources of resources, coordination with other human services programs, needs assessment, planning, evaluation and reporting activities, organization structure of the Administering Agency, and estimated expenditures. (U.S. Department of Health, Education and Welfare, 1977: 3)

Title XX mandates that these reports be made available for public review and comment. For the planning cycle of fiscal year 1976, changes in eligibility criteria were the most likely consequence of the public review process. In 1976, for example, twenty states and the District of Columbia changed eligibility levels during the planning cycle—nine states and the District lowered eligibility requirements, while twelve states raised them. Federal approval of the CASP reports is not necessary under Title XX, although a copy of each state's report is filed with HEW.

Title XX promotes a decentralized approach to social service planning and delivery. Approximately 1,300 different service programs are supported through Title XX in the fifty states and the District of Columbia. In order to develop a national perspective on Title XX service delivery, HEW has formulated a typology of forty-one general types of social services.[d] Of the forty-one services, Alaska offers the fewest (thirteen) and Maryland offers the most (thirty-four). The average number of Title XX services provided by the states and the District during fiscal year 1976 was twenty-five and one-half.

In the Title XX typology of social services, housing maintenance activities may be included in "chore services," "housing improvement services" or "home management services." For fiscal year 1976, thirty-seven states offered chore services, forty-five states committed Title XX funds to housing improvement services and forty-four states provided home management services. Three states (Delaware, Mississippi, and South Dakota) offered none of the three housing-related services; Hawaii offered only chore services; seventeen states offered two and the other thirty states and the District offered all three services. Most states offering these services provide them directly. In thirty-eight of the states offering housing improvement services during the last quarter of 1976, the service was provided directly by employees of the appropriate state agency; sixteen states purchased the service from public sources and an additional nineteen states purchased the service from the private sector.

A wide variety of state-sponsored programs are grouped together in the three housing-related categories. In some states, for example, chore services may be limited to housekeeping assistance, errand running, or grounds maintenance. In other states chore services also may include assistance with minor and infrequent repairs. Thus, simply locating a state offering housing-related programs, singly or jointly, does not necessarily mean that a state sponsoring housing improvement services, per se, has been located.

As a result, it is not possible to estimate with certainty the scope of or expenditures for housing maintenance or repair services under Title XX. This caution must be kept in mind when reviewing the data shown

[d] Based on the Comprehensive Annual Service Plan filed by each state, activities with similar characteristics were grouped under a "common standard service description"; programs that did not evidence commonality with services offered in the other states were grouped in the "other" category of the HEW typology. For a more complete taxonomy of Title XX Social Services see Project Share (1978). National data are published only for the forty-one general types of service categories.

in Table 8-1. Only those services specifically categorized as housing improvement are included in the tabulations. Hence, the estimates shown in Table 8-1 are close to being "worst-case" estimates and represent the minimum expenditure of Title XX for housing maintenance-repair services.

During July-September, 1976, thirty-nine states offered services specifically directed toward "home improvement." The scale and the cost of the programs varied widely, as can be seen from columns 1–3 in Table 8-1. As few as ten (in the District of Columbia) and as many as 8,520 (in New Jersey) primary recipients were served by the housing improvement programs operating within the thirty-eight states and the District of Columbia. The cost of these programs varied between a low of $387 in Wyoming to a high of $1,040,430 in New York. The national per-capita expenditure was $89. In only three states (California, Florida, and Montana) was the average cost per recipient in excess of $200; in nine states (Alabama, Colorado, Georgia, Illinois, Missouri, North Carolina, North Dakota, Oregon, and Wyoming) the average cost was less than $50. As can be seen from the last column of Table 8-1, the involvement of Title XX funds in the area of housing improvement is minimal. Nationally, only 0.9 percent of all Title XX monies was allocated to housing improvement programs. Nevada, West Virginia, New Jersey, Maine, and Iowa committed the largest proportion of their Title XX funds to housing improvement services, yet in no state is the allocation greater than 5 percent. Even when the national expenditures for chore services and home management services—the other service categories potentially aiding in home maintenance services—are added in, the maximum expenditure for repair maintenance services is but 7 percent of the total Title XX expenditures for the last quarter of fiscal 1976.

The data just cited pertain to all recipients of Title XX housing services, regardless of age. The elderly's share of these services can be estimated indirectly if one accepts a series of assumptions. Nationally in fiscal 1976, there were 4,169,464 Title XX recipients who were adults; 425,175 of these were aged SSI recipients. If one assumes that the elderly are represented in the other eligibility categories in proportion to the number of persons below the poverty level who were elderly, an additional 496,690 Title XX recipients were aged. This method of estimation suggests that 22 percent, or approximately 922,000 recipients, were elderly. If one further assumes that elderly recipients consumed each type of Title XX service uniformly, then fewer than 16,000 recipients of housing improvement services were elderly, and nationwide, less than 0.1 percent of all Title XX monies was directed toward improving the physical environment in which older persons reside.

Table 8–1. Title XX Housing Improvement Services, by State: Last Quarter, FY 1976

State	Number of Recipients	Expenditures: Total	Expenditures: Per Capita	Total Title XX Budget	% Committed to Housing Improvement
Alabama	3,509	$ 156,264	$ 44.53	$ 13,358,025	1.2%
Alaska	45	6,918	153.73	1,204,238	.6
Arizona	49	2,475	50.51	5,365,344	.1
Arkansas	[a]	[a]	[a]	8,575,651	[a]
California	4,365	1,032,530	236.55	87,739,891	1.2
Colorado	1,381	61,916	44.83	11,239,940	.6
Connecticut	753	113,329	150.50	15,708,979	.7
Delaware	[a]	[a]	[a]	2,074,832	[a]
District of Columbia	10	10,186	1,018.60	3,645,003	.3
Florida	90	52,435	582.61	24,731,258	.2
Georgia	1,852	57,154	30.86	16,545,558	.3
Hawaii	[a]	[a]	[c]	3,543,261	[c]
Idaho	[b]	[b]	[c]	2,201,076	[c]
Illinois	511	10,200	19.96	31,496,122	[e]
Indiana	213	11,439	53.70	4,592,597	.2
Iowa	1,592	111,595	70.10	5,655,731	2.0
Kansas	[a]	[a]	[a]	6,997,938	[a]
Kentucky	805	136,717	169.83	12,000,153	1.1
Louisiana	804	112,894	140.42	9,946,188	1.1
Maine	786	88,626	112.76	3,952,707	2.2
Maryland	14	[d]	[c]	[d]	[c]
Massachusetts	1,637	192,213	117.42	24,397,607	.8
Michigan	7,662	559,911	73.08	50,426,262	1.1
Minnesota	2,399	225,901	94.16	22,593,297	1.0
Mississippi	[a]	[a]	[a]	3,269,691	[a]
Missouri	7,209	69,362	9.62	5,205,736	1.3
Montana	48	21,428	446.42	2,942,168	[a]

Nebraska	[a]	[a]	[a]	5,627,303	[a]
Nevada	569	42,321	74.38	1,110,733	3.8
New Hampshire	75	9,732	129.76	2,666,082	.4
New Jersey	8,520	919,488	107.92	31,548,810	2.9
New Mexico	[a]	[a]	[a]	3,138,955	[a]
New York	8,213	1,040,430	126.67	68,870,251	1.5
North Carolina	2,392	104,950	43.88	19,650,184	.5
North Dakota	110	$ 2,551	$ 23.19	$ 2,229,994	.1
Ohio	1,284	114,791	89.40	31,579,567	.4
Oklahoma	1,048	66,925	63.86	9,916,923	.7
Oregon	520	18,586	35.74	9,478,033	.2
Pennsylvania	4,317	436,649	101.15	25,580,527	1.7
Rhode Island	966	[d]	[c]	[d]	[c]
South Carolina	0	1,662	[c]	8,689,610	[c]
South Dakota	[a]	[a]	[a]	2,897,614	[a]
Tennessee	996	57,158	57.39	9,384,052	.6
Texas	[a]	[a]	[a]	44,455,685	[a]
Utah	42	6,404	152.48	4,515,069	.1
Vermont	159	21,554	135.56	2,614,649	.8
Virginia	2,330	145,843	62.59	13,870,522	1.0
Washington	[a]	[a]	[a]	15,067,460	[a]
West Virginia	1,466	141,407	96.46	4,403,401	3.2
Wisconsin	2,660	153,370	57.66	17,225,067	.9
Wyoming	10	387	38.70	1,499,463	[e]
U.S. Total	70,963	$6,317,702	$ 89.00	$715,429,207	.9

Source: Office of Human Development Services, Administration for Public Services (DHEW), 1978, *Social Services U.S.A.*, Publication No. (HDS) 78-02020.

[a] Service not provided.

[b] Data not provided.

[c] Entry was not calculated because of missing data.

[d] State did not submit cost data.

[e] Less than 0.1 percent.

Since the states' distribution of Title XX funds supposedly reflects the need for specific services within the states, one might be tempted to interpret the low allocation of Title XX funds to housing improvement as an indicator of the minimal need or demand for such services. At least two survey sources refute this contention, however. In Wayne County, Michigan, a survey of service priorities found that 57 percent of recipient respondents reported housing improvement services to be among the seven most needed; only 35.7 percent of service providers assigned housing improvement services such a high priority (Gutowski 1978). In a survey of the elderly in Rhode Island, residential repair and renovation service was the service needed, but not received, by the largest proportion of the elderly (Rhode Island Department of Elderly Affairs 1978). These and other surveys suggest that Title XX's supply of housing improvement services falls far short of the demand for such services. At its current level of support, Title XX housing improvement services are likely to have little effect on the conservation of housing units, including those owned and occupied by older persons. Title XX, however, is not the only funding mechanism supporting housing improvement services and, as discussed later in this chapter, few municipalities rely exclusively on Title XX for funding home improvement maintenance services.

Title III

Unlike Title XX, services funded by Title III of the 1975 Amendments to the Older Americans Act (Grants for State and Community Programs on Aging, Public Law 94-135) are targeted specifically at the elderly. Receipt of Title III services is contingent only on age, not income, although service provision to low-income and minority-group elderly is encouraged.

In many other respects Title III programs are similar to Title XX. Like Title XX, Title III provides for a service delivery system that is planned, coordinated, and implemented at the state level. States are not mandated to provide specific services but to develop "coordinated and comprehensive" service systems directed toward (1) securing and maintaining independence and dignity and (2) removing the individual and social barriers to economic and personal independence for older persons. A number of social services are recognized as being compatible with the overall objectives of the legislation, including those "services designed to assist older persons to obtain adequate housing."

A unique feature of Title III is the establishment of state and area agencies on aging, a network that is "uniform in design, but diversified in operation." In order to be eligible to receive Title III allotment, there must be a state agency designated to serve as the sole state agency on aging. The state agency is charged with the development of the state plan of service delivery and evaluation, the administration of the state plan, the coordination of all intrastate activities relevant to aging (including those funded from other sources, such as Title XX), and the division of the state into district areas, or "planning and service areas."[e]

The area agencies are the primary arena of activity under Title III. Area agencies have the following responsibilities:

1. Developing a "comprehensive and coordinated" system for the delivery of social services. As part of this activity, area agencies are expected to identify the need for specific types of social services and negotiate agreements with providers of social services to offer the needed services.
2. Establishing or maintaining information-referral centers.
3. Rendering technical assistance to providers of social services.
4. Making arrangements with child day care centers "so as to provide opportunities for older persons to aid or assist, on a voluntary basis, in the delivery of such services to children."
5. Establishing and working with an advisory board composed of Title III recipients and the general public.
6. Formulating an area plan covering the preceding five activities.

Note that area agencies do not provide social services per se, but coordinate or serve as brokers for the delivery of needed services. The service provider may be a program funded from other federal or state funds such as the use of CETA workers to make home repairs, or the use of a private nonprofit social service agency or a contracted private for-profit group. As with Title XX, the states and area planning units under Title III exchange a great deal of local flexibility for administrative-coordinating responsibility.

States submitting acceptable comprehensive planning and evaluation reports to the commissioner on aging are awarded grants to plan, coordinate, evaluate and administer these plans. Each state receives 0.5 percent of the total Title III allocation for the fiscal year ($287,200,000 for the fiscal year ending September 30, 1978), plus an additional amount equal to the percentage of the total population age

[e] A planning and service area is any unit of local government whose elderly population exceeds 50,000 persons or that contains more than 15 percent of the state's older population. In some of the smaller states (such as Rhode Island, Delaware, or the District of Columbia) or sparsely settled states (such as Alaska and North Dakota) the entire state is designated as a single state planning and service area.

sixty and over residing in the state. From a state's allotment, the state agency on aging may elect to pay up to 75 percent of the cost of administering area plans (not to exceed 15 percent of the total allotment) and 90 percent of the cost of providing social services as part of a "comprehensive and coordinated system" of service delivery. The 1975 Amendments of the Older Americans Act also require that the state must:

1. Provide at least 20 percent of Title III state planning and social service funds, or
2. Allocate 50 percent of its increase in Title III allotment for the four priority services of transportation, legal and other counseling, home services, and *home repair and renovation* (emphasis added).

During the second quarter of fiscal year 1978, a total of $2,028,973 for residential repair and renovation services was expended by at least forty-eight states, the District of Columbia, and U.S. territories. Approximately 60,000 older persons received such services; nearly half of these were low-income elderly and one-quarter were minority-group elderly. The average per capita expenditure was fairly modest—$34.57. Recipient profiles and expenditures patterns, by state, are shown in Table 8-2.

The number of recipients was fairly uniform across states.[f] With the exception of New York, New Jersey, and California, most states served fewer than 1,500 older persons. In a majority of states at least one-half of the recipients of Title III repair and renovation services were low-income elderly. The extent to which minority-group members received Title III housing assistance varied widely, ranging from less than 5 percent to 50 percent or more. For the most part, the proportion of minority-group recipients is high in states with large concentrations of older blacks or Spanish-speaking persons.

However, expenditure patterns varied widely, ranging from a low of $327 in Hawaii to a high of $257,098 in California. The average expenditure for residential repair-renovation services was $42,270 per state. Per capital expenditures were low for the most part. Only in five states did the cost per recipient exceed $150; in fourteen states, the average expenditure was less than $50. The exact nature of the repairs or renovations financed by Title III monies is not available, but, given the generally low per-capita expenditure patterns, it is improbable that major repairs were undertaken very often. It is more likely that Title III repair activities were limited to infrequent minor repairs

[f] As used in this discussion, "states" refers to all fifty states, the District of Columbia, the Virgin Islands, Guam, American Samoa, and the Trust Territories.

Table 8–2. Title III Residential Repair and Renovation Services: Number of Recipients and Expenditures, by AoA Region and State: FY 1978, Second Quarter

	Number of Recipients			*Expenditures*	
Region and State	*Total*	*Percent Minority*	*Percent Low Income*	*Total*	*Per Capita*
Region I	467	0[b]	61.5	$ 38,661	$ 82.79
Connecticut	185	ND	91.9	20,714	111.97
Maine	128	0	91.4	6,075	47.46
Massachusetts	ND[a]	ND	ND	ND	ND
New Hampshire	ND	ND	ND	ND	ND
Rhode Island	110	ND	ND	9,067	82.43
Vermont	44	ND	ND	2,805	63.75
Region II	29,958	28.2	36.5	$ 239,873	$ 8.01
New Jersey	6,318	11.6	19.4	88,669	14.03
New York	23,613	32.6	41.0	151,204	6.40
Puerto Rico	27	100.0	100.0	ND	ND
Virgin Islands	ND	ND	ND	ND	ND
Region III	3,758	20.4	77.9	$ 139,099	$ 37.01
Delaware	ND	ND	ND	ND	ND
District of Columbia	52	96.2	96.2	0	[c]
Maryland	140	ND	ND	16,556	118.26
Pennsylvania	1,547	14.0	75.1	76,927	49.73
Virginia	511	57.5	100.0	31,369	61.39
West Virginia	1,508	13.6	79.8	14,247	9.45
Region IV	3,656	18.4	42.2	$ 289,510	$ 79.19
Alabama	400	42.8	93.3	17,640	44.10
Florida	899	29.8	74.4	109,256	121.53
Georgia	398	26.4	90.2	68,510	172.14
Kentucky	1,041	ND	ND	ND	ND
Mississippi	40	27.5	55.0	ND	ND
North Carolina	749	ND	ND	79,348	105.94
South Carolina	79	94.9	100.0	6,533	82.70
Tennessee	50	84.0	80.0	8,223	164.46
Region V	5,154	20.5	71.2	$ 366,244	$ 71.06
Illinois	25	0	84.0	ND	ND
Indiana	1,706	31.5	75.0	100,685	59.02
Michigan	1,714	24.6	65.7	167,921	97.97
Minnesota	172	1.2	86.6	11,070	64.36
Ohio	658	8.1	54.4	31,952	48.56
Wisconsin	879	5.2	84.1	54,616	62.13
Region VI	6,729	50.5	79.0	$ 294,832	$ 43.82
Arkansas	282	54.6	99.6	49,336	174.95
Louisiana	1,305	48.9	81.9	130,456	99.97
New Mexico	1,651	54.3	89.0	28,601	17.32
Oklahoma	261	21.5	71.3	16,500	63.22
Texas	3,230	51.1	71.5	69,939	21.65
Region VII	3,858	10.1	70.5	$ 276,743	$ 71.73
Iowa	85	10.6	74.1	500	5.88
Kansas	919	11.6	75.7	126,251	137.38
Missouri	526	43.7	94.7	53,240	101.23
Nebraska	2,328	1.8	62.8	96,752	41.56

(continued)

Table 8–2. continued

Region and State	Number of Recipients: Total	Percent Minority	Percent Low Income	Expenditures: Total	Per Capita
Region VIII	1,445	3.0	26.7	$ 37,818	$ 26.17
Colorado	758	ND	ND	4,636	6.12
Montana	42	9.5	71.4	620	14.76
North Dakota	ND	ND	ND	ND	ND
South Dakota	176	ND	54.5	21,025	119.46
Utah	88	ND	ND	2,300	26.14
Wyoming	381	10.5	68.2	9,247	24.27
Region IX	3,206	4.9	5.4	$ 327,407	$102.12
American Samoa	ND	ND	ND	ND	ND
Arizona	33	51.5	100.0	9,377	284.15
California	3,033	ND	ND	257,098	84.77
Guam	ND	ND	ND	ND	ND
Hawaii	0	0	0	327	X
Nevada	ND	ND	ND	ND	ND
Trust Territory	140	100.0	100.0	60,605	432.89
Region X	460	3.5	78.7	$ 18,786	$ 40.84
Alaska	71	ND	ND	ND	ND
Idaho	120	1.7	98.3	1,107	9.23
Oregon	181	2.8	97.2	ND	ND
Washington	88	10.2	77.3	17,679	200.90
U.S. Total	58,691	25.5	48.3	$2,028,973	$ 34.57

Source: Unpublished data provided by the Administration on Aging, U.S. Department of Health, Education and Welfare.

[a] ND = no data provided by the state.

[b] Several state reports utilized a zero "0" coding. It is unclear from the reports available if this coding indicates that no recipients were served or no expenditures made or that the data were not available from the state's report.

[c] Unable to calculate per-capita expenditure from the available data.

(such as replacing broken windows, replastering, or fixing leaky plumbing) or general low-cost annual maintenance (such as cleaning gutters or putting up storm windows).

The per-capita expenditures for residential repair and renovation under Title III are not (for the most part) of the magnitude sufficient to upgrade substantially housing units occupied by the elderly or contribute significantly to the conservation of the housing stock nationally.

Farmers' Home Administration Programs

Both Sections 502 and 504 of the Housing Act of 1949 (Public Law 81-171) are administered by the Farmers' Home Administration of the Department of Agriculture and have as a common objective the provision of "decent, safe and sanitary" dwelling units for farm owners and others living in rural areas.[g] Section 502 provides for loans to low-income rural residents for the purpose of buying, building, rehabilitating, improving, or relocating a dwelling unit for permanent residency. Individuals of any age meeting the residency criteria are eligible for a Section 504 loan. To qualify for a Section 504 loan, the household must have income insufficient to buy or repair a decent housing unit (or to secure credit from conventional sources) but adequate for meeting the repayment schedule set forth in the Section 504 loan. Section 504 makes available loans and grants (or a combination of these) to households without sufficient incomes to qualify for a Section 502 loan. Section 504 loans and/or grants may be used *only* for repair-renovation work such as repairing roofs; supplying screens, storm doors, a needed heating system; repairing or supplying structural supports; or providing a sanitary water and waste disposal system. Because activities supported by Section 504 are limited to repair-renovation work and because the elderly receive special consideration in the award of grants, the remainder of this discussion focuses on Section 504.

Section 504 loans or grants may not exceed a total of $5,000. Loans are awarded to individuals without sufficient income to qualify for a Section 502 loan but with an income (from all sources, including welfare payments) to repay in whole or in part the Section 504 loan. A rural resident also may qualify for a Section 504 loan if he or she obtains a cosigner on the loan. The repairs to be undertaken with the Section 504 loan must be specified at the time of application and certified by the FmHA county supervisor as necessary and reasonable. Section 504 loans are made only to remove health or safety hazards; cosmetic repairs or new construction cannot be supported by Section 504 loans, nor can the loans be used to make repairs to those dwelling units of "such poor condition and quality that when the repairs are completed the dwelling unit would likely continue to be a substantial hazard to the health and safety of those who occupy the unit."

Section 504 grants are subject to the same restrictions and limitations as Section 504 loans, with two major exceptions. In comparison to loans with no age restrictions, grants are available only to individuals sixty-two years of age or older. The income of the older grant applicant must be so low that he or she cannot repay any part of a Section 504 loan. Older owner-occupants of unsafe or unsanitary housing units may qualify for a combination loan-grant if the household income is sufficient to repay part of the repair costs.

[g] Information on housing programs administered under the auspices of the Farmers' Home Administration was compiled from the various program operational manuals. The authors wish to thank the FmHA for provision of these materials.

Unlike Title XX or Title III support, the state or local governments are only involved minimally in the administration of Section 504. County supervisors are the only local officials typically involved in the application or award of a Section 504 grant and/or loan. All repair-renovation work supported by Section 504 is done by local, private contractors whose cost estimates are evaluated by the county supervisor as "reasonable."

Unfortunately, no data are available showing either the number or cost of Section 504 grants or Section 504 loans made to older persons in rural areas. During the period October 1, 1977 to March 31, 1978, a total of 1,471 loans for repair work were made by the Farmers' Home Administration at a total cost of $3,669,410 or $2,494.50 per capita recipient. Assuming that the number of older persons receiving Section 504 loans for repairs is in proportion to the rural poverty-level population aged sixty-five and over, approximately 1,180 loans were made to older persons.[h] Although relatively few older persons benefited from Section 504 loans (and probably from Section 504 grants as well), the average amount of the loan suggests that substantial repairs were made. Unlike the repair activity supported by Title XX or Title III, the repairs financed by Section 504 were likely to be of sufficient magnitude to significantly upgrade the housing units occupied by older recipients.

Other Non-HUD Programs

At least two other non-HUD programs provide support for repair-maintenance activities. Title IV of the Energy Conservation and Production Act (Public Law 94-385) provides for the establishment of a weatherization program to insulate the dwelling units of low-income persons, especially the low-income elderly. When grants are provided to the state for weatherization programs, the amount of the grant is determined by a formula that takes into consideration the number of low-income households in the state, the climate of the state, and the proportion of the total residential energy used in the state for heating or cooling. At least 90 percent of the grant funds must be expended for direct program costs such as the installation of weatherstripping, storm windows, or ceiling insulation.

The actual appropriations for the weatherization program have increased rapidly, from $27.5 million in fiscal year 1977 to $200 million in fiscal year 1979. The allocation in 1979 reflects expansion of the

[h] In 1976, 1,259,000 individuals in farm areas had incomes below the poverty level. Of these, 1,009,000 (or 80.1 percent) were sixty-five years of age or older (U.S. Bureau of the Census 1978). Estimate was derived by assuming that .all 1971 Section 504 loans were made to those in farm areas with poverty-level incomes and that 80.1 percent of loan recipients were elderly.

program as provided for in Title I of the National Energy Conservation Policy Act. This act also raises the cost limitation from $400 to $800 per dwelling unit and makes provision for modifications of existing furnaces to increase energy efficiency. As of September 1978, a total of 72,519 homes had received assistance under the weatherization programs. It is not possible to determine how many elderly homeowners participated in the state programs or what type of insulation services they received.

A second additional source of repair-renovation financing is provided by the Developmental Disabilities Act of 1975. Disabled individuals, including the elderly, may receive a wide variety of remedial services through the state Developmental Disabilities Council. The federal government pays 75 percent of the cost involved in nonpoverty areas and up to 90 percent in poverty areas. States are responsible for determining how grants awarded under the Developmental Disability Act are expended. Among the services a state may elect to offer is a home repair service, but costs of repairs may not exceed $250 per unit. The Developmental Disability Act is poorly funded, and most of the expenditures to data have been made for new construction of residential facilities or personal care service to the disabled.

Neither the weatherization programs, financed by the Energy Conservation and Production Act, nor the home repair program, financed by the Developmental Disabilities Act of 1975, are major federal home repair programs and make an extremely small contribution to the housing improvement-conservation movement.

Evaluation of the Programs

Although approximately 700,000 older persons annually benefit from non-HUD-supported repair services, the per-capita expenditures of these programs tend to be extremely low. Despite the research showing that housing conditions have a significant impact on the well-being and life satisfaction of older persons (Berghorn et al. 1978), and that older persons prefer to remain in a familiar environment (Field 1972), social service programs such as Title XX and Title III have not made a substantial commitment to upgrade the housing units *currently* occupied by the elderly.

Evaluating the effect and success of the programs discussed by the criteria specified in the preceding chapter is problematic for several reasons: An older person may receive a service financed from a number of different sources making it difficult to credit one funding source with an improvement in living conditions, should one be noted.[i] Further-

[i] This problem is exacerbated in the present context. Records on program recipients are maintained for each program separately, and data are not available on the cluster of services (or their financing mechanisms) consumed by households headed by the elderly.

more, because most of the programs discussed in this chapter allow for extensive flexibility or discretion at the state level, summarizing the success of these programs at the national level may be misleading.

To the extent that these programs, particularly Title XX or Title III, sponsor home repair-maintenance activities, they clearly foster housing improvement or stock preservation—two of the five evaluation criteria identified in the preceding chapter.[j] The flaw in this approach is not the obtained effect but the relatively low priority assigned to housing repair services in a multiservice program. With reference to such broad-ranging programs, the question of equity or equal opportunity pertains not only to the distribution and mix of services offered but also to equality of access for all in need. In almost all of the programs described, low-income and minority groups dominate the recipient profile.

None of the programs involving federal-state-local coordination are characterized by administrative simplicity. Particularly at the state or local level, the responsible agencies must not only identify the matrix of needs within the community, but also piece together the funding necessary to provide needed services. While the programs administered by the various federal departments and agencies tend to function in isolation from one another, the actual meshing of these programs occurs only on the local level. To some extent the lack of administrative simplicity operates as both an advantage and a disadvantage to the local service provider. The next section considers how different localities draw on a number of federal programs to provide support for home repair activities.

FUNDING HOME REPAIR ACTIVITIES

Title III mandates that the area agencies on aging coordinate service activities in such a way as to:

1. Facilitate accessibility to and utilization of all social services provided within the geographic area served by each system by any public or private agency or organization;
2. Develop and make the most efficient use of social services in meeting the needs of older persons; and
3. Use available resources efficiently and with a minimum of duplication.

In delivering home repair-maintenance services to the elderly, a variety of funding sources is available, including (but not limited to)

[j] The evaluation criteria used in Chapter 7 were (1) housing improvement, (2) equal opportunity, (3) housing stock preservation, (4) administrative simplicity, and (5) cost.

the programs discussed in Chapter 7 and the preceding section of this chapter. At the local level, none of these programs are likely to be funded at a level necessary to support a comprehensive program of repair assistance. A 1975–1976 survey of area agencies on aging conducted by the Mayors' Task Force on Aging shows that the majority of home repair services for older persons are supported from a variety of sources (McNickle 1976).[k]

Fifty-six cities were surveyed in this study to determine the range of services and their funding available to urban elderly residents. Of the thirty-four cities (60.7 percent) providing a home repair service for the elderly, fifteen relied exclusively on one funding source (two from Title III only, three from Title XX, three from community development funds, one from Community Service Administration, two each from private or county funds, and one each from state funds, Community Service Administration funds, and unspecified HUD sources.) Of the remaining nineteen cities, eleven relied on two sources, three on three sources, and five on four or more sources. For those cities relying on two or more sources, Title III funds were most often included in the list of supporting programs. Title III funds were used in conjunction with Title XX services, CETA workers, private, city, and county monies and/or community development grants from HUD. In those cities not using Title III funds to provide home repair services, CETA funds or workers were frequently used jointly with community development funds to support the service. None of the thirty-four cities offering some type of home repair service allocated revenue sharing funds for this purpose.

The Mayors' Task Force on Aging Survey shows at least in urban areas, that federally supported programs are coordinated in order to provide housing repair services. In sheer number of programs supported, it is not HUD programs but Title III funds that form the bulwark of support. HUD-supported housing repair services, however, typically reach more individuals and provide greater per-capita expenditures.

SUMMARY

From the preceding review of non-HUD programs directly supportive of housing maintenance services, two conclusions are obvious: Because of the role assigned to state and local governments in delivering housing repair-maintenance services, there is considerable interstate variation in the scope, availability, and organization of such services. Even those states channeling Title XX or Title III monies into housing repair services commonly make only a superficial commitment to up-

[k] This research was supported by the Administration on Aging, Grant No. 90-A-431.

grading of housing currently occupied by the elderly. As a result, local areas frequently need to rely on a variety of federal and nonfederal funds to provide needed housing maintenance services. Out of necessity a level of coordination and integration may exist at the local level that is only an ideal at the federal level.

REFERENCES

Berghorn, F.J.; D.E. Schafer; G.H. Steere; and R.F. Wiseman. 1978. *The Urban Elderly: A Study of Life Satisfaction.* New York: Universe Books.

Field, M. 1972. *The Aged, the Family, and the Community.* New York: Columbia University Press.

Gutowski, M.F. 1978. "Integrating Housing and Social Service Activities for the Elderly Household." In R.P. Boynton, ed., *Occasional Papers in Housing and Community Affairs,* pp. 110–30. Publication No. HUD-497-PDR. Washington, D.C.: Governnment Printing Office.

McNickle, L. 1976. Services for the Urban Elderly in Selected Cities. Washington, D.C.: National League of Cities and U.S. Conference of Mayors.

Project Share: A National Clearinghouse for Improving Management of Human Services. 1978. *Trends in Taxonomies.* Report prepared for the Offices of Planning and Evaluation and of Human Development Services, Department of Health, Education, and Welfare, by Bowers and Associates, SHR-0002614. Washington, D.C.: Government Printing Office.

Rhode Island Department of Elderly Affairs. 1978. "An Analysis of Social Data Affecting the Lives of Rhode Island's Older Population." Providence, R.I.: Rhode Island Department of Elderly Affairs.

U.S. Department of Agriculture. n.d. "Section 502 Rural Housing Loan Policies, Procedures, and Authorizations." Manual of the Farmers Home Administration. Fm HA Instruction 444.1. Washington, D.C.: Government Printing Office.

———. n.d. "Title 7 Loan and Grant Programs," Manual of the Farmers Home Administration. Fm HA Instruction 1904-G. Washington, D.C.: Government Printing Office.

U.S. Department of Health, Education and Welfare. 1977. "First Annual Report to Congress on Title XX of the Social Security Act". Washington, D.C.: Government Printing Office.

———. 1978. "Social Services U.S.A., July-September, 1976." Publication No. (HDS) 78-02020. Washington, D.C.: Government Printing Office.

❋ *Chapter 9*

New Initiatives in Housing Services

The material presented thus far suggests literally dozens of policy initiatives that might be undertaken to improve the physical environment of elderly households. In this chapter, the primary focus is on two broad groups of the elderly identified as having particularly severe problems, groups comprising a large number of households who currently receive little assistance. The strengths and weaknesses of several alternative possibilities of assistance are discussed. A full set of programs is not recommended, however, because the exact elements in such programs depend on considerations beyond the analytic ones presented. From this material, one conclusion is inescapable: a mix of programs is required to aid a group as diverse as the elderly in improving their housing circumstances. Finally we address an issue critical to effective program implementation: the coordination at the local level of resources flowing from federal agencies.

TWO GROUPS IN NEED

Homeowners

This book has documented a number of facts about elderly homeowners. Many are very poor; about 0.5 million live in units with one or more of the five dwelling deficiencies examined in Chapter 3; 30 percent of elderly homeowners with mortgage debt spend more than 35 percent of their income on housing, as do 10 percent of the much larger group without mortgage debt.

We have seen that over the two-year period 1974–1976, there was a modest increase in dwelling deficiencies by those households who remained in the same unit over the period. We have also seen that the elderly are concentrated primarily in the older dwelling units, in the nation's inner city areas and in neighborhoods with comparatively high incidence of physical problems. In effect, the elderly, with their low rates of maintenance and repair activity, are concentrated in those neighborhoods that are in the greatest need of assistance if deterioration is to be stemmed and neighborhoods saved from destruction. Furthermore, the determinants of dwelling condition and maintenance activities have been seen to be varied and complex, ranging from the physical limitations of the household, to household composition, to income. This implies an equally varied policy response.

In examining the housing assistance to the elderly, older homeowners were found to receive comparatively little. Only a small share of rehabilitation funds from block grants, the Section 312 program, Farmers Home Administration, and HEW-supported programs were available. The elderly are not now singled out as a special element in the major federally sponsored neighborhood preservation programs.

There is no question that on equity alone, homeowners merit a greater share of assistance. It is also evident that such assistance can be provided so as to treat the superior asset holdings of homeowners in such a way as to produce equity between owners and renters. It is important, in this regard, to structure the programs so they will be flexible enough to treat owners, in both strong and weak asset and income conditions, fairly.

Rural Elderly

The rural elderly (and nonelderly, for that matter) live in much lower quality housing than their urban counterparts. Improvement is essential but difficult to achieve because of problems in the rural housing "delivery system," which has myriad elements: builders and firms willing to do rehabilitation, financial institutions, materials suppliers, and government agencies that deliver the already available programs. Improvement is also difficult both because of the extent of the problems of individual units and because of the lack of readily available substitute housing. In these cases, improvement may mean new construction, which is not only costly but potentially risky if future demand is not assured.

Another matter needs resolution: How is the desirability of the various options to be judged? Essentially, the same criteria are to be used here as were employed in the review of existing programs. These five are: (1) effects on the quality of housing occupied by the recipient, (2) equity, (3) effects on the housing stock at large, (4) administrative simplicity, and (5) cost. The equity criterion judges the program's merits in terms of the treatment of both of those eligible for the subject program and those ineligible. For example, in examining a program to assist homeowners, the concern is not only with the homeowner who receives assistance but also with the degree of assistance provided to similarly situated renters under alternative programs.

THE POLICY CONTEXT

It is important, but often forgotten, that any program resulting from a new policy initiative must be designed to mesh smoothly with existing programs. The long and sometimes acrimonious debate on welfare reform has highlighted the problems of interrelationships among various cash and in-kind transfer programs that provide benefits to the same households.[a] Clearly, communities have become sensitive to this as they set policies. Still, in cases where program interrelationships are less obvious or minimal but equity questions enter, the perspective for analyzing the proposal program is often not broad enough.

This analysis is predicated on the idea that the existing programs will continue. And, while detailed initiatives are not presented in this chapter, it is recognized that, prior to suggesting implementation of new programs, careful work is essential in order to assure proper coordination. For example, any change to the Section 8 housing assistance program, such as expanding it to include elderly homeowners, would require modification of the housing assistance plans so that individual communities would submit the changes as part of the application process for Community Development Block Grant funds. Also, the kind of programs undertaken by metropolitan areas to implement their plans for promoting racial and economic residential integration, the so-called areawide housing opportunity plans,[b] could be affected.

It is equally apparent that such program initiatives must be consistent with the programs of other agencies and other levels of government. While the programs of Farmers Home Administration are important to rural areas, interagency coordination has been less than perfect between HUD's Section 8 program and FmHA's Section 515 program (Housing Assistance Council 1977). It is clear that any housing initiative must be examined fully for its direct and indirect relations to other programs. Coordination of funding and program design is essential at the federal level, and coordination of implementation is essential at the local government level.

[a] For an overview, see Levitan and Taggart (1976: Chap. 3); also, Khadduri, Lyall, and Struyk (1978).

[b] See Listokin (1976) for a description of AHOPs and their utilization to date.

A more fundamental problem than new program integration is the improvement in the coordination of *existing* programs. Expenditures made from Title XX and Title III HEW funds are, in effect, independent of HUD and Farmers' Home Administration programs. The burden is presently on the local community to coordinate these activities despite federal agency planning guidelines that create powerful incentives to the contrary. The final section examines this knotty problem.

OPTIONS FOR ELDERLY HOMEOWNERS[c]

In this section, three program options for assisting homeowners are evaluated by applying the five criteria noted above. They include: insurance of reverse mortgages, a type of Section 8 or housing allowance for homeowners, and the provision of in-kind maintenance services to homeowners. These could be considered either as individual options or as various sets of options.

Each option is designed to deal with a different aspect of the elderly homeowners' housing needs, in recognition of the diversity of this group. What the options have in common is that each would cost considerably less per household served than the rental programs currently offered by the Department of Housing and Urban Development. It should also be noted that each could be used as an explicit tool for neighborhood revitalization and stabilization including preventing displacement (Myers 1978), although they would function better as a part of a concerted program such as in the Urban Homesteading, Neighborhood Housing services, or Neighborhood Strategy Areas.

Reverse Annuity Mortgages

Many elderly people do not wish to move because they have paid off all, or most, of the indebtedness on their houses. Some, however, although they have the asset of a mortgage-free home do not have enough income to adequately meet operating expenses and other obligations. The reverse annuity mortgage (RAM) allows the homeowner to take advantage of increased equity to obtain the additional income necessary to meet operating expenses, thereby helping elderly homeowners recover the equity in their homes without having to sell them.

There is considerable potential demand for RAMs. In 1976, 6.4 million elderly owner-occupants for whom the Census has information owned their homes free and clear. Of these 3.8 million lived in homes

[c] Some of the material presented here appears in Welfeld and Struyk.

valued at over $20,000; 1.6 million in dwellings valued at over $35,000. Among low-income households—those with less than $4,000 annual income—there were 0.75 million elderly-headed households living in units valued at over $20,000. Incremental income might be especially important for this group in sustaining dwelling maintenance (Struyk 1979, Tables 2-4). Several versions of RAMs already exist. The following paragraphs describe conventional RAMs, double RAMs, and lifetime annuity RAMs.

Conventional Reverse Annuity Mortgages. RAMs are now being offered by some state-chartered financial institutions. For example, a Cleveland savings and loan association is pioneering a RAM that lends homeowners up to 80 percent of the value of their homes in monthly payments over five to ten years. The homeowner pays interest as the loan grows and begins repaying principal after the funds are fully advanced. The loan is for thirty years, with the home as collateral.

An alternative method involves receipt of level monthly payments that draw down on the equity of the house; no loan repayment is required until the property is disposed of. The latter is more common and was discussed by the Federal Home Loan Bank Board (FHLBB) in its proposals on mortgage instruments.[d] The FHLBB, in its December 1978 regulations, permits its member institutions to write either type of RAM—either of fixed or of indefinite term (12 CFR, Parts 545, 555).

Fixed-term arrangements do not address the problem of homeowners with limited incomes after the equity is reduced. Once the loan is exhausted, the household is thrown back on its own resources and may even have to begin repaying the loan. Under reasonable assumptions on appreciation in housing values, the household could borrow against this "new" equity; but the potential problem remains. Still, moderate-income households may find RAMs an attractive vehicle for making major improvements in their units or raising their incomes without any governmental incursion.

The Double Reverse Annuity Mortgage. The inability of the lower-income elderly to take advantage of RAMs is unlikely to force the elderly out of their homes. Despite steeply rising operating expenses, a sharp increase in ownership among the elderly—with the sharpest increase among single elderly women—occurred from 1970 to 1975. Nevertheless, the large number of houses with multiple deficien-

[d] Under this type of RAM, interest on the implicit loan continues to accrue. If the principal and deferred interest become greater than the value of the property, the lender requires the household to pay additional interest before sale of the property.

cies occupied by the elderly points to the fact that retaining the home may come at the expense of maintaining it.

HUD could make RAMs work for lower-income homeowners by cosigning the note after appraising the borrower's property and financial situation. For the type of RAM in which repayment is scheduled before the property is sold, HUD could agree to be liable for the monthly repayment if it were more than 20 percent of the borrower's income and some percentage of liquid assets. As a condition of HUD's guarantee, the term of the annuity would have to be at least ten years and the repayment period would have to be at least twenty-five years. As a further condition, the borrower would have to keep the house in good repair during the entire period. As security for any payment made on behalf of the borrower, HUD would require a second mortgage with amortization to begin after the RAM loan is paid.

The HUD mortgage would be repayable at the earliest of the following events:

1. The property is sold or transferred, *or*
2. The owner ceases to occupy the house, *or*
3. The owner dies, *or*
4. The first RAM is repaid.

In the first three events, the full amount plus interest would be due. In the last event, the borrower would be required to repay the HUD loan on the same basis as the RAM. If the borrower's income is insufficient, HUD would allow the balance over 20 percent of the borrower's income to accrue.

To illustrate, assume a $20,000 ten-year annuity loan on a $25,000 house at 8 percent interest over thirty years is made to a household headed by a person sixty-eight years old whose annual income is $4,800. The borrower would receive $177 per month for ten years but would have to allocate at least 30 percent of the net annuity (annuity less interest on the accrued balance) to housing expenses. The monthly repayment, to begin when the borrower is seventy-eight, would be $146.34. Assuming no assets and no rise in income, the household could pay $80 per month (20 percent of its income); the government would pay $66.34. If the household lives in the unit for another ten years, the government's total outlay is $7,961. At an interest rate of 6 percent, the outstanding balance on the annuity loan would be approximately $10,800; the outstanding balance on the first mortgage would be approximately $17,536. Thus, the total debt on the property would equal $28,336. Note that even with this federal assistance, the low-income problem is not solved after the tenth year.

Under a second type of RAM—where no repayment is required until sale unless the charges for loan principal plus cumulative interest exceed the value of the property—assistance would begin only when the total debt exceeds the asset, and it would be limited to payment of housing expenses (including debt service) over 25 percent of income. Total exposure is difficult to judge because it hinges on the rate of property appreciation relative to the rate of interest on the loan. By limiting the loan-to-value ratio to 60 to 70 percent, HUD could reduce its exposure substantially, but this would also significantly reduce the number of households who would receive monthly annuity payments large enough to induce them to apply for a RAM.

Lifetime Annuity RAM. Neither RAM discussed thus far is fully satisfactory: the conventional RAM leaves the household with considerable uncertainty and the double RAM would be both difficult to explain and administer and in some forms would not guarantee incremental income to the household as long as it lived in the unit. A preferable option would be for the household to be given an annuity based on the value of its property and its life expectancy. (Note that it is the household's life expectancy, assuming that both spouses are above some minimum age, not the life expectancy of the head of the house.) Under this scheme, the household would face no uncertainty. HUD's role would be to insure the RAMs, thereby spreading the risk of some households' living beyond their actuarial expectancy. Further, HUD could guarantee payments adjusted for inflation with appreciation in the value of the home covering the increased monthly payments. The program would create its own reserves, with funds built up from those dying before the actuarial expectancy paying for those with greater longevity. All payments stop when the house is transferred, sold, no longer permanently occupied by the household, or both the husband and wife are dead. A lump sum settlement is made to survivors upon transfer or sale, which might be for the full amount or some fraction thereof, depending on the status of reserves. It is important to note that the regulations issued by the FHLBB make no provision for insuring individual member institutions against the possibility of having a disproportionately large number of very long-lived RAM purchasers. Savings and loan associations are allowed to pass annuity business through to an insurance company that would then bear the risk, but this may result in higher charges to the household.

Evaluation. Only lifetime RAMs are evaluated, using the five criteria discussed earlier, because they are predominant on several grounds. Still, this proposal may be difficult for the elderly to understand, and for HUD to administer. On balance, the plan seems feasible, but perhaps the Federal Home Loan Bank Board should test it before national implementation.

Housing Improvement and Stock Preservation. Based on current actuarial tables, the average sixty-five-year-old person can expect to live to be seventy-nine. Hence the expected RAM term will be long, and the monthly payment will, in many instances, be modest. For example, a seventy-year-old widow with a $20,000 lifetime annuity RAM and annual income of $2500 would receive $42 per month or an 18 percent income increment at a 9 percent mortgage interest rate. However, the typical monthly payment to elderly owner-occupant participants in the Experimental Housing Allowance Program (EHAP) was about $65, and this modest payment stimulated substantial additional repair and maintenance expenditures. It is important to remember that annual physical inspections were part of EHAP, and it is unclear how much repair and maintenance activity resulted from the knowledge that such inspections were going to be made. Combining the results from EHAP and the analysis of Chapter 5, which showed a low income-elasticity of repairs, suggests the inspections are important. Still, there is no doubt that better care of dwellings results from additional income.

Equity. Equity poses no problems since each householder's payments depend on his or her own loan amount and life expectancy. Presumably every household has an equal chance of enjoying a longer stream of payments than that for which it contracts.

Administrative Simplicity. Actual program administration would be straightforward. The private financial institution writing the mortgage would service the mortgage and, if members of the household died prior to the expected date, the undistributed loan proceeds would be sent to the agency administering the insurance (FHA, FNMA, or GNMA). If a household lived beyond expectation, the financial institution would draw funds from the administering agency.

A more challenging problem is consumer acceptance. In the past, the elderly have been hesitant to use deferred property tax payment provisions in those states that have them, possibly because of the way in which the deductions on interest on the mortgage would be treated for tax purposes; obviously the elderly would prefer to have a stream of deductions rather than having them massed at the end of the mortgage period.[e] Assuming the tax problem is surmountable, there seem to be

[e] For a discussion of this point see Peat, Marwick, Mitchell and Co. (1977).

two advantages to the lifetime annuity RAM. First, there is no uncertainty about the length of payment; the household will never have to worry about when the payments end. Second, RAMs would be for no more than 70 or 80 percent of the equity in the home, thus ensuring a strong maintenance incentive and a modest estate for transmission to one's heirs—a motivation among the elderly that appears to be quite strong (Blinder 1976).

Costs. Since there is no subsidy involved with RAMs, servicing and administration fees would be covered by service charges on the loan itself.

Modified Section 8

Extending the Section 8 program to homeownership is an alternative for low-income elderly for whom lifetime annuity RAMs are not practical but who wish to remain homeowners. If Section 8 is extended, it needs to be modified to allow current owners to remain in and maintain their homes. Because the program would focus on maintaining the existing stock, the modified program would assist only with operating expenses, that is, for utilities, property taxes, and repairs. In fact, 83 percent of all elderly multiperson homeowner families and 93 percent of all elderly single-person homeowners own their own homes free and clear.

Table 9-1 presents some figures on the cost of a Section 8 program designed to assist elderly homeowners with operating expenses only. In particular, it shows the number of elderly homeowners eligible for Section 8 in 1976 who live in mortgage-free dwellings and who spend over 25 percent of their income for housing. It also shows the average monthly housing expenses in excess of 25 percent of income. About 1.4 million households qualify for the program, most of whom are elderly individuals living alone.[f]

These figures can be used to compute crudely the cost of a national program. One estimate that provides a clear upper boundary to the relevant cost range assumes the subsidy will equal current excess operating expenditures. (Excess expenditures are defined as those over 25 percent of income). In an actual program, of course, some households will be found to be spending more than is deemed reasonable, and they would receive only a partial payment.

Program costs would also be sensitive to the expected participation rate. Solid information on this point is available from the supply component of the Experimental Housing Allowance Program now

[f] This estimate is doubly conservative because 25 percent of income is being used, not the 35 percent figure justified earlier.

Table 9–1. Excessive Housing Burden of Elderly Owner-Occupants Who Own Their Homes Free and Clear[a]

	Husband-Wife Couples		*Single Individuals*		*Other Households*	
Income	*Average Excess Expense*[b]	*Number of Households*	*Average Excess Expense*[b]	*Number of Households*	*Average Excess Expense*[b]	*Number of Households*
Under $2,000	$67	72,000	$49	158,000	$56	17,000
$2,000–$3,999	36	184,000	34	528,000	33	25,000
$4,000–$5,999	39	168,000	27	106,000	28	27,000
$6,000–$7,999	34	43,000	55	28,000	40	12,000
Over $8,000	21	10,000	0	0	52	3,000

Source: 1976 Annual Housing Survey, unpublished tabulations.

[a] "Excess housing burden" is defined as operating costs, including taxes, greater than 25 percent of income.

[b] Monthly housing expense.

[c] Numbers in thousands.

operating in Green Bay (Brown County) Wisconsin and South Bend (St. Joseph County) Indiana. The figures presented in Chapter 7 showed a fairly low rate of participation, based on two years of experience. For the present calculations, the assumption of a participation rate of 33 percent appears warranted. Combining these elements yields an average aggregate annual cost of payments to recipients of about $210 million, or $461 per year per participating household, in 1976 prices.[g]

The program would have to have an inspection system to ensure that houses are kept in good repair. A related problem is that units suffering most from deferred maintenance will cost the most to bring into the program. Hence, nonparticipation may be disproportionately high among those needing the assistance most. The use of "one-time" RAMs to finance needed basic repairs seems natural for households unable to bear the burden of a regular rehabilitation loan. If RAMs were deemed undesirable for some reason, granting of loans using CDBG funds (possibly with a recapture provision) might be employed.

Evaluation

Housing improvement and stock preservation. The findings of EHAP are relevant here. Based on the findings reviewed in Chapter 7, improved housing and greater maintenance outlays can be anticipated.

Equity. The low cost per unit would enable the program to cover a large proportion of the needy. A potential source of inequity might arise from the treatment of mortgage debt. This problem could be eliminated, however, by simply limiting the maximum subsidy payment to the fair market rents (FMRs) for operating expenses only, minus 25 percent of household income for all income-eligible elderly homeowners. As long as Section 8 assistance to homeowners is limited to the elderly, questions of equity with other owners who might be treated differently will not arise. If this program were enacted on a general basis, it would presumably apply to condominiums as well as to other fee-simple ownership arrangements.

Administrative simplicity. The program involves the same administration as the existing Section 8 program. It would require the administrative burden of establishing another set of FMRs for out-of-

[g] A more generous program could add an amount for maintenance to the operating expenses. If the subsidy is applied to operating expenses plus $300 per year for maintenance, the number of eligible households doubles and the average subsidy per recipient rises to $499 per year.

pocket expenses, but this would be easier to compute than the current rental FMRs. The FMRs could be computed as a standard utility component and as property taxes. The tax component would be based on actual tax payments in order to avoid inequities arising from local tax relief. The EHAP experience suggests few administrative problems.[h]

Cost. As noted earlier, the subsidy cost would be quite modest—approximately $500 per year per household assisted. This is much less than the subsidy under the Section 8 existing program, which must cover capital as well as operating costs.

House Care for the Aged

The housing occupied by elderly homeowners is, on the average, older than that occupied by others and often in greater need of maintenance and repair. The nearly 0.5 million houses with multiple structural deficiencies occupied by the elderly represent evidence of an unmet need. Unfortunately, the detailed analysis of maintenance and repair activities of elderly homeowners reported earlier indicates that increases in income do not necessarily bring corresponding increases in such activity. Complicating the matter even further is a discrepancy in homeowners' and housing experts' perceptions of what is a serious deficiency. When a deficiency is not perceived, it will not be corrected. Specific grants—housing allowance or Section 8—do well in converting subsidies into housing. But can we do better still by creating programs to ensure adequate maintenance?

Programs to ensure adequate maintenance can take two forms—preventive or curative. Preventive maintenance and repair averages about $25 per month for all homeowners, although expenditures are often infrequent but large (Mayer 1976). Doubling the cost for the elderly who live in units needing greater repair would require a total federal outlay for a continuous maintenance program of only about $550 per year per household, assuming the poor contribute $5 per month. This is approximately the same as the cost of the inexpensive modified Section 8 program. The real problem, however, is the administration of such a program.

[h] Implied in the text is an administrative arrangement different from that employed in EHAP. In EHAP, the cost of adequate housing (FMR) is the same for both owners and renters; the income of homeowners is adjusted by adding to it an imputed income from the household's equity in the house, which is computed from appraisal and mortgage data. The proposed program would set a separate FMR for owners and not impute income from the equity, although there would be a ceiling on total assets including equity. This would lead to considerable simplification in the income certification process. For a thorough discussion of the points, see Lowry (1974).

A number of communities have set up small programs (Handy Andy, Mr. Fix-It) to repair steps, railings, roofs, and plumbing—jobs that some elderly cannot do themselves. Generally, these programs are financed through the state and local grant programs of Title III of the Older Americans Act or Title XX of the Social Security Act (Jacobs and Rabushka 1976). These programs usually provide one-time assistance rather than continuing help, and coverage is very thin.

Given the nation's goal of preserving the existing housing stock, there should be direct federal interest in a more systematic program. The Department of Housing and Urban Development might try to encourage local housing authorities to provide maintenance and repair services for elderly homeowners within reasonable distances from HUD projects. Alternatively, HUD could set up a formal program using local housing authorities or other local agencies as the delivery agent. Before such an effort, the type of repair services to include and the actual cost of providing them must be determined. Past demonstrations in Baltimore and Pittsburgh, and a current one in Baltimore funded by the Ford Foundation and HUD, will provide information on this point (Ahlbrandt 1978).

In the Baltimore demonstration, participants were reluctant to sign up. Hence a nominal one-time fee was charged to contract for the services. The next step with the systematic approach is an inspection of the unit prior to signing the contract. Where only maintenance is required, the contract is signed; where rehabilitation is needed, arrangements for these major tasks must be made prior to signing. The contract entitles the household to an annual inspection, needed minor repairs, and a small number of "emergency" calls each year. The demonstration program is functioning smoothly, but it is still too early to determine the extent to which the repair and maintenance services being made under the program are substituting for work that would have been done otherwise. HUD is now launching a national evaluation to test this model more fully (Struyk 1979a).

Many cities are trying to cure the effects of deferred maintenance with funds from community development block grants. Des Moines, Iowa, has a program that grants low-income elderly people up to $1,500 for certain emergency repairs of code items for those in target areas. The program is a major part of the city's effort to stem housing abandonment. A study had concluded that households headed by low-income elderly and widows in Des Moines had high rates of abandonment. None of the participants in the new program have abandoned their homes, although one-third stated that without a grant they may have abandoned it within one to three years (Jacobs and Rabushka 1976:181–82).

Baltimore has used Comprehensive Employment and Training Act (CETA) funds to hire public service employees such as carpenters to work on jobs for very low income recipients. Boston offers cash rebates of up to one-half the cost of improvements, as well as technical assistance and an exemption from property tax reassessment. Technical assistance is especially valuable to assure the elderly that they are not being overcharged for repairs. A recent survey found an extremely wide disparity in charges (multiples of up to 20 to 1) for the same job (Jacobs and Rabushka 1976:176–77).

It is impossible to select one particular program as a model, both because of the absence of detailed analyses of these programs and because of the variety of local housing and neighborhood situations. However, a few general principles of program design seem clear. Admission to the preventive program should depend on a unit's being brought up to some minimum standard, not necessarily in full compliance with local codes. In this phase, community development block grants to local governments could be used to make grants or loans to the elderly poor. For those who have the options, RAMs or recasted existing first mortgages to finance repairs could be used. A large amount of administration would be needed to bring households into the program and to assist them in making repairs. A network of assistance is essential and local housing authorities, Neighborhood Housing Services Agencies, and/or the network established by the Administration on Aging are the obvious candidates. Finally, such a program may provide economies of scale: a large number of participants allows efficient scheduling and staffing. For this reason, if funding is limited, the program should be geographically targeted, both in specific cities and specific neighborhoods.

Evaluation

Housing improvement and stock preservation. The program is designed to lead to long-term improvement in the housing quality of elderly-occupied units, which will ultimately assist in the preservation of the stock. The extent to which this goal is accomplished depends on the net increase in maintenance generated. Eventually, its success will have to be evaluated in relation to the amount of maintenance generated by housing allowance or a modified Section 8. The argument in favor of in-kind services is that all of the funds in this program go for housing, whereas there is substantial leakage under an earmarked transfer approach. In-kind maintenance, though, may simply exchange one form of leakage for another, if maintenance under the program is simply a substitute for maintenance that would have been done anyhow.

Equity. The major impediment to equity is the problem of getting units up to the minimum standard necessary to enter the program. The lowest-income households will frequently be those least able to qualify and those most in need. Another equity consideration is whether homeowners who are not income-eligible should be allowed to participate if they are willing to pay the cost of services delivered. Two arguments favor their inclusion: First, the problems of arranging for repairs to be made—both real (for example, impairments make this difficult) and imagined (that is, fear of having strangers in the house)—are not unique to the poor, so that packages of services may assist higher income households preserve their housing. Second, greater participation would help achieve the badly needed economies of scale.

Administrative simplicity. The program would be difficult to administer, particularly in its early stages. Recruiting households to participate has proven difficult in the past, and the effort of bringing units up to minimum standards—involving other programs—could be especially difficult. Furthermore, dwelling inspections, including careful discussions of which deficiencies the program would repair, and efficient scheduling are critical. Income eligibility would have to be determined. All of these factors point to a program that will have a high administrative burden and the procedures of which must be carefully worked out on a pilot basis before full implementation.

Cost. Neither of the first two demonstrations generated conclusive cost data, and the ongoing demonstration has not yet reached a steady state of operation. It is clear, however, from the evidence in hand that annual costs per household, including outreach, will not exceed $500 (in 1978 prices). These costs are exclusive of income certification and are based on programs in compact geographic areas, two facts that argue for greater expenses. Hard data should be available in 1979.

THE RURAL ELDERLY

There are fundamental differences in the task of delivering housing assistance in rural and urban areas. These must be recognized before policy options can be intelligently discussed. These differences can be divided into two broad, but related, areas: those having to do with the structure of the housing market and those that more directly affect the delivery of housing services.

Turning first to the structure of the market, the rural market has more homeownership than the urban market. Among the elderly, 74 percent of those in metropolitan areas were homeowners in 1976 while the equivalent figure was 83 percent outside of metropolitan areas. (A similar pattern exists for the nonelderly.) A second comparison is the lack of suitable substitute housing in many instances in rural areas. Unlike most urban areas where there is consistently a selection of vacant units from which a household might choose, this is often not the case in small towns or in the countryside. This can be a special problem when it is necessary to move to a unit meeting certain standards in order for the household to participate in the Section 8 program.

A third difference concerns the quality of the housing stock. The intensity of the deficiencies in a substantial number of rural units, documented in Chapters 3 and 4, suggests that it may be more economical, in the long term, to assist households in such dwellings by providing replacement housing. The incidence of this circumstance is much less frequent in urban areas, especially if one considers the cost of demolishing the old dwellings as part of the replacement cost. A fourth difference is the difficulty of "market aggregation" in rural areas, for example, the problem of developing sufficient demand to support minimal levels of multifamily housing construction or to justify a residential financial specialist on the staff of local banks.

Many of the "delivery system" problems are associated with the special characteristics of rural markets just enumerated. There are others, however, that are associated with the delivery of government programs in such areas. In this regard, the comments of a 1978 HUD task force dealing with the delivery of services in rural areas are enlightening. The general conclusion of the task force is that available resources either have not been provided efficiently or have not been provided at all because of (1) deficiencies in the delivery system and (2) a failure to make full and imaginative use of existing authority and resources. This is in large part a result of the failure of government administrative machinery to take into account and adapt its procedures, forms, and communications to the capacities of these smaller communities and rural areas and their modes of administration and doing business. Included here is the capacity of business enterprise operating in these areas as well as the capacities of the government entities.

Two passages from the report provide further details:

> Testimony before the Task Force indicated that one of the basic problems impeding the meeting of housing needs in rural areas is simply that incentives for housing production are not as great in low density areas as they are in higher density areas. The small builders that generally do business in rural areas often have considerably less resources than the developers with which HUD has had the bulk of its experience. In

> addition, the size of projects in rural areas has almost always been considerably smaller and, therefore, less rewarding than the size of projects elsewhere. Finally, capital resources are scarcer in rural areas than they are elsewhere and it is therefore essential that capital resources for these areas have access to the secondary markets. . . .
>
> As a general matter, the provision of increased assisted rental housing through the Section 8 and Public Housing programs will necessitate a more flexible approach to the administration of these programs in rural areas and small communities. The method of allocating assisted housing funds, the delivery mechanism for bringing these funds to the communities, the evaluation of unusual arrangements for scattered site multi-family projects and the provision for financing for the Section 8 program all require creative and flexible administrative capabilities in both HUD central and field offices (HUD 1978, "Report of the Task Force").

The task force's report recommends a number of specific changes in the administration of HUD programs to overcome these problems and others that it discovered, but it is far too early to know if they will be successfully implemented.

The Farmers Home Administration has the advantage of a county agent system in the delivery of its programs. But poor training, lack of interest by some agents, and a program mix that focused in the past on the nonpoor have historically produced uneven and modest assistance to the rural poor.

All of these points highlight the challenge of providing housing assistance to the rural elderly. They also suggest some important distinctions that can be used to develop a classification of various needs. Four characteristics stand out: the condition of the dwelling unit, the availability of substitute housing, the likely future demand for housing in a specific location, and the extent of market aggregation. Combining these elements yields four cases of particular interest. Each begins with the condition of the dwelling:

1. The deficient but salvagable dwelling. The elderly-occupied dwelling requires rehabilitation; there is likely to be continuing demand for it; rehabilitation is economically justifiable.
2. The deficient but unsalvagable dwelling. The elderly-occupied dwelling requires rehabilitation but rehabilitation is not economically justified because of the extremely poor condition of the unit.
3. The deficient but unfeasible to salvage dwelling. The elderly-occupied dwelling requires rehabilitation; the rehabilitation could be justified over the long run, but future demand is uncertain.
4. The nondeficient elderly-occupied dwelling that does not require rehabilitation.

All of these situations assume that the elderly occupant is capable of living in his or her own unit (very likely a single-unit structure) and wants to continue to do so. Some households, of course, will not meet this condition. For them, a less demanding rental alternative is needed.

The following discussion of options is less rigorous than that of the previous section. The programs available for dealing with each of the foregoing four situations are discussed. A final section discusses options when the single unit becomes too much for the elderly to maintain. Where present programs are found wanting, a modification or an alternative is provided. It is presumed that both HUD and FmHA will work to make the best use of the existing programs in rural areas.

The Deficient but Salvagable Dwelling

If the dwelling is badly deficient, continuing demand seems likely, and the rehabilitation is rational economically, in theory assistance is possible for both owner- and renter-occupied units under present programs. In particular, the Section 312 rehabilitation loan and the rehabilitation segment of Section 8 could be used. In practice, neither are utilized in rural areas, another instance of administrative problems.

For owners with adequate assets, RAMs are a possibility although their use in rural areas does not seem likely in the near future. For those for whom RAMs are impractical, a grant for rehabilitation is possible. The value of the grant (plus accrued interest charged at the federal borrowing rate) would be recaptured at the time of sale. To encourage the borrower to maintain the unit and to protect the government's interest, the grant would be for a minority of the value of the unit after rehabilitation. This arrangement would also allow the property to be part of the estate passed on to heirs. The property could even appreciate at a rate slightly less than the federal interest rate on long-term borrowings for the expected holding period of the household without this basic relationship being disturbed. Thus the program costs the government nothing (aside from administration), increases the quality of the recipients' housing, and helps to preserve the existing housing stock. Realistically, however, it is not administratively simple. Income certification, inspection of the dwelling after rehabilitation to see that minimum standards are met, and placement of a lien on the property are all required.

For rental properties, the Section 8 rehabilitation program seems to be the proper vehicle with its guaranteed future demand. But, its complexity has been an impediment even to the sophisticated urban developers. Simplification will be necessary to make it operable in rural areas.

The Deficient and Unsalvagable Dwelling

This encompasses cases (2) and (3); in neither case can rehabilitation be justified. Is nothing then to be done to assist those who live in such units and who are unwilling to relocate? Most homeowners are adament against selling, in this case for little profit, and moving into a rental unit. For many renters substitute housing close enough to work or friends is simply not available; a change of dwelling may mean moving to another neighborhood or a nearby town. One solution to this problem is to make greater use of mobile homes.

The idea of using mobile homes as part of an overall housing strategy is certainly not new (Drury 1972; Morris and Woods 1971; MacFall and Gordon 1973). Two arguments have, however, been consistently advanced against mobile homes. One has been that their quality has been low, frequently to a degree which makes them unsafe. While some manufacturers did produce poor-quality units in the past, the production of mobile homes is now regulated; and since 1975 the Department of Housing and Urban Development has had an aggressive research program for cost-effective improvements in the safety, livability, and durability of mobile homes. The longer loan periods—up to 15 years—now permitted under Title I mortgage loans attest to the improvements.

A second argument is that mobile homes depreciate quickly. This makes them an expensive form of housing despite their low capital costs; additionally, it means that if used by housing agencies to house the poor, they would have to be replaced frequently. It is true that the full cost of mobile homes is high. Analysis of the costs of a typical mobile home and the "average" single family home insured under FHA's Section 203 (b) program in 1972 are shown in Table 9-2. The figures in the table make two important points: (1) the monthly costs of the two dwellings are quite close, even though the mobile home has 744 square feet of living space compared to 1,200 in the conventional dwelling; and, (2) the equity in the mobile home after 15 years is only about one-fifth that in the conventional unit, exclusive of any appreciation.[i]

The depreciation of mobile homes accounts for most of the difference in full long-term costs of mobile and conventional homes that is reflected in the equity figures. An important point, often omitted in such discussions, is the sensitivity of mobile home to structural degradation from relocation. Research supported by HUD shows that reloca-

[i] Phillip Weitzman, who produced these figures, assumes no appreciation for the conventional unit, so that the $8,941 reported in the table is the repayment to principal. For the mobile home, the equity is based on resale data compiled in a study by the First National City Bank.

Table 9–2. Comparison of Mobile Home and Conventional Housing Costs for 1972 (in Constant Dollars)

Type of Home	*Conventional Financing*[a]	*FHA Insured*[b]
	Average monthly costs of possession[c]	
$7,000 mobile home	$155	$155
$20,500 home	$170	$191
	Present value of the stream of housing costs[d]	
$7,000 mobile home	$20,354	$19,384
$20,500 home	$24,102	$24,706
	Move in Cost[e]	
$7,000 mobile home	$1,674	$418
$20,500 home	6,525	$2,045
	Equity after 15 years	
$7,000 mobile home	$1,050	$1,050
$20,000 home	$8,941	$5,270

Source: Phillip Weitzman, "Mobile Homes: High Cost Housing in the Low Income Market," *Journal of Economic Issues* 10(3) (September 1976):582, Appendix.

[a] Mobile home: 7 percent add-on for ten years after 20 percent down payment. Conventional homes: 7.5 percent for a thirty-year mortgage after 25 percent down payment.

[b] Mobile home: 8 percent for a twelve-year mortgage after 5 percent down payment. Conventional home: 8 percent for a thirty-year mortgage after 5 percent down payment.

[c] The sum of down payment, furniture, closing costs, and total monthly outlays, less tax savings and resale averaged over 180 months.

[d] Discounted at 6 percent.

[e] Down payment, closing, and furniture costs.

tions produce the equivalent degradation of at least five years of occupancy for the first two moves of a single-wide mobile home and a greater rate thereafter. For the double-wides, degradation rates are much greater (South West Institute 1979).

These facts bear heavily on the use of mobile homes to assist the elderly presently living in units that are economically unfeasible to rehabilitate. Since the unit would not be relocated, and since the rate of structural degradation to the stationary mobile home is low, the home could be relied upon to provide housing for the elderly as long as they wanted to live in them. Furthermore, the life of the unit coincides with the projected demand for housing at that location; the mobile home is cheaper over a fifteen-year period if there is no market value for the conventional unit at the end of the period, that is, in the absence of any capital appreciation. Here is a remarkable complementing of need and potential solution.

Fortunately, the 1978 amendments to the Section 8 housing assistance program permit HUD to assist owner-occupants of mobile homes.

(Rental units are already included in the program.) The legislation permits subsidy payments in the amount of the difference between 25 percent of the household's income and expenditures for principal and interest, utilities and site rents. The regulations implementing the law, however, limit the subsidy to the rent of the site or mobile home "pad." Thus, while the vehicle for implementing the use of mobile homes already exists in law, program regulations would have to be modified for full use.

Obviously a major consideration is the subsidy cost involved. A 12 foot by 60 foot single-wide mobile home in 1977 cost about $12,500, including site installation. Operating expenses for the unit in the same year are roughly estimated to be $1,200 or $2,100 depending on whether the unit is in a trailer park or on the owner's own site.[j] For a household with $6,500 income, this implies a first-year subsidy cost of $1,075 or $1,950—substantially less than the cost associated with building a new Section 8 unit. To be more realistic, for an elderly person with $2,500 income per year the first year subsidy is $2,075 or $2,950—a substantial expenditure but still cheaper than the available alternatives. Of course, these costs would be reduced if the household could contribute to the down payment.[k]

Another concern is what the potential use of a program might be. The best an analyst can do in this regard is to provide some crude indicators. In 1976, there were 136,000 elderly homeowners outside of SMSAs with incomes below the poverty line living in units without complete plumbing; another 76,000 lacked full kitchens. There were an additional 119,000 elderly homeowners in units with these deficiencies among those with incomes between the poverty level and twice that level of income. If only 20 percent of these units fall into the category defined as unfeasible for rehabilitation because of poor dwelling condition or lack of future market demand, then some 66,000 households could be served by such a program.

Dwellings Not Needing Rehabilitation

Most dwellings in rural areas are in this category. In addition, in the absence of the type of "neighborhood effects" that sometimes discourage investment in urban areas, the degree of dwelling maintenance might seem to depend more directly on the demand by potential

[j] The operating figures were obtained from a phone survey made by HUD staff in the Division of Building Technology to mobile home industry representatives in Virginia, Florida, Texas, California, North Dakota, Michigan, Pennsylvania, and Kentucky. The survey was not scientifically constructed, but the information is viewed as generally reliable in the aggregate.

[k] The cost could also be reduced by a recapture provision at the time of sale; this is not included in the current legislation.

consumers in the marketplace. Still, it does not follow, given some incremental demand, that landlords (owners or renters) will be more responsive in supplying services than their urban counterparts. Both the urban and rural investor must consider the rate of return—in both annual profit *and* capital gains. Rural markets can and do decline much like certain urban neighborhoods.

In this light, real incremental maintenance on units occupied by the poor elderly will likely to be forthcoming only on rental units under fairly long-term contracts like those available under the part of Section 8 program that utilizes existing dwellings. Participation in the Section 8 program by public housing authorities in rural areas has gradually increased from very low levels in 1976 (HUD 1978, "A Summary of Findings"). There has been some attempt to form regional housing authorities or for state housing agencies to administer Section 8 in rural areas to obtain more comprehensive geographic coverage. There is presently little information on the extent of effective coverage, however. Likewise, only skimpy evidence exists on the operation of the program in rural areas, although HUD is mounting an evaluation of the rural component.

For homeowners, most of the options discussed in the previous section are applicable. The one exception is the delivery of in-kind maintenance services. It seems doubtful that the clients for such a program would be numerous enough and sufficiently concentrated spatially to keep the full costs at an acceptable level.

When the Home Is Too Much to Maintain

The dominance of the single-unit structure in rural areas means that a greater share of the rural elderly will find it difficult to continue to live in their traditional, preretirement unit because of the more demanding maintenance such units entail. The higher rate of institutionalization of rural elderly, other factors being held constant, has been documented (Dunlop 1976). Among rural elderly *renters,* about 60 percent of non- single-person households live in single-unit structures and even 40 percent of one-person households live in such dwellings. This contrasts with about 20 and 10 percent, respectively, in metropolitan areas. Of course, rural homeowners universally live in single-family homes.

Certainly some additional housing alternative should be available. The construction of small housing projects for the elderly who are still capable of living independently is the obvious solution. There is a double emphasis here: the projects must generally be small to permit sufficient market aggregation close to the original homes of the occupants, and the projects should provide little in the way of support services because of the high costs per recipient of such services when the fixed cost component is amortized over a few recipients.[l]

While the prescription appears simple enough, it has been indeed difficult to fill in the past. As noted earlier from the task force report, the financial incentives typically work to make large projects profitable. In addition, there is little in the way of technical assistance to help the small developer or a nonprofit organization work its way through the program regulations—for either Section 202 or Section 8 new construction programs. It is true that some states are providing some aid (four are participating in a joint HUD/USDA demonstration) and the Housing Assistance Council (funded by HUD) provides help and seed money; but these efforts are very small in comparison to the need.[m] The task force report cited some cases of funding a single developer to develop multifamily housing in several different rural locations, and other innovative ideas. Again, the question is whether the concerned agencies can restructure the administration of their programs to deliver the services to rural areas. What needs to be done is all too clear. How it is done is the crux of the problem.

THE OVERARCHING PROBLEM

Although the options presented in the preceding section describe specific policy initiatives, there remains an overarching problem that impedes the effective and efficient delivery of housing services to the elderly from either new or ongoing programs. That problem, plaguing numerous aspects of bureaucratic endeavors, is duplication and lack of coordination between housing programs originating from different federal agencies. Because HUD and HEW fund the vast majority of housing assistance programs, these two departments bear primary responsibility for resolving the issue of avoiding duplication of efforts through coordination.

As noted in the beginning, HUD and HEW operate with very different mandates that are discrete legislatively but overlap substantially in implementation. The primary focus of program support from HUD is housing in the strict sense of the word. HUD's programs address themselves to the distribution, provision, and maintenance of physical structures. In pursuit of this fundamental goal, HUD's programs benefit the inhabitants of these dwelling units. While this is a desirable effect, it is never the sole rationale behind a program. HUD's programs

[l] This point is documented in another context in Weissert (1978). Also see Urban Systems Research and Engineering (1976).

[m] For succinct description of HAC see the brochure by the Housing Assistance Council (n.d.).

may benefit only the quality of the housing stock or both the housing stock and individuals, but programs from which only individuals benefit are outside the legal mandate of HUD.

In housing, HEW's priorities are the reverse of HUD's. HEW's concern is individuals, not buildings. A program toward providing home maintenance services has as its primary objective the upgrading of the living environment of those in need. That the quality of the housing stock improves as well is both an unnecessary and unexpected side effect from HEW's perspective. HEW formulates and delivers housing assistance services without regard to the effect on the conservation of the housing stock.

While the distinction between housing as a physical structure and housing as a service consumed by occupants facilitates the establishment of administrative boundaries, the distinction is, at best, an abstract concept. Individuals act and react with their immediate environment continuously; individual housing units provide both shelter and housing services simultaneously.

Because the distinction between physical housing and housing services is artificial at the service delivery level, both HUD and HEW provide similar housing repair and maintenance services under different justifications. In effect, these programs duplicate one another. Because different organizational structures are required to administer similar HUD and HEW service programs, duplication not only lacks cost effectiveness but also presents the service user (most often the local community) with complex bureaucratic mazes to unravel.

At this point in the narrative, it would be reasonable to offer three recommendations similar to the three identified by Thompson (1976) in a survey of housing services available to the handicapped: maintain the existing situation with all its inherent duplication; provide funds to HUD for the provision of housing services; provide funds to HEW for the provision of housing per se. A fourth alternative might borrow language from Title III of the Older Americans Act and encourage HUD and HEW to "facilitate accessibility to and utilization of" all services, whether housing or social services.

We are not, however, going to make any of these recommendations. While each of the four recommendations is quite reasonable, they are not practical. The first option can be dismissed readily as an ineffective ostrich-with-its-head-in-the-sand alternative. The other three options demand somewhat more consideration. Empowering HUD to provide housing services or HEW to provide housing units chips away at the authority and territoriality currently invested in the two departments. Neither department is likely to support a proposal that diminishes its authority. Without departmental backing the chances of such a proposal succeeding are slim.

Much more likely to be enacted is a resolution calling for (or requiring) HEW-HUD coordination and cooperation in the delivery of all types of housing assistance. Previous experience with task forces and interdepartmental agreements on this topic demonstrates the futility of yet another such resolution. Previous agreements between HUD and HEW indicate that both departments are aware of the problem and are "committed" to finding a solution. However, translation of the ideas in these documents into practical, workable strategies of cooperation has been lacking.

Rather than propose one of the four alternatives listed above, we endorse an approach that is more realistic and more likely to accomplish the objective of fostering HUD-HEW coordination. We propose that states coordinate housing services delivery through a single planning-funding application. Consider the complexity a community faces when it wants to establish a housing repair-maintenance program for low-income elderly. Funds are sought from three sources. Under the current system the community would prepare a housing assistance plan (HAP) as part of a community development block grant application submitted to HUD. In a HAP, the local area would describe the current housing situation, identify housing assistance needs of low-income households and formulate both an annual and a three-year action program and program goals.[n] The same municipality applying for Title XX support from the Social Security Administration would submit a Comprehensive Annual Services Program (CASP). Through that plan the local government (or its agency) would notify HEW of the services needed in the area, the details of an appropriate service plan, the group to be served, and ways it intends to coordinate provision of services. If this same municipality also submits an application to the Administration on Aging for Title III funds to support the housing service program, an area plan would have to be prepared. In this area plan (ultimately included as part of the state plan), the designated area agency on aging would identify and justify the need for the housing assistance service, as well as other services. Because funds for housing assistance are administered by numerous agencies at the federal level, the local community is literally pushed into several separate planning modes.

In order to eliminate costly duplicate planning and coordinating exercises, we propose that the local community prepare but one service delivery plan. A community applying for federal support would prepare only a HAP, the most detailed of the three existing planning exercises in the area of housing services. Under a revised HAP

[n] These HAPs are briefly discussed in Chapter 7. A more complete discussion is in South West Institute (1979).

strategy the community would provide HUD with its comprehensive plan for dealing with the housing and housing maintenance problems of the elderly. A revised HAP would be recognized as fulfilling the planning requirements for Title III and Title XX support as well as for the various HUD programs. The revised HAPs would be reviewed only by HUD, but acceptable plans would be eligible for support through HEW funds also. HUD would assume responsibility for brokering acceptable proposals through the federal bureaucracy. The revised HAP proposal fills in part a need identified previously by Lawton for a more systematic local community-based structure that could plan and organize the pooling of multiple sources of subsidies (1978: p. 64).

In a revised HAP (or any other planning strategy) a central issue is how to establish realistic goals. A major problem faced repeatedly by state and local governments in developing and planning for social programs is the uncertainty of federal support from year to year. HUD is now providing local jurisdictions with an estimate of the amount of resources they can expect to have over the three-year planning period based on conservative assumptions about congressional action. HEW could easily provide the states with similar information and require them to prepare similar allocation plans.

The revised HAP strategy has several advantages that recommend its adoption. Because the need for multiple planning and review exercises would be negated, our proposal is economical on both the local and federal levels. Moreover, implementation of this proposal would eliminate the artificial distinction maintained by HEW and HUD between housing as a physical structure and housing as a social service. Furthermore, the revised HAP strategy is compatible with the current situation in which planning and coordination, by default, are reserved to the local level.

SUMMARY

Through various legislative initiatives, including the Housing Act of 1959, the Older Americans Act of 1965, and the Social Security Act, the government, at various levels, has assumed increasing responsibility for the care and well-being of its older citizens. This commitment has proven to be a costly one: in 1978, federal expenditures for the elderly exceeded $107 billion, of which $1.2 billion was allocated for housing services.[o] In spite of this sizable outlay, decent and affordable

[o] Estimates of the total federal expenditure for older persons are from U.S. Office of Management and Budget (1978). Estimates of total expenditures on the elderly from HUD were derived from the product of the average outlay per unit under each program times the number of elderly occupied units. The former data are from Part I, U.S. Department of Housing and Urban Development 1979, *Justification for 1980 Estimates* (Wash., D.C.: Department of Housing and Urban Development). Mimeograph.

housing is frequently outside the grasp of several distinct groups within the older population. The rural elderly and older homeowners, in particular, have slipped through the net of federal housing programs. Yet to propose new and costly programs is foolhardy in an era characterized by a "Proposition 13" mentality and demands for a balanced federal budget.

In this chapter we have described several new policy initiatives we believe are compatible with the twin objectives of providing decent housing for those elderly overlooked by existing housing programs and containing the cost of long-run programs. Each of our proposals (reverse annuity mortgages, a modified Section 8 program, and housing support programs customized to the situation of the rural elderly) is intended to meet the housing needs of different groups in the older population, but a common rationale unifies the set of proposals. When poorly housed older persons are relocated to newly constructed units, the public sector may incur both direct and indirect costs: the direct cost of financing construction and underwriting occupancy costs and the potential indirect cost in "soft markets" of allowing units previously occupied by the elderly to deteriorate and eventually be withdrawn from the inventory of existing dwelling units. Substantial savings can be realized by providing the elderly with either the services or the capital necessary to maintain or upgrade the housing units they own. Each of our proposals is, in effect, a variation on this theme. Housing stock conservation also tends to brake the process of economic decline found in blighted areas—where the elderly are overrepresented—and potentially minimizes the need of other types of federal relief in the neighborhood.

The cost-effectiveness of housing services provided to the elderly also is compromised by duplication in program initiatives. Operating from discrete legislative mandates, HEW and HUD nonetheless support similar types of home repair and maintenance programs. Because of this duplication, the total administrative costs of these programs are needlessly high. We do not, however, offer as solutions to this problem plans to foster greater coordination between HUD and HEW or to locate responsibility for housing services exclusively in one department. Rather, we recommend that local communities be relieved of the burden of preparing different but similar planning reports for HUD and HEW. Under our proposal a single planning statement would be prepared by the responsible local agency and submitted only to HUD for review. Plans approved by HUD would be eligible for funding either through HUD programs or through HEW programs. By eliminating duplicative planning and review exercises, administrative costs would be reduced while multiple funding channels would be preserved.

In testing the policy implications contained in our previous analyses we have been guided by two principles. First, there is no single housing program, new or old, that can address adequately the housing needs of a group as diverse as the elderly. The bundle and mix of available housing services must be diverse and interrelated, but flexible. Second, the housing needs of the elderly do not exist and cannot be met adequately in a social vacuum. For the most part, the elderly are not isolated in their own communities but rather are members of age-heterogeneous neighborhoods and communities. Housing services cannot be provided to the elderly at the expense of their neighbors' needs or at the expense of their neighborhoods' development. Thus, responsible housing initiatives for older citizens must be compatible with and supportive of quality of life in the total community.

REFERENCES

Ahlbrandt, R.S., Jr. 1978. "Home Maintenance Programs: A Necessary Ingredient for Neighborhood Preservation?" Pittsburgh: University of Pittsburgh. Unpublished

Blinder, A.S. 1976. "Intergenerational Transfers and Life Cycle Consumption." *American Economic Review* 66: 87–93.

Drury, M.J. 1972. *Mobile Homes: The Unrecognized Revolution in Housing.* New York: Praeger Publishers.

Dunlop, B. 1976. "Determinants of Long-Term Care Facility Utilization by the Elderly: An Empirical Analysis." Washington, D.C.: Urban Institute Working Paper 963-35.

Gutowski, M. 1978. "Integrating Housing and Social Service Activities for Elderly Households." *Occasional Papers in Housing and Community Affairs.* Vol. 1.

Housing Assistance Council. 1977. "HUD Section 8/FmHA Section 515 Program." Washington, D.C.: Report to the Department of Housing and Urban Development.

———. n.d. "Housing Assistance Council: Housing Programs for Rural America." Washington, D.C.

Jacobs, B., and A. Rabushka. 1976. *The Elderly Homeowner: A Proposal for Further Study.* Washington, D.C.: U.S. Department of Housing and Urban Development, Office of Policy Development and Research.

Khadduri, J.; K. Lyall; and R. Struyk. 1978. "Welfare Reform and Housing Assistance: A National Policy Debate." *Journal of the American Institute of Planners* 44: 2–12.

Lawton, M.P. 1978. "The Housing Problems of Community-Resident Elderly." *Occasional Papers in Housing and Community Affairs*, HUD-497-PDR. Washington, D.C.: Government Printing Office.

Levitan, S.A., and R. Taggart. 1976. *The Promise of Greatness.* Cambridge, Mass.: Harvard University Press.

Listokin, D. 1976. *Fair Share Housing Allocation.* New Brunswick: Center for Urban Policy Research.

Lowry, I. 1974. *Equity and Housing Objectives in Homeownership Assistance.* Santa Monica: The Rand Corporation, WN-8715-HUD.

MacFall, E.A., and E.Q. Gordon. 1973. *Mobile Homes and Low-Income Rural Families.* Washington, D.C.: Office of Economic Opportunity.

Mayer, N. 1976. *Homeownership: The Changing Relationship of Costs and Income.* Washington, D.C.: Congressional Budget Office.

Morris, E.W., and M.E. Woods. 1971. "Outlook for the Future." In *Housing Crisis and Response: The Place of Mobile Homes in American Life.* Ithaca, N.Y.: State College of Human Ecology.

Myers, P. 1978. *Neighborhood Conservation and the Elderly.* Washington, D.C.: The Conservation Foundation.

Peat, Marwick, Mitchell and Co. 1977. *AMI: Tax, Accounting Origination, Servicing.* Washington, D.C.: A Report of the Federal Home Loan Bank Board.

South West Institute. 1979. "Analytical Evaluation of Transportation Effects on Mobile Homes." Report to the U.S. Department of Housing and Urban Development. San Antonio: South West Institute Report to HUD.

Struyk, R. 1979a. "The Housing and Income Needs of Older Americans." In K. Scholen, ed., *Unlocking Home Equity.* Madison:

———. 1979b. "Testing the Concept of Providing In-Kind Maintenance Services to Elderly Homeowners." Washington, D.C.: The Urban Institute.

Thompson, M.M. 1976. *Housing and Handicapped People.* Washington, D.C.: The President's Committee on Employment of the Handicapped.

U.S. Conference of Mayors. 1977. "Guide to Preparing Housing Assistance Plans." Washington, D.C.: U.S. Conference of Mayors.

U.S. Department of Housing and Urban Development. 1978a. *Report of the Task Force on Rural and Non-Metropolitan Areas.* Washington, D.C.

———. 1978b. "A Summary of Findings from HUD Research on Rural Housing and Community Development Program." Washington, D.C.: Division of Housing Research.

Weissert, W.G. 1978. "Cost of Adult Day Care: A Comparison to Nursing Homes." *Inquiry*: 10–19.

Urban Systems Research and Engineering. 1976. *Evaluation of the Effectiveness of Congregate Housing for the Elderly.* Washington, D.C.: U.S. Government Printing Office.

Weitzman, P. 1976. "Mobile Homes: High Cost Housing in the Low Income Market." *Journal of Economic Issues* X, no. 3: 582.

Welfeld, I., and R. Struyk. 1979. "Housing Options for the Elderly." *Occasional Papers in Housing and Community Affairs.* Vol. 3.

Index

About the Authors

Raymond J. Struyk has spent most of the 11 years since completing graduate studies at Washington University doing research on the economics of housing. Prior books, done while on the staff at the Urban Institute, include *Urban Homeownership: The Economics Determinants, Housing Policy for the Urban Poor*, and the *Web of Urban Housing*. Since 1977 he has been the Deputy Assistant Secretary for Research at the Department of Housing and Urban Development; his duties have included oversight of the Department's research on ways to improve and expand federal housing assistance for the elderly.

Beth J. Soldo combines interests in gerontology, sociology and demography. Upon completion of her graduate work at Duke University, she joined the staff of the Center for Population Research, Georgetown University. As a Senior Research Scholar, she has directed studies of the living arrangements and health of the elderly, future mortality trends among the older population and factors affecting the appropriateness of institutionalized placements. She is the author or co-author of numerous research reports and journal articles and is a regular participant in the meetings of the Gerontological Society.